Neural and Massively
Parallel Computers

Neural and Massively Parallel Computers

The Sixth Generation

BRANKO SOUČEK
Department of Mathematics
University of Zagreb

and

MARINA SOUČEK
National and University Library, Zagreb

A Wiley-Interscience Publication
JOHN WILEY & SONS
New York • Chichester • Brisbane • Toronto • Singapore

Library of Congress Cataloging in Publication Data:

Souček, Branko.
    Neural and massively parallel computers: the sixth generation /
Branko Souček and Marina Souček.
      p.   cm.
    "A Wiley-Interscience publication."
    Bibliography: p.
    Includes index.
    ISBN 0-471-63533-2
    1. Neural computers. 2. Parallel processing (Electronic
computers) I. Souček, Marina, 1960- . II. Title.
QA76.5.S6573 1988
004'.35–dc19   88-723
                                               CIP

Printed in the United States of America

10 9 8 7 6 5 4 3 2

PREFACE _____

Leading laboratories around the world are pushing research toward brain-like computers: sixth generation. The sixth generation, described in this book presently offers the following categories of machines: adaptive and learning systems, artificial neural systems, neural computers, adaptive goal-directed expert systems based on genetic mutation algorithms, event-train computers, transformation (mapping) systems, associative memories and processors, fuzzy and pseudo-associative systems, hypercubes, array processors, programmable connection machines, concurrent systems including Transputer family and OCCAM language, and computers in neurobiology and behavior. The electronics computer market is approaching $1000 billion annually, and it will be commanded by those who are now designing or producing sixth-generation devices and systems, based on very large-scale and wafer-scale integration.

The goals of the sixth generation are truly intelligent computing, measurement, control, robot, or information systems. Although we cannot expect to build a computer that emulates the brain, we could emulate many logical and intelligent functions of neural and behavioral systems. The research is interdisciplinary involving computer science/engineering, physiology, linguistics, logic, and psychology. This research generates new architectures, algorithms, components, systems and applications. Actually an entire new and rapidly growing discipline has been created called:

Psychological/intelligent/neural/knowledge engineering

By treating biological and technological systems alike, the discipline both advances and opens new job profiles and businesses. To be attractive for the market, consumer goods and industrial hardware of all kinds must be wrapped in to a psychological/intelligent/neural/knowledge package which includes: natural

v

interface to the user based on nonrestricted dialogue, speech, and image; features of adaptability, learning, sensing the environment; human-like behavior, offering the user a new sensation of mind and body, new experiences, happenings, and pleasures. These require quality and status associations. As a result, psychological intelligent/neural/knowledge engineering is turning out to be a pillar of super-industrialism and modern economy.

Psychological/intelligent/neural/knowledge engineering is composed of the following technologies:

- Intelligent systems measurement and analysis
- Intelligent systems modelling and simulation
- Intelligent-system design and interfacing
- Intelligent-system coding, programming, and training
- Intelligent-system application

This book is designed to serve as a textbook/reference in psychological/intelligent/neural/knowledge engineering and its related technologies.

The first of four parts "Sixth-Generation Computers," gives an overview of four groups of systems:

- Systems based on automatic programming and knowledge engineering; these systems represent the continuation of the fifth generation.
- Systems emulating or matching human behavior, with the elementary features of perception, learning, and cognition.
- Systems emulating brain-behavior functions. Different brain models are examined, models which approximate animal and human neural and behavioral processes; new computer architectures are being created, based on these models.
- Computers applied in neurobiology and behavior, in research laboratories as well as in health and recreation institutions—new multibillion-dollar professional and home market is open.

The purpose of this part of the book is to define the state of the art and detect future trends in psychological/intelligent/neural/knowledge engineering.

Part II, "Computer Models of Brain and Behavior," starts with an overview of neural and behavioral simulation. This part also describes selected models of biological information-processing systems. Five models are shown in detail: insect, bird, synaptic junction, brain windows, and brain-window language. Each system uses its unique coding: time intervals, frequency patterns, all-or-none signals, fuzzy adaptable windows, or message quanta. The codes and architectures are based on digital elements, analog elements, and nonlinear coupled oscillators. The behavior is programmed in the form of time sequences of events. The adjustable sets explain the context switching and the relation between the brain and the behavior.

This kind of coding and programming is of interest for hardware and for software designers; study of the bio-signals shows that there are many different ways to present information beyond the binary system used in present-day computers.

The third part, "Neurocomputers and Genetic Systems," describes systems that directly emulate neural structures and networks, and genetic crossover algorithms. This part presents the concept of adaptive learning systems, which comes from biological models. Concrete examples presented include the perceptron, the neocognitron, NETtalk, a parallel network that learns to read aloud, bidirectional associative memories and fuzzy cognitive maps. Large-scale artificial neural systems are described, including MARK, ANZA, and DELTA. MARK was developed for DARPA and contains 250,000 distributed processing elements. These systems can recognize similar as well as identical patterns, and they can generalize and draw conclusions. As an example of genetic systems, an adaptive rule-based expert and goal-directed system is presented; event-train processing systems are also described. These systems are direrectly influenced by biological codes and architecture; the future will see more and more systems of this kind.

The fourth part, "Associative and Parallel Computers, Concurrent Systems," describes major avenues: digital transformation systems; pseudoassociative memories; associative and fuzzy associative memories and processors; associative random access memory; massively parallel systems, including the hypercubes, DAP and MPP systems and the connection machine with programmable routes between thousands of processors; hypercube programming; Transputer family and OCCAM language. These systems are influenced by distributed processor/memory biological architectures. They operate at a much higher speed than classical computers. Associative and massively parallel processors present important blocks in many intelligent systems. These include artificial intelligence machines, real-time expert systems; airborne surveillance and trajecting systems; data base machines; intelligent instruments and control systems.

Brain-like computers are here to stay. Many devices, systems, applications, and services are now available. For further advance the strong interaction between computer and brain-behavior sciences is necessary. We have a partial understanding of how cognition, perception, memory, and learning work. Advancement is achieved through many parallel breakthroughs. This book describes variety of breakthroughs: three levels of man-made intelligence; five theories and computer models of brain behavior; seven learning algorithms; 12 categories of machines, following different principles of operation; and intelligent real-time, on-line, robot and process control systems, and concurrent computers.

The book has been written as a textbook for students, as well as a reference for practicing engineers and scientists. Treatment is kept as straightforward as possible, with emphasis on functions, systems, and applications. A minimal background—like that offered to undergraduates—is assumed, although many fundamentals are reviewed. We use this book to teach these courses:

Neural/Knowledge Engineering
Parallel Computers and Concurrent Processes
Intelligent Systems

The boundaries among computer generations are blurred. To leave room for flexible interpretation, the term "sixth generation" used throughout this book, may be understood as "the sixth generation and related techniques."

We would be happy to exchange ideas, programs and supporting teaching/consulting material. Our contact address is: Department of Mathematics, University of Zagreb, P.O.B. 187, 41001 Zagreb, Yugoslavia.

Zagreb, Yugoslavia   BRANKO SOUČEK
June 1988   MARINA SOUČEK

ACKNOWLEDGMENTS ───────────

We acknowledge the encouragement, stimulating atmosphere, discussions, and support received from our teachers, friends, and colleagues. Here, we can only name a few:

P. Brajak, I. Bratko, A. D. Carlson, F. Cellier, B. Furht, S. R. Hameroff, F. J. Hill, F. Jović, G. A. Korn, D. Koruga, H. Kraljević, R. H. Mattson, V. Milutinović, B. Ostojić, P. Papić, G. R. Peterson, M. Petrinović, S. Prešern, J. W. Rozenblit, A. Scott, T. Triffet, D. Vrsalović, B. P. Zeigler, A. Železnikar.

We thank the following institutions where we performed the experiments described in the book:

Department of Mathematics, University of Zagreb
Department of Data Processing, National and University Library, Zagreb
Department of Data Processing, Zagreb Bank
Department of Electrical and Computer Engineering, University of Arizona
Department of Neurobiology and Behavior, State University of New York at Stony Brook
Brookhaven National Laboratory
Institute Rudjer Bošković

To write a book like this one, it was necessary to borrow some data from the manuals of computer/system manufacturers. We should like to thank the following companies for giving us permission to adapt material from their publications:

Goodyear Aerospace Corp.
Hecht-Nielsen Neurocomputer Corp.

INMOS Group of Companies
Intel and iPSC
Intellicorp
TRW

We are grateful to the *Journal of Theoretical Biology* and *Microprocessing and Microprogramming* for allowing us to reprint the material from our papers published in these journals.

Special thanks to John Wiley's editors and reviewers and to Mrs. B. Grdović and Miss J. L. Main, for assistance during preparation of the manuscript for the publisher. We are grateful to Mrs. L. Van Horn for an outstanding job in supervising the copyediting of the manuscript.

CONTENTS _____

PART I

SIXTH-GENERATION COMPUTERS

Knowledge Engineering and Automatic Programming

Systems Emulating Human Behavior

Systems Emulating Brain-Behavior Functions

Computers in Neurobiology and Behavior

————————————————————————

CHAPTER 1

Knowledge Engineering and Automatic Programming

INTRODUCTION AND SURVEY

The sixth-generation computer project establishes cooperation between science and engineering. This chapter starts with definitions of structure, phases, and goals of the sixth-generation project. Because the sixth generation is emerging gradually from the fifth generation, we give an overview of the fifth generation, of artificial intelligence, and of expert systems; the following major trends are detected:

- A number of parallel computer architectures are under development for expert-system applications, based on a large set of small processing/memory elements.
- Expert-system shells have been developed which take care of the linguistic and reasoning mechanisms for drawing conclusions from knowledge.
- Commercial hardware/software systems are becoming available that simplify and speed up expert-systems development and application.
- New areas of applications for artificial intelligence are open, including process control, instrumentation, robotics, software engineering, system design, and testing.

The chapter also examines the trends in automatic programming systems and neural computers. The trend of switching from software into hardware simplifies the programming procedure. The ultimate systems are those that do not require programming—learning systems. Machine learning and automatic programming present two major bridges into the future of computing.

1.1. THE SIXTH-GENERATION PROJECT

The sixth-generation project[1-3] marks the end of the eighties. The key words are *brain-like computers*. Although we cannot expect to emulate the brain, we could emulate many intelligent functions that exist in biological systems. The brain and biological intelligence are among the most complex areas in science. Many different disciplines are needed to attack these problems. The sixth-generation project establishes cooperation between the following scientific disciplines: logic, linguistics, psychology, physiology, and computer science and engineering. This cooperation is outlined in Figure 1.1. The project is divided into three areas: science, technology, and applications.

Science should provide the answers to questions, such as these: What are intelligence, the mind, cognition? How do we think, see, hear? What are the

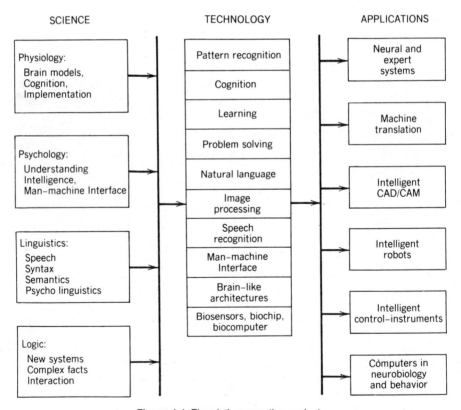

Figure 1.1 *The sixth-generation project.*

architecture and building materials of the brain? What controls behavior? How does the memory operate?

Technology should process the information received from science and develop new techniques for learning, cognitive thinking, pattern recognition, and decision making. New hardware architectures, new algorithms, and new building materials are envisaged; these will be much different from those used in the first through the fifth computer generations.

Applications of the sixth generation overlap with the applications of classical computers, with many new dimensions added. For example, a present-day robot is only a programmed mechanical manipulator. The sixth-generation robot is equipped with fine sensors connected to a knowledge base and behaves more like a living organism.

The goals of the sixth generation are outlined in Figure 1.2a. These goals must be integrated into one coherent system. The integration is presented with the bus structure of Figure 1.1. All the participating groups will have to interface to the bus structure. Technology must be able to link to the bus of physiology, psychology, linguistics, and logic and to the bus of applications. This book attempts to provide the necessary links.

We define three levels of man-made intelligence:

- Artificial intelligence (AI)
- Brain-behavior intelligence (BBI) or Neural Intelligence (NI)
- Molecular intelligence (MI)

Artificial Intelligence (AI). Basically a branch of applied mathematics (logic) which provides rule-based software packages called expert systems. Computers optimized for expert systems are called fifth-generation computers. The fifth generation project started in the early eighties.

GOALS

Physiology	Psychology	Linguistics	Logic
A brain model which approximates human/animal cognitive processes.	Clarification of the nature of understanding.	Understanding the processes of speech, syntax, semantics, language.	New logic is needed, suitable for learning and inductive inference.

Technologies

Feature extraction; knowledge representation; learning; intelligent programming; application generations; language processing; image processing.

Figure 1.2a *Sixth-generation project goals.*

Brain-Behavior Intelligence (BBI).   Seemingly mimics intelligent behavior in man and in animals and approximates some of the brain functions. In the brain a signal fired from one neuron can trigger a cascade of thousands of other neurons; consequently BBI hardware has been designed to use a massively parallel structure with a high interconnectivity between a large number of simple processors. Programming is frequently replaced by learning and training; presently the hardware solutions are based on large-scale integration (LSI) and wafer-scale integration (WSI) and are called sixth-generation computers. The sixth generation project started in the late eighties. An alternative name for BBI is *neural intelligence (NI)*.

Molecular Intelligence (MI).   Based on the premise that the cytoskeleton within the living cell represents the molecular level of cognition and information processing. Research in this direction could result in an interface between biological and technological information devices; ultimate goals would be the design of biosensors, biochips, and biocomputers. Useful results are expected by the early nineties, as a tail of the sixth generation or possibly as a start of the seventh generation.

The relation between the sixth-generation project and AI, BBI and MI is shown in Figure 1.2b. Presently, research development and marketing are focused on BBI, but there are strong overlaps with AI and MI.

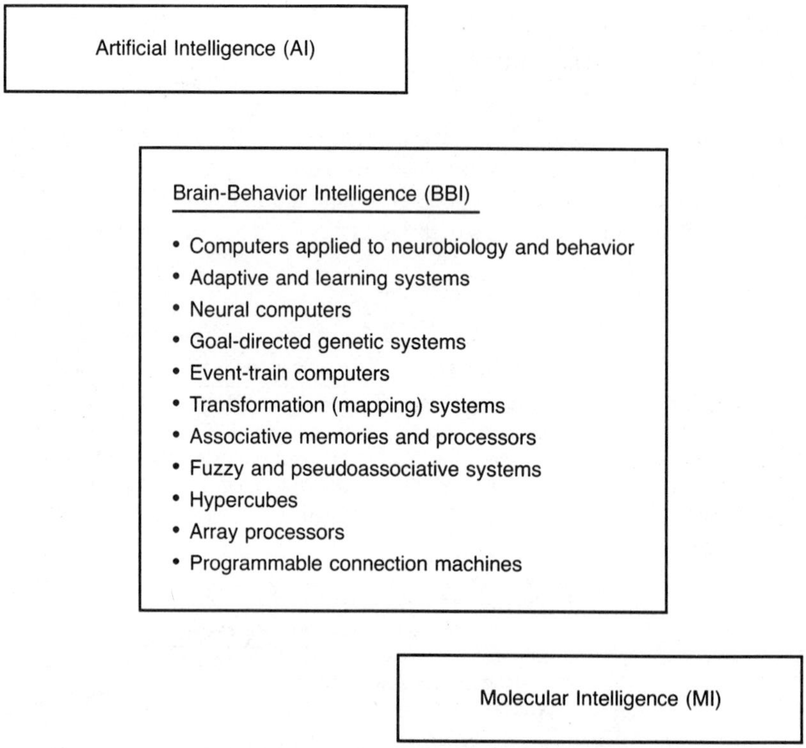

```
┌─────────────────────────────────────────┐
│                                         │
│   Artificial Intelligence (AI)          │
│                                         │
└─────────────────────────────────────────┘
```

```
┌─────────────────────────────────────────────────┐
│                                                 │
│   Brain-Behavior Intelligence (BBI)             │
│                                                 │
│   • Computers applied to neurobiology and behavior │
│   • Adaptive and learning systems               │
│   • Neural computers                            │
│   • Goal-directed genetic systems               │
│   • Event-train computers                       │
│   • Transformation (mapping) systems            │
│   • Associative memories and processors         │
│   • Fuzzy and pseudoassociative systems         │
│   • Hypercubes                                  │
│   • Array processors                            │
│   • Programmable connection machines            │
│                                                 │
└─────────────────────────────────────────────────┘
```

```
┌─────────────────────────────────────────┐
│                                         │
│   Molecular Intelligence (MI)           │
│                                         │
└─────────────────────────────────────────┘
```

Figure 1.2b   *The sixth-generation project.*

The sixth generation gradually emerges from the fifth generation. While the fifth generation concentrates on artificial intelligence, the sixth generation covers artificial intelligence, brain-behavior intelligence, and molecular intelligence. Major advances in artificial intelligence are goal-driven adaptive expert systems, and very high speed real-time expert systems. These systems, based on newly developed genetic algorithms and associative memories, are described in detail in Chapters 13 and 17. Major advances in brain-behavior intelligence include neuro-computers, learning systems, associative and massively parallel systems, described in Chapters 11–22. Molecular intelligence is in its infancy, but its time is coming. We associate two terms with the fifth and sixth generation:

Knowledge engineering
Psychological/intelligent/neural/knowledge engineering

Knowledge Engineering (KE) marks the fifth generation. It signals the shift from mere data processing to an intelligent processing of knowledge. KE deals with the symbolic manipulation and symbolic reasoning.

Psychological/Intelligent/Neural/Knowledge Engineering (PINK engineering) marks the sixth generation, and is much broader than KE. It covers advanced, adaptive, real-time, symbolic reasoning as well as fuzzy reasoning, based on massively parallel global synthesis. Its products are knowledge-ware, psycho-ware, and neuro-ware. These products define an entirely new market with new kinds of consumer goods and industrial hardware. The features of PINK engineering products include natural interface to the user based on nonrestricted dialogue; speech and image; interface through the brainwaves and neural signals; human-like behavior offering to the user a new sensation of mind and body, new experience, happenings and pleasures; sensing the environment and based on the sensory data, self-organization, adaptation, and learning; and automatic programming. PINK engineering bypasses present day bottlenecks, such as knowledge acquisition and software development. In general, PINK engineering opens the door to superindustrialism, with psychoware, neuroware, and knowledge ware being three major new markets.

In parallel, new *PINK services* are growing. They include: generation and distribution of knowledge; intelligent libraries; PINK books, video disks, and television; intelligent, self-adaptable, learning tools in the area of repair and maintenance; much higher-level research and service for computers, neurobiology, and behavior; home care and home birth services; homelike nursing centers for the elderly; new rehabilitation, leisure, and pleasure activities; PINK tourism; and services for personal growth which open new avenues in sensing the environment, thinking, and direct communication between people. The tools, consumer goods, and services have become soft-edged, suitable for human touch. In this way the lost balance between man and nature is being restored.

The epoch after 1960 has been called the Information Society. The primary occupation in the United States has become clerical, the key resource is information, and many activities are in the service area. Society is now moving beyond the clerk, information and plain services. With PINK engineering and services, and the sixth-generation project, a new epoch is here. Should we call it the *PINK Society*?

Psychological: balance with nature, peace, and spiritual values

Intelligent: natural, artificial, brain behavior and molecular intelligence

Neural: brain-like computers, sensors, biotechnologies

Knowledge: mind, learning, perception

Many of these goals are included in the sixth-generation project.

In Japan, the sixth generation is an official national project of high priority. The project identifies two goals: conversion of materials and conversion of information.

Conversion of materials involves studies of molecular recognition and transformation of substances for the balanced organization of technological solutions that produce useful products and byproducts. Science and technology will mimic the mechanisms of living organisms. Such organisms perform useful work without polluting and simultaneously produce byproducts that enrich the environment.

Conversion of information involves studies of learning mechanisms, memory, motor control, sensation, and thought. Information is processed in a manner similar to that of living organisms (i.e., using artificial neural networks and biosensors). Living organisms sense their environment to come up with an internal representation of it. That personal information base then can assist the organism to learn, recognize, remember, think about, and create new strategies for coping. A detailed understanding of these processes results in new technologies for artificial intelligence, brain-behavior intelligence, and molecular intelligence.

1.2. ARTIFICIAL INTELLIGENCE AND EXPERT SYSTEMS

The sixth generation is gradually emerging from the fifth generation. For this reason we give here a short overview of the fifth generation and of artificial intelligence.

There are many ways to define artificial intelligence, including the following:

Nilsson[4]: Artificial intelligence should be thought of as applied logic.

Winston[5]: Artificial intelligence is the study of ideas that enable computers to be intelligent.

Rajaram[6]: Artificial intelligence can be defined as the discipline of building computer systems capable of solving problems which, if done by humans, would be considered intelligent activity.

Artificial intelligence is present in all parts of the fifth-generation computer, in hardware as well as in software (see Figure 1.3).

The core of the system is a knowledge base. It contains all of the relevant domain-specific information, permitting the system to behave as an intelligent

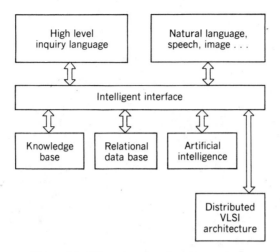

Figure 1.3 *Fifth-generation computer systems.*

specialist. The main processing element of the system is an artificial-intelligence module, or inference machine; it controls the deductive process and implements the most appropriate strategy of reasoning for the problem at hand. The knowledge base and inference machine are connected through intelligent interfaces to intelligent input-output units, relational data bases, and intelligent programming language units. Some of the above functions are supported by special-purpose hardware; the others are realized as software packages. The whole concept of the fifth generation is based on advances in logic and in linguistics.

In the past years, most of the activity in artificial intelligence was in software. Computer programs have been written which perform expert diagnoses of infectious diseases, discover the chemical structure of complex organic compounds from mass spectrogram data, understand limited amounts of speech and natural language text, solve mathematical problems at expert level, and perform other human-like activities. The best known examples are the systems for chemical analysis,[7] medical diagnosis,[8] and mineral exploration.[9] The common name for these kinds of software packages is *expert systems*. The program structure of the expert system is different from the program structure of classical software products; the difference is outlined in Figure 1.4.

Classical software products are based on sequential computation. The programs are composed of a number of modules which are interconnected, forming a deterministic, fixed calling sequence. This sequence is defined at the time of programming and remains unchanged.

An expert system is based on parallel computation. The subsystem is composed of a number of modules which are prepared at the time of writing of the software package but are not connected. The calling of the modules depends on the data environment. A particular condition in the data environment calls the necessary module; as several conditions could occur at the same time, several modules can

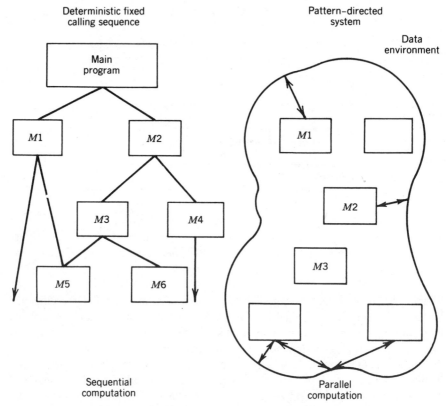

Figure 1.4 *Deterministic fixed calling sequence in classical software packages, and pattern directed calling of modules in expert systems.*

be called for execution. For this reason, single-processor computers are not the right tools for expert systems.

The expert system generates results by using production rules. The production rules are identical to the rules that a human expert would use to solve the same problem. Early expert systems used several hundred production rules; the number of rules in more complex systems could run into the thousands or even tens of thousands. It is conceivable that such large systems may require hours of computing time to execute a single circle of production-system execution. The solution to the time problem is parallel computing. A number of parallel computer architectures has been developed for expert-system applications (DADO[10]; the Connection Machine[11]; GF11 from IBM; Butterfly from Bolt, Beranek, and Newman Inc.; iPSC from Intel; and others). See Chapters 15 to 22.

Most of these machines would comprise a very large set (on the order of hundreds or thousands) of very small processing elements. Each processing element would contain its own processor and a small amount of memory (one to four kbytes). The major difference between the systems would be the interconnection (bus-based, DMA channel-based, binary tree structure, programmable interconnections, etc).

Even if the right hardware were available, the design of expert systems would be a complex achievement. For this reason, the major effort is concentrated on the design of software tools to speed up expert-system development.

A major step forward is the TEIRESIAS/MYCIN system[12], which attempts to fully automate the acquisition and explanation of knowledge provided by a human expert unsophisticated in computer technology. The system is split into two parts (see Figure 1.5):

MYCIN: a rule-based consultant program performing diagnoses of bacterial infectious diseases

TEIRESIAS: a front-end interface used to transfer the expertise of a medical doctor to the MYCIN

The split architecture of this system has served as a model for organizing current and future expert systems. The modern systems are composed of two parts: a *knowledge subsystem* and a *shell*, the linguistic and reasoning mechanism that interprets and draws conclusions from knowledge. The shells present the major tools to speed development of expert systems. A developer can produce a full-fledged expert system without having to create the linguistic and reasoning components from scratch.

Commercial shells are now available on the market. They run on mainframes as well as on microcomputers. The packages include Personal Consultant for Texas Instruments Computers and several packages for the IBM Personal Computer: M.1 from Teknowledge; Expert-Ease from Expert-Ease; Insight Knowledge System from Level 5 Research, and The Intelligent Machine Model from General Research.

The Knowledge Engineering Environment (KEE) package from Intelli-Corp incorporates two reasoning mechanisms: *backward chaining*, which starts with a hypothesis and ends with a supporting fact, and *forward chaining*, which starts with a fact and then finds a rule whose application is verified by the fact.

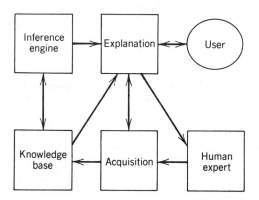

Figure 1.5 *The structure of TEIRESIAS/MYCIN.*

Figure 1.6 shows an example of using the KEE system to simulate a factory production line. The availability of such systems opens the door for mass application of expert systems.

1.3. EMERGING EXPERT SYSTEMS

Figure 1.7 lists eight areas for which expert systems exist or are under development. Many new areas will be added to the list every year.

An excellent example of an early expert system is DENDRAL.[7] The purpose of the system is to work like a knowledgeable chemist. The system matches two pieces of information, a chemical formula or structure, and a spectrogram measured on the chemical sample.

Figure 1.8 shows these two pieces of information: chemical structure and measured spectrogram. The system is exposed to a large number of such pairs and correlates the structure and the shape of the spectrogram. In this way the system learns the rules and the facts. After the learning phase is finished, the system can be used as an expert. A sample with an unknown structure is used to

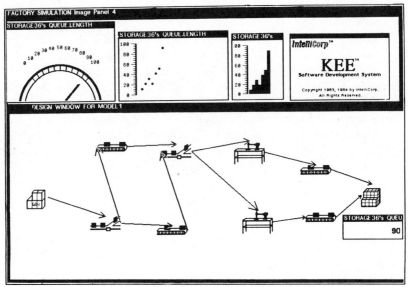

In this display, Intellicorp's KEE system is simulating the operation of a factory production line. Graphical symbols (icons) represent the conveyor belts, diverter belts, and machine tools (lower box). The symbols, in turn, are associated with units (not shown) describing the operation of the individual components. The dial (top left) shows the present size of the output queue. The bar charts (top center) represent changes in the queue size over time.

Figure 1.6 *Simulation of the operation of a factory production line. Copyright ©1986 by IntelliCorp Inc. All Rights Reserved.*

Emerging Expert Systems:

1. Home (Games, Advice, Aids)
2. Professional (Scientists, Physicians, Engineers)
3. Technical (Diagnosis of failure, repair)
4. Military (Situation Assessment, Planning)
5. Design of LSI and VLSI Chips
6. Signal Interpretation (Visual, Speech, Experiments, Medical)
7. Intelligent Agents (Aids use of complex computer systems)
8. Office Automation (Common office procedures and functions)

Figure 1.7 *Emerging expert systems.*

measure the spectrogram, which is then entered into the expert system together with the question: what is the structure? The expert system then suggests the chemical structure which was previously unknown.

Figure 1.9 shows an expert system for command and control of a robot.[6] The system has two inputs: human and sensory elements. Such a system has the following capabilities:

1. The system could be initialized by a human towards a particular task.
2. The sensors provide an image of the work place which calls for transformation of the environment model.

Such a robot or control system becomes a goal-seeking mechanism with a high degree of flexibility.

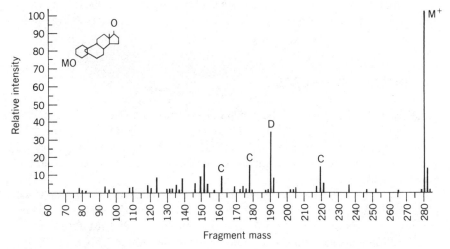

Figure 1.8 *Operation of the expert system DENDRAL[7] (finding the molecular structure of organic chemicals using a mass spectrogram).*

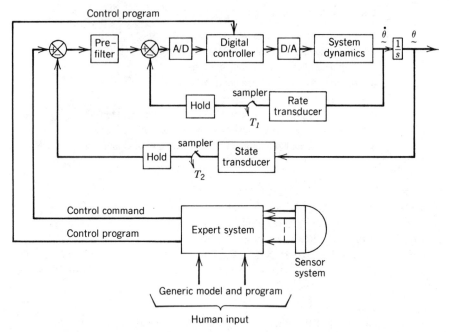

Figure 1.9 *Expert system for command and control of a robot*[6]. *By permission of N.S. Rajaram.*

Figure 1.10 presents an expert system used as an intelligent programming tool.[13] Although the system would not synthesize programs automatically, it has the capability of aiding programmers in various stages of program production, such as design, coding, debugging, and testing. The system is composed of several major units, each an expert system for a subdomain of the program development process.

1.4. INTELLIGENT BUSES

In the example of Figure 1.10 the domain of expertise is divided into subdomains, each supported by a specialized expert system. Each unit of the system, while acting as an advisor in its own specific subdomain, can communicate and consult with other units if necessary. Communication between expert systems is an open area for investigation.

Most problems existing in engineering and in applied science are multidisciplinary in nature. These problems are investigated by teams of specialists addressing different parts of a large project. It is possible that the expert systems specialized for different subdomains cooperate on the same project. This could become reality only if a communication standard is agreed upon. The problem is similar

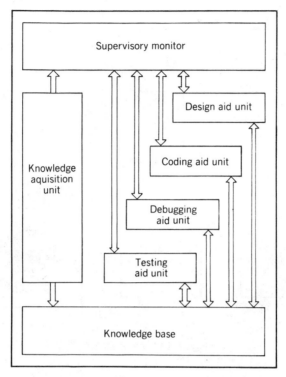

Figure 1.10 *A knowledge-based programming support tool.* [13] *By permission of M.T. Harandi.*

to the standardized communication through interface buses on a chip, card device, or subroutine level. An expert-system bus would enable the formation of expert-system conferences, councils, and design teams. The ultimate goal would be the creation of regional, national, and global knowledge bases and inference engines. This kind of technology could be a major step in the history of mankind. Figures 1.11 and 1.12 outline the idea of such an expert-system bus.

The cost of acquiring the knowledge base tends to dominate all other hardware and software costs. To expedite knowledge acquisition and problem specification, new tools have been designed and implemented. These tools present the interface bus between the system and the user. Lewis and Lynch[14] describe the graphic system developed in General Electric Company.

The new system is a workbench for exploring the use of AND/OR trees in an improved user interface for entering, modifying, analyzing, and documenting rules. The AND/OR tree serves as mechanism for direct graphic documentation of the rule-set; for explaining HOW, HOW-NOT, WHY, and WHY-NOT questions about conclusions and facts; for displaying execution traces of forward or backward chaining inference mechanisms; for modifying inference strategies; and for teaching the rule-base to the user.

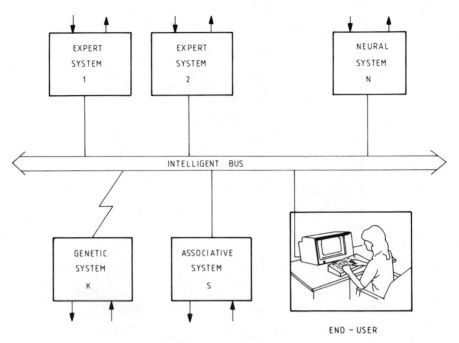

Figure 1.11 *Intelligent bus.*

Software bus = Protocol for transmitting data packets
from one software package to another
= network of independent software components

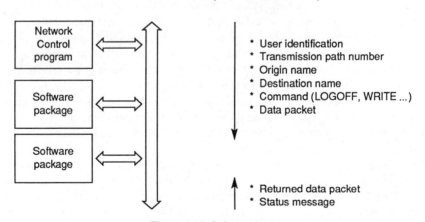

Figure 1.12 *Software bus.*

The problem of drafting AND/OR trees is neatly solved with a simple computer-aided-graphics rule-entry system.

The current experimental system is implemented under VAX/VMS using an ordinary VT100 alphanumeric terminal and a high-speed color graphics display. This kind of system will tremendously reduce the knowledge-acquisition cost and error rate. It will enable the user to modify nodes and connecting arcs and to follow the execution of inference engines. As users can verify correctness visually, they could have full responsibility for and control of the knowledge base. This is the best way to transfer use of expert systems from artificial intelligence experts and closer to end-users.

1.5. WILL NEURAL COMPUTERS REPLACE EXPERT SYSTEMS?

Most classical computers are single-processor, sequential machines. Sixth-generation computers are multiprocessor parallel machines: associative, massively parallel, neural, genetic, etc. A detailed description of these machines is given in Parts III and IV of the book. Here we discuss the links between classical computers and sixth-generation computers. Artificial intelligence and expert systems present such links because they use both kinds of machines.

Which applications will stay on classical computers alone, and which applications will migrate into the sixth generation? Will neural computers replace expert systems? To answer these questions, we look into human intelligence and the human brain.

The human brain is divided into two hemispheres, left and right. Evidence shows that the left hemisphere of the brain is specialized to deal with "sequential tasks" and the right hemisphere is specialized to deal with "parallel tasks." Sequential tasks use simple logic and a small portion of the available data at any given time. If a problem can be successively decomposed into simple and relatively independent parts, it can be solved on a sequential machine similar to a classical computer or the left hemisphere of the brain. Sequential tasks include logical reasoning, sequential mathematical operations, planning, language understanding and production, scheduling, and small rule-based expert systems.

Parallel tasks use all the available data at the same time. The logic of such tasks cannot be decomposed into independent parts but instead requires a global synthesis. Parallel tasks require a large number of linked processors operating in parallel, such as a sixth-generation computer or the right hemisphere of the brain. Parallel tasks include image processing, parallel mathematical operations, body or robot coordination, fuzzy expert systems, large rule-based expert systems, pattern recognition, analog and fuzzy reasoning and learning.

There is room in computer research and applications for both classical sequential computers and for sixth-generation parallel computers; they are not in competition. Each group is specialized for separate tasks, similar to the specializations of the left and right hemispheres of the brain (see Figure 1.11).

1.6. AUTOMATIC PROGRAMMING

Since the early 1980s the end user frequently has spent more money on software products than hardware. As a result, new tools have been developed to automate application software design. Martin[15] lists the following tools:

Simple query languages
Complex query languages
Report generators
Graphical languages
Application generators
Very high-level languages
Parametrized application packages

These tools markedly improve the efficiency of application program development.[16] IBM claims that its application generator ADF, if used instead of the COBOL, increases the productivity by 27 times. UNIVAC claims similar results for its application generator called MAPPER.

Automatic programming is an obvious direction for both sequential machines as well as for highly parallel machines.

The idea of using parallel processing to solve the problem is to break the problem into chunks that then can be written into a parallel-processing language, such as Occam. It is also necessary to have simulation tools that permit programmers to trace the execution of programs on parallel processors. The operating system is also a major design issue, since memory management and interprocessor communication are critical to the functioning of the programming languages.

All applications could be divided between two main classes: regular and irregular.

Regular applications are characterized by a crystalline structure in time and space. The structure is static and can be mapped easily onto the topology of hardware.

Irregular applications are asymmetric and sometimes unpredictable in time and space. This means that optimal mapping of the process structure onto the topology of the hardware is a much more difficult problem than it is for regular applications.

Tools have been developed to decompose an application in terms of functions, tasks, and data, and to determine inherent parallelisms. The degree to which an application is decomposed and structured for processing is termed granularity.[17]

Large-grain parallel processing typically involves dividing the processing into functions and tasks; medium-grain programming involves further destructuring of tasks; and fine-grain programming takes parallel procedures to the instruction level. The large- and medium-grain solutions are being mounted now, while fine-grain systems exploiting parallelism just start with applications.

For concurrent parallel computers, application generators must solve the problems of an immense variety of hardware architectures, communication structures, synchronization for resource sharing, run-time support, and host/target distribution of activities.

Three approaches are present today:

- *Parallel control flow.* All processing modules are called at the same time. They execute in parallel, and the control module waits until all processing procedures are complete before continuing. Concurrent Pascal and Ada support this kind of parallel operation.
- *Graph reduction.* Enables the parallel operations to be performed without any explicit instruction from the program. Each mode in a program graph is represented as a packet specifying identifiers, functions, operators, data, and pointers to other packets. These features are found in PROLOG and HOPE.
- *Data flow.* Reflects at hardware level the parallelism inherent in inference processing.

According to Kolbezen[18] the central idea of data flow architecture is a network of processing elements set up to reflect the logical structure of the task to be carried out where items of data flow between the elements which operate at their own pace, and wait until each has a complete set of intermediate inputs before it "fires." There are two techniques for the control of such a network. In the totally data-driven approach, each element waits passively for data to arrive, whereas in the demand-driven regime each element issues requests "upstream" for data when it is ready for it. In general a dataflow computer or computer subsystem has three requirements:

- Store representations of program graphs,
- Implement some form of data tokens to flow through the graphs, and
- Provide suitable instruction processing facilities.

A measure of "controlled" parallelism can be incorporated into procedural programming languages. This approach was pioneered in Concurrent PASCAL, Concurrent C, Pascal-Plus, Modula, and so on and has been incorporated into the real-time language ADA.

The most fully developed implementation of parallelism into procedural languages is OCCAM, where each module is regarded as a communicating sequential process, which may run on its own, possibly dedicated, processing element.

Other languages include: CSP, PARLANCE, TASK, NSL, PCL, CLU, MOD, PLITS/ZENO, FLOWGRAPH, LIMP, CCS, ELLA, AXON, CMLISP and so on.

In system software and in application software one can detect an important trend which could be called "switching from software to hardware." The trend is obvious in two areas:

- Control operations presently performed by system software (scheduling, I/O control, compilers, interupts, etc.) are moving in hardware.
- Special purpose microsystems with almost everything burned into ROMs, or

into hardware including the application software (word processing systems, accounting systems, inventory control systems, process control systems, neural computers, fuzzy associative processing, etc.).

Switching from software to hardware covers the following features:

1. Timesharing and multiprogramming
   Memory scheduling
   Processor and task scheduling
   Priorities
   Swapping
   Protection
2. File and list management
   Searching
   Sorting
   Comparisons
   Swapping
   Copying
   Indexing
3. Direct higher-order language execution, reducing the need for compilers, assemblers, editors, and debugging programs
4. Fault protection and detection
   Memory protection
   Diagnosis
   Some self repair
5. Fast computational sequences based on large read-only memories and on large sets of micro instructions

Switching from software to hardware simplifies the programming procedure. The ultimate systems are those that do not require programming: adaptable learning systems, artificial neural networks, and neurocomputers. These systems are based on learning or training. Machine learning and automatic programming present two major bridges into the future of computers (see Chapters 11–22).

REFERENCES

1. Science and Technology Agency, *Promotion of Research and Development on Electronic and Information Systems that May Complement or Substitute for Human Intelligence.* STA, Tokyo, 1985.
2. R.E. Chapman, *Biologically-Related Computing (Japan's Sixth Generation)*, Background Paper. Technicom International Corporation, Falls Church, VA, 1985.

3. B.R. Gaines, Sixth generation computing: A conspectras of the Japanese proposals. *Sigart News*. **95**, 39–44 (1986).

4. N. Nilsson, *Principles of Artificial Intelligence*. Tioga, Palo Alto, CA, 1980.

5. P.H. Winston, *Artificial Intelligence*. Addison-Wesley, Reading, MA, 1984.

6. N.S. Rajaram, Design of intelligent systems with cooperating knowledge based components. In *Proceedings of Trends and Applications: Automating Intelligent Behavior, Applications and Frontiers*. IEEE, New York, 1983.

7. B.G. Buchanan and E.A. Feigenbaum, DENDRAL and Meta-DENDRAL: Their application dimension. *Artif. Intell.* **11**, 5–24 (1978).

8. E.H. Shortcliffe, *Computer Based Medical Consultations: MYCIN*. Am. Elsevier, New York, 1976.

9. R. Duda, L. Gashnig, and P.E. Hart, Model design in the PROSPECTOR consultant system for mineral exploration. In D. Michie (ed.), *Expert Systems in the Microelectronic Age*. Edinburgh Univ. Press, Edinburgh, 1979, pp. 153–167.

10. S.J. Stolfo, *Knowledge Engineering: Theory and Practice*. In *Proceedings of Trends and Applications: Automating Intelligent Behavior, Applications and Frontiers*. IEEE, New York, 1983, pp. 97–104.

11. D. Hillis, *Connection Machine*. MIT Press, Cambridge, MA, 1986.

12. R. Davis, *Applications of Meta-Level Knowledge to the Construction, Maintenance and Use of Large Knowledge Bases*, Rep. No. STAN-CS-76-552. Computer Science Department, Stanford University, Stanford, CA, 1976.

13. M.T. Harandi, A knowledge-based programming support tool. In *Proceedings of Trends and Applications: Automating Intelligent Behavior, Applications and Frontiers*. IEEE, New York, 1983, pp. 233–239.

14. J.W. Lewis, and F.S. Lynch, GETREE: A knowledge management tool. In *Proceedings of Trends and Applications: Automating Intelligent Behavior, Applications and Frontiers*. IEEE, New York, 1983.

15. J. Martin, *Application Development Without Programmers*. Savant Institute, 1981.

16. M. Souček, *Automatic Programming*. Informator, Zagreb, 1986.

17. J.V. Hornstein, Parallel processing attacks real-time world. *Mini-Micro Syst*. Dec., pp. 65–77 (1986).

18. P. Kolbezen, Language considerations of parallel processing systems. *Informatica* **ii**, (2) 36–43 Ljubljana (1987).

CHAPTER 2 ———————————————————

Systems Emulating Human Behavior

INTRODUCTION AND SURVEY

Cognitive psychology has developed models of human behavior, perception, and learning, and has linked them with brain physiology. According to the sixth-generation project proposal, [1,2] there are still many problems to be solved in the future:

1. Clarification of the nature of understanding. People integrate knowledge to understand objects or ideas, recall typical examples from experience, and generate analogies by modifying them by deductive inference. The means by which people prevent malfunctioning, lighten mental strain, use creative cognition and language must be understood.
2. Modeling of intelligent functions. Models must be constructed for visual perception, linguistic meaning, long-term memory, learning, and cognitive development.
3. Investigation of the human-computer interface in terms of cognitive science.
4. Integration of psychological and physiological research.

This chapter's primary purpose is to compare the intelligent behavior of humans with that of computers. Humans are by far superior in the area of perception, while the computer is better in the area of high-precision calculation. Capacities of input-output channels, memory, and perception are given for both the human brain and the computer. Knowledge in this area opens new directions in the computer design.

We also show that the brain preprocesses sensory data into compact units, increasing the information content per unit. The data is then memorized in the form of associative units with common denominators.

We analyze possibilities for human-computer interfaces. These include communication based on brain waves and on correlations between speech, vision, and brain patterns. Descriptions of experiments leading towards mind-reading machines close the chapter.

2.1 PERCEPTION

The brain generally reacts not to what it observes directly but to the difference between what is expected and what actually occurs. In effect, the brain is making hypotheses about the world, and it changes them when unexpected occurrences contradict these working models. This phenomenon is termed *adaptation*. We can define *understanding* as a locking procedure between the unexpected hypotheses and the sensory data stream.

If we look at Figure 2.1, we believe that we see the spiral. Take a pencil and carefully follow the broken curve. Soon you will realize that the curve is not the spiral but is composed of small segments which belong to the concentric circles. Figure 2.1 is an example illustrating the basic feature of human perception. The sensory data stream received by the brain is greatly simplified and locked with the hypothesis, which is formed earlier on the basis of past experience.

Perception, as defined in psychology, presents a process of forming in the brain a complex model of the world, a model that is different from the sensory data stream. Based on experience, the brain compares the expected model with the received data. The main features are selected; unimportant details are neglected.

The same data stream can produce two different models or conclusions, if the brain has two hypotheses. Figure 2.2 may present either a vase or two faces staring at each other. What is received depends upon what is hypothesized; incorrect hypotheses lead to illusions, as in Figure 2.1. On the other side, the hypotheses help build the image of the world even if the data are incomplete or buried in "noise". So long as the sensory data stream can provide an occasional data point that reinforces the hypotheses, the process of understanding can proceed successfully.

Figure 2.1
Fraser's spiracle—an example of perception.

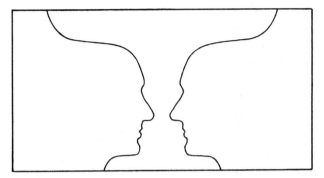

Figure 2.2 *Input sensory data locked with two hypotheses. The figure might be either two faces staring at each other or a vase.*

In the area of perception, the human brain is by far better than any computer. In most cases, it is impossible to incorporate perception into the computer. The computer has difficulty even recognizing one sound from another, one simple drawing from another. Perception and context-switching are areas in which computer-system designers must learn from nature.

How perception, context-switching, and understanding operate in humans is unknown. Because animals exhibit similar features, we can sometimes learn by analyzing animal brains and behavior, which are much simpler. For example, context-switching has been observed in firefly communication and has been related to the relatively simple logic and architecture of the firefly brain. For details of experiments and findings, see Chapters 9 and 10.

2.2 HUMAN-COMPUTER INTERFACES

In the past, computer systems have been designed with efficient use of technology in mind. Saving in hardware was a very important issue. As hardware becomes less expensive, design is now more oriented towards human factors. One of the main goals is a friendly human-computer interface, enabling easy-going communication. Figure 2.3 shows the basic logical parts involved in human computer communication.

From the human side, the communication is divided into four parts:

1. The brain and the central nervous system, supporting cognition, perception, and long-term memory
2. Short-term memory, used for temporary storage of sensory data
3. A communication channel for internal information transmission
4. Sensory and motor logic, as an interface with the environment

Equivalent part on the computer side are as follows:

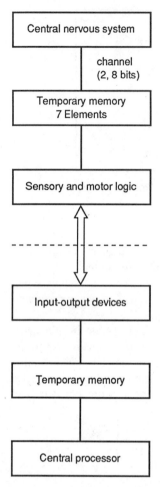

Figure 2.3
Human-computer interface.

1. The central processor and the main memory, with stored program
2. Short-term buffer memory, used for temporary storage of data
3. Data communication channels
4. Input/output peripheral units, interfacing the computer to the environment (in the case discussed here, the environment is a human)

The optimal communication form for humans is an interactive dialogue. The most frequent form is a written dialogue; however, the dialogue can also be based on the use of speech, images, and even brain waves (EEG). We can design a good human-computer interface if we understand both sides; so far, at least two aspects are known: the capacity of human perception, and the capacity of human short-term memory.

2.3 CAPACITY OF HUMAN PERCEPTION

Performing a large number of experiments, psychologists have succeeded in establishing the sensitivity level of human perception[3,4]. The simplest experiments are those involving a linear scale. In one experiment, students were asked to look at a point displayed on a linear scale for a short period of time. The students' task was to estimate the position of the point on the scale. In other experiments, students were asked to distinguish between different colors, or to distinguish between the sounds of different frequencies. After each experiment, the students were asked what they had seen or heard. The goal of each of these experiments was to find out the relation between the input information and the information recognized by the student.

In all experiments, if the students were asked to distinguish between a small number of choices, the answer was correct. However, if the number of choices in one experiment were more than seven, students could not recognize choices precisely; thus, the answers were incorrect. The conclusion is that the natural scale of human sensitivity has seven levels. If two levels differ by less than 1/7, humans have difficulty in distinguishing between them without technical aids. This fact readily explains why we use the scale of seven basic colors in paintings and the scale of seven basic tones in music.

The results of linear one-dimensional experiments are shown in Figure 2.4. The input information, as well as the recognized information, is coded in bits. Two alternatives ask for one-bit coding, four alternatives ask for two-bit coding and, in general, N alternatives ask for $\log_2 N$ bits of coding. For seven alternatives, it is necessary to have 2.81 bits. This experiment shows a relatively low level of

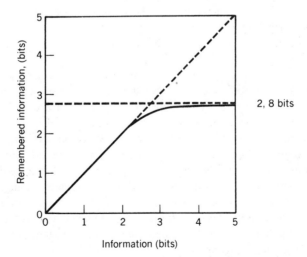

Figure 2.4 *Capacity of the human perception channel. The limit is 2.8 bits for each dimension, or seven discrete levels.*

sensitivity of the perception channel: only 2.81 bits. In reality, sensitivity is much higher, because we do not receive the information only in one linear and absolute scale.

Sensitivity is increased if the student answers on a relative rather than an absolute scale. The sensitivity also increases if the student makes decisions one after another. This mode of operation is typical for dialogue between humans as well as for human-computer dialogue.

Multidimensional coding of input information also increases the sensitivity level. Instead of distinguishing between the points on linear scale, students were asked to distinguish between points inside a square. The experiment found that each new dimension increases the sensitivity level. However, the increase is not quadratic (7^2) in the case of two dimensions, and it is less than the power of three (7^3) in the case of three dimensions.

2.4 CAPACITY OF SHORT-TERM MEMORY

Information storing in humans is divided into at least two categories: *long-term memory* (LTM) and *short-term memory* (STM). Ericsson and Chase [5] define LTM and STM in the following way:

When the new information is perceived and attended to, it is kept available for a short time but then is irrevocably lost unless it is attended to again, or rehearsed. This temporary storage system is called short-term memory (STM). The amount of information that can be held at one time in STM is severely limited for normal people. To be stored permanently, information has to be placed in long-term memory (LTM), which consists of an essentially unlimited and permanent base for storing information. Information in LTM can be retrieved only by precise retrieval cues, and failure in retrieval is the major cause of loss of information in LTM. For normal people it requires conscious effort and considerable time to commit unrelated information to LTM in a form that makes it avialable for retrieval.

Fairly early in psychology, attempts were made to measure the capacity of STM. The most common procedure was the memory-span task, in which an experimenter presents a number of items to be recalled in order. The items are presented at a fairly rapid rate (1 item per second) to minimize the amount of information converted to LTM. The interesting conclusion was that the memory span is limited and is approximately the same for many types of symbols: around 7 different digits or consonants and slightly fewer (5) or (6) for colors, visually presented geometrical designs, and words. Miller [6] summarized this research by saying that STM has the capacity to retain 7 plus or minus 2 symbols or chunks. A chunk is a collection of symbols, such as a phone number, that acts as a memory unit: all the symbols of the chunk are forgotten or retrieved together, and there is a single retrieval cue for the chunk.

It is interesting that the memory capacity does not depend on the information complexity of individual chunks: in one experiment, simple information-poor chunks are used, and the memory capacity is seven; in another experiment complex information-rich chunks are used, and the memory capacity is again seven. Only when chunks become very complex does the short-term memory store less then seven elements. The results of experiments are shown in Figure 2.5.

These experiments show that the memory is designed to maximize the information content for each chunk that is remembered. Hence, humans will learn in the best way if they are confronted with a limited number of chunks which can be distinguished from each other, and if each chunk is rich in information. Humans are not skillful when dealing with a large number of information-poor chunks, such as remembering a long string of numbers.

The best way of learning is to classify the information into chunks and then to remember the whole chunk as one element. (The chunk should keep the items that are related in some way.) These relations within the chunk are identical to the associations. Through association, one item of the chunk recalls the other items of the same chunk. In this way, the brain optimizes the information content or the number of information bits in the chunk. Chunking in short-term memory has been investigated for many years.[6-11]

The brain uses the process of association in short-term memory. In the sensory stream, data are coded in one way. Through the formation of association groups, the memory data are coded in another way. Multi-dimensional associations are possible with overlaps between the group. For example, Ericsson and Chase[5] report that a student, SF, remembers the number 3492 as "3 minutes and 49.2 seconds, near world-record time for running a mile. " Table 2.1 lists individuals with allegedly exceptional memory; SF's performance of remembering 80 digits is remarkable.

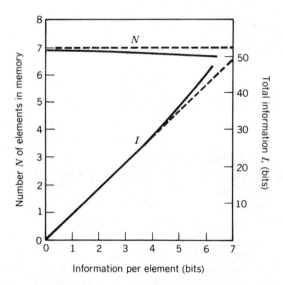

Figure 2.5 *Capacity of temporary memory. The limit is seven elements, regardless of the information content of each element.*

TABLE 2.1 Digit Spans of Memory Experts

Investigator	Memory Expert	Digit Span
Binet[11]	Inaudi	< 12
	Diamondi	< 12
	Arnould	< 12
Muller (1911)	Ruckle	18
Luria[7]	S	< 20
Hunt and Love[8]	VP	17
Hunter[9]	Aitken	15
Ericsson and Chase[5]	SF	80

Reprinted from Ericsson and Chase[5]. Courtesy and Copyright ©1982 by American Scientist.

Newell and Rosenbloom[10] found that the speed of retrieval of numerical matrices is closely related to the extra study time spent beyond that required for memorization alone. Thus, it will be the relations between different retrieval times of a subject that will give information about the memory structure, rather than the absolute retrieval times.

In digital computers, the simplest way to store the data is to keep the same kind of coding in the sensory data stream and in the memory. Most of the memories are externally addressable (ROM, RAM, disk). Only recently, new types of computing systems become available, based on code transformation between the sensory stream and the memory, or designed around associative, content-addressable memories (see Chapters 11–20).

2.5 COMPUTER VERSUS HUMAN

Although the computer cannot be compared with humans, some of its features have similar features in man. Figures 2.6 and 2.7 list some of the interesting features. Three areas are examined: memory, input/output channels, and speed of operation.

A human can store up to 10^{12} information items. The memory is organized on the principle of association; data retrieval is fairly slow (5 to 50 bits/second). Humans have strong preprocessors between the sensors and the memory, which compress and transform the sensory data into more meaningful form. The central system and the long-term memory deal only with highly preprocessed information. The main features of the brain are associative organization, self-adaptability, learning, and perception. It is estimated that long-term memory could acquire 10,000 chunks of information per year.

The modern computer has large (10^{10} bits) and fast (10^8 bits/sec) memories. It can process data with a high precision that is literally unthinkable for humans. Yet, the computer knows only the tasks which are described in programs written by humans.

Humans receive and send information at a moderate speed. Yet, we have a variety of sensory channels which are very flexible and which have a large dynamic range ($1:10^9$). The computer receives and sends information at a high speed. The most frequent modes of operation are written text, images, and manual data entry.

Human Brain	Computer Processor
Memory capacity of 10^{12} bits	Memory of 10^{10} bits
Associative organization	Direct addressing
Slow, 5–50 bits/second	Fast, up to 10^8 bits/second
Strong preprocessors	Very accurate, no errors
Eye has 10^8 receptors, but	
10^6 optical fibers	Does only what the
Adaptable in learning	program specifies
Human Input	**Computer Output**
Multichannel	Presently mostly graphical
Very flexible	Limited capability to
	generate speech
Slow	
Wide dynamic range 1:10^9	Very fast
Human Output	**Computer Input**
Multichannel	Presently mostly manual
	(keyboard)
Multidimensional	Limited capability to
	understand speech
Slow	
Very flexible	Very fast
	Limited flexibility

Figure 2.6 *Brain versus computer.*

Human Input	Computer Output
Eye	Graphic display (image, text)
Ear	Synthesized speech
Nose	– – –
Skin	Special output (for blind)
Human Output	**Computer Input**
Hand	Many devices, based on
	manual control
Voice	Devices to understand limited
	number of spoken words
Moving head, leg	Mechanical devices in
	simulators
Electrical signals	Laboratory experimental
	devices—to control arti-
	ficial organs, or to read
	and analyze brain waves

Figure 2.7 *Input-output channels: computer versus human.*

New modes have been developed, enabling the computer to hear, speak, and see. However, there is still a long way to go to improve these modes of operation.

Better understanding of human behavior, sensory modes, and motor logic will influence many technological areas (see Figure 2.8). Technologies do exist in each of the areas shown, but they could be substantially improved.

2.6 EVOKED RESPONSES

It has been known for a long time that the brain generates waves called *electroen-cephalograms* (EEG). An EEG is a slow electromagnetic wave that pervades the brain tissue. It can be recorded either with electrodes implanted in the brain or with an array of thin electrodes affixed to the scalp.

Of special interest are experiments with *evoked responses*. The evoked responses or *event-related potentials* (e.r.p) result from a stimulus applied to a person. The stimulus can be an electrical pulse, a light flash, a sound, a touch, and so on. The stimulus can also be a word or sentence that the observed person himself or herself is saying or hearing. By averaging many such responses, it is possible to cancel out the background activity of the brain and extract the electrical activity specifically associated with the stimulus. The result is a wave representing the brain's response.

In experiments performed by Chapman and his group at the University of Rochester, subjects were shown words grouped into six categories by connotations. For example, "good" words might be "peace," "beauty," or "love." "Bad" words might be "war," "crime," or "drug." Each word-type gave rise to a distinctive e.r.p. pattern. The computer and pattern-recognition programs have been used to guess the correct word-type from the patterns; the results are better than those for random guesses.

Some research groups looked at how the pattern of electrical potentials shifts over space and time as the meaning of a word changes. It has been found that different spatial and temporal patterns of the electromagnetic waves were generated

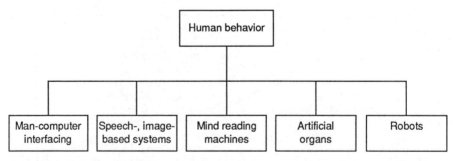

Figure 2.8 *Computer engineering areas that are influenced by advances in human behavior study.*

in response to nouns and verbs of similar sound (for example, "the rose" versus "he rows").

The e.r.p.s triggered by verbal stimuli have been related to several different aspects of language processing.[12-14] It has been found that if a subject reads a sentence that ends with an unexpected word, a negative wave shows up 400 milliseconds after the appearance of the word. This wave is called the N400 component. The closer in meaning the word is to the expected sentence ending, the smaller the N400 wave. One likely interpretation of these findings would assume that N400 amplitude reflects the extent to which a word is unpredictable or unexpected, regardless of whether or not it is incongruous with a preceding context.

In their experiment, Kutas and Hillyard [14] presented 321 sentences to subjects, one word at a time, on a video terminal controlled by a microcomputer. Words were presented once every 700 ms for a duration of 132 ms; sample sentences are shown in Figure 2.9. Scalp electrical activity was recorded, and e.r.p. waveforms were calculated. The N400 amplitude was indeed sensitive to the semantic relationship between the eliciting words and the expected best composition.

According to Kutas and Hillyard, these results are in agreement with the hypothesis that the N400 component reflects the extent to which a word is semantically

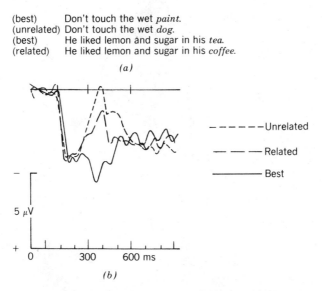

(best)   Don't touch the wet *paint.*
(unrelated) Don't touch the wet *dog.*
(best)   He liked lemon and sugar in his *tea.*
(related)   He liked lemon and sugar in his *coffee.*

(a)

– – – – – –Unrelated

— — — Related

———— Best

5 μV

0   300   600 ms

(b)

Figure 2.9 *(a) Two examples of sentences with high contextual constraints completed by low Cloze probability words. Above each experimental sentence is the same sentence terminated by its best completion, which was or was not semantically related to the word that was actually presented in the sentence below. (b) Grand average e.r.p.s from Pz for the best completions (solid waveform), the semantically related (large dashed waveform), and the semantically unrelated (small dashed waveform) low Cloze probability words. Reprinted by permission from* Nature **307**, *161–163 (1984). Copyright ©1984 Macmillan Magazines Limited.*

primed, rather than its being a specific response to contextual violations. If the N400 amplitude proves to be a valid index of semantic priming, it should become possible to investigate the timing and the spread of activation within semantic networks and knowledge schemata and to identify automatic and attentional components of processing.

In another group of experiments, subjects were shown several panels with images displayed in repetitious mode, as in television, with the repetition rate high enough to avoid flicker. To the eye, all the images looked steady, although different repetition rates were used in each panel. The computer measured the e.r.p. and was able to guess into which panel the subject was looking.

If the computer could read and understand the e.r.p. patterns which are related to particular stimuli, this ability could open the door to many questions and speculations: Is it possible for the operator to look at a particular panel and have the computer understand a specific "wish" calling the necessary subroutine for that wish from the program library to start action? Will it ever be possible to build a "mind-reading machine," as shown in Fig.2.10, which will be able to recognize some simple e.r.p.s?

Figure 2.10 *"Mind-Reading Machine"?*

2.7 THE DIALOGUE

Natural human-computer communication is based on speech and images, and is constantly developing. In the meantime, simpler written dialogue enables efficient interactive communication with the computer. The interactive dialogue is used in both classical sequential machines and in new parallel computers; the most flexible is the natural language-based dialogue. Other modes include [15] programming-style dialogue; instruction and response; menu selection; displayed formats; form filing; panel modification; query by example; long-distance dialogue; and hybrid dialogues.

An example of the hybrid dialogue is the software package T-ask. It is oriented towards business applications, banking, and library systems and has three modes of operation:

- Maintenance mode, used in the initialization
- Query mode, used for efficient data storage and retrieval
- Catalogue mode, used to store the dialogue structure for future applications

T-ask can operate in the English language, as well as in other languages. Figure 2.11 shows a dialogue in the Croatian-Serbian language in Zagreb Bank[15]:

First window:

Top: Menu of applications
Middle: 19, 2, 18, 16, selected items
Bottom: Body of the dialogue for checking accounts

Second window:

Displays selected checking accounts. The high efficiency in preparing and using the dialogue is obvious.

A special kind of dialogue is the long-distance dialogue. A large number of data bases are distributed around the world. These data bases supply the bibliographic reference data for libraries as well as commercial data, drawings, marketing, technical, and scientific data. An entire information industry has developed to sell the data, whose market value is in the billions of dollars. A long-distance data network is the neural network of a modern society. We show a simple example of a dialogue with one such network: EURONET DIANE.

EURONET DIANE has a number of host centers in large cities. Each center is specialized for gathering and storing a specific kind of data. End users communicate through terminals, display units, printers, or modems connected to the telephone network. The dialogue with the network is divided into three steps:

1. Identification and start of the dialogue
2. Data-base search
3. Termination of the dialogue

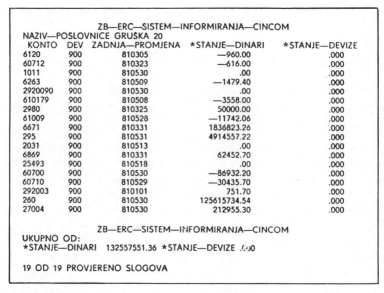

```
               ZB—ERC—SISTEM—INFORMIRANJA—CINCOM
ODABERI IMENA PODATAKA
01 POSLOVNA—JEDINICA   02 KONTO                  03 KONTO—3—CIF
04 POSLOVNICA          05 POSL—JED               06 PODRN
07 DUGUJE—DEVIZE—P     08 POTRAZUJE—DEVIZE—P  09 DUGUJE—DINARI—P
10 POTRAZUJE—DINARI—P  11 ZADNJA—PROMJENA—P  12 DUGUJE—DEVIZE
13 POTRAZUJE—DEVIZE    14 DUGUJE—DINARI          15 POTRAZUJE—DINARI
16 ZADNJA—PROMJENA     17 DEVIZA                 18 DEV
19 NAZIV—POSLOVNICE    20 KONTO—4—CIF            21 OZNAKA
22 ST—RACUN            23 ST—VRNA                24 ST—DOTV
25 ST—RORO             26 ST—STOPA               27 ST—POSL
28 ST—SALDO            29 ST—SALDO—KTE           30 ST—ZAD—PROM
31 ST—BROJ—PROM        32 ST—MTS—NO              33 ST—RAD—MJEST
34 ST—SEQ—BROJ         35 GR—RACUN               36 GR—IME—ADRESA
37 GR—BR—PTT           38 GR—OOUR                39 ST—DOMICIL
40 ST—STARI—BROJ       41 ST—NOVI—BROJ           42 MAT—BROJ
43 NAZIV—KOMITENTA     44 SJEDISTE               45 ADRESA—KOM
**JOŠ PODATAKA**


19, 2, 18, 16

               ZB—ERC—SISTEM—INFORMIRANJA—CINCOM
UNESI NAČIN SELEKCIJE
POSLOVNICA JD 12109
POTRAZUJE—DINARI — DUGUJE—DINARI = *STANJE—DINARI
POTRAZUJE—DEVIZE — DUGUJE—DEVIZE = *STANJE—DEVIZE
UKUPNO *STANJE—DINARI, *STANJE—DEVIZE


kraj
```

```
                ZB—ERC—SISTEM—INFORMIRANJA—CINCOM
NAZIV—POSLOVNICE GRUŠKA 20
  KONTO   DEV  ZADNJA—PROMJENA  *STANJE—DINARI   *STANJE—DEVIZE
  6120    900      810305          —960.00          .000
  60712   900      810323          —616.00          .000
  1011    900      810530              .00          .000
  6263    900      810509         —1479.40          .000
  2920090 900      810530              .00          .000
  610179  900      810508         —3558.00          .000
  2980    900      810325         50000.00          .000
  61009   900      810528        —11742.06          .000
  6671    900      810331       1836823.26          .000
  295     900      810531       4914557.22          .000
  2031    900      810513              .00          .000
  6869    900      810331         62452.70          .000
  25493   900      810518              .00          .000
  60700   900      810530        —86932.20          .000
  60710   900      810529        —30435.70          .000
  292003  900      810101           751.70          .000
  260     900      810530     125615734.54          .000
  27004   900      810530        212955.30          .000

                ZB—ERC—SISTEM—INFORMIRANJA—CINCOM
UKUPNO OD:
*STANJE—DINARI  132557551.36 *STANJE—DEVIZE .000

19 OD 19 PROVJERENO SLOGOVA
```

Figure 2.11 *Checking-account dialogue in the Croatian-Serbian language.*

```
EURONET   0041437
02223344DXXXXXN000000000012
COM

PLEASE ENTER YOUR PASSWORD
XXXXXXX CONNECTION ACCEPTED   11:49:   :17

? BASE ENERGY
? FIND CARBOURANT AND REPLACEMENT
       1   2904 CARBOURANT
       2   6089 REPLACEMENT
       3    785 1*2

? FIND ALCOHOL
       4 16654 ALCOHOL
       5    38 3*4

? SHOW

? STOP
SESSION TERMINATED AT 12:02:28

LIBPAD
```

Figure 2.12 *Long-distance dialogue: EURONET DIANE.*

An example of the dialogue is shown in Figure 2.12: the user is looking for fuel to replace gasoline. The first five lines present the connection to the selected system, followed by the identification. After that, the user must select one of many data bases. In the example, BASE ENERGY is chosen. Now the user selects the key words: CARBURANT and REPLACEMENT. The words are labeled 1 and 2, and their Boolean product is labeled 3. The data-base search shows 785 references with both key words. The user now narrows the search, by using the key word labeled 4 = ALCOHOL. Again the label 5 presents the product of 3 and 4. The data-base search shows 38 references containing this product. If the user wants, the system will show selected references. When the search is finished, the user STOPs the dialogue and consults the library for another possible service.

In designing the dialogue it is necessary to understand the principles of perception; human-computer interfaces; the capacity of short-term memory; and human and computer response times. Speech, images (and in special cases evoked responses) are entering the market, resulting in hybrid operations.

REFERENCES

1. Science and Technology Agency, *Promotion of Research and Development on Electronic and Information Systems that May Complement or Substitute for Human Intelligence.* STA, Tokyo, 1985.

2. R. E., Chapman, *Biologically-Related Computing (Japan's Sixth Generation)*, Background Paper. Technicom International Corporation, Falls Church, VA, 1985.

3. J. Martin, *Design of Man-Computer Dialogues,* Prentice Hall, Englewood Cliffs, NJ, 1973.

4. B. Shackel, The ergonomics of man/computer interface, In *Infotech State of the Art Report: Man/Computer Communication,* Infotech, England, 1979, pp' 299-385.

5. K. A. Ericsson and W. G. Chase, *American Scientist* **70**, 607-615 (1982).

6. G. A. Miller, The magic number seven, plus or minus two, *Psychol. Rev.* **63**, 81-97 (1956)

7. A. R. Luria, *The Mind of a Mnemonist.* Avon, 1968

8. E. Hunt and T. Love, How good can memory be? *On Coding Processes in Human Memory*, A. W. Melton and E. Martin (eds,), Winston, Washington, DC, 1972.

9. I. M. L Hunter, An exceptional memory. *Brit. J. Phsychol,* **68**, 155-164 (1977).

10. A. Newell and P. S. Rosenbloom, Mechanisms of skill acquisition and the law of practice. In *Cognitive Skills and Their Acquisition*, J. R. Anderson (ed.), Erlbaum, Hillsdale, NJ, 1981.

11. A. Binet, *Psychologie des grands calculateurs et joueurs d'echecs.* Librarie Hachette, Paris, 1894.

12. M. Kutas and S. A. Hillyard, *Science* **207**, 203-205 (1980).

13. M. Kutas and S. A. Hillyard, *Mem. Cognit.* **11**(5), 539-550 (1983).

14. M. Kutas and S. A. Hillyard, *Nature*, **307**, 161-163 (1984).

15. M. Souček, *Automatic Programming.* Informator, Zagreb, 1986.

CHAPTER 3 ⎯⎯⎯⎯⎯⎯⎯⎯⎯⎯⎯⎯⎯

Systems Emulating Brain-Behavior Functions

INTRODUCTION AND SURVEY

A number of efforts are under way to build computers and systems influenced by models and theories of the brain. Although the beginning was very slow, the design of brain-like systems is now turning into an avalanche. Both laboratory-built as well as commercial brain-like systems are becoming available, with outstanding features. The primary purpose of this chapter is to examine those information-processing models of the brain which could directly influence the development of sixth-generation computers.

The first coding layer in the living system is the layer of the cell. Two codes are present within the cell: fixed genetic code, corresponding to the read-only memory in a computer; and programmable microtubule code, corresponding to read/write memories. These codes are based on molecular structures. We will examine the possibility of using genetic and microtubule codes and molecular structures to design the biochip.

Above the molecular layer is a neural network layer. The operation of this layer is explained with brain theories and models. Several Nobel Prizes have been delivered in the area of brain-behavior research and modeling. The theory and modeling proceeds on several levels: neuron, network and connection, feature maps and feature extraction, brain windows and coding languages, and cooperative action.

Can computer architects learn from nature? Advances have been achieved in areas where barriers between the life sciences and computer science/engineering have been dissolved. Brain models suggest a mixture of different modes of information presentation. Many projects are in progress, following brain models: cognitrons, adaptive learning systems, neurocomputers, associative memories, fuzzy logic systems, massively parallel systems, and genetic systems. An avalanche of new brain-like systems is under way.

3.1 GENETIC CODE

The primary layer of coding in biological systems is a *genetic code*, stored inside the nucleus of every cell. It contains genetic information included in the amino-acid sequences of protein molecules. The nucleus of each cell contains the complete program necessary to develop a living organism. The genetic code presents an extremely efficient packing of information.

In the period between 1944 and 1953, several experiments identified DNA as the primary genetic material. The double helical, base-paired structure of DNA was discovered in 1953 by Francis Crick and James Watson. This structure provided knowledge of several requisite features of primary genetic material, including stable information storage and faithful self-replication.

The code is composed of coding elements and coding words. The coding elements present the building blocks of the genetic code. Four deoxynucleoside triphosphates have been identified as coding elements and labeled *U*, *C*, *A*, and *G*. Hence the genetic code is a base-four code, as opposed to the base-two (binary) code used in digital computers. The names of the four coding elements are *A*—Aderine; *C*—Citosin; *G*—Guarin; and *U*—Uracil.

An adjacent sequence of three coding elements constitutes a code word; the coding word is composed of three positions. Each position in the word is filled by one of four coding elements. The total number of contributions, or different coding words, is 4 x 4 x 4 = 64.

Each code word specifies an amino acid. With 64 available three-element sequences, there should be 64 amino acids. In reality, though, only 20 amino acids have been identified. Clearly, the code is degenerate, and more than one word is used to specify an amino acid.

The genetic code is shown in Figure 3.1[1]. At the bottom, 20 amino acids are listed. At the top, three-element sequences or words are shown. From Figure 3.1 we can read the coding sequence for each amino acid. Examples:

Methionine—met: A U G

Aspartic acid—asp: G A U but also G A C

Glutamic acid—glu: G A A but also G A G

The genetic code is universal. A given code word or codon specifies the same amino acid throughout the biological kingdom.

3.2 MICROTUBULE CODE

The secondary layer of coding in biological systems is a microtubule code, stored in the cytoplasm within every cell. Microtubules (MT) are cylindrical, gridlike

First position (Read down)	Second position (Read across)				Third position (Read down)
	U	C	A	G	
U	phe	ser	tyr	cys	U
	phe	ser	tyr	cys	C
	leu	ser	stop	stop	A
	leu	ser	stop	trp	G
C	leu	pro	his	arg	U
	leu	pro	his	arg	C
	leu	pro	gln	arg	A
	leu	pro	gln	arg	G
A	ile	thr	asn	ser	U
	ile	thr	asn	ser	C
	ile	thr	lys	arg	A
	met	thr	lys	arg	G
G	val	ala	asp	gly	U
	val	ala	asp	gly	C
	val	ala	glu	gly	A
	val	ala	glu	gly	G

ala — alanine	gly — glycine	pro — proline
arg — arginine	his — histadine	ser — serine
asn — asparagine	ile — isoleucine	thr — threonine
asp — aspartic acid	leu — leucine	trp — tryptophan
cys — cysteine	lys — lysine	tyr — tyrosine
gln — glutamine	met — methionine	val — valine
glu — glutamic acid	phe — phenylalanine	

Figure 3.1 *The genetic code. From Sampson*[1] *reprinted by permission of John Wiley & Sons, Inc. Copyright ©1985.*

polymers which comprise cilia, flagella, and the structural skeleton of living cells. Their functions include cellular orientation and structure, and guidance of membrane and cytoplasmic movements.

According to Hameroff and Watt,[2] neuronal microtubules can be linked to many features of behavior and intelligence:

Evidence has linked neuronal MT to trophism and differentiation as well as to conscious perception, behavior, and intellect. Theorized processes which could explain these apparent information functions occurring within MT include cooperative resonance among spatially arrayed proteins, and propagated conformational changes along MT protofilaments. Propagated changes along helical row axes as well as longitudinal protofilaments would imply that polymer subunits within cylindrical grid-like MT structure, connecting proteins, and intracellular trabecular networks could provide programmable switching matrices for information transfer via Boolean logic. Calcium-dependent conformation states coupled to charge or energy quanta could be a medium of information transfer among the four nanometer (nm), 55,000 dalton MT subunits (tubulin), with programming by genetic or environmental effects. Transduction of information signals by ATPase mechanical proteins would result in temporal and spatial control of protein mechanical functions and cellular activity. In the nervous system, parallel computing in neuronal MT arrays may be coupled to action potentials or $2+$ calcium ion (Ca^+) flux. Such coupling could result in cooperative resonances, field fluctuations, and interference patterns which might comprise conscious awareness functions within the brain.

The microtubule itself is an assembly of thirteen longitudinal protofilaments, each of which consists of a series of dimers of alpha and beta monomers (Figure 3.2). Electron occupancy of either monomer may correlate with coherent dipole oscillations. The patterns of oscillation phase can function as specific sites of protein binding and transport, orchestration of biomolecular activities, and information and memory storage. Interaction and interference in these patterns can process information as in a computer.

The microtubule coding system is composed of coding elements and words. The coding elements are three-state elements. The coding words are formed from four coding elements.

A number of microtubule associated proteins (MAPs) can bind to the outside of the microtubule cylinder (Figure 3.3). Among these are dynein and kinesin, which can contract in the presence of biochemical energy supplied by ATP. The MAPs can transport substances along the length of the microtubule at rates of up to 400 mm per day. According to Hameroff, [2] the orchestration of directional transport of specific enzymes or precursors via a sliding filament can be thought of as a function of the on-off states of the tubulin dimers which anchor the sidearm proteins.

For example, if a row of subunits anchoring one sidearm protein is on (occupied) and the other is off (unoccupied), then the sidearm points to an unopposed "on"

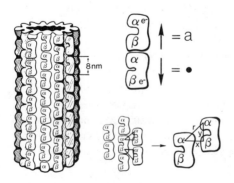

Figure 3.2
Left: microtubule (MT) structure. Right: MT tubulin subunits comprised of two and three monomers. Reprinted by permission from Hameroff and Watt.[2].

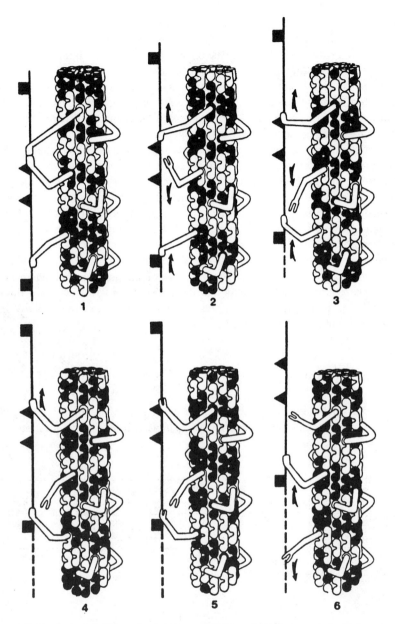

Figure 3.3 *Computer/robot-like microtubule model of axoplastic transport. A single column of MAP sidearm protein in a "bucket brigade" model of axoplasmic transport of a sliding filament carrying specific enzymes of precursors is portrayed. Reprinted by permission from Hameroff and Watt.*[2]

subunit (see Figure 3.3). In this example, genetic information would be considered a program, and changes in state (ion flux, charge gradient, action potential) would be considered execute commands. The on-off states within each microtubule could provide for transductional information processing.

The matrix grid of microtubule subunits and associated proteins resembles the operation of computers, cellular automata, and robots. It seems that microtubules are at least partially responsible for biological communication, regulation, information processing, and cognitive and thought processes.

Genetic and microtubule codes are summarized in Figure 3.4. These two digital codes and associated analog information interactions present the basic level of intelligence: the level of the cell. This intelligence level is subdivided into layers: digital (genetic code); analog (molecular interaction); digital (microtubular codes); and analog (ion flux, charge gradient, action potential). The mixture of digital and analog layers might be one of the basic features of biological architectures for intelligence.

There are many more layers between DNA and neurons. For example, there is a highly localized system of membrane specializations around synapses that involves neurotransmitter receptors and the cytoskeleton. However, we limit the discussion on microtubules here because of the on-going research activity in the area of microtubules and the biochip.

3.3 THE BIOCHIP

Genetic and microtubule codes show the fascinating world of biological intelligence based on biomolecules—intelligence on the single-cell level. The question is, can

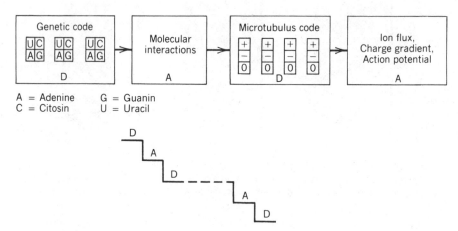

Figure 3.4 The basic level of intelligence: the level of the cell. Mixture of digital (D) and analog (A) information layers.

we build a chip and a computer based on biomolecules? Very little has been done in this direction, but the name has been coined: *biochip*.

The concept of the biochip takes into account two basic aspects of molecular biology:

- Biopolymers can self-assemble.
- Molecules like DNA can store, replicate, and transmit information.

In such a device, DNA properly coded would be inserted into a cell, which would make the desired biomolecules and assemble them into a computer. The cell and the computer within it will find numerous applications: restoring the sight to the blind and hearing to the deaf, putting real intelligence into machines, reproducing intelligent systems, and so forth. The applications also include biosensors, biobatteries, robot vision, neuronal interfaces, and artificial intelligence.

Due to the molecular size of the elements in biochips, packing densities can be increased by orders of magnitudes. At present, the highest-density semiconductor chip approaches one million transistors on an area 4 mm square, with spacing between elements of about 1.5 microns. By means of new materials and advanced lithographic techniques, it may be possible to increase the density four times, with a spacing of 0.2 micron, this seems to be the limit. Yet with biomolecules, one can envisage three-dimensional devices with capacity several orders of magnitude better than in semiconductor devices.

The first molecular device was patented in 1974 by Aviran and Seiden, of IBM's Yorktown Heights research center, and Ratner of Northwestern University. They noted that a number of organic molecules can exist in two or more stable states, depending on the distribution of charges within the molecule. For example, hemiquinones (molecules involved in biological electron transport) have two stable electronic states. By applying a voltage across the molecule, one can convert it reversibly from one state to another and use the molecule as a binary device.

Even more revolutionary devices have been envisaged, based on soliton propagation and on microtubules. No one has yet built a working biochip. Still, major companies in Japan and in the United States (e. g., IBM, General Electric, Hughes Aircraft, Hitachi, Sharp, Suntory, and others) are investigating various phases of biomolecular computing.

Of even greater interest is the use of genetically engineered compounds as sensors. Such a device would harness the pattern-recognition ability of some proteins for detecting specific molecules at low concentration. Such a device could sniff out chemicals in the environment and serve as a biosensor.

The first interdisciplinary conference on the biochip was held in 1984 in Santa Monica, California, and was funded by the National Science Foundation. Since then, molecular computing has been a subject of many conferences. Significant problems still remain; the most obvious is the question of how to hook up molecular-scale circuits to a conventional scale conductor. Many questions have to be answered before research in biochip turns into development and production. Still, if biochips do materialize, they will be used to design the ultimate computer.

3.4 BRAIN THEORIES AND MODELS

Brain theories are concerned with developing mathematical models of neurons and the brain. Several Nobel Prizes have been delivered in the area of brain-behavior research and modeling:

> Hodgkin-Huxley: Physiological model of propagation of electrical signals along the axon of a neuron
> Katz: All-or-none model of synaptic junction
> Hubel and Wiesel: Feature-extraction model of visual cortex
> Lorenz, Tinbergen: Goal-directed behavioral models

Theories and modeling proceed on several levels: those of the neuron, network and connections, feature maps and feature extraction, brain windows and coding languages, and cooperative action. All of these theories and models are supported at least in part by experimental evidence. Here we give a short summary of these models. A detailed description of brain-behavior models follows in Part II of this book.

3.4.1 The Neuron

Neural cells, or *neurons*, present the basic unit of the brain structure. There is a large variety of neurons with different features. Neurons transmit electrochemical impulses from one to another via long fibers called *axons*[3-5] (Figure 3.5). These impulses travel along the axon until they reach a junction, or *synapse*, with another neuron. At this point, chemical transmitters released from the axon terminal, called the *end plate*, cross the synaptic gap and excite or inhibit the target neuron. If the excitation from several synaptic inputs exceeds a certain threshold, the target neuron generates an impulse of its own.

The main purpose of the neuron is signal amplification and processing. Usually a very great number of input signals converge upon a single neuron: in Pyramid, cells up to 10^3 connections; in Parkinje cells, up to 10^5 connections. Each neuron has one output with many branches, called *dendrites*. Dendrites are connected to many places, forming neural networks.

The first model of a neuron was suggested by McCulloch and Pitts.[6] In this model, the neuron is considered as a triggering device with a threshold. When the sum of the input signals exceeds this threshold, an output with the value "true" is obtained; otherwise, the output is "false." This is a highly simplified model, yet it has been used to explain many neural functions, using Boolean algebra. The model is known by the name "formal neuron" (Figure 3.6).

Using this model, we can compare the neural network, or the brain, to technical communication networks, or computers, dealing with binary information. This is a simplified approach. In reality, the neuron is not only a logical gate, but also an analog computing device that integrates and processes the event-trains. Because the synaptic junction has a much longer time constant than the spacing between pulses

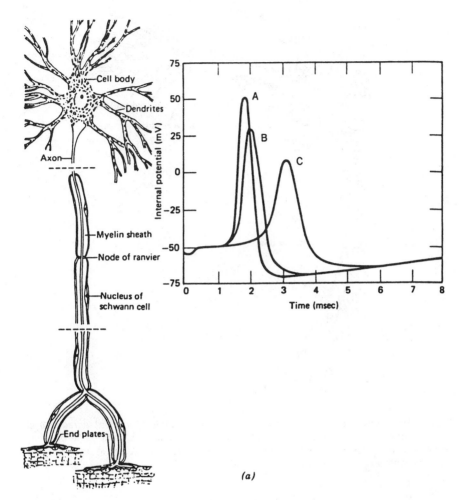

Figure 3.5a *Left: motor neuron. The cell body fans out into a number of twigs, the* dendrites, *which make synaptic contact with other nerve fibers. Nerve action potentials arise in the initial, unsheathed region of the axon and travel to the end plate, which is embedded in the muscle fibers. The transmitter is released at the end plate to activate the muscle fiber membrane.* [3] *Right: three action potentials recorded on the oscilloscope screen. Potential (A) in axons with normal ionic medium. Potentials from axons in which a quarter (B) and half (C) of the potassium was replaced with sodium.* [4]

in the train, a temporal summation occurs. New pulses pile up on the remains of the previous pulses thereby yielding the so-called "slow potential" on the dendrite. The resulting magnitude of this dendritic depolarization is proportional to the average frequency at which pulses arrive at the synapse. Similarly, the action potential frequency of the next neuron connected to this dendrite is proportional to the slow potential on the dendrite. In this way, neurons operate as event-train/analog

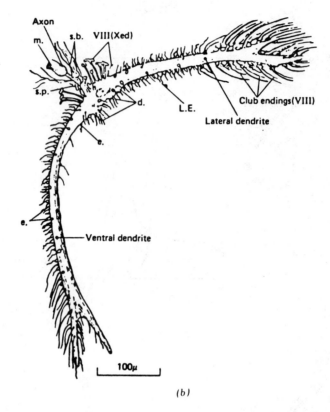

(b)

Figure 3.5b *Mauthner cell from brain of goldfish. An example of mosaic segregation of different types of synaptic endings from different sources on specific parts of the dendritic zone of a neuron; m:myelin sheath of Mauthner cell axon; s.b.: bundle giving origin to spiral fibers; h:axons hillock; d:small dendrites; e:small end bulbs.*[5]

voltage/event-train processors. A detailed description of event-train processing and of related computer systems is given in Chapter 14.

3.4.2 Networks and Connections

The neurons are interconnected via special formations called synapses. Two main types of synapses are now distinguished:

- *Excitatory Synapses* increase the postsynaptic depolarization, or bring the neuron closer to triggering.
- *Inhibitory synapses* decrease the depolarization and make the triggering less likely.

The synapses and networks can be considered as a third layer of information coding and memory. (The first layer is genetic code, and the second layer is

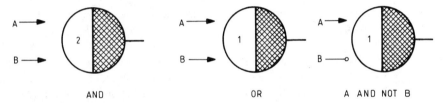

Figure 3.6 *Some McCulloch-Pitts cells.*

microtubule code.) The first and the second layer rely on biomolecular structures and present the basis for a chemical theory of memory and intelligence. The network-synaptic layer is explained by the connections established in the system. Hence, this layer presents the basis for a "connectionist" theory of memory and intelligence. The connectionist theory has been introduced by several authors and is used to explain many features of the brain as well as of behavior.

In one version of the connectionist theory,[7] the inhibitory connections are hardwired but the excitatory connections are not. Instead, excitatory connections show the feature of plasticity with variable coupling strengths. The coupling strengths are formed according to the associative learning law originally introduced by Hebb.[8] Hebb first formulated the law as follows: if neuron *A* repeatedly contributes to the firing of neuron *B*, then *A*'s efficiency in firing *B* increases. By changing the strength of connections, the neural network learns and memorizes.

A large number of models has been developed within the frame of connectionist theory (Figure 3.7 shows one plastic connection explaining learning). Practical devices have been designed on this principle with limited features of learning and classifying patterns. The devices are named *perceptrons*.[9] Early connectionist models represent an extreme case, in which every single element of the memory field has a semantic interpretation.

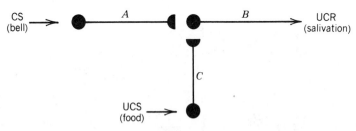

Figure 3.7 *Plastic connection based on Hebb's law explains Pavlovian learning. When a dog is presented with food it salivates. When the dog hears a bell it does not salivate initially. But after hearing the bell simultaneously with the presentation of food in several consecutive occasions, the dog is subsequently found to salivate when it hears the bell alone. Hebb's law: when a conditional stimulus (bell) is repeatedly paired with an unconditional stimulus (food) which evokes an unconditional response (salivation), the conditional stimulus gradually acquires the ability to evoke the unconditional response. For details see Chapter 11.*

In contemporary brain theories, memories are not specifically localized. When lesions were made in various parts of the brain in an accident, the level of performance sustained depended on the amount of damage and to a much lesser extent, on the exact location of lesion. The information related to a given behavioral task seems to be distributed and not localized. This fact must be taken into account when analyzing the models based on connectionist theory. Connectionist theory presents the basis for learning systems and for neural computers, described in Chapters 11 and 12.

3.4.3   Feature Extractors

Hubel and Wiesel[10] found that in a cat's visual cortex they could identify a class of single neurons whose firing rates were related to certain basic features of an image, such as the orientation of edges or bars. They called this kind of cell a "simple" neuron. A second class of cells was sensitive to the direction of motion of edges; these cells were called "complex" neurons. A third class of cells responded to even more elaborate stimuli, such as angles and corners. This class was labeled "hypercomplex" neurons. Examples of complex cell stimulus-response patterns are shown in Figure 3.8.

Simple, complex, and hypercomplex neurons are connected into a hierarchical structure; the sensory data stream is processed as it passes through this structure. The human retina contains over 100 million cones and rods which serve as primary receptors. The human optic nerve which carries information from the ganglion cells to the brain only contains about 1 million optic nerve fibers. This reduction of neural paths carrying information about an object received on the retina occurs through information processing by the network of cells in the retina. Many areas in

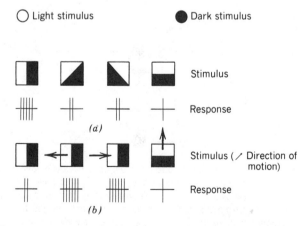

Figure 3.8 *Feature extractors: complex cells in a cat's cortex: (a) complex cell responding best to vertical bar (edge); (b) complex cell responding best to a moving vertical bar (edge).*

the brain are also able to process information in themselves. This finding presents the basis for the *feature extractor model*: for a particular sensory experience, the pattern of activity over the brain and neural system consists of only a few activated local areas, whereas the rest of the elements in the field are silent.

At present, science is not fully aware of the details of the feature detectors and their interconnections. Some authors support the idea of a continuum from simple to complex feature detectors. Stone et al.[11] propose the model based on the classification of the retinal ganglion cells as being *W*, *X*, and *Y* types. *X* cells are concerned with static and *Y* cells with dynamic features. *W* cells respond to either static or dynamic stimuli. Which model is correct, or to what degree each is correct, remains to be established. According to Braitenberg[12] it is difficult to translate the preceding sketch of feature detectors as seen by physiologists into a neural model compatible with the known anatomy. In trying to solve these difficulties, the first step is to establish a map of the visual cortex in which the relative sizes and positions of the various elements become apparent.[13] The entire question will have to be solved by anatomical techniques. It is not beyond technical feasibility to stain the fibers in order to determine their spacing in the cortex. It will then be seen whether the basic assumption (Hubel and Wiesel[10]) is correct.

3.4.4 Brain Windows and Language

Souček and Carlson[14,15] found that, in firefly communication, stimulation intervals and response latencies are clustered into islands. They named these islands "brain windows. " Upon receiving the stimulus, the firefly generates a sequence of time windows. Receive and send windows are interleaved in the sequence. Each receive window is related to specific behavior: courtship, mimicry, or patrolling. Fireflies will accept the stimulation flash only when the receive window is open; in this way they understand the flash's meaning. Fireflies will answer through one of the send windows and in this way send back coded information.

Response latency is a continuous (analog) function of the stimulus interval. This function is examined through the set of two-dimensional receive-send brain windows (Figure 3.9). In this way, a transition from continuous signaling to discrete coding is achieved, and a communication language is formed. The language is generated through the interaction of nonlinear oscillators with memory. The oscillators generate flexible, fuzzy, adjustable windows. In the case of courting behavior, the windows narrow, resulting in language with large coding distances and high selectivity. In the case of mimicry behavior, the windows widen, increasing the chance to establish communication with potential prey.

The transition from continuous signaling into a coded language is crucial in interfacing layers of biological information-processing systems. The receive-send windows also explain the programmed sequence of behavior. Nonlinear oscillator logic resulting in fuzzy windows might also be of interest in computer design. Brain windows are seen as a natural transition from fuzzy information processing to symbolic reasoning. For details, see Chapters 9 and 10.

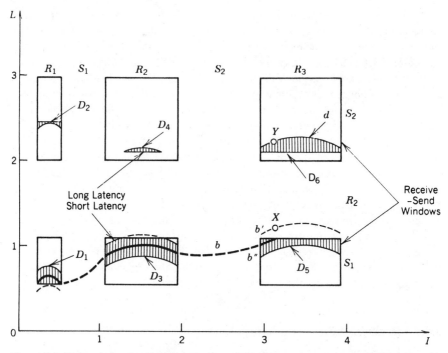

Figure 3.9 *Brain-window language of the firefly. The language is formed of dialects (shaded area); dialects are intersections between continuous belts (b, d) and discrete windows.*

3.4.5 Cooperative Action

Experiments with brain waves or EEGs suggest a correlation between brain patterns and some cognitive processes. An example is shown in Figure 2.9. This kind of experiment is used as a basis for a brain theory called "cooperative action."

According to cooperative-action theory, thoughts and perceptions are encoded in the changing patterns of an electromagnetic field rather than in the impulses of individual neurons. The model envisages a closed feedback loop: individual neurons are contributing to the common field; the field in turn influences the activity of the neuron. The situation is similar to that in an orchestra: each musician contributes to the total sound; the total sound is heard by each musician. The musician adjusts his or her playing on the basis of two sets of information: the melody he or she is supposed to play and which is written on the paper, and the sound received from the common field.

The EGG is a continuous wave extending in frequency from one hertz to a few kilohertz. The maximum of the EEG power spectrum is in the range between 3 and 50 hertz. It has been believed in the past that the EEG merely presents a random noise produced by the activity of neurons. The cooperative-action theory, based on experimental findings, claims that the electromagnetic field is the carrier of memory and cognition. The patterns are stored in some way in the field. When a stimulus is received, it produces the field, which is compared with the stored patterns. The pattern of the stimulus causes millions of brain cells to generate a similar pattern, which has somehow been stored in the chemical structure of these neurons. One way to explain the cooperative action is through resonance: A tuning fork "remembers" the frequency it is tuned at; placed in a variable sound field, the fork will produce the originally tuned pitch when it recognizes that frequency or a frequency which is merely similar (recognizing similar but not necessarily identical frequencies).

There is still a long way to go to prove the cooperative-action theory. The idea of field potentials is highly unconventional and not generally accepted. One hundred years of work on this signal has not yet elucidated its origin, let alone its function. One argument supporting the theory is the fact that the brain is composed of more than ten billion neurons. It is difficult to envision the network that would connect all of these neurons on a point-to-point basis. One possible answer is a connection through many intermediate synapses at a cost of time. Another possible answer is a contactless communication through the electromagnetic field. Through the field, a large population of neurons would be able to communicate simultaneously.

3.5 HIERARCHICAL GOAL-DIRECTED BEHAVIOR

Albus[16] has developed a model describing the brain and its behavior in the form of a hierarchical phyramid. The model follows the structure of a multilevel, multivariable feedback system. Multilevel systems are used for servomechanism process control.

Control systems are sensory-interactive and goal-directed. In the case of a servomechanism, the setpoint or reference input presents the command. Feedback from a sensing device, which monitors the state of the output, is compared with the command. In this way an error signal is generated which acts on the output. The error signal leads the output in the proper direction. Hence, the system seeks the goal set by the input command through the feedback information received from the sensing device.

A multivariable servomechanism is shown in Figure 3.10. The function H operates on the input variables in S and computes an output $P = H(s)$. The input vector S is divided into two vectors: C $(s_1, s_2, \ldots, s_i)$ is the command vector; F $(s_{i+1}, \ldots s_N)$ is the feedback vector. In building up a hierarchy of feedback systems, Albus has developed a model that would explain some brain and behavior functions. Albus uses the feedback hierarchy to support the model of behavior suggested by Tinbergen,[17] and explains the command and control of the behavior of the male three-spined stickleback fish.

In simple creatures like insects, fish, and birds, behavior is sufficiently stereotyped. The control hierarchies have only a few levels. Each level has an operator H, and the command and feedback vectors, C and F. The sensory system is simple, providing only few externally driven components in the F vectors at each level. The external variables that control behavioral patterns are the innate releasing

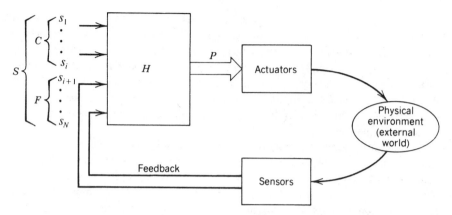

Figure 3.10 *A multivariable servomechanism. The reference or command input is the vector C consisting of the variables* s₁ *through* sᵣ*. The feedback is the vector F consisting of sensory variables* s_{i+1} *through* s_N*. The function H computes an output vector P consisting of* P₁ *through* P_L *that drives actuators, thus affecting the physical environment. Adapted from Albus.* [16]

mechanisms. Most of the behavior is internally driven (fixed action potentials, tropisms). Innate releasing mechanisms and tropisms have been studied extensively in a number of insects (i. e., digger wasp and various bees and ant species), several fish, and many birds (i. e., the herring gull, turkey, and golden-eye drake).

The hierarchical model presents the basis to build a sensory-processing goal-directed robot system. Using the multilevel, multivariable hierarchical feedback system, Albus explains many features of living or robot systems, including: goal-seeking as the natural form of behavior, sensory processing hierarchy, pattern recognition, internal world representation and the functions found only in higher animals and man; analogy between the brain and a military heirarchy, but with the vast interconnected network. Each sensory-motor system has its own set of overlaying hierarchies, that become increasingly interrelated and interconnected with each other at the higher levels. According to Albus the sensory feedback that enters each level of the behavior-generating hierarchy comes from a parallel sensory-processing hierarchy, as shown in Figure 3.11. Sensory data enter this hierarchy at the bottom and are filtered through a series of sensory-processing and pattern-recognition modules arranged in a hierarchical structure that runs parallel to the behavior-generating hierarchy. Each level of this sensory-processing hierarchy processes the incoming sensory data stream, extracting features, recognizing patterns, and applying various types of filters to the sensory data. Information relevant to the control decisions being made at each level is extracted and sent to the appropriate behavior generating modules. The partially processed sensory data that remains is then passed to the next higher level for further processing.

For a more specific explanation of the behavior hierarchy it is necessary to find the internal structure of the operators and to relate this structure to actual experimental findings. One could expect a large variety of structures for different

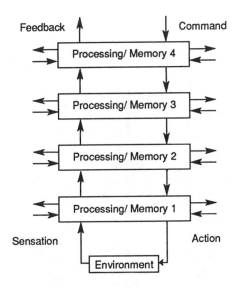

Feedback   Command

Processing/ Memory 4

Processing/ Memory 3

Processing/ Memory 2

Processing/ Memory 1

Sensation   Action

Environment

Figure 3.11
A cross-coupled processing-generating hierarchy.

species and behaviors. So far the study of behavior control has been done on the level of behavior observations.

Souček and Carlson,[14,15] in computerized experiments with fireflies, show a way to go the two steps further:

1. Behavior is specified through the communication flashing sequences. The sequences could be measured and quantized. Hence the behavior is not only described in general terms but also in numerical form.

2. The generation of the flashing sequences is related to the action of entrained oscillators. The oscillators produce a sequence of brain windows. Hence the behavior is related to the internal structure and operation of the firefly brain.

Figure 3.12 shows the behavior hierarchy for the Femme Fatale firefly. Each level of behavior generating hierarchy receives the command C from a higher level. It also receives the feedback F from the environment. The output from the operator H selects one of the possible subcommands on the next lower level.

For example, the level "SURVIVAL" selects the subcommand for the next lower level from the set C_2 (C_2', C_2'', C_2'''). Which subcommand is selected depends on the feedback vector F_3. In other words, $C_2 = H_3(F_3)$. Similarly the level "RE-PRODUCTION" selects the subcommand for the next lower level: $C_1 = H_2(F_2)$.

When the hormone level and blood chemistry indicate the proper time, and the air temperature is right, the command C_2 is selected. When $C_2 = C_2'$ indicates reproduction, and F_2 indicates that external stimuli are present in the form of light flashes, and the male is in the territory, the command C_1 is selected. When $C_1 = C_1'$ indicates "PATROLLING FLASHING," motor control, internal oscillator, and the lantern, execute this command.

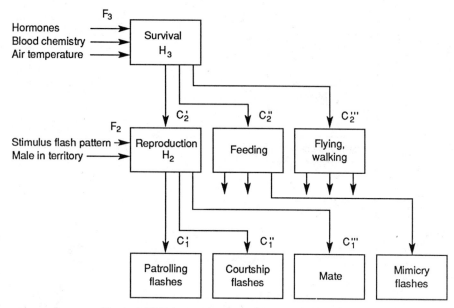

Figure 3.12 *The control hierarchy for the female firefly.*

Both commands and feedback are coded in a slow scale (chemical hormonal coding) and in a fast scale (pulse/time coding). Pulse/time coding is of special interest for behavioral patterns that are executed as time sequences of events. It seems natural that the time windows (brain windows) should be used in such sequences, to screen, check, or recognize the information, which is coded in the form of intervals. The brain-window logic and language are described in Chapters 9 and 10.

3.6 ARCHITECTURES INFLUENCED BY BRAIN MODELS

Can computer architects learn from nature? Katuro Fuchi, director of the Institute for New Generation Computer Technology (ICOT),[18] believes that we should have more research on human thinking processes but we already have some structures. For more than 2000 years man has tried to find the basic operation of thinking and has established logic. The result is not necessarily sufficient. What really is going on in our brain? It's a rather difficult problem.

Many researchers are skeptical of the relevance of brain models to computer science/engineering; this is especially so for models and theories that are vague and unproven. Nevertheless, a number of efforts are under way to build computers and systems influenced by brain models and theories, including projects at the Massachusetts Institute of Technology, the University of Utah, AT&T Bell Laboratories, California Institute of Technology, the University of Arizona, Carnegie-

Mellon, Johns Hopkins University, the University of Southern California, the National Bureau of Standards, Ohio State University and so on.

Advances can be achieved only by dissolving barriers between the life sciences and computer science/engineering. The result may be the formation of a new, fertile discipline which, by treating biological and technological systems as being alike in a fundamental way, advances both (Figure 3.13).

Figure 3.14 shows a robot developed for industrial applications.[19] This impressive achievement is modeled after a leg of an insect such as ant. It has been shown that the ant can learn its way through a complicated maze. After 25 experiments, ants follow the way to food and avoid dead-end roads. For computerized robots, however, it is still a long way to reach the performance of the leg and the brain of the ant. Similarly, Figure 3.15 shows a rat finding the way to the cheese. How does one build a robot to do the same task?

Here we discuss four possible ways to build a computer or a robot following architectures influenced by brain models:

- Microwave nonlinear oscillators
- Josephson junction devices
- Optical computing
- Molecular computing

A large set of nonlinear oscillators could be used to build a field-effect computer. However an oscillator is more complex and expensive than digital switching element.

Josephson junction naturally functions as a nonlinear oscillator. The problem with Josephson junction devices is that they operate only at liquid helium temperatures which are expensive to maintain.

Optical computing is now investigated in several laboratories, and the first results are promising. Optics are of special interest in the area of artificial neural networks and massively parallel systems. High parallelism and global communications properties of optics provide a new solution. In addition, research is showing that there are certain types of processing tasks, such as matrix operations, that are highly parallel and could lend themselves to solutions by optical processors. Some feel there may be a natural overlap between the needs of neural networks and the capabilities of optics. Optical computers of many designs, sizes, and functions are taking shape. The research and development concentrates on input and output devices, memories, interconnectors, and processors. One of the most promising components is the spacial light modulator, a transducer that converts a two-

Neural and behavioral experiments, data acquisiton, processing simulation, models, theories	Neural, genetic, event-train, associative, massively parallel computers

Figure 3.13 *PINK Systems, a new discipline in science, technology, and business.*

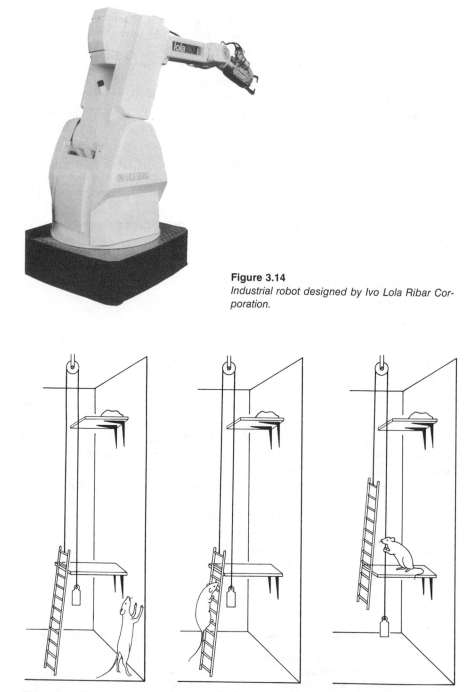

Figure 3.14
Industrial robot designed by Ivo Lola Ribar Corporation.

Figure 3.15 *The thinking rat. A white rat faces the tricky problem of getting cheese, which is placed on a high shelf with no ladder leading up to it. The rat climbs the first shelf, and then moves the ladder to reach the second shelf.*

dimensional pattern of light into a spatial pattern that can vary its brightness. This device could do both continuous and binary information processing and it could serve as a building block in neural networks and in numerical computers.

Molecular computing is based on the idea to replace silicon microcircuits with biochips. In biochips individual molecules or molecular chains would serve as the basic functional elements. Machines and tools able to directly manipulate matter on the submicron to nanometer size scale would be necessary to build a molecular computer. In 1981 the invention of the scanning tunneling microscope (STM) opened the door toward nanoscale machines. Manipulation of atomic sized structures on surfaces will lead to new frontiers in high density memories and to new devices operated on quantum-size effects. A new branch of technology is born: nanotechnology. According to Hameroff,[20] computing may soon exist in the nanoscale. Nano $= 10^{-9}$, one nanometer is a billionth of a meter, and one nanosecond is a billionth of a second. Subunits within biological protein assemblies (cytoskeletal polymers, organelles, membrane, proteins, virus coats) are of nanometer size scale and undergo conformational oscillations in the nanosecond time scale. Nanoscale excitations, which may be coherent and coupled to intraprotein dipole shifts, can generate communicative "collective modes" within protein assemblies and provide a substrate for biological information processing. Thus the "nanoscale" may be where living intelligence has evolved. Coincidentally, nanoscale devices including molecular computers, Feynman machines, and von Neumann replicators are becoming feasible through technologies such as scanning tunneling microscopy.

The described approaches might become very interesting in the future. Brain models suggest mixtures of different modes of information presentation, as outlined in Figures 3.16, 3.17, and 3.18. Many projects are already in progress: cog-

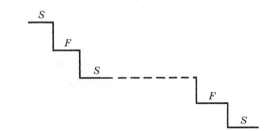

Figure 3.16 *Signal (S) and field (F) information layers.*

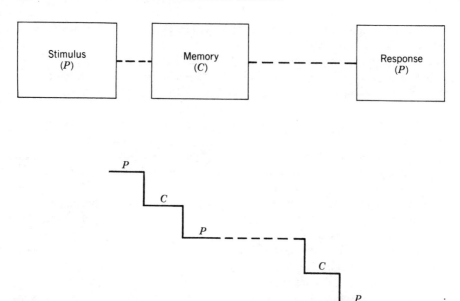

Figure 3.17 *Point (P) and continuous (C) information layers.*

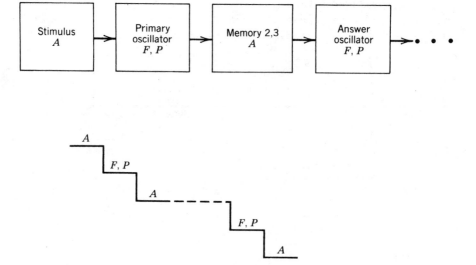

Figure 3.18 *Amplitude (A), frequency (F), and phase (P) information layers; the model of the firefly brain.*

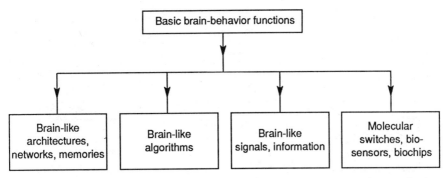

Figure 3.19 *New avenues in computer science/engineering that could benefit from research in brain behavior.*

nitrons and neocognitrons; adaptive learning systems; goal-directed systems; digital transformation systems; associative-memory based systems; and massively parallel systems. Brain-like systems following these lines are described in Parts III and IV of this book.

Areas that could directly benefit from brain-behavior research are outlined in Figure 3.19. The brain shows many modes of information processing, on the molecular level and on the macro-level. Classical computers focus only on one group of features: digital, deterministic, electrical. Sixth-generation computers include many new features (Figure 3.20). These new features will find their way into microcomputers first. A large number of different sixth-generation microcomputer systems are under way, both as stand-alone units and as units in tandem with mainframes. In this way, a two level coexistence is established (Figure 3.21): a microcomputers/mainframe coexistence, and a sixth-generation/fourth and fifth-generation coexistence.

	Fifth-Generation	Sixth-Generation	Seventh-Generation
Electrical	+	+	
Digital	+	+	
Deterministic	+	+	
Linear	+	+	
Parallel	+	+	
Optical		+	
Analog		+	
Random		+	
Nonlinear		+	
Time-coded		+	
Massively Parallel		+	
Self-adaptable		+	
Learning		+	
Brain-like		+	
Biochip-based			+

Figure 3.20 *Sixth-generation computers.*

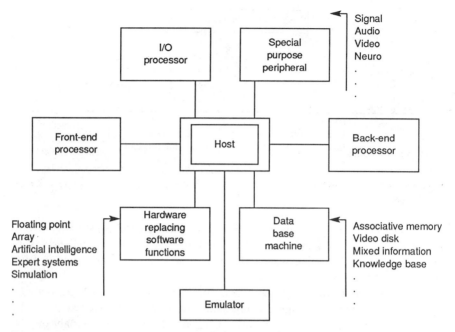

Figure 3.21 *Microcomputer/mainframe Coexistence; sixth-generation/fourth and fifth-generation coexistence.*

REFERENCES

1. J. R. Sampson, *Biological Information Processing*, Wiley, New York, 1984.
2. S. R. Hameroff and R. C. Watt, Information processing in microtubules, *J. Theor. Biol.* **98**, 549-561 (1982).
3. B. Katz, *How Cells Communicate*. Scientific American, New York, 1961.
4. P. Baker, *The Nerve Axon*. Scientific American, New York, 1966.
5. D. Bodian, *Cold Spring Harbor Symp. Quant. Biol*, **17**, (1952).
6. W. S. M. Culloch and W. Pitts, A logical calculus of the ideas imminent in nervous activity, *Bull. Math. Biophys.* **5**, 115-133 (1943).
7. S. Grossberg, *Studies of Mind and Brain*, Reidel Publ. Dordrecht, Netherlands, 1982.
8. D. O. Hebb, *The Organization of Behavior*, Wiley, New York, 1949.
9. F. Rosenblatt, *The Perceptron: A Perceiving and Recognizing Automation*, Proj. PARA, Cornell Aeronaut. Lab. Rep. 85-460-1, Cornell University, Ithaca, NY, 1957.
10. O. H. Hubel and T. N. Wiesel, Receptive fields, binocular interaction and functional architecture in the cat's visual cortex, *J. Physiol. London* **160**, 106-154 (1962).
11. J. Stone, B. Dreher, and A. Leventhal, Hierarchical and parallel mechanisms in the organization of visual cortex, *Brain Res. Rev.* **1**, 345-394 (1979).
12. V. Braitenberg, Charting the visual cortex, In A. Peters and E. G. Jones (eds.), *Cerebral Cortex*, Vol 3, Plenum, New York, 1985.

13. V. Braitenberg, Das Raster der neuralen Elemente in der Sehrinde und seine neurophysiologische Konsequenzen, In V. Herzau (ed,), *Pathophysiologie der Sehens*, Enke, Stuttgart, 1984.

14. B. Souček and A. D. Carlson, Brain windows in firefly communication, *J. Theor. Biol.* **119**, 47-65 (1986).

15. B. Souček and A. D. Carlson, Brain windows language of fireflies, *J. Theor. Biol.* **125**, 93-103 (1987).

16. J. Albus, *Brain, Behavior and Robotics*, McGraw-Hill, New York, 1981.

17. N. Tinbergen, *The Study of Instinct*, Oxford Univ. Press, London and New York, 1974.

18. K. Fuchi, S. Sato, and E. Miller, 1984. Japanese approaches to high technology R & D, *Computer* **17**(3), 14-18 (1984).

19. Products Manual, Ivo Lola Ribar Corporation, Belgrade, 1987.

20. S. R. Hameroff, *Ultimate Computing: Biomolecular Consciousness and Nanotechnology.*, Elsevier, Amsterdam, 1987.

CHAPTER 4 ────────────────────────

Computers in Neurobiology and Behavior

INTRODUCTION AND SURVEY

The best investment that we can make is the investment in our bodies and our minds. This is becoming possible due to the advances in physiology, psychology, and computer technology. A new multibillion-dollar area for marketing and for applications is being created: computers in neurobiology and behavior. This area includes systems for health and pleasure, mind-reading machines, human-computer interfaces, artificial organs, analyzers, stimulators and simulators for both professional and home use.

The primary purpose of this chapter is to examine those neural and behavioral signals and processes that could directly influence the development of new computing and measuring systems.

Behavioral biologists, neurophysiologists, and other life scientists and engineers are no longer restricted to simplistic descriptions of the trains of spikes or of continuous waveforms that constitute the basic signals in biocommunications. The development of a wide variety of computational techniques, the rise of computer models for framing and testing hypotheses, and the development of new theories have all engendered new interpretations, new questions, and new directions in the quantitative investigation of biocommunications. One can feel that trend in the study of both communication between living organisms and communication within living organisms.

Chapter 4 is adapted from Souček and Carlson, *Computers in Neurobiology and Behavior*, Wiley, 1976. Reprinted with permission.

65

Communication is a process of exchanging messages between two points using some kind of signal. First of all, it must be mentioned that the communication signal is normally distorted by random fluctuations, which are caused by ongoing biological activity; by the common "black-box" approach and the great complexity of the biological object; by the environment; and finally by the instrumentation used. Because of these distortions, the statistical approach to biocommunication signals processing must be the main method used in this domain.

This chapter gives an overview of biomedical and biocommunication signals and their computer processing. It is shown that virtually the same computer techniques can be used to study two fields: communication between living organisms and communication within living organisms.

This chapter reviews a number of typical problems and shows some of the solutions. The purpose of this chapter is to give a bird's eye view of the field, rather than to explain the techniques used. Numerous computer techniques used to solve the problems are then explained in detail in the chapters that follow.

Three functions are frequently used in biological data analysis: probability distribution, correlation function, and power spectra. These functions describe the random data in a similar way, as amplitude, signal shape, and signal frequency describe deterministic data.

The *probability distribution* describes the amplitude property of the random data. As the data fluctuate in a random fashion, the probability distribution shows which amplitude range is more probable and which amplitude range is less probable.

Correlation function describes the dependence of a signal at one instant of time on the signal at another instant of time. The difference between two time instants is called *time lag* or *correlation delay*. The correlation function is plotted as a function of the time lag. Maximal value of the correlation function shows the time lag for which the two signals influence each other the most.

The *power spectra* show the frequency composition of the signal. Each signal can be approximated with the mixture of sine waves of different frequencies and amplitudes. The power spectra show the amplitudes of the sine waves as a function of the frequencies.

All these functions and many others can be measured and calculated using laboratory computers. Each of the techniques used is described in a separate chapter.

In this chapter, we use the above definitions of the basic functions and, without going into details, we review a number of typical problems and show some of the solutions.

4.1 COMMUNICATION BETWEEN AND WITHIN LIVING ORGANISMS

Communication involves the production of a signal at a source, which stimulates a response in a receiver. In biology, communication is carried on at two distinct levels:

- Communication within living organisms, through neural processes
- Communication between living organisms, such as messages exchanged between two animals or between two humans

The purpose and modalities of these two levels of communication are quite different. Many times the researcher has to study both levels of communication to understand the biological system. One of the main tools in communication study is a digital computer. The communication is carried through signals and messages, and the computer can be used for many purposes: data acquisition, processing, system simulation, and comparison between theoretical and experimental results. Fortunately, the same computer techniques that are used in the field of communication between living organisms can be also used in the field of communication within living organisms, and vice versa.

A communicatory system involves a number of components which are represented somewhat after the fashion of communication engineers, as shown in Figure 4.1. The emitter sends the signal over the communication channel to the receiver.

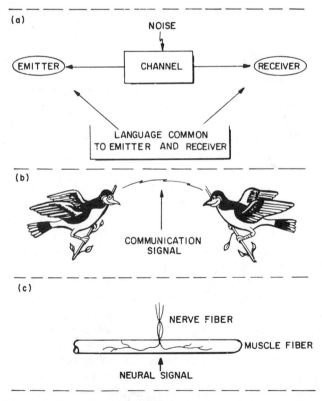

Figure 4.1 *Communication system: (a) information exchange between emitter and receiver through a noisy channel; (b) external communication between two living organisms; (c) internal communication through neural processes.*

The signal incorporates the message, which is based on the code held in common with the receiver. The meaning to the recipient is dependent on the context of the signal. The meaning can probably be operationally defined as the response selected by the recipient from all responses open to it.

During the transmission of information over the communication channel, noise is added to the signal. One of the tasks of biological communication study is to distinguish the basic signal from the noise. The always-present noise in biological systems is a reason that biological messages are coded in a special way. Rarely will the messages be coded using available signal elements in an optimal way. Rather, a large degree of redundancy occurs.

From the signal point of view, biological communication can be divided into two groups: point (discrete) processes and continuous processes. From the system point of view, biological communications can also be divided into two groups: internal communications through neural processes and external communications between two living organisms.

Four combinations of processes are described in the following sections. Descriptions and examples of neural processes are quoted from the review by Škvařil.[1]

4.2 NEURAL POINT PROCESSES

The nerve cell is considered as the basic functional element of the nervous system. Its basic property common to all living cells is the ability to build and maintain a concentration gradient for different substances on both sides of membrane surrounding the cell. Often these substances are electrically charged, and therefore a potential difference appears across the membrane.[2] The changes in an environmental condition act on the neuron in such a way that its membrane potential is sometimes decreased to a value known as the threshold. When this is the case, this potential markedly decreases and then returns again to the preceding resting potential (the duration of this transient change is about 1 msec, and the voltage of this drop is about 70 mV). This event, known as the *action potential* or *spike*, spreads along the whole neuronal body, including its processes. The spike could be transferred to other neurons in synaptical contact with the originally charged neuron. This impulse activity represents the basic mechanism of information transmission in the nerve system.[3,4] Therefore, the analysis of it is of considerable importance.

Action potentials or spikes taken from a single neuron may be considered as a sample function of a point process, the basic characteristic of which is the histogram of the intervals between consequent events. It is an estimate of the probability density function of the mentioned intervals considered as a sample of a random variable (see Figure 4.2). If the studied series of events corresponds to the renewal process, then the knowledge of this density alone is sufficient for the description of the process.[5]

The second stage in the description is represented by the problem of the approx-

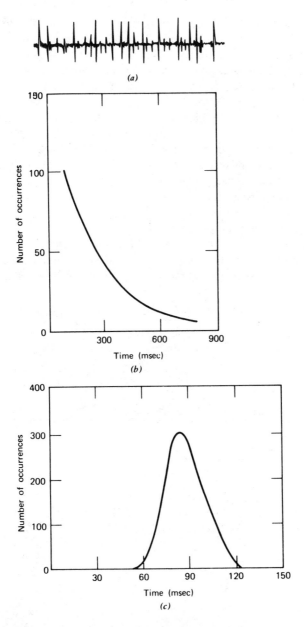

Figure 4.2 (a) *An example of the action potentials of a single neuron recorded by a micro-electrode and reproduced from a CRT screen.* (b) *Example of histograms of intervals between consecutive spikes of the spontaneous activity of a single neuron.* (c) *Another example of an interval histogram.*

imation of this experimental histogram by some general type of distribution, like the gaussian or exponential characterized by only a few parameters. A similar problem is encountered in deciding if two experimental histograms are produced by identical generators (homogeneity of population). Sometimes simpler statistics are sufficient for the detection of spontaneous changes of the activity observed. The mean value estimated by the arithmetic mean, the variance estimated by the squared deviation, or the coefficient of asymmetry or excess could be typical representatives of these simple statistics (see Figure 4.3).

To detect the influence of the repetitive stimulation of the observed activity, the *dwell histogram* is most frequently evaluated. It resembles an estimate of the conditional probability density function that an event occurs in a certain time, if a stimulus is applied in time zero. When the stimulus is not influencing the activity observed and other certain assumptions are fulfilled, the dwell histogram is uniformly distributed over the interstimulation period.[6] Therefore, in some cases the evaluation of the experimental dwell histogram, that is, the acceptance or rejection of the hypothesis about the influence of the given stimulus, may be stated on the basis of the "naked eye" approach only (see Figure 4.4*a* and *b*).

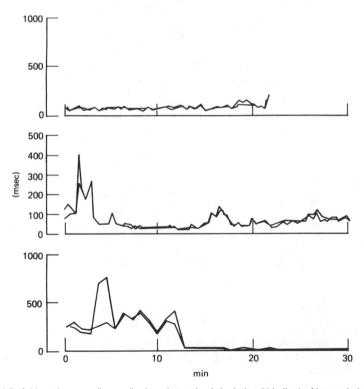

Figure 4.3 *Arithmetic mean (heavy line) and standard deviation (thin line) of intervals between consecutive spikes of the spontaneous unit activity of a single neuron, as a function of time after the application of a particular dose of drug. Three examples are given.*

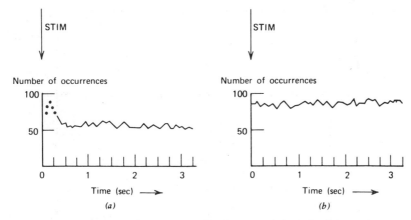

Figure 4.4 *Dwell histograms of two neurons:* (a) *shows a strictly defined dependence on the stimulus;* (b) *is not influenced.*

To detect the dependencies and hidden periodicities in one series of events, the estimate of the *autocorrelation function* (also known as the postfiring interval distribution, renewal density function, or expectation density function) is sometimes evaluated.[7] This estimate of a conditional probability density function is like the dwell histogram, but the role of stimulus is fulfilled consequently by each analyzed event in the latter case (see Figure 4.5).

To detect the mutual dependence of two series of events, other functions like the crosscorrelation function or the distribution of forward and backward recurrence times can be used.[7] The first approach is similar to the dwell-histogram method described above (events of one process are considered as the stimuli); the second one is described later.

To present other examples of the electrophysiological phenomena reduced to the point process and evaluated by the mentioned methods, the series of the interval histograms between the QRS complex of ECG (Figure 4.6) and the histograms of the intervals between consecutive breathing (Figure 4.7) are shown.

4.3 BEHAVIORAL OR COMMUNICATION POINT PROCESSES

Communication is considered as the basic functional element of animal and human behavior. Its basic property common to all living organisms is the ability of organisms to support themselves and to adapt and to survive as a species. By any reasonable definition of the term *communication*, there can be no doubt that not only humans but also animals communicate with each other.

Most critical from the point of view of natural selection is the presence of species-specific information. Another critical type of form is sexual information, used to distinguish between males and females. Next is individual information, used to distinguish a particular individual in the social group. Communication messages can also be motivational; for example, the singer is in a reproductive

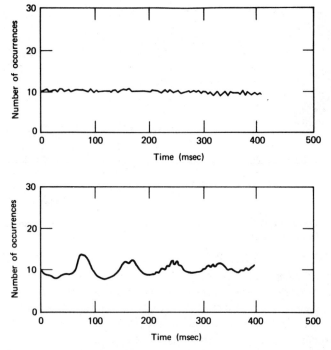

Figure 4.5 *Autocorrelation functions of the spontaneous impulse activity of the same neuron used in Figure 4.2.*

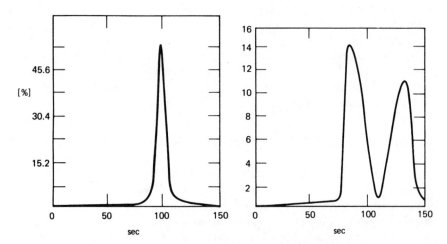

Figure 4.6 *Histograms of the intervals between the consecutive QRS complexes in ECG.*

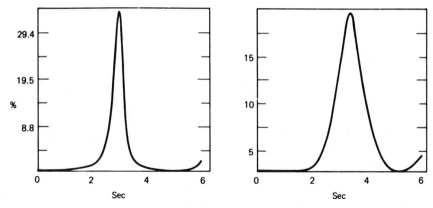

Figure 4.7 *Histograms of the intervals between the consecutive instants of inspiration, moments of which are determined by a chest movement controlled switch.*

condition. Another message can be environmental, such as when the singer is within his territory and has no mate.

Communication involves the production of a signal by an individual or a group, which stimulates a response in a receiver. In general, our discussion assumes sender and receiver to be of the same species. Here are a few examples of sensory stimuli comprising the signal:

- A sequence or pattern of sounds
- A sequence or pattern of light flashes
- A display of gestures, body position, facial expressions or
- An emission of odors

The processes described above can be either discrete (or point processes) or continuous processes.

Figure 4.8 presents an example of acoustical point processes, katydid chirping. Adult males of the true katydid produce different sequences of chirps; each chirp consists of two or more pulses.

Figure 4.8*a* shows the calling sound, whose function is to attract mature females. Figure 4.8*b* shows the alternating sound: if two male katydids are close enough, they will respond to each other's songs. One male will be the leader, and it will increase its chirp rate. The other male, the follower, will try to sing in such a way that the chirps of the two will be in alternation. Figure 4.8*c* shows the aggressive sound produced by two males who fight an acoustical war over the same territory. Figure 4.8*d* shows the disturbance sounds produced whenever the katydids are handled.

Computers are becoming the basic tools in measuring and analyzing communication point processes. Computers are used for direct data acquisition, latency and amplitude histogram generation, correlation analysis, and power spectra analysis.

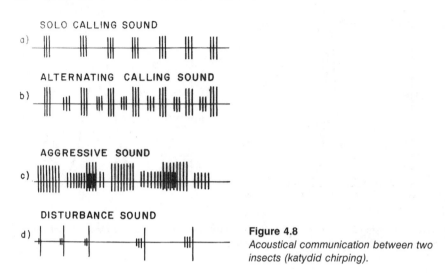

Figure 4.8
Acoustical communication between two insects (katydid chirping).

Figure 4.9 shows an example of the correlation analysis of katydid calls. Such techniques can be used to detect the periodic component buried in random noise.

Figure 4.10 presents an example of a point process with light flashes used for communication purposes. This exchange of light flashes is used for a courtship communication between male and female fireflies. Much of the basic information transmitted from one member of the species to another member is contained in the interflash interval of male flashes and in the female's flash-response latency. Precise time discrimination is needed to recognize the species-specific signal and to identity the correct partner.

Computers are used not only to measure and analyze communication signals but also to simulate communication processes. Computer modeling presents a significant step in closing the gap between animal communication and behavior on one side and neural-structure study on the other side.

4.4 NEURAL CONTINUOUS PROCESSES

The EEG is a typical example of a continuous neurophysiological signal. Contrary to neuronal unit activity that is recorded by microelectrodes taking the electric potentials from a very small neighborhood of a cell, EEG activity is taken from the surface of the scalp or from the depth of the brain by relatively large electrodes. In our review, the term EEG has broader meaning; it is used for electrical activity of the brain recorded by the macroelectrode. The presence of different tissues between the local generators of the electrical activity in the brain influences the potential observed at the surface.[8] Thus, the activity of single neurons is not more discernible in an EEG record representing the filtered sum of the activity of a large

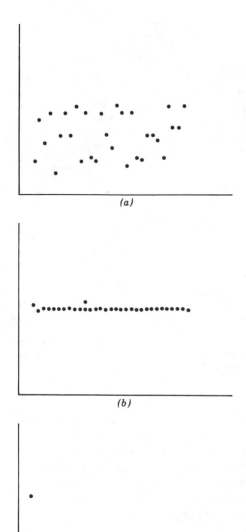

Figure 4.9
Computer analysis of insect calls (katydid chirping): (a) interchirp intervals displayed as a function of the chirp serial number; (b) simple correlation function of interchirp intervals: this example proves that this function is of no use for interval analysis; (c) modified correlation function of interchirp intervals: the analyzed process is periodic and we can determine the period of the process. For details, see Section 14.1.

set of individual generators. These generators must be synchronized to produce the periodical activity that is sometimes observed.

The evaluation of this activity is the domain of very skilled specialists, and the procedures are very subjective and always time-consuming. The application of computers in this task is therefore important but difficult.

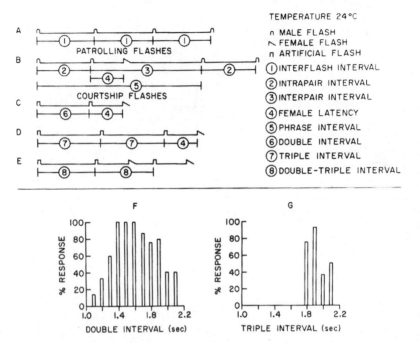

Figure 4.10 *Flashing sequences used for firefly communication: (a-e) different flashing sequences and definitions of intervals; (f) measured probability distribution of "double intervals"; (g) measured probability distribution of "triple intervals."*

The amplitude histogram, representing (under some conditions) the estimate of the first-order probability density function of the process analyzed, is one of the simplest first-order statistics used in connection with both spontaneous and evoked EEG activity (see Figure 4.11).[9] Some parameters characterizing the form of this histogram are often evaluated. For example, on the basis of the coefficient of asymmetry, the typical waveform in an EEG can be automatically detected.[10] In further processing, we may try to approximate such histograms with some theoretical distributions (for instance, with a normal one) to simplify its description.[11]

Estimation of the ensemble mean in chosen time relative to the stimulus represents the most famous statistic evaluated in the domain of the evoked activity in EEG. It is a powerful tool for the detection of the evoked response, that is, the changes in slow electrical activity of the chosen part of the brain subject to a given stimuli. This method enables one to extract a response of very small amplitude (signal) hidden in the additive random spontaneous activity (noise) (see Figure 4.12). This technique is useful for the detection of some irregularities in the transmission of a signal in the brain as it is caused by a tumor, or to differentiate the sensory function,[12] and is useful as a clinical method.[13,14] A theoretical approach to the problem of the evoked response detection is presented in comprehensive form in Bendat,[15] Sayers,[16] and partially in Ruchkin.[17] In connection with the evoked

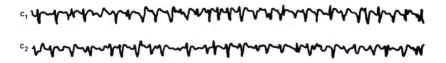

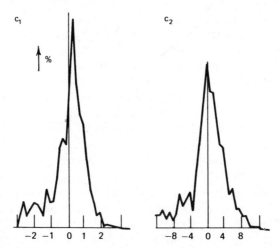

Figure 4.11 *Amplitude histograms of EEG together with the parts of the original EEG records. Frequency of sampling is 60 samples/second.*

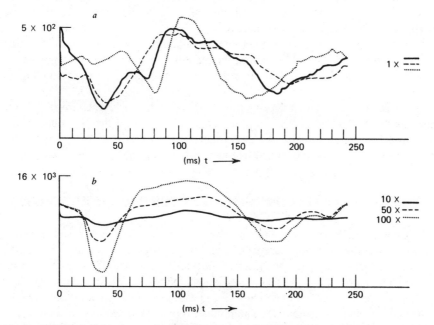

Figure 4.12 (a) *Individual, superimposed records of the EEG activity following the stimulus;* (b) *emerging of the evoked response by summing the shown number of individual records.*

response, processing the evaluation of the standard deviation in all points of the evoked response can be presented as an example of simple second-order statistics. This standard deviation plays an important role in estimation of the validity of the evoked response evaluated simultaneously (biodata).

Auto and cross-correlograms and the corresponding spectral density functions are the most often used second-order statistics in connection with EEG processing.[18,19] Correlograms are evaluated by convolution; spectral density functions were formerly computed as their Fourier transform. Nowadays, spectral density is evaluated directly by digital filtering or by using the fast Fourier transforms.

Further interpretation of these statistics is rather difficult, mainly because the assumptions under which these functions are evaluated do not hold, and because the error due to the finite time of observation is neglected.[20] Both the correlation function and spectral density functions are equal, insofar as the description of the stationary stochastic processes is concerned. Some examples of correlograms and spectrograms, together with the EEG evaluated, are presented in Figures 4.13 and 4.14.

The relationship between the power of the EEG activity in different frequency bands is in some cases very important, from the clinical point of view, and thus the spectral density function may soon become an important clinical characteristic. By means of spectral analysis, the different stages of sleep, for example, or different levels of vigilance, can be recognized.[21-23]

Modeling seems to be important in the descriptions of EEG activity by their correlograms. Often it is possible to approximate the experimental correlation function by an analytical function and, on that basis, to define the normal process giving the same autocorrelation function.

The continuous signal can be reduced to the point process for some tasks, which enables a substantial simplification of the recording. Activity observed is reduced to the instants when the signal crosses zero (mean) level, as shown in Figure 4.15.[6,24]

Evaluation of the mutual dependence of the two activities of the different types, such as the evaluation of the two-dimensional histogram of the amplitude of the observed EEG and evaluation of the instants of the occurrence of spikes from a single neuron, must be mentioned in concluding of this short review.

4.5 BEHAVIORAL OR COMMUNICATION CONTINUOUS PROCESSES

A typical example of a continuous communication signal is the sound wave. Acoustical communication based on sound-wave modulation is used in human speech, in birds' singing, and in terrestrial and aquatic animal communication. Insects frequently use a pulse modulation of the sound wave, producing short chirps. We have described these chirps as an example of the point process. On the other side, mammals and birds use amplitude, frequency, and phase modulation of the sound wave, producing a continuous communication signal. Computers present a major tool in studying continuous communication processes.

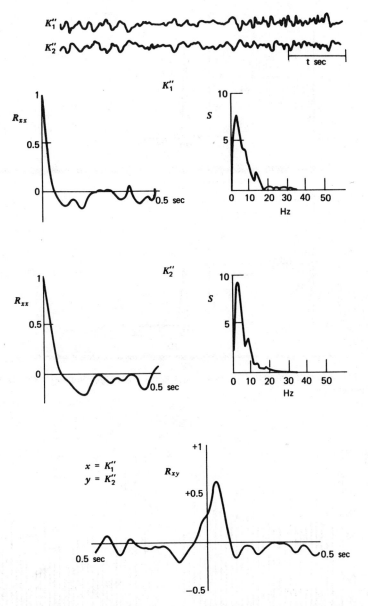

Figure 4.13 *An example of two original EEG records taken from the two different parts of the brain and their autocorrelograms* (R_{xx}), *spectrograms* (S), *and crosscorrelogram* (R_{xy}).

An example of the continuous communication process is presented in Figure 4.16. Figure 4.16*a* presents a recording of the bird song.[25] The amplitude of the sound is recorded as a function of time. It is very difficult and often impossible to provide any conclusion based on the direct observation of such a continuous signal. Different computing techniques are used to transform the signal in more meaningful forms.

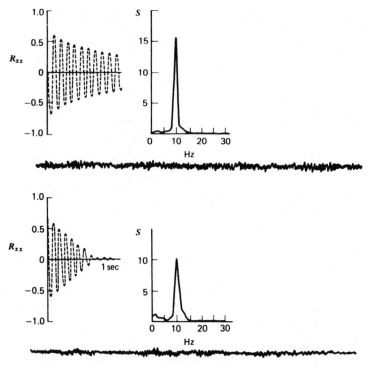

Figure 4.14 *Examples of periodic EEG activity and corresponding autocorrelograms* (R_{xx}) *and spectrograms* (S).

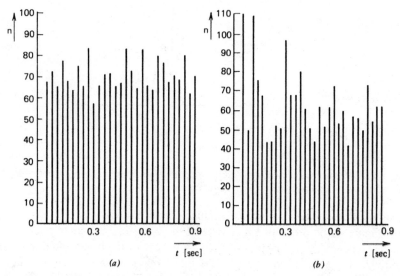

Figure 4.15 *Dwell histogram of the EEG zero level crossing instants relative to the stimulus;* (a) *evoked response is absent,* (b) *evoked response is present.*

AMERICAN GOLDFINCH

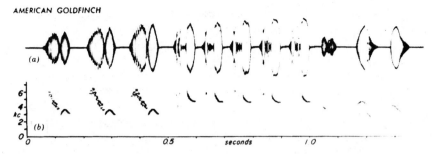

Figure 4.16 *Acoustical continuous communication process: (a) amplitude of the sound as a function of time; (b) power spectrum of the same signal as a function of time.* [25]

Figure 4.16*b* shows the power spectrum of the same signal as a function of time.[25] Such *sonagrams* are produced through the procedure of measuring the frequency content of the signal at various time intervals and are identical to the mathematical procedure of Fourier transforms.

Digital machines can be used in many phases of continuous communication signal analysis. The most elementary phase includes computer-controlled experiments, signal sampling, and data acquisition. The most elaborate phase involves the application of computers for sonagram pattern recognition. By defining to the computer the message code for each sonagram, one can write the program to accept and analyze the sonagrams and to decode the message. Such techniques are especially of interest in studying human-machine communication through speech.

REFERENCES

Neural Processes

1. J. Škvařil, Short review of the basic types of biomedical signals and their computer processing. In B. Souček (ed.), *Data Processing*. Jurema, Zagreb, 1969, p. 111.

2. J. Bures, M. Petran, and J. Zachar, *Electrophysiological Methods in Biological Research*. Academia, Prague, 1967.

3. W. L. Nastuk, *Physical Techniques in Biological Research*, Vol. 3. Academic Press, New York, 1964.

4. T. C. Ruch and J. F. Fulton, *Medical Physiology and Biophysics*. Saunders, Philadelphia, PA, 1960.

5. D. R. Cox and P. A. W. Lewis, *The Statistical Analysis of Series of Events*. Methuen, London, 1966.

6. I. Krekule, Zero crossing detection of the presence of evoked response. *Electroencephalogr. Clin. Neurophysiol.* **25,** 175–176 (1968).

7. G. P. Moore, D. H. Perkel, and J. P. Segundo, Statistical analysis and functional interpretation of neuronal spike data. *Annu. Rev. Physiol.* **28** 493–522 (1966).

8. C. E. Hendrix, Theory of transmission of electric fields in cortical tissue, two models for the origin of the alpha rhythm. Ph.D. dissertation, University of California, Los Angeles (1964).

9. M. G. Saunders, Amplitude probability density studies on alpha and alpha-like patterns. *Electroencephalogr. Clin. Neurophysiol.* **15**, 761–767 (1963).

10. T. Radil-Weiss, I. Krekule, and L. Chocholová, Epileptoid EEG activity during chloralose anaesthesia in rats. *Physiol. Bohemoslov.* **16**, 23–27 (1967).

11. J. Campbell, E. Bower, S. J. Dwyer, and G. V. Lago, On the sufficiency of autocorrelation functions as EEG descriptors. *IEEE Trans. Biomed. Eng.* **BME-14**, 49 (1967).

12. E. R. John, D. S. Ruckin and J. Villegas, Experimental background: Signal analysis and behavioral correlates of evoked potential configuration in cats. *Ann. N. Y. Acad. Sci.* **112**, 362–420 (1964).

13. D. R. Giblin, Somatosensory evoked potentials in health subjects and in patients with lesions of the nervous system. *Ann. N. Y. Acad. Sci.* **112**, 92–142 (1964).

14. I. Rapin, and L. J. Graziani, Auditory evoked responses in normal, brain-damaged, and deaf infants. *Neurology* **17**, 881–894 (1967).

15. J. Bendat, Mathematical analysis of average response values for nonstationary data. *IEEE Trans. Biomed. Eng.* **BME-11** 72 (1964).

16. B. McA. Sayers, *Signal and System Analysis*. Imperial College Press, University of London, 1968.

17. D. S. Ruchkin, An analysis of average response computations based upon aperiodic stimuli. *IEEE Trans. Biomed. Eng.* **BME-12** 87 (1965).

18. M. A. B. Brazier, and J. U. Casby, Crosscorrelation and autocorrelation studies of electroencephalography potentials. *Electroencephalogr. Clin. Neurophysiol.* **4**, 201–211 (1952).

19. J. S. Barlow, M. A. B. Brazier, and W. A. Rosenblith, The application of autocorrelation analysis to electroencephalography. *Proc. Natl. Biophys. Conf., 1st, 1957* pp. 622–662 (1959).

20. R. S. Daniel, Electroencephalographic correlograms ratios and their stability. *Science* **145** (1964).

21. J. S. Rhodes, D. Brown, M. Reite, and W. R. Adey, Computer analysis of chimpanzee sleep records. In *Symposium Sleep Mechanisms*. Lyon, France, 1963.

22. V. S. Rusinov et al., *Gagra Symposium*. 1965.

23. T. Radil-Weiss, D. O. Walter, D. Brown, and W. R. Adey, EEG manifestations of sleep and wakefulness in rat studied by spectral analysis. *Electroencephalogr. Clin. Neurophysiol.* **18**, 516 (1965).

24. J. P. Ertl, Detection of evoked potentials by zero crossing analysis. *Electroencephalogr. Clin. Neurophysiol.* **18**, 630–631 (1965).

25. C. H. Greenewalt, *Bird Song Acoustics and Physiology*. Smithsonian Institution Press, Washington, DC, 1968.

GENERAL REFERENCES

Alexander, R. D., *Science* **114**, 713 (1964).

Altmann, S. A., *Ann. N. Y. Acad. Sci.* **102** (Art. 2), 338 (1962).

Altmann, S. A., in E. L. Bliss (ed.), *Roots of Behavior*. Harper, New York, 1962, pp. 277–285.

Anonymous. *Mathematics and Computer Sciences in Biology and Medicine.* H. M. Stationery Office, London, 1965.

Armstrong, E. A., *A Study of Bird Song.* Oxford Univ. Press, London, 1963, p. 6.

Baerends, G. P., *Arch. Neerl. Zool.* **13**, 401 (1958).

Barnett, S. A., *The Rat: A Study in Behaviour.* Aldine, Chicago, IL, 1963, p. 98.

Bartholomew, G. A., and N. E. Collias, *Animal Behav.* **10**, 7 (1962).

Bossert, W. H., and E. O. Wilson, *J. Theor. Biol.* **5**, 443 (1963).

Bühler, K., *Sprachtheorie.* Fischer, Jena, 1934.

Busnel, R.-G. (ed.), *Acoustic Behavior of Animals.* Elseuer, Amsterdam, 1963.

Collias, N. E., in W. E. Lanyon and W. N. Tavolga (eds.), *Animal Sounds and Communication.* American Institute of Biological Sciences, Washington, DC, 1960, p. 387.

Darwin, C., *The Expression of the Emotions in Man and Animals.* Murray, London, 1872.

Frings, M. R., and H. W. Frings, *Sound Production and Sound Reception by Insects: A Bibliography.* Pennsylvania State Univ. Press, University Park, 1960.

Goodall, J., *Natl. Geogr. Mag.* **124**, 293 (1963).

Griffin, D. R., *Listening in the Dark: The Acoustic Orientation of Bats and Men.* Yale Univ. Press, New Haven, CT, 1958.

Hess, E. H., *New Directions in Psychology.* Holt, New York, 1963.

Hockett, C. F., *Curr. Anthropol.* **5**, 166 (1964).

Jakobson, R., *Shifters, Verbal Categories, and the Russian Verb* (mimeogr.). Department of Slavic Languages and Literatures, Harvard University, Cambridge, MA, 1957.

Jakobson, R., in T. A. Sebcok (ed.), *Style in Language.* Wiley, New York, 1960, pp. 350–377.

Jesperson, O., *Language: Its Nature, Development, and Origin.* Norton, New York, 1964, p. 123.

Jinde, R. A., *Animal Communication.* Blaisdell, New York, 1964.

Jinde, R. A., in D. McK. Rioch and E. A. Weinstein (eds.), *Disorders of Communication.* Williams & Wilkins, Baltimore, MD, 1964, pp. 62–84.

Kainz, F., *Die "Sprache" der Tiere. Tatsachen—Problemschau—Theorie.* Enke, Stuttgart, 1961.

Kellogg, W. N., *Porpoises and Sonar.* Univ. of Chicago Press, Chicago, IL, 1961.

Köhler, F., *Z. Bienenforsch.* **3**, 57 (1953).

Lenneberg, E. H. (ed.), *New Directions in the Study of Language.* MIT Press, Cambridge, MA, 1964, pp. 65–88.

Lenneberg, E. H., in J. S. Fodor and J. J. Katz (eds.), *The Structure of Language.* Prentice-Hall, Englewood Cliffs, NJ, 1964, pp. 579–603.

Lindauer, M., *Communication Among Social Bees.* Harvard Univ. Press, Cambridge, MA, 1961.

Lindauer, M., *Annu. Rev. Psychol.* **13**, 35 (1962).

Linsdale, J. M., and P. Q. Tomich, *A Herd of Mule Deer; A Record of Observation, made on the Hastings Natural History Reservation.* Univ. of California Press, Berkeley, 1953.

Lissmann, H. W., *J. Exp. Biol.* **35**, 146 (1958).

Lorenz, K., in B. Schaffner (ed.), *Group Processes: Transactions of the First Conference.* Josiah Macy, Jr. Found., New York, 1955, p. 179.

MacKay, D. M., in H. von Foerster (ed.), *Cybernetics*. Josiah Macy, Jr. Found., New York, 1952, p. 224.

Marler, P., in P. R. Bell (ed.), *Darwin's Biological Works: Some Aspects Reconsidered*. Cambridge Univ. Press, London, 1959, pp. 150–206.

Marler, P., *J. Theor. Biol.* **1**, 295 (1961).

Marler, P., in *Vertebrate Speciation: A Conference*. Univ. of Texas Press, Austin, 1961, pp. 96–121.

Marler, P., in R.-G. Busnel (ed.), *Acoustic Behavior in Animals*. Elsevier, Amsterdam, 1963, pp. 228–243, 794–797.

Mason, W. A., and A. J. Riopelle, *Annu. Rev. Psychol.* **15**, 143 (1964).

McElroy, W. D., and H. H. Seliger, *Sci. Am.* **207**, 76 (1962).

Möhres, F. P., *Naturwissenschaften* **44**, 431 (1957).

Moles, A., in R.-G. Busnel (ed.), *Acoustic Behavior of Animals*. Elsevier, Amsterdam, 1963, pp. 112–131.

Mowrer, O. H., *Learning Theory and Personality Dynamics*. Ronald Press, New York, Chap. 24.

Ruesch, J., in R. R. Grinker (ed.), *Toward a Unified Theory of Human Behavior*. Basic Books, New York, 1956, p. 37.

Schaller, G. B., *The Mountain Gorilla: Ecology and Behavior*. Chicago Univ. Press, Chicago, IL, 1963, p. 272.

Schneirla, T. C., in M. R. Jones (ed.), *The Nebraska Symposium on Motivation*, Vol. 7. Univ. of Nebraska Press, Lincoln, 1959, pp. 1–42.

Sebcok, T. A., *Behav. Sci.* **7**, 430 (1962).

Sebcok, T. A., *Language* **39**, 448 (1963).

Sebcok, T. A., *Language* **39**, 465 (1963).

Sebcok, T. A., in P. L. Garvin (ed.), *Natural Language and the Computer*. McGraw-Hill, New York, 1963, pp. 47–64.

Sebcok, T. A., *Am. Anthropol.* **66**, 954 (1964).

Sebcok, T. A., *Science* **147**, 492 (1965).

Sebcok, T. A., A. S. Hayes, and M. C. Bateson (eds.), *Approaches to Semiotics*. Mouton, The Hague, 1964.

Shannon, C. E., and W. Weaver, *The Mathematical Theory of Communication*. Univ. of Illinois Press, Urbana, 1949, p. 117.

Slama-Cazacu, T., *Language et Contexte*. Mouton, The Hague, 1961.

Smith, W. J., *Am. Nat.* **97**, 122 (1963). Cf. Schneirla (1959).

Stankiewicz, E., in T. A. Sebcok, A. S. Hayes, and M. C. Bateson (eds.), *Approaches to Semiotics*. Mouton, The Hague, 1964, pp. 239–264.

Tavolga, W. N. (ed.), *Marine Bio-Acoustics*. Macmillan, New York, 1964.

Thorpe, W. H., *Annu. Rev. Psychol.* **12**, 27 (1960).

Thorpe, W. H., *Bird-Song: The Biology of Vocal Communication and Expression in Birds*. Cambridge Univ. Press, London, 1961.

Thorpe, W. H., *Nature (London)* **197**, 774 (1963).

Thorpe, W. H., *Learning and Instinct in Animals*. Harvard Univ. Press, Cambridge, MA, 1963.

Tinbergen, N., *Study of Instinct*. Oxford Univ. Press, London, 1951.

Tinbergen, N., *The Herring Gull's World*, rev. ed. Basic Books, New York, 1961, p. 112.

Tinbergen, N., Z. *Tierpsychol.* **29**, 411 (1963).

Trager, G. L., *Stud. Linguist.* **13**, 1 (1958).

Wenner, A. M., *Science* **138**, 446 (1962).

Wenner, A. M., *Sci. Am.* **210**, 117 (1964).

Wilson, E. O., and W. H. Bossert, *Recent Prog. Horm. Res.* **19**, 792 (1963).

Wood-Gush, D. G. M. *Annu. Rev. Psychol.* **14**, 175 (1963).

Wynne, Edwards, V. C., *Animal Dispersion in Relation to Social Behaviour*. Hafner, New York, 1962, p. 16.

Zinkin, N. I., in R.-G. Busnel (ed.), *Acoustic Behavior of Animals*. Elsevier, Amsterdam, 1963, pp. 132–180.

PART II ————————————————————————

COMPUTER MODELS OF BRAIN AND BEHAVIOR

CHAPTER 5 —————————————————————

Simulation and Modeling

INTRODUCTION AND SURVEY

The first step toward any experiment is the design of the experiment. This plan can be done analytically if the system is linear, deterministic, and involves a small number of parameters. For more realistic, nonlinear, and nondeterministic systems and parameters, the experiment design can be done through simulation and modeling. The objective of the experiment design is to predict how a system under study will perform by conducting studies on the model of the system. We define a model as the body of information about a system for the purpose of studying the system. Different models of the same system are possible, depending on the nature of the information that is gathered. One physical system can be modeled with another physical system, or it can be represented as a mathematical model, in which activities are described by mathematical functions and interrelations of variables. Mathematical models can be simulated by electronic computers.

System simulation is the technique of solving problems by following changes in a dynamic model of a system over a period of time. The simulation does not attempt to solve the equations of a model analytically; instead, it observes the way in which all variables of the model change with time.

Since the advent of electronic analog computers about two decades ago, the analog computer has been widely used for simulations. Recently, many modeling techniques using digital computers were introduced. Many programming systems, called digital simulators, have also been written for continuous-system simulation, industrial dynamics, probability simulation, servicing and queuing, discrete-system simulation and so forth.

Chapter 5 is adapted from Souček and Carlson, *Computers in Neurobiology and Behavior*, Wiley, 1976, Reprinted with permission.

In this chapter, we concentrate on the techniques suitable for data simulation and for experiment design.[1-3] Generation of continuous and discrete deterministic processes is shown first; simulation of random data and systems is explained next. Special attention is given to the most widely used Monte Carlo techniques; such techniques may be used to recognize and possibly minimize experimental difficulties, or to prove interrelations between different parameters of a system.

5.1 DETERMINISTIC DATA SIMULATION

5.1.1 Sine-Wave Generation

Sine-Wave generation has many applications in the laboratory. Sine waves are produced by any physical system that can be described through a differential equation of the harmonic oscillator:

$$\frac{d^2x}{dt^2} = -w^2 \cdot x \tag{5.1}$$

Differential equation 5.1, with initial conditions $x = U$; $dx/dt = 0$, at the moment $t = 0$, has the solution

$$x(t) = U \cdot \cos wt \tag{5.2}$$

Such an equation describes the motion of the mass hanging on a spring without friction; or electrical voltage, inductance-capacitance circuit; or elastic deformation of a solid, or internally controlled behavior, and so on.

Although there are many different ways to build sine-wave generators, the most instructive way will be by making an electronic model of equation 5.1. Such a model is shown in Figure 5.1a.

Let us suppose that the function d^2x/dt^2 is available. Using this function as input to the integrator, we obtain $-dx/dt$ at the output of integrator number 1. Integration of $-dx/dt$ yields x at the output of integrator 2. Applying x as the input to the amplifier with the gain w^2, we obtain the output $-w^2x$. According to equation 5.1, $-w^2x$ equals d^2x/dt^2. Hence, by closing the loop we form the harmonic oscillator described by Equation 5.1.

Initial conditions may be set on either integrator or on both. Integrator 1 generates dx/dt. No initial-condition circuit is necessary for integrator 1, since the initial condition is $dx/dt = 0$. Integrator 2 generates x. Hence, the initial-condition circuit is necessary to supply the voltage $x(0) = U$. At $t = 0$, the contact $\overline{S}$ should be open, and at the same time the contact S should be closed. The output x, according to equation 5.2, will be the cosine wave. Hence, the output $-dx/dt$ will be the sine wave.

In the above example, gains of the integrators have been chosen to be 1. In a

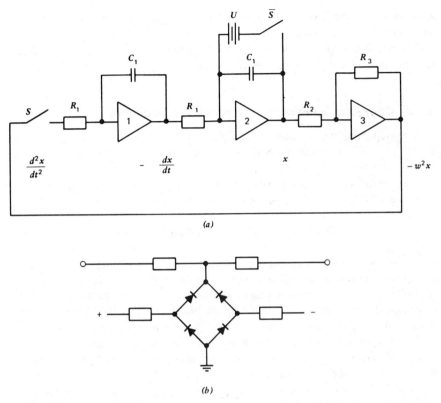

Figure 5.1 *Simulation of the harmonic oscillator, using operational amplifiers and integrators:* (a) *linear parts;* (b) *nonlinear part.*

general case, integrator 1 will have a gain $1/R_1C_1$ and integrator 2 will have a gain $1/R_1C_1$. Hence, the circuit will be described by the equation

$$\frac{d^2x}{dt^2} = \frac{1}{R_1C_1} \cdot \frac{1}{R_1C_1} \cdot \frac{R_3}{R_2} \cdot x \qquad (5.3)$$

producing the sine wave of the frequency

$$w_o^2 = \frac{1}{R_1C_1} \cdot \frac{1}{R_1C_1} \cdot \frac{R_3}{R_2}$$

For proper operation of the circuit, the time constants of the integrators must be $1/R_1C_1 \gg 2\pi/w_0$; and the cut-off frequency w_e of amplifiers 1,2, and 3 must be $w_e \gg w_0$.

Further modifications of the circuit can improve sine-wave accuracy: slight regeneration can be achieved by adding the feedback resistor between output 3 and input 2; amplitude control can be achieved through the degenerative feedback from output 1 to input 1, including a nonlinear element in the loop.

The circuit provides a way to generate a sine or cosine wave for use as a forcing function in analyzing the response of systems.

5.1.2 Computer Simulation of a Harmonic Oscillator

In digital computer simulation, the time scale t is divided into discrete intervals $T, 2T, \ldots, NT$. To make the equivalent of the integrator, we have to design the system with the following properties.

If at the instant NT the input IN(NT) is presented to the system, with the initial condition OUT[(N-1) · T], then the new output of the system must be

$$OUT(NT) = IN(NT) + L \cdot OUT[(N - 1)T] \tag{5.4}$$

Equation 5.4 presents the simplest definition of a digital integrator. The value OUT[(N-1)T] presents the accumulated result up to the instant (N-1)T. The value IN(NT) represents the contribution of the signal arriving at the instant NT. The coefficient L represents the leakage from the integrator. Typically L is slightly less than 1, showing that the integrator would eventually discharge due to leakage. Many physical and biological integrating processes can be simulated with integrators, as defined in equation 5.4. Ideal integrators, which would only accumulate the result and never leak, can be described by L = 1.

Figure 5.2a shows the symbol for the integrator. It is fully described by its initial condition OUT[1 · T], and by the leakage L. Figure 5.2b shows the digital equivalent for the harmonic oscillator, and follows the basic structure of Figure 5.1.

Equation 5.4 can be programmed in the following way:

$$OUT = IN + L * OUT \tag{5.5}$$

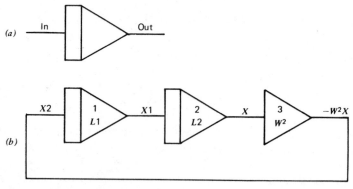

Figure 5.2 *Block diagram of the harmonic oscillator simulation:* (a) *integrator;* (b) *simulation chain.*

This is a typical programming equivalence statement: the new value of OUT is equal to the sum of the new value of IN, and of the old value of OUT multiplied by L.

The whole system in Figure 5.2 can be described by three such equations: two for integrators (units 1 and 2), and one for the amplifier (unit 3, with the gain w^2):

Output of the first integrator (unit 1):

$$X1 = X2 + L1 \cdot X1 \tag{5.6a}$$

Output of the second integrator (unit 2):

$$X = X1 + L2 \cdot X \tag{5.6b}$$

Output of the amplifier (unit 3):

$$X2 = -(w^2) \cdot X \tag{5.6c}$$

The program based on equations 5.6a, b, and c is shown in Table 5.1. This program simulates the harmonic oscillator, for 300 time intervals. The produced signal X as a function of time is displayed on the scope and shown in Figure 5.3.

Figure 5.3a shows the result of the first run, with parameters $W = 0.1$, $L1 = 1$, $L2 = 1$ (see the second part of Table 5.1). Because the integrators have no leakage, an ideal sine wave is generated.

Figure 5.3b shows the result of the second run, with parameters $W = 0.1$, $L1 = 0.99$, $L2 = 0.99$. Because of the leakage in the integrators, a dumped sine wave is generated.

System simulation is the technique of solving a problem by following the changes in a dynamic model of a system over a period of time. The simulation does not attempt to solve the equations of a model analytically. Instead, it observes the way in which all variables of the model change with time.

Sometimes we as programmers are not interested in the structure of the system, and we treat the system as a unit box. If we know that such a unit always generates, say, a sine wave, we will program the output using the sine function, which is available as a part of the language library.

5.2 RANDOM DATA AND PROBABILITY DISTRIBUTIONS

Data representing a random physical phenomenon cannot be described by an explicit mathematical relationship, because each observation of the phenomenon will be unique. In other words, any given observation will represent only one of many possible results which might have occurred.

Figure 5.4 represents a sequence of pulses with random amplitudes produced by an experiment. Measuring the amplitude of one particular pulse will not produce significant information, because amplitudes vary in an unpredictable way. What we *can* measure is the distribution of amplitudes. The distribution is obtained by

TABLE 5.1

```
LIST
10 REM HARMONIC OSCILATOR AS SIN WAVE GENERATOR
20 REM TIME UNIT T=1
30 REM INITIAL CONDITIONS
60 X2=.05
70 X1=0
80 X=0
90 REM CIRCULAR FREQUENCY W
95 PRINT "ENTER W,L1,L2"
100 INPUT W,L1,L2
110 W2=W↑2
120 REM INTERVAL COUNTER N
130 N=0
150 REM TIME INCREMENTING LOOP
160 REM FOR 300 TIME INTERVALS
200 FOR N=1 TO 300
210 X1=X2+L1*X1
220 X=X1+L2*X
230 X2=-W2*X
300 REM SCALING DATA FOR DISPLAY INTO 0 TO 1 RANGE
310 T=3.300000E-03*N
320 S=.5+.5*X
330 PLOT T,S
340 DELAY
350 NEXT N
400 STOP

RUN
ENTER W,L1,L2
?.1,1,1

READY.

RUN
ENTER W,L1,L2
?.1,.99,.99

READY.
```

counting how many times each possible amplitude occurs in a sample. The fraction of all observations that took a particular value is called its probability.

If a stochastic variable can take on different values $x_i, (i = 1,2,3. . n)$ and the probability of the value x_i being taken is P_i, the set of numbers $P_i(i = 1,2,. . n)$ is said to be a *discrete probability function*. Since the variable must always take one of the values, P_i, it follows that

$$\sum_{i=1}^{n} P_i = 1$$

Table 5.2 for example, represents data gathered on the amplitudes of pulses produced in experiment for a sample of 1000 pulses. The third column in Table 5.2

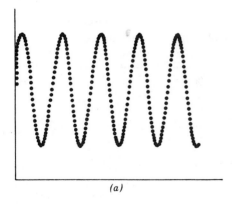

(a)

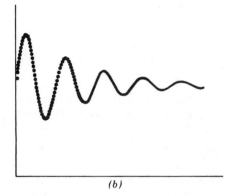

(b)

Figure 5.3
Sine wave simulated on a digital comput-
er: (a) *constant amplitude, no leakage;* (b)
dumped amplitude due to leakage.

is the estimate of the probability of a pulse having amplitude x_1, derived by dividing the number of pulses having amplitude x_1 by the total number of observations. In practice, there is more interest in deriving the cumulative distribution, F_r, which defines the probability that the observed value is less than or equal to x_r. The cumulative distribution function at the point $x_r(r = 1,2, \ldots ,n)$ is given as

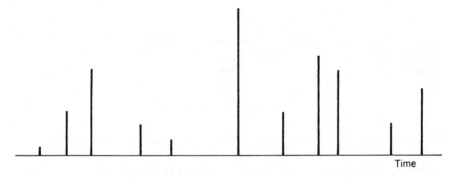

Time

Figure 5.4 *Sequence of pulses with random amplitude.*

TABLE 5.2

Amplitude	Number of Pulses	Probability P	Cumulative Probability F
1	2	0.002	0.002
2	18	0.018	0.020
3	30	0.030	0.050
4	103	0.103	0.153
5	157	0.157	0.310
6	210	0.210	0.520
7	180	0.180	0.700
8	151	0.151	0.851
9	119	0.119	0.970
10	30	0.030	1.000

$$F_r = \sum_{i=1}^{r} P_i \tag{5.7}$$

The fourth column in Table 5.2 represents the cumulative distribution for the case shown. The probability distribution and the cumulative distribution are presented graphically in Figure 5.5.

In the experiment shown, amplitudes have been grouped into only ten classes. If the number of classes is very large or infinite, then the amplitude x becomes a continuous variable that can be described by its probability density function $f(x)$. The probability that x falls in the range x_1, x_2 is given by

$$\int_{x1}^{x2} f(x)dx \qquad f(x) \geq 0 \tag{5.8}$$

The integral of the probability density function taken over all possible values, according to the intrinsic definition of a probability density function, must be

$$\int_{-\infty}^{\infty} f(x)dx = 1 \tag{5.9}$$

A related function is the cumulative distribution function which defines the probability that an observed value is less than or equal to x. If $F(x)$ is the cumulative probability distribution function, then

$$F(x) = \int_{-\infty}^{x} f(x)dx \tag{5.10}$$

From its definition, $F(x)$ is a positive number ranging from 0 to 1, and the probability of x falling in the range x_1, x_2, is $F(x_2) - F(x_1)$. Figure 5.6 illustrates a probability density function and the corresponding cumulative or integral distribution function.

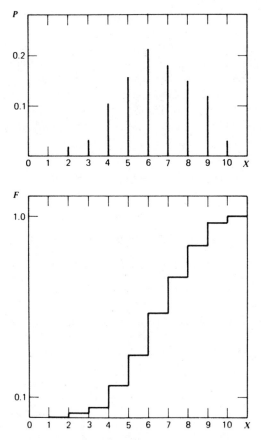

Figure 5.5 *The probability distribution* P *and the cumulative distribution* F.

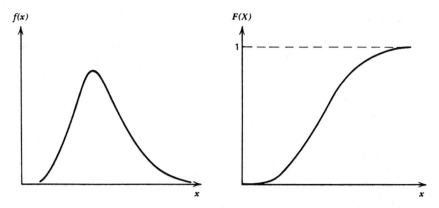

Figure 5.6 *The probability density function* f(x) *and the cumulative or integral distribution function* F(x).

The formation of the probability distribution function from experimental data has been shown. When the function is formed, we are interested in seeing if it can be expressed by an analytical expression. There are large numbers of analytical expressions for probability density functions. We discuss three basic analytical expressions for probability functions which are of particular interest.

The simplest probability density function is a uniform distribution, as shown in Figure 5.7a. The uniform distribution describes the case when there is equal probability for the observed quantity to have any value between A and B. The uniform distribution can be expressed by

$$f(x) = \frac{1}{B - A} \text{ for } A < x < B \qquad (5.11)$$

$$F(x) = 0 \text{ otherwise}$$

A special case is the uniform distribution with parameters $A = 0$, $B = 1$:

$$f(x) = 1 \text{ for } 0 < x < 1 \qquad (5.12)$$

$$f(x) = 0 \text{ otherwise}$$

Such a distribution, as will be shown, presents the basis for the Monte Carlo simulation.

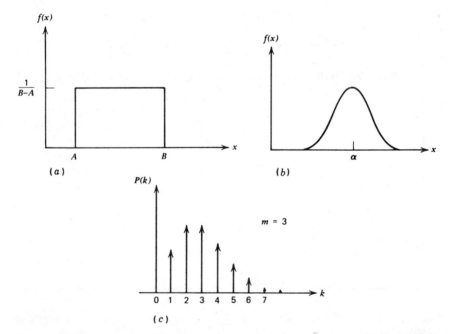

Figure 5.7 Basic probability density functions: (a) uniform; (b) normal or gaussian; (c) Poisson distribution.

The most frequently used continuous probability distribution function is the normal or gaussian distribution, as shown in Figure 5.7b. The gaussian distribution has a bell-like shape and is defined by two parameters, α (mean value) and σ (standard deviation), through the expression

$$f(x) = \frac{1}{\sigma\sqrt{2\pi}} \exp[-(x - \alpha)^2/2\sigma^2] \qquad (5.13)$$

The most frequently used discrete probability distribution is a Poisson distribution, as shown in Figure 5.7c. The Poisson distribution is defined by one parameter, m (mean value), through the expression

$$P(k) = \frac{e^{-m}}{k!} m^k \qquad (5.14)$$

A probability distribution describes the behavior of a stochastic variable. It shows the result of a number of observations, considering only the values assumed by the variable and not the sequence in which they occurred. In carrying out a simulation that involves stochastic variables, the reverse problem arises. It is necessary to generate a sequence of numbers in which the successive values are random but have the distribution that describes stochastic variables. In other words, the numbers should be generated in a random sequence, as in the real experiment shown in Figure 5.4.

5.3 MONTE CARLO TECHNIQUES

The *Monte Carlo method* is a technique for direct simulation of random phenomena and random data. Direct computer simulation of random phenomena permits estimation of a much wider variety of statistics than the analytical methods, and is not restricted to linear systems.

Modern experiments often investigate complex systems which produce a large quantity of data, often of a random character. A variable representing the outcome of random activity is said to be a *stochastic variable*. Although the exact sequence of values taken by a stochastic variable is not known, the range of values over which it can vary, and the probability with which it will take the values, may be known or assumed to be known. Stochastic variables are therefore discussed in terms of functions which describe the probability of the variable taking various values.

As an example, one can consider an experiment producing a sequence of pulses, amplitudes of which fluctuate in a random fashion. Such random pulses are known to physicists and chemists working with radiation detectors, as well as to biologists measuring neuroelectrical signals. Such random signals pass through the system and produce random outputs. Direct simulation of a system with random inputs is frequently the only possible method for conducting realistic laboratory-process studies and for estimating the output.

The Monte Carlo method and generation of random sequences can be introduced in the following way. Various devices and techniques exist for producing such sequences. The simplest random process is the one described by a uniform discrete probability distribution where the choice is between n different numbers. An honest roulette wheel that has n sections will generate such a sequence. Because of this analogy, the name "Monte Carlo," with its associations with roulette, has become a general term used to describe any computational method using random numbers.

A Monte Carlo simulation requires sequences of random numbers which are drawn from a distribution that, in general, is not uniform. Methods for directly generating random numbers with a particular distribution are not usually available. Methods do exist, however, for generating random numbers with a uniform distribution. Fortunately, there is a simple way for transforming uniform distribution into the required distribution. As a result, most of the nonuniformly distributed sequences used in Monte Carlo simulation are generated through the transformation of uniformly distributed sequences.

5.3.1   Transformation of Random Variables

A system with input x and output y is described by its transfer function $y = g(x)$. For a given x, and a known transfer function, one can determine the value of y. If the input x is a random variable, the output y will also be a random variable. If input x has a distribution function $f_1(x)$, then output y presents a new random variable whose distribution function, $f_2(y)$, is a function of $f_1(x)$ and $g(x)$. The easiest way to determine the output-distribution function, $f_2(y)$, is as follows: if there is a one-to-one correspondence between x and y, then the probability that the input variable is in the range $x, x + dx$ must be equal to the probability that the output variable is in the range $y, y + dy$ (Figure 5.8).

$$f_1(x)dx = f_2(y)dy \qquad (5.15)$$

$$f_2(y) = f_1(x) \cdot \frac{1}{dy/dx} = f_1(x) \cdot \frac{1}{|g'(x)|}$$

The output distribution, $f_2(y)$, is a function of $f_1(x)$ and of the derivative of the transfer function, $g(x)$. The absolute value of the derivative is taken because the distribution function cannot have negative values. From the above expression, one can find the transfer function $g(x)$, which will transform a given distribution, $f_1(x)$, into a new desired distribution, $f_2(y)$:

$$g'(x) = \frac{f_1(x)}{f_2(y)}$$

$$(5.16)$$

$$g(x) = \int \frac{f_1(x)}{f_2(y)} \, dx$$

Of special interest is the generation of a given distribution through the transformation of a uniform distribution, and vice versa. If

$$f_2(y) = K = const$$

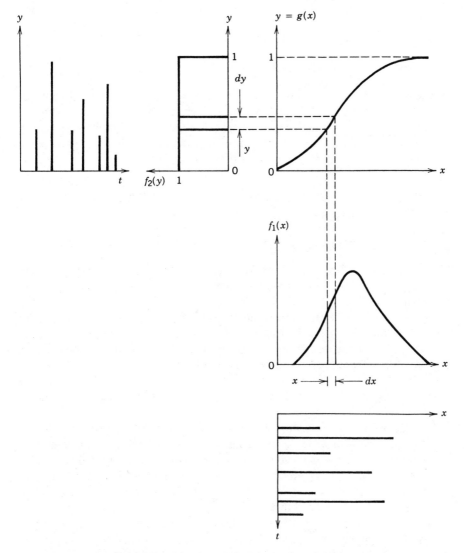

Figure 5.8 *Transformation of the random variable.*

then

$$g(x) = \frac{1}{K} \int f_1(x)dx = \frac{1}{K}F_1(x) + C \qquad 5.17$$

$F_1(x)$ is the cumulative or integral distribution function of the variable x. The constant C can be obtained from boundary conditions for $g(x)$. If the uniform distribution is defined in the interval between 0 and 1, then $K = 1$, and from the boundary condition

$$g(x)_{x=\infty} = 1 = 1 \cdot 1 + C$$

$$C = 0$$

$$g(x) = F_1(x) \tag{5.18}$$

The transformation can go both ways. Usually a uniformly distributed sequence of random numbers is available. Applying such a sequence, y, on a transfer function, $g(x) = F_1(x)$, a new sequence x is generated, with the probability density function $f_1(x)$. It is important to remember that the transfer function $g(x)$, is the same as the cumulative or integral distribution $F_1(x)$.

5.4 EXAMPLES OF SIMULATION OF EXPERIMENTAL AND THEORETICAL DATA

5.4.1 Uniform Distribution

Generate a series of pulses at time intervals $T = 1,2,3,. . .$ The pulses should have random amplitudes, uniformly distributed in the range 0 to 1. The program is shown in Table 5.3.

Statements 60 to 90 serve to allocate the space for the array D. This array will be used to sort the generated pulses and to prove that the distribution is uniform.

Statement 100 initiates the loop to generate 5000 random pulses. Actual generation of one random number is done in statement 120.

Statements 140 to 160 display the first 20 random pulses on the scope. For further pulses, the time scale is out of the scope range, and display is stopped. The display is shown in Figure 5.9a.

Statement 200 scales random amplitudes into integers in the range 0 to 25. Statement 210 uses those integers to address the array D. When a random pulse addresses the array, one is added to the content of a selected array channel. In this way, the frequency of occurrence or amplitude distribution is formed. This part of the program (statements 100 to 230) is repeated 5000 times, and 5000 random amplitudes are generated and then sorted.

The rest of the program is used to display the distribution $D(I)$. The display is shown in Figure 5.9b. Note that the array D is dimensioned for 50 items, and that statement 200 sorts the amplitudes in only 25 amplitude channels. The display shows that random pulses are uniformly distributed over 25 amplitude channels.

5.4.2 Simulation of the Experiment

Generate a series of pulses at time intervals $T = 1,2,3. . .$ The pulses should have random amplitudes, with the amplitude distribution as shown in Table 5.2. The program is shown in Table 5.4.

Statements 10 to 400 present virtually the same program as in Table 5.3.

Statement 410 to 455 are used to form the transformation curve, which is identical to integral or cumulative distribution. The cumulative distribution from

Table 5.2 is described with 10 points in statement 610. Statement 440 reads these points and places them into array $C(I)$ (cumulative distribution). This part of the program presents initialization and is called from the main program at statement 91. The main program then continues at statement 95.

The major point of the program is transformation of a random variable. Statement 120 generates a random number between 0 and 1. Statement 121 switches the program to the line 460, where the actual transformation is performed in the following way: the random number R is compared with the cumulative distribution $C(I)$. The values $C(I)$ grow from 0.002 to 1, the right-hand column of Table 5.2. Comparison proceeds through the loop, as long as $R < C(I)$. When the value of R intersects the $C(I)$ value, the index I is read out. The transformed value of R is equal to the index, $R = I$. In this way the transformed random number is formed. Statement 520 returns control back to the main program at line 130.

TABLE 5.3

```
LIST
10 REM GENERATION OF RANDOM PULSES
20 REM AT TIMES T=1,2...5000
30 REM WITH RANDOM AMPLITUDES UNIFORMLY DISTRIBUTED
40 REM BETWEEN 0 AND 1
50 REM SPACE ALLOCATION FOR DISTRIBUTION
60 DIM D(50)
70 FOR I=1 TO 50
80 D(I)=0
90 NEXT I
95 REM PULSE GENERATING LOOP
100 FOR T=1 TO 5000
120 R=RND(1)
130 REM SCALING T AND R FOR DISPLAY
140 X=T/20
145 Y=.5*R
150 PLOT X,Y
160 DELAY
170 REM SORTING PULSES INTO 25 AMPLITUDE CHANNELS
180 REM TO FORM AMPLITUDE DISTRIBUTION
200 I=INT(25*R)
210 D(I)=D(I)+1
230 NEXT T
240 INPUT A
250 CLEAR
300 REM DISPLAY OF THE DISTRIBUTION FUNCTION
310 FOR I=1 to 50
320 X=1/50
330 Y=2.000000E-03*D(I)
340 PLOT X,Y
350 DELAY
360 NEXT I
400 STOP
```

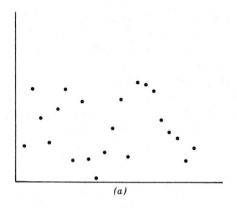

(a)

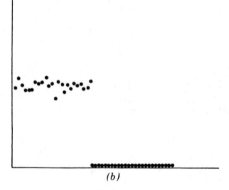

(b)

Figure 5.9
Simulation of random pulses with amplitudes uniformly distributed between 0 and 25: (a) first 20 pulses; (b) probability distribution measured into 50 amplitude channels.

Figure 5.10a shows the first 20 transformed values displayed on the scope. Figure 5.10b shows sorted pulses. Note that the distribution shown in Figure 5.10b is the same as the distribution shown in the *P* column in Table 5.2. This step presents the checking procedure, to make sure that all steps have been performed correctly.

5.4.3 Random Time Intervals

Generate a series of random time intervals. The probability distribution of the time intervals should follow the Poisson distribution.

The basic properties of arrivals in the Poisson pattern are that they are random and independent. There are no simultaneous arrivals. The mean arrival rate L is constant.

The probability distribution of intervals is given by

$$f(t) = L \cdot exp(-Lt) \qquad (5.19)$$

TABLE 5.4

```
LIST
10 REM GENERATION OF RANDOM PULSES
20 REM AT TIMES T=1,2...5000
30 REM WITH RANDOM AMPLITUDES FOLLOWING
40 REM EXPERIMENTAL DISTRIBUTION (DATA STATEMENT)
50 REM SPACE ALLOCATION FOR DISTRIBUTION
60 DIM D(50)
70 FOR I=1 TO 50
80 D(I)=0
90 NEXT I
91 GO TO 410
95 REM PULSE GENERATING LOOP
100 FOR T=1 TO 5000
120 R=RND(1)
121 GO TO 460
130 REM SCALING T AND R FOR DISPLAY
140 X=T/20
145 Y=.1*R
150 PLOT X,Y
160 DELAY
170 REM SORTING PULSES INTO AMPLITUDE CHANNELS
180 REM TO FORM AMPLITUDE DISTRIBUTION
200 I=R
210 D(I)=D(I)+1
230 NEXT T
240 INPUT A
250 CLEAR
300 REM DISPLAY OF THE DISTRIBUTION FUNCTION
310 FOR I=1 TO 50
320 X=I/50
330 Y=2.000000E-03*D(I)
340 PLOT X,Y
350 DELAY
360 NEXT I
400 STOP
402 REM
406 REM
408 REM
410 REM FORMING THE INTEGRAL OR CUMULATIVE DISTRIBUTION
420 DIM C(10)
425 RESTORE
430 FOR I=1 TO 10
440 READ C(I)
450 NEXT I
455 GO TO 95
456 REM
457 REM
```

TABLE 5.4 (cont.)

```
458 REM
460 REM TRANSFORMATION OF RANDOM VARIABLE
470 FOR I=1 TO 10
480 IF R<=C(I) GO TO 510
490 NEXT I
500 REM TRANSFORMED RANDOM NUMBER IS
510 R=I
520 GO TO 130
550 REM
560 REM
570 REM
600 REM EXPERIMENTAL DISTRIBUTION
610 DATA 2.000000E-03,.02,.05,.153,.31,.52,.7,.851,.97,1
```

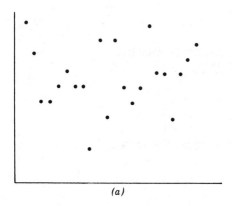

(a)

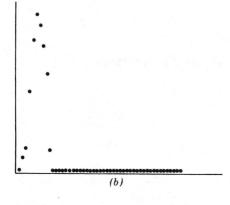

(b)

Figure 5.10
Simulation of the experiment: (a) first 20 pulses with random amplitudes; (b) probability distribution.

By integrating equation 5.19, we obtain the integral distribution

$$F(t) = Y = 1 - exp(-Lt) \tag{5.20}$$

Equation 5.20 should be used to transform a uniform distribution into the Poisson distribution. This time the transformation equation is a simple one and yields an analytical answer. Solving Equation 5.20 for t gives

$$t = -\frac{1}{L}log(1 - Y) \tag{5.21}$$

Equation 5.21 works as follows. Generate a uniformly distributed number Y. Substitute the number into equation 5.21. The result is a random interval t, with a Poisson distribution.

Table 5.5 shows a simple program based on Equation 5.21. This program

TABLE 5.5

```
LIST
10 REM GENERATION OF RANDOM INTERVALS,
20 REM WITH POISSON DISTRIBUTION
30 REM MEAN VALUE L
40 INPUT L
50 REM SPACE ALLOCATION FOR DISTRIBUTION
60 DIM D(50)
70 FOR I=1 TO 50
80 D(I)=0
90 NEXT I
95 REM INTERVAL GENERATING LOOP
100 FOR N=1 TO 1000
120 R=RND(1)
125 T=(LOG(1-R))/L
130 REM SCALING T AND N FOR DISPLAY
140 X=N/20
145 Y=.2*T
150 PLOT X,Y
160 DELAY
170 REM SORTING INTERVALS INTO CHANNELS
180 REM FOR INTERVAL DISTRIBUTION
200 I=INT(5*T)
210 D(I)=D(I)+1
230 NEXT N
240 INPUT A
250 CLEAR
300 REM DISPLAY OF INTERVAL DISTRIBUTION FUNCTION
310 FOR I=1 TO 50
320 X=I/50
330 Y=2.000000E-03*D(I)
340 PLOT X,Y
350 DELAY
360 NEXT I
400 STOP
```

follows the same structure as the program shown in Table 5.3. The program reads in the mean value L of the Poisson distribution and generates 1000 random intervals. The transformation operation based on Equation 5.21 is programmed in statement 125.

Figure 5.11a shows the display of the first 20 intervals. Figure 5.11b shows the interval distribution function. As expected, the distribution follows the Poisson law, Equation 5.19.

5.4.4 Normal Distribution

Normal or gaussian distribution is very frequently needed in simulation. Fortunately, it can be easily generated on the basis of the central limit theorem. Form the sum X, of random variables $X1$, $X2$,. . . , XN. It can be proved that the sum X will have gaussian distribution, regardless of the distributions of the variables $X1$, $X2$, . . . , XN.

We shall show the generation of gaussian distribution through a triple summation of the uniform distribution. The program is the same as in Table 5.3, except for statement 120.

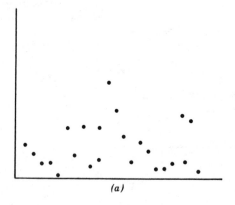

(a)

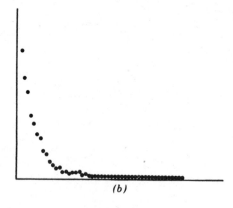

(b)

Figure 5.11
Simulation of random time intervals, following Poisson arrival pattern: (a) first 20 random intervals; (b) probability distribution of the intervals.

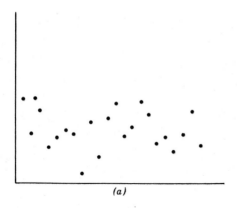

(a)

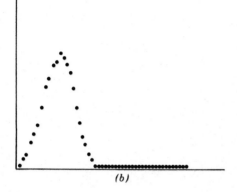

(b)

Figure 5.12
Simulation of random pulses with gaussian distribution: (a) first 20 pulses; (b) probability distribution.

$$120\ R = \frac{1}{3}(RND(1) + RND(1) + RND(1))$$

Figure 5.12a shows the first 20 amplitudes generated by the program. Figure 5.12b shows the sorted amplitudes forming the normal distribution. If one uses more then three random numbers to form the sum, a still better gaussian distribution will result.

REFERENCES

1. B. Souček, *Minicomputers in Data Processing and Simulation,* Wiley, New York, 1972.
2. G. Gordon, *System Simulation,* Prentice-Hall, Englewood Cliffs, NJ, 1967.
3. S. Deutsch, *Models of the Nervous System,* Wiley, New York, 1967.

CHAPTER 6

Time Coding In Insects

INTRODUCTION AND SURVEY

A time axis is a perfect information carrier. Time intervals are noise and drift immune, and they cannot be attenuated or amplified. The behavior of living systems and of machines is naturally programmed into the time axis as a sequence of events. It is not surprising that information processing in living systems is heavily oriented towards time coding. The use of time coding is also increasing in sixth-generation systems. This chapter presents an example of the time coding used in insect communications. Insects use time coding for courtship, alternating, and aggressive communication.

Alternating and aggressive communication patterns are present in many species. A theory[1] has been developed which explains these two modes of communication. The theory covers both central neural control and phonic interaction between two partners. A concrete example, katydid chirping, is shown here in detail. Upon receiving acoustical stimuli from the partner, a male katydid generates a characteristic response function with three parts, which regulates solo-overlapping chirps, partially delayed chirps, and alternating chirps. Each partner is considered an element in a closed feedback loop and is described through its response period versus stimulus-period curves. In the alternating mode the communication loop converges toward a stable operating point, whereas in the aggressive mode stability is never achieved. Based on this theory, computer models[1] have been designed simulating both deterministic and random components of the communi-

---

Chapter 6 is adapted from Souček and Carlson, *Computers in Neurobiology,* Wiley, 1976. Reprinted with permission.

cation signal. Computer-simulated chirping sequences are in excellent agreement with field-measured data.

In this chapter, two functions are introduced for the first time, following Souček[1]: response function and transfer function. The *response function* describes the inherent built-in timing program. Upon receiving acoustical stimuli, an animal generates a response function which determines the phases and the timing of the behavior to follow. The *transfer function* describes the input-output relationship, the magnitude of the stimulus versus the magnitude of the response. The transfer function is very useful in describing the interaction between two partners or elements in a communication loop. Each partner or element can be described through its transfer function. Simple plotting of two transfer functions on the same diagram can be used to explain different patterns of communication feedback.

6.1 EXAMPLE OF KATYDID CHIRPING

6.1.1 Basic Definitions

Adult males of the northern true katydid, *Pterophylla camellifolia* (Fab.) (Orthopteria; Tettigoniidae), produce three kinds of sound, termed calling, aggressive, and disturbance signals.

The *calling* song consists of two to four pulse chirps (Figure 6.1a) and its assumed function is to attract mature females.

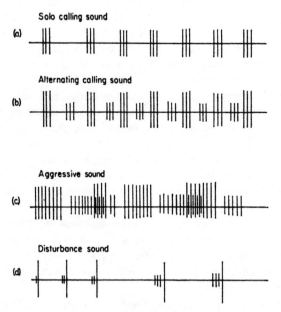

Figure 6.1 *Solo, alternating, aggressive, and disturbance sounds in northern true katydid* Peterphylla camellifolia (Fab.) (Orthoptera; Tettigoniidae).

If two male katydids are close enough, they will respond to each other's songs. One male will be the leader and will increase its chirp rate. The other male, the follower, will try to sing in such a way that the chirps of the two will be in *alternation* (Figure 6.1*b*).

The *aggressive* sounds are made up of multipulsed chirps (Figure 6.1*c*). The leader, by increasing his chirp rate, has started an acoustic "war" with the follower. The follower squeezes his chirps in between the leader's, which results in many overlapping chirps. Eventually the acoustically "defeated" katydid might leave the area.

The *disturbance* sounds consist of very short chirps produced at irregular rates; these are produced whenever male or female katydids are handled (Figure 6.1*d*).

Alternating and aggressive chirping can be explained through some kind of excitatory and inhibitory effects of the sound of one katydid on another, as suggested by Alexander[2] and Jones.[3] Shaw[4] has produced large numbers of measurements, concentrating on the effects of one male's song on another male's song. Huber,[5] Ewing and Hoyle,[6] Jones,[3] Wilson,[7] Shaw,[4] and Heiligenberg[8] have all suggested that the acoustical output of crickets and katydids is controlled by a neuron oscillator or pacemaker. The pacemaker is sensitive to sensory inputs, which could turn it on or off.

Recently, theories have been developed to explain both firefly flashing communication[9] and bird duets.[10] Although there are great differences between katydids, fireflies, and, especially, birds, there are also some similarities in their communication patterns.

In this chapter, we analyze katydid alternating and aggressive chirping. A theory has been proposed to explain solo calling, alternating calling, and aggressive sounds. Based on this theory, a computer model was designed to simulate katydid chirping sequences. The experimental findings used for the model and the theory are based mostly on the data measured by Shaw.[4] For this reason, the definitions of parameters are identical to Shaw. These definitions are explained in Figure 6.2.

The time measured between beginnings of successive chirps will be called the chirp *period*.

The time measured between the end of one chirp and the beginning of the next will be called a chirp *interval*.

The leader katydid's chirp presents a stimulus to the follower katydid; the follower's chirp reciprocally stimulates the leader.

The time between a stimulus chirp and a responder's chirp is called the *response* period or interval.

The time between a responder's chirp and the next stimulus chirp is called the *stimulus* period or interval.

6.1.2   Review of Experimental Findings

The most extensive experimental data dealing with the phonoresponse of the true katydid have been published by Shaw.[4] To find the basis for a theoretical model,

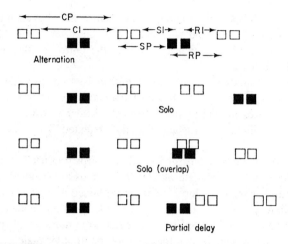

Figure 6.2 Definition of periods and intervals; CP, chirp period; CI, chirp interval; SP, stimulus period; SI, stimulus interval; RP, response period; RI, response interval. Open box: katydid chirp. Dark box: stimulus chirp.

it was necessary to examine this experimental data carefully. The basic findings are as follows:

1. A single male produces a solo calling song at approximately a constant average rate and with a chirp duration of about 0.2 seconds (temperature 24 to 28°C).

2. Two males produce sounds in alternation. Excitatory and inhibitory effects of the sound of one katydid on another regulate the alternating chirping sequence.

3. The leader's chirp period and response period are functions of the stimulus period produced by the follower. The measured data are presented in Figure 6.3a.

4. The follower's chirp period and response period are functions of the stimulus period produced by the leader. The measured data are presented in Figure 6.3b.

5. The mean response interval of the leader is shorter and less variable than the mean response interval of the follower.

6. The response period of the leader in some cases is only slightly longer than the duration of the follower's chirp, which means that the leader in some cases could start chirping only slightly later than the follower. Such cases are called *partial delay* and are denoted with *PD* in Figure 6.2 and in Figure 6.3a.

7. No cases of partial delay have been found in the measured data for the follower.

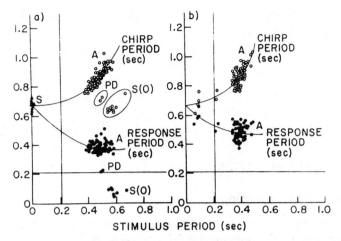

Figure 6.3 *Graphic analysis of acoustical interaction during alternating calling by a pair of P. camellifolia males, as measured by Shaw:[4] (a) leader; (b) follower. The letters on the graphs mark the groups of points corresponding to the following types of acoustical responses: A, alternation; S, solo; PD, partial delay; S(O), solo involving overlap of a follower's chirp and a leader's chirp.*

8. The response period of the leader in some cases is shorter than the duration of the follower's chirp. That means that the beginning pulses of the leader's chirp are overlapped with the ending pulses of the follower's chirp. Such cases are called *solo overlap*, and are denoted with *S(0)* in Figure 6.2 and in Figure 6.3*a*.

9. Two katydids chirp mostly in alternation. From time to time they lose the antiphony and enter the partial delay and solo overlap modes. After one or more overlapping chirps, the alternating antiphony is achieved again.

10. The first solo chirp interval is the shortest interval of all.

11. If the distance between two katydids is shortened (i.e., the sound is greater), they will enter the aggressive mode of chirping. It seems that, for entering into the aggressive mode, not only acoustical but also other kinds of nonacoustic stimuli are needed. Aggressive chirps have a longer duration (up to 0.6 sec or more).

12. In the aggressive mode, the percentage of alternations is decreased and the percentage of solo overlaps is increased.

13. In the aggressive mode, the mean chirp interval of solos is about one half of the mean chirp interval of solos in alternating calling.

14. In the aggressive mode, the response intervals of alternations of the leader are somewhat longer than in alternating calling, and somewhat shorter for the follower than in alternating calling.

15. If the katydid is stimulated with electronically produced chirps, the chirp

duration can be varied. There is a shortening of the response interval if the chirp duration is longer.

16. If the stimulus is short, the stimulus intensity has no effect on the response interval.

If the stimulus is long (say, 0.6 sec.), the decrease of stimulus intensity to or below 55 Db shortens the response interval almost to zero. The sixteen effects listed above have been used as a basis for the theory and computer modeling.

6.2 RESPONSE FUNCTION

6.2.1 Alternating Chirping

Figure 6.2 presents four possible combinations of leader-follower acoustical interaction: alternation, solo, solo overlap, and partial delay.

Alternation is the most frequent mode of interaction. The leader's chirps are roughly halfway between the follower's chirps, and vice versa.

In the solo mode, the leader chirps one or more times during a very long follower chirp period. In a normal alternating calling song, only a leader produces solo chirps (by definition).

In the solo-overlap mode, the leader starts chirping before the follower's chirp ends, and the two chirps partially overlap. Again, as shown in Figure 6.2, the follower's chirp period is greatly extended.

In partial delay, the leader chirps almost immediately after the follower. In normal alternation, only the leader sings in partially delayed mode.

The proposed model must explain all these modes of acoustical interactions. Three functions are the basis of the model: time function, threshold function, and response function (Figure 6.4).

The *time function* is started every time the male katydid chirps. It can be explained by any integrating process that can be used to measure the time elapsed after the chirp.

The *threshold level* is compared with the time function. In solo chirping, when the time function reaches the threshold level, a new chirp is produced. As a result, the time function is reset and a new process is started. By adjusting the threshold level, the chirp rate can be controlled.

The *response function* is generated in the male katydid when receiving an acoustical stimulus from another male. The response function is crucial for the explanation of both alternating and aggressive sounds. The response function is added to the threshold, and in this way the crossover point with the time function is changed.

The response function has a spikelike shape, with three parts (see Figure 6.4). First, the negative part of the response function explains the solo-overlapping chirps. Second, the flat part explains partially delayed chirps. Third, the positive part explains the normal alternating chirps.

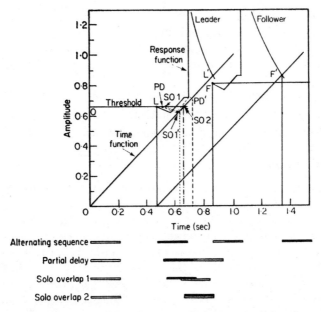

Figure 6.4 *Time function, response function, and threshold: horizontal scale presents actual time, as observed in experiments; vertical scale presents relative amplitudes.*

A typical normal alternating sequence is shown in Figure 6.4. The leading male chirps at time 0 and starts its time function. The follower in this example chirps 0.47 sec later and starts its time function. When the leader hears the follower's chirp, the leader generates the response function. The leader's response function starts at point L and intersects the time function at point L'. At that point (0.86 sec) the leader chirps again, resets its time function to zero, and starts a new time function.

The follower hears the leader's chirp and generates its response function. The follower's response function starts at point F and intersects the follower's time function at point F'. As a result, the follower now chirps and the whole sequence is repeated. The leader's response period is $LL' = 0.39$ sec. The follower's response period is $FF' = 0.47$ sec.

The period OL presents the stimulus period for the leader. If this period is approximately zero, the response function exponentially fades out to zero, and the time function intersects the threshold itself, producing the solo chirp period of 0.66 sec. As the stimulus period becomes longer (point L is moved right), the interaction point is on a higher part of the exponential function, and the chirp period is longer. This explains the exponential relationship between chirp period (OL') and stimulus period (OL) and also between response period (LL') and stimulus period (OL), as shown in Figure 6.3.

Without noise and disturbances, the leader and the follower would produce a stable alternating chirping sequence, as dictated by the two response functions arriving at instants L and F, respectively.

In the computer model, the leader is called katydid #1, and the follower is katydid #2. Each of them has three parameters, which can be adjusted:

- Low-level threshold $L1$ (leader) and $L2$ (follower)
- Amplitude of the response function $A1$ and $A2$
- Time constants of the tail of the response function, $T1$ and $T2$

6.2.2 Partial Delay

Because of noise or disturbance, the standard alternating mode of chirping can be changed into the partial delay, solo, or solo-overlap modes of chirping.

Partial delay is shown in Figures 6.2 and 6.3. Note that the leader's response period is very short, only slightly longer than the duration of the follower's chirp. The resulting leader's chirp period is shorter than in the alternating mode. The model explains these facts with the flat part of the response function. One case of the partial delay mode of chirping is shown in Figure 6.4 (dashed parts).

The leader has started to chirp at time 0. Without any interaction, the next leader's chirp would occur at 0.66 sec, when the time function intersects the threshold. The follower chirps 0.51 sec after the leader. The leader generates its response function, which starts at point PD and intersects the time function with its flat part, at point PD'. As a result, the leader's chirp period is 0.72 sec. This value is larger than 0.66 sec, but smaller than the periods produced in the normal alternating mode. The bottom part of Figure 6.4 shows that the leader chirps immediately after the follower.

Note that as the length of the stimulus period OL increases from 0 to 0.5 sec, the chirp period OL' becomes longer. However, when the stimulus period of OL becomes longer than 0.5 sec, the response function intersects the time function at point PD' rather than at point L'. The resulting chirp period O–PD' is substantially shorter.

Since the probability of the partial delay mode occurring is low, the flat part of the response function is short. In Figure 6.3, there are only two cases of partial delay.

6.2.3 Solo Overlap

A case of the solo-overlap chirping mode is presented in Figure 6.4 (dotted parts). The follower's chirp occurs 0.53 sec after the leader's chirp. The leader generates the response function, which starts at point $SO1$ and intersects the time function at point $SO1'$. The resulting chirp period is the shortest period of all, its value being only 0.63 sec. The bottom part of Figure 6.4 shows that the leader's chirp is overlapped with the follower's chirp.

The extreme case of solo overlap is the response function generated at point $SO2$. This function immediately intersects the time function, resulting in a chirp period of 0.66 sec (dash-dotted part of Figure 6.4).

The bottom part of Figure 6.4 shows that the leader's and the follower's chirps are completely overlapped. The negative part of the response function is longer than the flat part; hence, cases of occurrences of solo-overlapping mode are more probable than for the cases of partial delay.

Note that in the solo-overlap mode, the response period is shorter than the duration of the follower's chirp, and the produced chirp periods are the shortest of all. The first solo overlap period is only 0.63 sec. Other solo overlap chirp periods are between 0.63 and 0.66 sec. The solo-overlap cases are clearly distinguishable in Figure 6.3.

6.3 TYPICAL SEQUENCE AND NOISE

Table 6.1 shows the regions of interest, as determined from Figures 6.3 and 6.4. Typical observed sequences in alternating calls are as follows. Leader and follower are chirping in alternating mode. Because of noise or disturbance, they enter the partial delay mode. Partial delay is followed by the solo-overlap mode, which is usually followed by the solo chirps of the leader. The next step again establishes the normal alternating sequence.

The computer model behaves in the same way. Table 6.2 presents one typical sequence produced by the computer model. The disturbance has forced the sequence into the partial delay mode. Table 6.2 shows the standard transition path: partial delay, solo overlap, solo, alternation.

The same sequence is shown in Figure 6.5. The leader chirps at time 0; the follower chirps at 0.50 sec later. The leader generates the response function $L1$, which intersects the leader's time function 0.21 sec later, and the leader chirps in the partial delay mode. Now the follower generates the response function $F1$, which intersects the follower's time function 0.61 sec later, and the follower chirps in alternating mode. The leader generates the response function $L2$, which intersects the leader's time function 0.03 sec later, and the leader chirps in the solo overlap mode. The leader starts a new time function. In the meantime, the response function $L2$ exponentially fades out to zero, and the leader's time

TABLE 6.1
(all periods in sec)

Mode	Stimulus Period	Response Period	Chirp Period
Alternation	0 to 0.50	0.66 to 0.38	0.66 to 0.88
Partial delay	0.50 to 0.53	0.20 to 0.23	0.70
Solo overlap	0.53 to 0.66	0.10 to 0	0.63 to 0.66

Leader's threshold $L1 = 0.66$
Leader's response-function amplitude $A1 = 0.68$
Leader's time constant $T1 = 0.15$ sec
Follower's threshold $L2 = 0.81$
Follower's response-function amplitude $A2 = 3.1$
Follower's time constant $F2 = 0.1$ sec

TABLE 6.2
(all periods in sec)

Stimulus Period	Response Period	Chirp Period	Chirps
0.5	0.21	0.71	1
0.21	0.61	0.82	2
0.61	0.03	0.64	1
0.61	0.69	0.65	1
0.69	0.32	1.01	2
0.32	0.46	0.78	1
0.46	0.42	0.88	2
0.42	0.41	0.83	1
0.41	0.45	0.86	2
0.45	0.4	0.85	1
0.4	0.46	0.86	2
0.46	0.4	0.86	1
0.4	0.46	0.86	2

function intersects the threshold level 0.66 sec later. This results in the solo chirp by the leader. The follower hears the solo chirp and generates the response function *F2*, which intersects the follower's time function 0.32 sec later, and the follower chirps in alternating mode. The leader now generates the response function *L3*, which intersects the leader's time function 0.46 sec later, and the leader chirps in alternation. Both leader and follower are now in the alternating mode; this mode will be repeated a number of times. A new disturbance could start the whole transient sequence again.

The sequence presented in Figure 6.5 and in Table 6.2 is generated by the computer model in the case of a "noiseless" environment. In actual biological systems noise is always present. In the model, the noise is added to the threshold

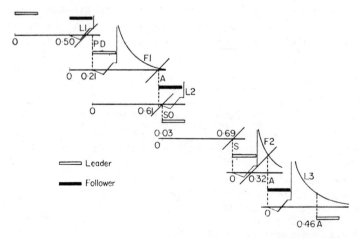

Figure 6.5 *Transition path: alternation; partial delay; solo overlap; solo; alternation.*

level. Sequences produced by noisy computer models are presented in sorted form in Figure 6.6. A very good agreement between the measured results, Figure 6.3, and the model-produced results, Figure 6.6, is obvious. In both cases, one can clearly distinguish the regions of alternation, partial delay, and solo overlap in the leader. Both measured and computer-model-produced results show that the follower maintains the alternating mode of chirping only. In Figure 6.3*b* and 6.6*b* one can distinguish those follower's chirps that are involved in the leader's partial delay mode. Their stimulus period is around 0.2 sec (duration of the chirp).

Figure 6.7 presents the results of another pair of computer-modeled katydids. In this model, the response function is slightly modified. The flat part responsible for partial delay is shortened. The negative part responsible for solo overlaps is extended. As a result, there are only two cases of partial delay in Figure 6.7. The theoretical results presented in Figure 6.7 are in even better agreement with the experimental data in Figure 6.3.

6.4 STABLE SEQUENCE, SLIDING SEQUENCE, AND TRANSFER FUNCTION

The basis for alternating and aggressive chirping is acoustical interaction between two male katydids. Each katydid can be considered as an element in a closed

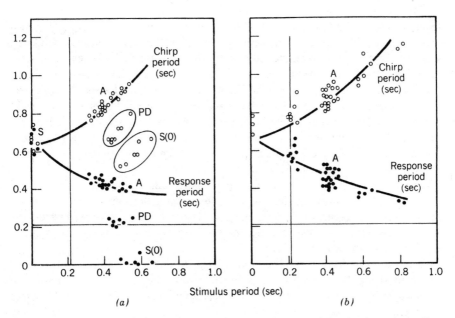

Figure 6.6 *Computer-produced data simulating acoustical interaction in alternating calling. Marked areas are identical to those found in experimental data presented in Figure 6.3.*

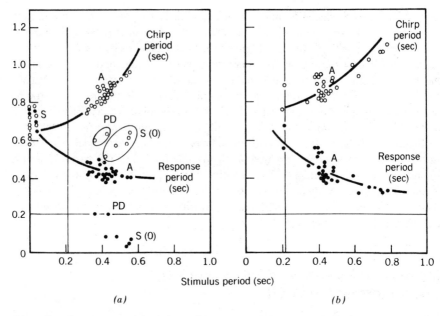

Figure 6.7 *Computer-produced data. Response function is modified in such a way that it emphasizes the solo overlap mode over partial delay mode. Compare this theoretical data with experimental findings in Figure 6.3.*

feedback loop, having its input drive force (stimulus period) and responding to it with a measurable output (chirp period). One of the ways to study this feedback loop is to determine the input-output transfer functions for each element. Noiseless computer models have been used for this task. Obtained response-period versus stimulus-period curves are plotted in Figure 6.8, for both leader and the follower.

From Figure 6.4, it is clear that the response period of the leader $R1$ is identical with the stimulus period of the follower $S2$. Also, the response period of the follower $R2$ is identical with the stimulus period of the leader $S1$. In Figure 6.8 the curve marked "leader" presents $R1$ as a function of $S1$. Similarly, the curve marked "follower" presents $R2$ as a function of $S2$.

The leader curve has three distinguishable parts: alternation, partial delay, and solo overlap. The shape of this curve is, in a sense, the same as the response-period curves in Figures 6.3, 6.6, and 6.7. The follower's curve is, in fact, the same shape, except for the fact that the partial delay and solo overlap parts are high up out of the frame of Figure 6.8.

The two curves have only one common point, H; this is the stable operating point of the alternating calls. In a noiseless environment, the parameters of alternating calls would be exactly as dictated by the operating point H: $S2 = R1 = 0.39$ sec; $S1 = R2 = 0.47$ sec.

If for any reason the songs were to start with the parameters of point A, a drift towards the stable point H would occur in the following aspects: the leader sings

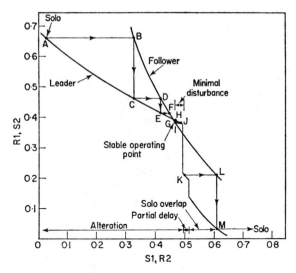

Figure 6.8 *Response period–stimulus period curves for leader and follower. The two curves intersect at the stable operating point* H.

at $A(R1 = 0.67$ sec). As $R1 = S2$, for $S2 = 0.67$ the follower's response is 0.31 (point B). As $R2 = S1$, for $S1 = 0.31$ leader's response is 0.46 (point C), and so forth. The sequence would drift through the path A, B, C, D, E, F, G, H. These eight chirps represent the transition. All subsequent chirps will have the parameters of the stable operating point H. Similarly, if the sequence begins at point J, it will drift through the path J, I, H, again ending up in the same operating point H.

An entirely different situation occurs if the sequence starts at point K (partial delay). From point K, it will drift into point L (alternation for the follower) and then to point M (solo overlap for the leader).

The next step would lead to a very long response, $R2$, which is longer than the chirp period of the leader. As a result, in the next step the leader produces a solo chirp. The solo chirp period of the leader is 0.66 sec (see threshold level in Figure 6.4). That means that after point M the next leader's point will be A. The detailed sequence K, L, M, A is shown in Table 6.2 and in Figure 6.5. From point A, the sequence drifts to the stable operating point H.

Note that the stable operating point H is distant from the partial delay region of the follower, but very close to the partial delay region of the leader. As a result, noise or disturbance takes the sequence from point H to point K, producing partial delay, solo overlap, and solo parts in the leaders' chirps. Simultaneously, the follower is in the alternating mode of chirping.

Another mode of operation is shown in Figure 6.9. The parameters are as follows: $L1 = 0.66$; $A1 = 0.68$; $T1 = 0.15$; $L2 = 0.81$; $A2 = 7$; $T2 = 0.1$. The resulting two curves never intersect. There is no stable point, and the sequence constantly drifts through the points A, B, C, D, E, F, G, H, I, and then back to

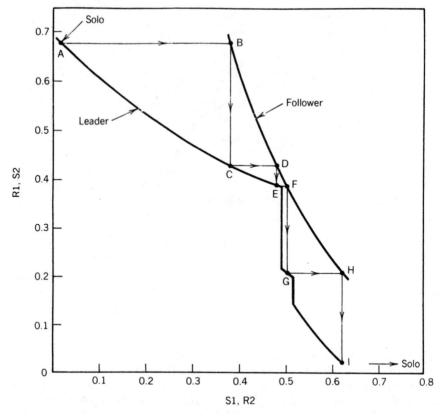

Figure 6.9 *Response period–stimulus period curves, without the stable operating point. Such a combination results in a continuously "sliding" sequence.*

A. Again, the leader passes through its partial delay (G), solo overlap (I) and solo (A) modes, but the follower does not. One detailed sliding sequence is presented in Table 6.3. Results of the sliding sequence with noise are shown in Figure 6.10.

6.5 AGGRESSION

By changing the threshold and the height of the response function (Figure 6.4), both the leader's and the follower's transfer curves can be shifted up and down. Figure 6.11*a* presents a case in which the follower's solo overlap operating region has a stimulus period $S2$ of similar duration to the leader's solo period. In this case, both the leader and the follower will go through partial delay and solo overlap sequences. The parameters are as follows: $L1 = 0.66$; $A1 = 0.68$; $T1 = 0.15$; $L2 = 0.83$; $A2 = 0.50$; $T2 = 0.10$.

TABLE 6.3
(all periods in sec)

Stimulus Period	Response Period	Chirp Period	Chirps
0.47	0.39	0.86	1
0.39	0.5	0.89	2
0.5	0.21	0.71	1
0.21	0.62	0.83	2
0.62	0.02	0.64	1
0.62	0.68	0.65	1
0.68	0.38	1.06	2
0.38	0.43	0.81	1
0.43	0.48	0.91	2
0.48	0.39	0.87	1
0.39	0.5	0.89	2
0.5	0.21	0.71	1
0.21	0.62	0.83	2
0.62	0.02	0.64	1
0.62	0.68	0.65	1
0.68	0.38	1.06	2

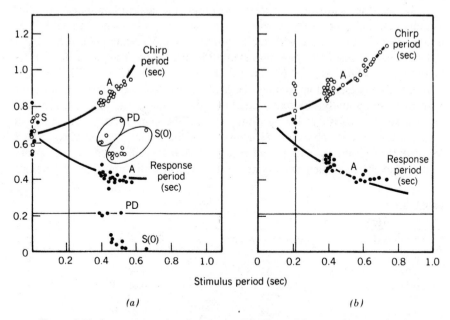

Figure 6.10 *Computer-produced data, resulting from sliding sequence and noise.*

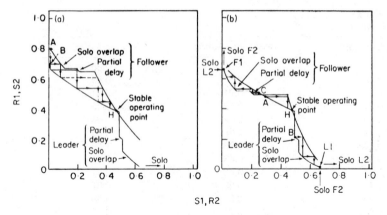

Figure 6.11 *Response period–stimulus period curves:* (a) *solo overlap and partial delay regions of the follower are close to the solo chirp period of the leader;* (b) *solo overlap and partial delay regions of the follower are close to the stable operating point.*

If the sequence starts at point *A*, it will follow the full-line transition path, including the follower's partial delay. Such a sequence is presented in Table 6.4.

If the sequence starts at point *B*, it will follow the dashed-line transition path, including the follower's solo overlap. Such a sequence is presented in Table 6.5. In both cases, the sequence will stabilize at the same operating point *H*.

Of special interest is the case presented in Figure 6.11*b*. The parameters are as follows: $L1 = 0.66$; $A1 = 0.68$; $T1 = 0.15$; $L2 = 0.66$; $A2 = 3$; $T2 = 0.1$.

In all cases presented up to now, the leader's and follower's transfer functions have been substantially different. This time, the two response functions are very much alike. Point *H* is a stable operating point. If the sequence starts at point *A*, it will drift toward the stable point *H*. However, if the sequence starts at point *B*, it will drift through the leader's partial delay and solo overlap into the leader's solo mode. Also, if the sequence starts at point *C*, it will drift through the follower's

TABLE 6.4

(all periods in sec)

Stimulus Period	Response Period	Chirp Period	Chirps
0.8	0.02	0.82	2
0.02	0.67	0.69	1
0.67	0.21	0.88	2
0.21	0.53	0.74	1
0.53	0.39	0.92	2
0.39	0.43	0.82	1
0.43	0.45	0.88	2
0.45	0.4	0.85	1
0.4	0.47	0.87	2
0.47	0.39	0.86	1
0.39	0.47	0.86	2
0.47	0.39	0.86	1

TABLE 6.5
(all periods in sec)

Stimulus Period	Response Period	Chirp Period	Chirps
0.6	0.04	0.64	1
0.6	0.7	0.65	1
0.7	0.09	0.79	2
0.09	0.61	0.7	1
0.61	0.35	1.96	2
0.35	0.45	0.8	1
0.45	0.43	0.88	2
0.43	0.41	0.84	1
0.41	0.46	0.87	2
0.46	0.4	0.86	1
0.4	0.47	0.87	2
0.47	0.39	0.86	1

partial delay and solo overlap into the follower's solo mode. Such a case is presented in Table 6.6.

Note the follower's chirps: first, $F1$ with the response period of 0.03 sec, and second, $F2$ solo chirp with the chirp period of 0.65 sec. This sequence results in a stimulus period for the leader of 0.68 sec.

Now the leader produces two chirps: the first chirp $L1$ is a response to the stimulus $F2$. The second chirp $L2$ is the leader's solo chirp, with a chirp period of 0.65 sec. Chirp $L2$ presents a stimulus for the follower. In this way, the following sequence is established: $F1$, $F2$, $L1$, $L2$, $F1$, $F2$, $L1$, $L2$, ... Since both leader and follower produce solo chirps, the case presented in Figure 6.11b could be used to explain aggressive chirping.

TABLE 6.6
(all periods in sec)

Stimulus Period	Response Period	Chirp Period	Chirps
0.26	0.5	0.76	1
0.5	0.21	0.72	2
0.21	0.53	0.74	1
0.53	0.09	0.63	2
0.09	0.61	0.7	1
0.61	0.03	0.65	2 $F1$
0.61	0.69	0.66	2 $F2$
0.69	0	0.69	1 $L1$
0.69	0.66	0.65	1 $L2$
0.66	0.02	0.69	2
0.66	0.68	0.66	2
0.68	0	0.68	1
0.68	0.66	0.65	1
0.66	0.02	0.69	2
0.66	0.68	0.66	2
0.68	0	0.68	1

Noise has been added to the system presented in Figure 6.11*b*, and a small part of the produced sequence is shown in Table 6.7. Note the many overlapping chirps, as well as solo chirps in the leader and the follower. A computer-generated sequence in Table 6.7 is very similar to observed aggressive sequences.

As the aggressive mode of chirping has received only minor attention in the past, new experiments are in preparation to concentrate on this mode of operation.

6.6 MODEL BASED ON RESPONSE FUNCTION AND TRANSFER FUNCTION

Alternating and aggressive chirping sequences have been analyzed for true katydids. A theory has been developed here that explains both central neural control as well as phonic interaction between two partners. It is possible to explain all experimental findings through three functions: time function, threshold function, and response function. The response function is generated in a male katydid on receiving acoustical stimuli from another male. The response function has a spikelike shape, with three parts. First, the negative part explains solo overlap chirps. Second, the flat part explains partially delayed chirps. Third, the positive part explains the normal alternating chirps.

Each katydid is considered as an element in a closed feedback loop and can be described through its response-period versus stimulus-period curves. In an

TABLE 6.7
(all periods in sec)

Stimulus Period	Response Period	Chirp Period	Chirps
0.6	0.05	0.65	1
0.05	0.66	0.72	2
0.66	0.	0.66	1
0.66	0.66	0.65	1
0.66	0.06	0.73	2
0.06	0.63	0.69	1
0.63	0.03	0.67	2
0.63	0.66	0.63	2
0.66	0.06	0.72	1
0.06	0.62	0.69	2
0.62	0.04	0.66	1
0.04	0.75	0.8	2
0.75	0.	0.75	1
0.75	0.73	0.72	1
0.73	0.	0.74	2
0.73	0.64	0.64	2
0.64	0.09	0.73	1
0.09	0.66	0.76	2
0.66	0.	0.66	1
0.66	0.64	0.63	1

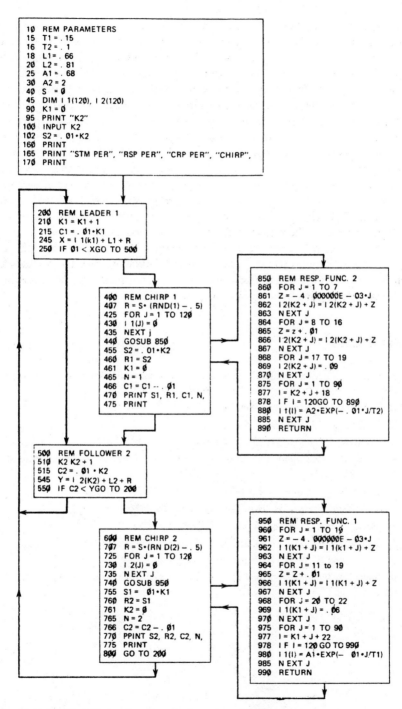

```
10   REM PARAMETERS
15   T1 = . 15
16   T2 = . 1
18   L1 = . 66
20   L2 = . 81
25   A1 = . 68
30   A2 = 2
40   S  = Ø
45   DIM I 1(120), I 2(120)
90   K1 = Ø
95   PRINT "K2"
100  INPUT K2
102  S2 = . 01•K2
160  PRINT
165  PRINT "STM PER", "RSP PER", "CRP PER", "CHIRP",
170  PRINT
```

```
200  REM LEADER 1
210  K1 = K1 + 1
215  C1 = . Ø1•K1
245  X = I 1(k1) + L1 + R
250  IF Ø1 < XGO TO 500
```

```
400  REM CHIRP 1
407  R = S• (RND(1) − . 5)
425  FOR J = 1 TO 120
430  I 1(J) = Ø
435  NEXT j
440  GOSUB 850
455  S2 = . 01•K2
460  R1 = S2
461  K1 = Ø
465  N = 1
466  C1 = C1 − . Ø1
470  PRINT S1, R1, C1, N,
475  PRINT
```

```
850  REM RESP. FUNC. 2
860  FOR J = 1 TO 7
861  Z = − 4. ØØØØØØE − 03•J
862  I 2(K2 + J) = I 2(K2 + J) + Z
863  N EXT J
864  FOR J = 8 TO 16
865  Z = z + . Ø1
866  I 2(K2 + J) = I 2(K2 + J) + Z
867  N EXT J
868  FOR J = 17 TO 19
869  I 2(K2 + J) = . Ø9
870  N EXT J
875  FOR J = 1 TO 9Ø
877  I = K2 + J + 18
878  I F I = 120GO TO 89Ø
88Ø  I t(I) = A2•EXP(− . Ø1•J/T2)
885  N EXT J
89Ø  RETURN
```

```
500  REM FOLLOWER 2
510  K2 K2 + 1
515  C2 = . Ø1 • K2
545  Y = I 2(K2) + L2 + R
55Ø  IF C2 < YGO TO 200
```

```
600  REM CHIRP 2
7Ø7  R = S•(RN D(2) − . 5)
725  FOR J = 1 TO 120
730  I 2(J) = Ø
735  N EXT J
74Ø  GO SUB 95Ø
755  S1 =  Ø1•K1
760  R2 = S1
761  K2 = Ø
765  N = 2
766  C2 = C2 − . Ø1
77Ø  PPINT S2, R2, C2, N,
775  PRINT
8ØØ  GO TO 200
```

```
950  REM RESP. FUNC. 1
960  FOR J = 1 TO 1Ø
961  Z = − 4. ØØØØØØE − 03•J
962  I 1(K1 + J) = I 1(k1 + J) + Z
963  N EXT J
964  FOR J = 11 to 19
965  Z = Z + . Ø1
966  I 1(K1 + J) = I 1(K1 + J) + Z
967  N EXT J
968  FOR J = 2Ø TO 22
969  I 1(K1 + J) = . Ø6
970  N EXT J
975  FOR J = 1 TO 9Ø
977  I = K1 + J + 22
978  I F I = 120 GO TO 99Ø
980  I 1(I) = A1•EXP(− Ø1•J/T1)
985  N EXT J
99Ø  RETURN
```

Figure 6.12 *Simulation program. Katydid (N = 1) = leader; katydid (N = 2) = follower. K_1, K_2, time interval counters; S_1, S_2, stimulus periods; C_1, C_2, chirp periods; R_1, R_2, response periods; $I_1(K_1)$, $I_2(K_2)$, response functions; R, random noise; X, comparison level for leader; Y, comparison level for follower.*

alternating mode, the two response curves intersect at a stable operating point, which is near the partial delay region of the leader, but far away from the partial delay region of the follower. Because of disturbance or noise, the communication loop drifts out of the stable point, through the leader's solo chirps, and back to the stable point. In the aggressive mode, the two response curves are in a position such that the communication loop drifts constantly from solo chirps in the leader to solo chirps in the follower and vice versa. A disturbance moves the communication out of this pattern, which explains the numerous solos by both leader and follower in the aggressive mode. This theory has been used to design a computer model for alternating and aggressive communication. Computer-simulated chirping sequences are in excellent agreement with field-measured data.

A katydid's chirping sequences are composed of deterministic and random components. As a result, two programming techniques have been used: continuous-system simulation for the deterministic components, and the Monte Carlo technique for the random components. These techniques have been adopted for application on a laboratory minicomputer.[11] The complete simulation program in flow-chart form is shown in Figure 6.12. Response function and transfer function principles can be directly applied to brain-like computer design.

REFERENCES

1. B. Souček, Model of alternating and aggressive communication with the example of katydid chirping. *J. Theor. Biol.* **52**, 399–417 (1975).
2. R. F. Alexander, *Annu. Rev. Entomol.* **12**, 195–526 (1967).
3. M. R. R. Jones, *J. Exp. Biol.* **45**, 15–30 (1966).
4. K. C. Shaw, *Behaviour* **31**, 203–259 (1968).
5. F. Huber, *The Physiology of the Insect Control Nervous System.* Academic Press, New York, 1965.
6. A. Ewing and C. Hoyle, *J. Exp. Biol.,* 139–153 (1965).
7. D. M. Wilson, *Symp. Soc. Exp. Biol.* **20**, 199–228 (1965).
8. W. Heiligenberg, *Z. Vergl. Physiol.* **65**, 70–97 (1969).
9. B. Souček and A. D. Carlson, *J. Theor. Biol.* **55**, 339–352 (1975).
10. B. Souček and F. Vencl, *J. Theor. Biol.* **49**, 147–172 (1975).
11. B. Souček, *Minicomputers in Data Processing and Simulation.* Wiley, New York, 1972.

CHAPTER 7

Frequency Pattern Sequences

INTRODUCTION AND SURVEY

Sequential behavioral patterns present the basis for animal or human communication. For precise study of such patterns, large amounts of data must be analyzed. Statistical analysis of the motor patterns can best be accomplished using a programmed digital computer. Developed methods and computer programs can be used to analyze any coded behavioral pattern or neural spike pattern in general.

The pattern could be a sequence of chirps or sounds used in acoustical communication. It could also be a sequence of flashes used in firefly communication, a sequence of displays describing animal behavior, or the like. Here we study the organization of bird songs and speech recognition systems.

A bird song is a sequence of frequency patterns. Each pattern or syllable is obtained through the Fourier transform of the acoustical signal. The frequency pattern obtained through the Fourier transform has several properties that make it useful as a feature extractor: (1) the modulus of the Fourier transform is invariant to positional shifts; (2) Fourier transforms are unique, in that every signal pattern has a different Fourier transform; (3) the Fourier transforms facilitate data compression, because a pattern can be adequately described by just a few Fourier coefficients; and (4) in the case of image processing, a rotation in the input plane corresponds to an equal rotation in the Fourier plane.

The duetting songs analyzed here are composed of four syllables or patterns for the female and up to 20 syllables for the male. Transition probabilities between syllables, pairs, triplets, and subsequences have been measured. Programmed associative memory is used to efficiently store and display hundreds of songs in the form of one single tree. The tree pattern is a new method to present both the communication process and behavioral control. As the songs are displayed in a sorted and comparative way, one can read from the tree the basic message units, decision-making points, and variations in songs, frequencies, and probabilities of transitions.

This chapter describes both sequential pattern analyzing methods and concrete computer programs. The programs are tested on the example of bird song analysis,[1] but they can be used to analyze other sequential patterns as well.

The model of a bird singing developed by Souček and Vencl[1] suggests the following:

- Storage of the songs is in the form of frequency patterns (syllables).
- Sequences are overlaid in the tree structure.
- Associative storage is used in sequence generation and in pattern recognition.

These features suggest a new brain-like computer architecture: the associative storage of frequency patterns/sequences. As a candidate for associative storage, the logic of coupled nonlinear oscillators should be considered, storing the frequency coefficients.

7.1 BASIC ELEMENTS OR SYLLABLES

7.1.1 Example of the Bird Song

Study of bird songs provides much information about the sequential organization and control of a behavior which functions as communications.[2–6] Recently, theories have been developed to explain firefly flashing communication,[7] and also to explain katydid chirping communication.[8] Although there are great differences between katydids, fireflies, and birds, there are also some similarities in their communication patterns. The present chapter gives an account of song organization and duetting in the white-crested jay thrush (family Timaliidae, *Garrulax leucolophus patkaicus*).

A bird song is expressed as a series of elements of varied frequency lying between 1.5 and 8 kHz. The individual elements of the song are called *syllables*. Syllables result from waveform analysis of acoustical records through continuous sampling and Fourier transformation. Four different syllables are found in the female song, coded 1 to 4, and twenty syllables are found in the male song, coded 5 to 25. For details on experimental data see Vencl and Souček.[9]

A syllable can be recognized as a continuous trace on the sonogram which is separated from other traces of the same individual by 75 msec or more. Two adjacent syllables in the song form a pair, and three syllables form a triplet. Syllable, pair, triplet, and song definitions are outlined in Figure 7.1.

One of the basic questions in sequential behavioral analysis is how strong the influence of a given syllable, pair, or triplet is on the element (syllable), which will appear *N* time-positions later in the sequence. The presented computer programs

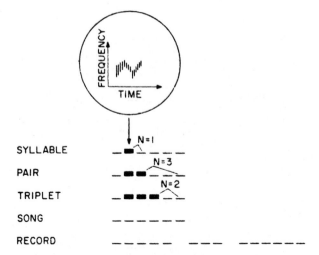

Figure 7.1 *Definitions of syllables, pairs, triplets, songs, and records.*

are written in such a way that the experimenter can select any value for the distance N. However, in reality only the distances 1, 2, and 3 are of interest.

The analyzed record is composed of 141 duetting songs and contains approximately 3000 syllables. By coding the female syllables with codes 1 to 4 and the male syllables with codes 5 to 25, a digital record has been produced as the input to the computer. By introducing the digital computer in bird communication study, it was possible to provide many classes of analysis with high statistical accuracy. Special attention is given to the study of motor patterns of each individual and to the study of message switching between individuals during duetting.

The study is based on recordings of one pair of birds in the summer season. Songs were recorded at 9.5 cm/sec, on a UHER-4200 Report stereo tape recorder using a UHER M517 microphone. Frequency spectra defined as syllables were produced on a Kay electric sonagraph. Coded sonagrams were preanalyzed on a minicomputer in BASIC language. Final analysis was performed in FORTRAN language.

7.1.2 Analysis of Syllables

The computer program for analysis of syllables is presented in Figure 7.2. It reads the record and produces the transition matrix one syllable by one syllable. Table 7.1 shows the matrix for the distance between syllables $N = 1$. The program reads the data and analyses two syllables at a time, $D(K)$ and $D(K + N)$. The values of those syllables, $X = D(K)$ and $Y = D(K + N)$, are used to address the matrix $\mathbf{P}(X, Y)$. The addressed location is used as a counter. Whenever the analyzed two syllables produce the values X and Y, one is added to the location $\mathbf{P}(X, Y)$. This operation is repeated, until the end of the record is reached. The program then prints the frequency tables, such as Table 7.1. The table displays the transition

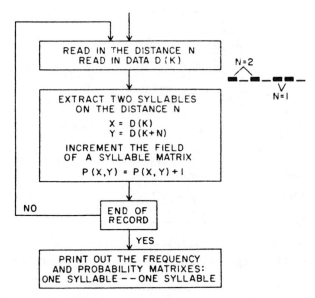

Figure 7.2 Syllable analysis program.

frequencies from syllable X (first element, vertical) into syllable Y (next element, horizontal). It also displays row and column sums, as well as a total sum. The total sum is used to normalize the frequency matrix, producing a new probability matrix, as shown in Table 7.2. Note that in the probability matrix, only the transitions with the probabilities higher than 1% are displayed.

From the frequency Table 7.1, we see that the most frequent transition is from syllable 22 (male) into syllable 1 (female). This transition occurs 353 times. From probability Table 7.2, one can read that this transition presents 12% of all analyzed transitions.

Note that transitions from male syllables (5 to 25) into female syllables (1 to 4) are very frequent. Also, the reverse is true. On the other hand, male-male transitions are almost nonexistent and can be treated as spurious events. At the same time, female-female transitions are very frequent: syllable $F3$ is followed by $F4$ 118 times; syllable $F4$ is followed by $F4$ 147 times. Hence, we can conclude that the male will not sing without an immediate female response; the female will sing without an immediate male response. Also, the female will repeat the same syllable, namely $F4$.

Table 7.3 shows the frequencies of syllable transitions for $N = 2$. Note very frequent transitions: $F1$ into $F1$ (with another syllable in between), 361 times; $F4$ into $F4$, 311 times; $M22$ into $M22$, 262 times. Also, one is able to see the diagonal over the whole matrix, showing the very frequent repetition of the same syllable (with another in between).

From the tables presented, one can always read conditional probabilities: given an element, what are the relative frequencies of the elements to follow? For

TABLE 7.1

N = 1
One Syllable - One Syllable
Frequencies

Next Element

1ST	2ND	3RD	SUM	1	2	3	4	5	6	7	8	9	10	11	12	13	14	15	16	17	18	19	20	21	22	23	24	25
1	0	0	463		2	2			86				3			6	3						23		266	26	32	
2	0	0	138		3	3	6	4		15						1	7									78	20	
3	0	0	316		4	118	10		3	26	2	3	2			14	21	9								9	79	2
4	0	0	585		2	147	43	14	60	16	36	38				11	18	44	1		1	20	10	19		1	93	10
5	0	0	57		3	11	42				1																	
6	0	0	110	91			18					1																
7	0	0	100		12	41	46					1																
8	0	0	18			4	14																					
9	0	0	40			5	34		1																			
10	0	0	44			4	34				1							5										
11	0	0	0																									
12	0	0	0																									
13	0	0	33			16	17																					
14	0	0	50	18		8	19									1												
15	0	0	57			7	48									1												
16	0	0	1															1										
17	0	0	16	15																		1						
18	0	0	1																			1						
19	0	0	20				20																					
20	0	0	40		1	24	14		1																			
21	0	0	27			7	20																					
22	0	0	356	353	132	22			1																		
23	0	0	155		7	179	38	1																		1	
24	0	0	225																								1	
25	0	0	14			1	12	1																				
SUM =			2866	478	161	341	648	59	105	101	18	41	45	0	0	33	50	59	1	15	1	20	41	27	268	115	225	14

TABLE 7.2

N = 1
One Syllable - One Syllable
Probabilities *100

1ST	2ND	3RD	SUM										Next Element															
				1	2	3	4	5	6	7	8	9	10	11	12	13	14	15	16	17	18	19	20	21	22	23	24	25
1	0	0	16	16					3																9			1
2	0	0	4																									
3	0	0	11				4	1																		2	2	
4	0	0	20				5			2		1	1														3	
5	0	0	0				1																					
6	0	0	3		3																							
7	0	0	3			1																						
8	0	0	0																									
9	0	0	1																									
10	0	0	1				1																					
11	0	0	0				1																					
12	0	0	0																									
13	0	0	1																									
14	0	0	1																									
15	0	0	1				1																					
16	0	0	0																									
17	0	0	0																									
18	0	0	0																									
19	0	0	0																									
20	0	0	1																									
21	0	0	0																									
22	0	0	12	12																								
23	0	0	5		4																							
24	0	0	7			6	1																					
25	0	0	0																									
SUM =	0	0	100	16	5	11	22	2	3	3	0	1	1	0	0	1	1	2	0	0	0	1	0	9	4	7	0

TABLE 7.3

N = 1
One Pair - One Syllable
Frequencies

Next Element

1ST	2ND	3RD	SUM	1	2	3	4	5	6	7	8	9	10	11	12	13	14	15	16	17	18	19	20	21	22	23	24	25
1	6	0	61	61																								
1	22	0	212	210		1																		*8				
1	24	0	22	1	5	16																						
2	23	0	71		61	10																						
3	4	0	70		39		3	2		10	5	2				1	4				1			7			34	1
3	24	0	50			11				12	7	3				2	6		1					6			15	2
4	4	0	72		1	29																						
4	5	0	32			9	30										1											
4	7	0	40			2	26		1																			
4	9	0	29			1	19					1																
4	17	0	26			1	26											5										
4	15	0	27			1	26																					
4	24	0	70		54	16																						
5	4	0	29				8	6	1	1		9	1			1	2								2		1	1
6	1	0	76			1		1	59	11	1	9	2				2							2	8		1	
7	3	0	20				6	2		6	1														2		1	1
7	4	0	29				14	5	9	6	1														2		1	1
9	4	0	21				6	5	9		1																	
10	4	0	26				3	2	1	2	12	1	4				1	2		5								
15	4	0	32			1	1	3	17	1	1	1				1	21											
22	1	0	309																	5	1		6	245		10	1	2
23	2	0	98			3	4			8						1	2						1		66		26	
24	3	0	123			2	57	1		6						7		2				3			45		11	
24	4	0	26			24			1	1														1				6
0	0	0	0																									
SUM =			1586	272	68	140	288	25	88	58	14	27	12	0	12	15	34	1	5	1	2	7	18	247	86	142	7

137

example, from Table 7.1, one can read that, given syllable 23, the probability that syllable 2 will follow is 132/155.

7.2 PAIRS

A computer program for analysis of pairs is presented in Figure 7.3. Here the patterns are analyzed with a repertoire of up to 25 different syllables. Hence, they could form $25 \times 25 = 625$ different pairs. Without a computer, the analysis of pairs would be very limited. The computer program is written in such a way that it selects, out of all possible pairs, only the most probable pairs. The program, in fact, investigates the probability matrix one syllable by one syllable (Table 7.2). It compares the probability for each transition with bias probability P_o. The experimenter can choose any value for the bias probability P_o. If the probability of a transition $P(J, I) \geq P_o$, the pair J, I is inserted into a list of most probable pairs. For example, for $P_o = 1\%$, one can see from Table 7.2 that the list of pairs will look as follows:

$$\text{1st pair} = 1, 6 \text{ (probability 3)}$$

$$\text{2nd pair} = 1, 22 \text{ (probability 9)}$$

$$\text{3rd pair} = 1, 24 \text{ (probability 1)}$$

$$\text{4th pair} = 2, 23 \text{ (probability 2), and so forth}$$

The program now prepares the space for a new matrix = one pair-one syllable, as shown in Table 7.4. The vertical column presents the list of most probable pairs; the horizontal column presents the syllable following after the pair.

The transition frequency for a given pair-syllable combination is obtained in the following way (Figure 7.3). The program reads three subsequent data values, $D(K)$, $D(K + 1)$, and $D(K + 1 + N)$. The values $X = D(K)$ and $Y = D(K + 1)$ are treated as a pair. The value $Z = D(K + 1 + N)$ is the syllable following the pair at a distance N.

The new pair XY is compared with all pairs on the list of most probable pairs. If such pair is on the list, the matrix element $P[(X, Y), Z]$ is increased by one.

After the whole record is analyzed, the frequency matrix one pair-one syllable is printed, as shown in Table 7.4. Dividing all values of Table 7.4 with the total number of analyzed transitions, one finds transition probabilities, as shown in Table 7.5. Again, only probabilities above 1% are displayed. The most frequent pair-syllable transitions are as follows:

- Pair (22,1) is followed by syllable 22 in 15% of all transitions.
- Pair (1,22) is followed by syllable 1 in 13% of all transitions.
- Pair (24,3) is followed by syllable 4 in 3% of all transitions.

Pair-syllable matrices will prove very useful in explaining the basic sequences of songs.

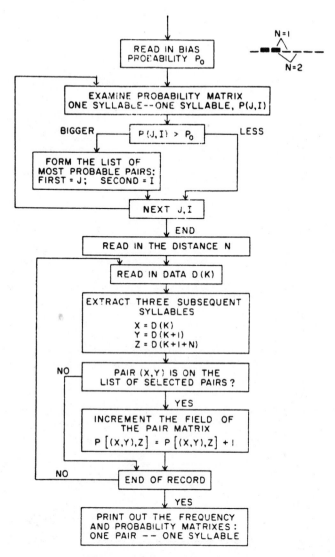

Figure 7.3 *Pair analysis program.*

7.3 TRIPLETS

The computer program for analysis of triplets is presented in Figure 7.4. Here the patterns are analyzed with a repertoire of 25 syllables, and the number of possible triplets is so big that it would be impossible to make any analysis without the help of a computer. Again, out of all possible triplets, the computer selects only the most probable triplets. The program investigates the probability matrix one pair-one syllable, Table 7.5, and compares each value with the bias probability P_o. If

TABLE 7.4

N = 1

One Syllable - One Syllable
Probabilities *100

				Next Element																								
1ST	2ND	3RD	SUM	1	2	3	4	5	6	7	8	9	10	11	12	13	14	15	16	17	18	19	20	21	22	23	24	25
1	6	0	3	3																								
1	22	0	13	13																								
1	24	0	1			1																						
2	23	0	4		3																							
3	4	0	4																									
3	24	0	3			2																						2
4	4	0	4																									
4	5	0	1				1																					
4	7	0	2				1																					
4	9	0	1				1																					
4	10	0	1				1																					
4	15	0	1				1																					
4	24	0	4			3	1																					
5	4	0	1																									
6	1	0	4						3																			
7	3	0	1						1																			
7	4	0	1				1																					
9	4	0	1																									
10	4	0	1																									
15	4	0	2															1										
22	1	0	19						1																15		1	
23	2	0	6																							4		
24	3	0	7				3																					2
24	4	0	1				1																					
0	0	0	0																									
SUM =			100	17	4	8	18	1	5	3	3	1	0	0	0	0	0	2	0	0	0	0	0	1	15	5	8	0

TABLE 7.5

N = 1
One Triplet - One Syllable
Frequencies

				Next Element																								
1ST	2ND	3RD	SUM	1	2	3	4	5	6	7	8	9	10	11	12	13	14	15	16	17	18	19	20	21	22	23	24	25
1	6	1	61			1		1	47					1												1	8		
1	22	1	200						10														5		154	7	24	16
1	24	3	16																									2
2	23	2	42		2		3			7														1		27		
3	4	24	32			25	7																					
3	24	3	34				13	1		3		7	1			4		1									12	1
4	5	4	24				8	4		1						1		2										
4	7	4	24				14	2		6	1																	
4	9	4	18				6	3	8		1	9	4					1										
4	10	4	18				1	2		1			1											2			1	1
4	15	4	23				30	1		1						2	1	17						1			5	
4	24	3	42				11			3																	4	
4	24	4	16																									
6	1	6	45	45																								
7	4	4	11							5		1	1															
15	4	15	16				2																	1			1	
22	1	6	16	16			16																					
22	1	22	211	209		1										1												
22	1	24	20	1	5	14																						
23	2	23	64		55	9																	3					
24	3	4	49				3			7	1	1												3			33	
24	3	24	30			23	7																					
24	4	4	15							2	1																12	
0	0	0	0																									
0	0	0	0																									
SUM =			1028	271	62	73	121	14	65	36	4	18	8	0	0	8	3	21	0	0	0	0	5	7	155	42	111	3

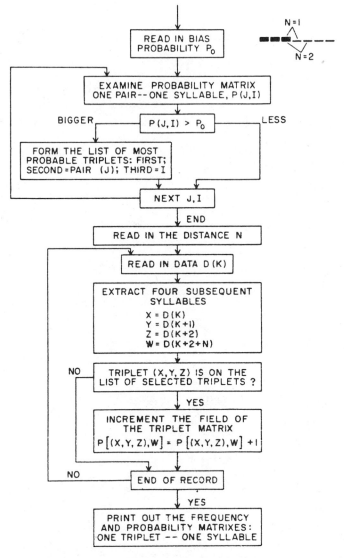

Figure 7.4 *Triplet analysis program.*

the probability of a transition $P(J, I) \geq P_o$, the triplet is inserted into the list of most probable triplets. For example, for $P_o = 1\%$, one can see from Table 7.5 that the list of triplets will look as follows:

1st triplet: pair (1,6), syllable 1 = 1,6,1 (probability 3)

2nd triplet: pair (1,22), syllable 1 = 1,22,1 (probability 13)

3rd triplet: pair (1,24), syllable 3 = 1,24,3 (probability 1)

4th triplet: pair (2,23), syllable 2 = 2,23,2 (probability 3), and so on

The program now prepares the space for a new matrix: one triplet-one syllable, as shown in Table 7.6. The vertical column presents the list of most probable triplets; the horizontal column presents the syllable following after a triplet.

The transition frequencies for a given triplet-syllable combination are obtained in the following way (Figure 7.4). The program reads four subsequent data values, $D(K)$, $D(K+1)$, $D(K+2)$, and $D(K+2+N)$. The values $X = D(K)$, $Y = D(K+1)$, and $Z = D(K+1)$ are treated as a triplet. The value $W = D(K+2+N)$ is the syllable following the triplet at a distance N.

The new triplet X, Y, Z is compared with all triplets on the list of most probable triplets. If such a triplet is found, one is added to the matrix element $P[(X, Y, Z), W]$.

Table 7.7 presents the probability matrix for $N = 1$. The most frequent triplet-syllable transitions are as follows: (22, 1, 22)1 in 20% of all transitions; (1, 22, 1)22 in 14% ; (23, 2, 23)2 in 5% , and so on. Note the strong tendencies of the male to repeat his syllable and of the female to repeat her syllable.

7.4 ASSOCIATIVE TREES

Although transition matrices are useful for many discussions, for a more detailed picture the time information will be needed. For this reason, a computer program was written which superimposes the songs. Each song is split into the time intervals $T1, T2,\ldots,T50$. One time interval belongs to one syllable. The program overlays the songs in such a way that the time interval $T1$ of all the songs is synchronized. The program then counts the frequency of occurrence of a syllable at a given time interval. To show the dependence on the preceding syllables, the overlaying technique produces branches whenever a new song differs from those songs already forming the overlying tree. For example, for

$$Song1: 1, 1, 2, 3, 4, 4$$
$$Song2: 1, 1, 3, 4, 4$$

The overlay will look as follows:

$$\frac{syllable}{frequency}\ \frac{1}{2} \rightarrow \frac{1}{2} \rightarrow \frac{2}{1} \rightarrow \frac{3}{1} \rightarrow \frac{4}{1} \rightarrow \frac{4}{1}$$

$$\rightarrow \frac{3}{1} \rightarrow \frac{4}{1} \rightarrow \frac{4}{1}$$

Note that for time $T1$ and $T2$, both songs follow the same pattern, but after $T2$ the songs are different, producing two separate branches in the overlaying tree. As a result, the frequencies (lower number) for the first and second nodes are 2, whereas for higher nodes the frequencies are 1. The tree program is shown in Figures 7.5 and 7.6. The program reads in one song at a time. It compares

TABLE 7.6

N = 1
One Triplet - One Syllable
Probabilities *100

1ST	2ND	3RD	SUM	\# Next Element																								
				1	2	3	4	5	6	7	8	9	10	11	12	13	14	15	16	17	18	19	20	21	22	23	24	25
1	6	1	5						4																		2	
1	22	1	19																						14		1	
1	24	3	1																							2		
2	23	2	4																									
3	4	24	3			2	1																					
3	24	3	3				1																					
4	5	4	2				1																					
4	7	4	1				1																					
4	9	4	1																									
4	10	4	1																									
4	15	4	2															1											
4	24	3	4			2	1																					
4	24	4	1				1																					
6	1	6	4		4																							
7	4	4	1																									
15	4	15	1				1																					
22	1	6	1	1																								
22	1	22	20	20																								
22	1	24	1		1																							
23	2	23	6		5																							
24	3	4	4		2																							
24	3	24	2																									3	
24	4	4	1																									1	
0	0	0	0																									
0	0	0	0																									
SUM =			100	26	6	7	11	1	6	3	0	1	0	0	0	0	0	2	0	0	0	0	0	0	15	4	10	0

TABLE 7.7

N = 1
One Syllable - One Syllable
Frequencies

Next Element

1ST	2ND	3RD	SUM	1	2	3	4	5	6	7	8	9	10	11	12	13	14	15	16	17	18	19	20	21	22	23	24	25
1	0	0	459	361	32	58	4																					
2	0	0	135	3	79	42		1		1												1	1	9	1	1	3	7
3	0	0	309	12		113	63	4	1	21	6	2	8			3	5	3			1	1		9	2	1	55	1
4	0	0	547	5	8	111	311	6	1	22	7	7	1			3	8	13	1		3	3	2	8		2	25	4
5	0	0	55				16	14	1	2								1										3
6	0	0	109			1	41	6	68	25	1	1	20				3								2	10		
7	0	0	86				41	6		25	1	4														9		
8	0	0	13				4	3			1	1	1					1										
9	0	0	35			1	11	10	11		1	4	1			1												
10	0	0	41				8	2	2	2	18	6						2										
11	0	0	0																									
12	0	0	0																									
13	0	0	30				16	1								3	8						22		2			
14	0	0	48			1	3		2			1				13	4	2					22		2			
15	0	0	52			1	8	5	2	1		2				2	27							2		2	2	
16	0	0	1				1																					
17	0	0	16			1												9				6					
18	0	0	1																		1							
19	0	0	18				2															15	1					
20	0	0	38			1	15		2								16				1			3			1	
21	0	0	26				17		2	2								4					3	3				
22	0	0	342	1		1	11		18											6			6	2	262	16	32	
23	0	0	132		4	3	11			10						2	3	3					2	2	72	23	
24	0	0	214			4	112			9						7		3					4	4	1	1	72	
24	0	0	14				3	5	4									0										1
SUM =			2721	382	123	338	647	59	104	101	17	41	43	0	0	32	50	59	1	15	1	20	41	27	268	113	225	14

ANALYSIS PROGRAM:

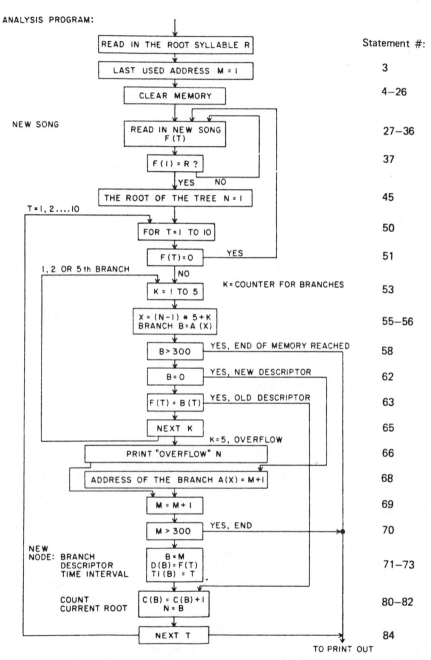

	Statement #:
READ IN THE ROOT SYLLABLE R	
LAST USED ADDRESS M = I	3
CLEAR MEMORY	4–26
READ IN NEW SONG F (T)	27–36
F (I) = R ?	37
THE ROOT OF THE TREE N = I	45
FOR T = I TO IO	50
F (T) = O	51
K = I TO 5	53
X = (N–I) * 5 + K / BRANCH B = A (X)	55–56
B > 300	58
B = 0	62
F (T) = B (T)	63
NEXT K	65
PRINT "OVERFLOW" N	66
ADDRESS OF THE BRANCH A(X) = M+I	68
M = M + I	69
M > 300	70
B = M / D (B) = F (T) / TI (B) = T	71–73
C (B) = C (B) + I / N = B	80–82
NEXT T	84

NEW SONG

T = I, 2 .... IO

I, 2 OR 5th BRANCH

K = COUNTER FOR BRANCHES

YES   NO

YES

NO

YES, END OF MEMORY REACHED

YES, NEW DESCRIPTOR

YES, OLD DESCRIPTOR

K = 5, OVERFLOW

YES, END

NEW NODE: BRANCH / DESCRIPTOR / TIME INTERVAL

COUNT CURRENT ROOT

TO PRINT OUT

Figure 7.5 *Tree generating programmed associative memory. For program statement labels see Table 7.10.*

PRINT OUT:

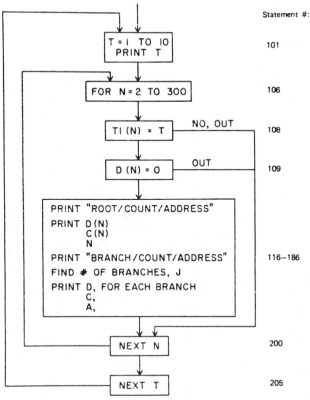

Figure 7.6 *Print-out program. For program statement labels see Table 7.11.*

the first syllable of the song, $F(1)$, with the root syllable R. One can choose any root syllable. If the song starts with the selected root syllable, it will be analyzed; otherwise, the program reads in a new song sequence.

The next step is the overlaying procedure. The new song series is compared with the tree structure formed up to this moment. The analysis starts for time interval $T1$ and proceeds until the end of a song is reached. For each time interval, the syllable of the song is compared with the tree structure for this time interval. An example of the tree produced using this technique is shown in Figure 7.7. The program allows up to five branches to go out from each node of the tree. The new syllable is treated as a descriptor for searching the tree. The syllable investigates five branches, with the following possible outcomes:

- The branch is empty ($B = 0$). In this case, the new descriptor takes this branch from now on. Each branch keeps the following information:

    Address A, pointing to the origin of the branch

    Descriptor D, syllable

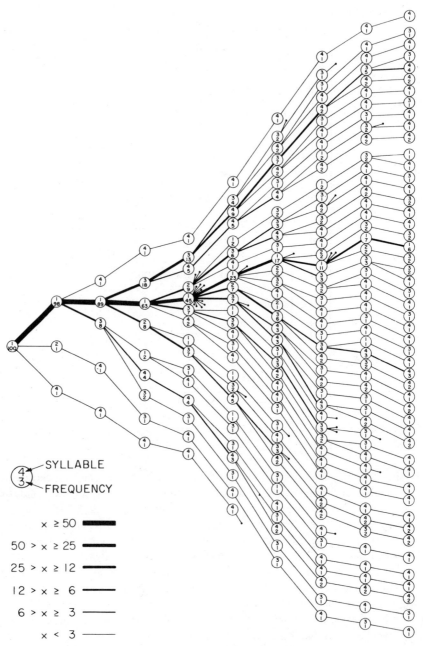

Figure 7.7 *Female transition tree. Tree stores only female portion of sequences beginning with* F₁. *Tree contains 100 duets (frequencies are percentages). Tree is formed by the summation of common syllable types at each node in a time period. Reading the tree from left to right, 10 time periods are given,* T = 1 to 10. *If a new syllable type is uttered, a branch is formed. Pins symbolize the termination of a sequence. Repetition of* F₁ *gives a strong major pathway or branch.*

Time interval of the branch T

Frequency counter C

- The branch is occupied with the descriptor that is identical to the one being analyzed. In this case, the frequency counter C of this descriptor is incremented by one.
- The branch is occupied with a different descriptor. In this case, analysis proceeds on the next branch.

Note that computer memory cannot be allocated to the branches in advance. The branches take the memory locations from a common space as they are added to the tree. In fact, the tree is organized as a programmed associative memory; the search is based on the content of a cell, rather than on the address of the cell. [10]

After analysis the printout program produces the results; this program is shown in Figure 7.6. The program prints out all the branches for $T = 1$, then for $T = 2$, and so on. Each branch is described with the following information: descriptor = syllable; frequency; connectors to the preceding nodes; connectors to the following nodes.

Figure 7.7 presents a female tree. Figure 7.8 presents a duet tree. One is able to identify the structure of the songs that are repeated many times (heavy lines), as well as many rare variations, especially toward the end of the song.

Note that the tree keeps the songs of the whole experiment. Each individual song can be recognized on the tree. The tree method presents, in fact, the most efficient way to store hundreds of behavioral sequences. The tree compares and sorts the patterns at the same time. One can read directly from the tree the transition frequencies between individual syllables, including the time dependence. The tree also displays pairs, triplets, and longer subsequences, and their time dependence.

One can conclude that the tree presents an actual model of the behavior under analysis. The tree not only keeps all the information from the experiment, but also displays all the characteristic features of the patterns, subpatterns, probabilities of transitions, branching points, and time dependence.

Here are a few examples of how to read the information from the female tree in Figure 7.7. The female songs are produced by extracting the female syllables from duets. Whenever a song ends at a time T, a pin is inserted in the tree node at the time level T. The left-hand node, 1/100, shows that the tree is composed of the songs starting with syllable 1, and that 100 songs are analyzed.

The top branch presents a rare song: 1,1,4,4. This song has occurred only one time. The second branch presents the song 1,1,1,3,3,3,3,3. The seventh node on this branch (3/2), reads 3 = syllable; 2 = frequency; i.e., two songs. One song ends at this node (see the pin), whereas the second song proceeds for one more time interval (node 3/1).

Next are a few examples dealing with the duet tree, Figure 7.8. The first node, 22/89, shows that songs starting with syllable 22 are displayed, and that 89 songs are stored in the tree. The heavy branch presents the most frequent sequence: 22,1,22,1,22,1. At the time $T = 6$, on this branch one finds the node 1/64, with few outgoing branches. The first top branch shows that one song ends here. The second branch points to the node 20/2, showing that in two songs the next syllable was 20. The third branch points to the node 23/2, showing that in two songs the next syllable was 23. The fourth branch points to the node 22/40, showing that in forty songs the next syllable was 22, and so on.

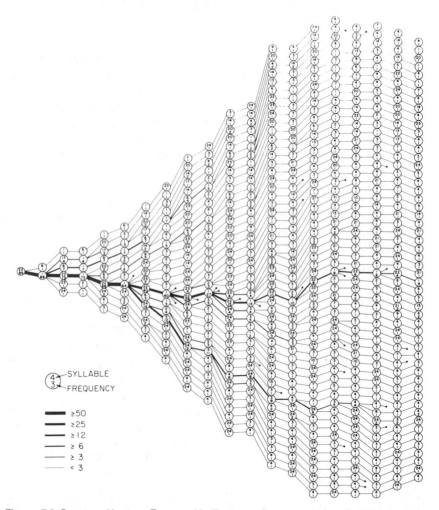

Figure 7.8 *Duet transition tree. Tree graphically stores all sequences from the study beginning with M$_{22}$. The tree contains 89 such sequences. The tree is formed by overlapping of common syllables at nodes. Nodes occur at each time period (from left to right T = 1 to 20). Branching occurs if the sequence is different at any node. Syllable type is given as the top value. Bottom value is the frequency of occurrence at that node. Pins symbolize the termination of sequences. Lines connecting nodes are weighted. Overall branching pattern pictorially reveals the decision points and major sequence pathways. Many sequences are formed from an alternation of M$_{22}$ and F$_1$ and produce the thick trunk of the tree. At T = 10 to 11 and T = 12 to 13 major branching occurs, indicating decision points. At T = 6, M$_{24}$ initiates a major side branch.*

Note that after time $T = 6$, the two heavy branches occur:

$$22, 1, 22, 1, 22, 1$$
$$24, 3, 24, 3, 24, 3$$

In forty songs, the male has responded at time $T = 7$ with the usual 22, and the standard sequence 22,1,22,1 continues. In sixteen songs, however, the male has responded with 24, and a new subsequence is developed: 24,3,24,3.

This case shows definite interdependence between syllables produced by the male and those produced by the female. In a similar way one can examine different portions of the tree and follow subsequences and transitions.

7.5 THE SIGNIFICANCE OF THE TREE METHOD

In contrast to transition matrices, the tree stores all observed duet sequences preserving the relative time-dependent relationships between syllables. Each duet sequence is compared, counted, and displayed for analysis.

7.5.1 Female Songs

Figure 7.7 represents the transition tree for the female part of the duets beginning with F_1 only. F_2 was less frequent (43%) as the females' first call, whereas F_3 and F_4 were almost never given first. The most-frequently recurring sequences are identified by line weightings and counts at nodes. Rarer variations appear later in the duet. Sequences shorter than 10 syllables terminate as periods between nodes. Dominant features such as bound groups, subpatterns, transitional probabilities, and switch points are summarized as follows:

1. From the 100 sequences stored in the tree, 45%
    reach the time $T = 5$ as a repetition of F_1 (heavy branch).
2. Distributions of syllables relative to sequence time are given for $T = 1$, $T = 5$, and $T = 10$ in Figure 7.9. F_1 is the dominant syllable in the beginning of a

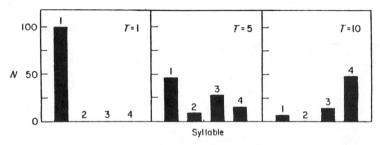

Figure 7.9 *Histograms showing distribution of syllables in female tree. At the beginning of the song (T = 1), syllable* F$_1$ *is dominant. In the middle of the song (T = 5), all syllables are possible. At the end of the song (T = 10), syllable* F$_4$ *is dominant.*

duet. At time $T = 5$, F_3 totals 29%. At time $T = 10$, F_4 composes 49% of the cases, whereas F_1 is quite rare (7%).

3. Figure 7.7 shows that many sequences (11%) terminate at time $T = 5$. $T = 5$ appears to be a decision point. Those sequences which continue past time $T = 5$ are likely to be composed of new units (44%), whereas only a few revert to previously given units (4%).

4. 52% of the sequences continue past $T = 5$ as a repetition of the same syllable type.

5. Linear dependencies exist. For example, F_1 and F_2 precede F_3 and F_4 98% of the time. F_1 follows F_2 less than 3% of the time.

6. Some syllables commonly occur together; they may be said to be coupled. They are expressed in Table 7.8 as a percentage of the total syllables at time periods $T = 1 - 2$; $T = 5 - 6$; and $T = 9 - 10$.

7.5.2 Duet Songs

Figure 7.8 represents a duetting transition tree composed of only those sequences beginning with M_{22}. Forty-eight duets, not sampled by this tree, begin with M_{23}; four begin with M_{24}; and none begin with any other male note. The base node indicates that 89 sequences were initiated by the male with M_{22}. By the time $T = 20$, the main pathways have dwindled and the appearances of rarer syllables are most frequent. Distribution data for the beginning, middle, and end of the tree are summarized in Figure 7.10. All rare events are denoted by R. The most common message units and their times of appearance are given in Table 7.9.

By introducing a digital computer into the study of animal communication, it was possible to provide many classes of analysis with high statistical accuracy. Special attention is given to the study of motor patterns of each individual, and to the study of message switching between individuals during bird duetting.

We found that the individual pattern of the female usually starts with syllable code 1 and exhibits a tendency of shifting toward syllables with higher code values. As a result, the female song usually ends with the syllable F_4. Also, the female frequently produces two syllables in a row, without waiting for the male's answer.

It was found that the individual pattern of the male usually starts with syllable

TABLE 7.8 Message Units and Time Period

Message unit	Time period		
	$T = 1-2$	$T = 5-6$	$T = 9-10$
$(1 \rightarrow 1)$	98	24	6
$(3 \rightarrow 4)$	0	18	15
$(4 \rightarrow 4)$	0	9	12
$(3 \rightarrow 3)$	0	12	6
$(1 \rightarrow 2)$	1	9	0
$(1 \rightarrow 3)$	0	9	1
$(1 \rightarrow 4)$	1	3	1

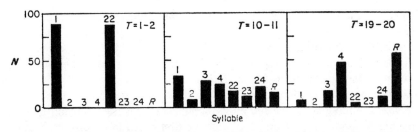

Figure 7.10 *Histograms showing distribution of syllables in the duet tree. At the beginning of the duet (T = 1 to 2), syllables F_1 and M_{22} are dominant. In the middle of the song (T = 10 to 11) many combinations are possible. At the end of the song (T = 19 to 20), syllable F_4 and rare male syllables become dominant.*

code M_{22}, has a tendency to shift toward syllables M_{23} and M_{24}, and then spreads over a variety of syllables with lower frequencies. The male initiates the song, and after that generates one syllable following each answer from the female side. Almost never does the male produce two syllables in a row without waiting for the female answer.

Programmed associative memory is used to efficiently store and display hundreds of songs in the form of one single tree. The tree pattern is a new method to present both the communication process and behavioral control. Since the songs are displayed in a sorted and comparative way, one can read from the tree the basic message units, decision-making points, variations of songs, frequencies, and probabilities of transitions. Each individual song can be recognized in the tree. The tree method presents the most efficient way to store hundreds of behavioral sequences.

Through inspection of the duet tree, it is found that the first message unit in most of the songs has a pattern of 22,1,22,1,22,1. At $T = 6$, major branching occurs, initiated by the male responding with a syllable which is different from 22.

Large numbers of songs will continue with the pattern 22,1, but other new message units are also initiated. If the male has responded with 24, a new message unit starts, with the pattern 24,3,24,3,24. This is an obvious case of peripheral

TABLE 7.9 Message Units and Their Times of Appearance

Message unit	T = 1–2	T = 5–6	T = 10–11	T = 15–16	T = 19–20
(4 → 4)	0	0	4	3	8
(4 → 3)	0	0	12	9	6
(22 → 1)	88	82	22	10	6
(24 → 3)	0	3	2	15	5
(24 → 4)	0	4	3	10	6
(23 → 2)	0	1	2	1	0
Terminations	0	0	2	0	2
New branches	0	0	2	0	
Rare transitions	0	5	14	20	22

influence. It shows the interdependence of syllables produced by the male and the female.

The actual tree program is shown in Table 7.10 and 7.11. The statement labels from Table 7.10 are also displayed next to the corresponding boxes on the flowchart in Figure 7.5. The statement labels from Table 7.11 are displayed in the same manner on the flowchart in Figure 7.6. Note the following details in the program: code 98 is used to identify the end of one song; code 99 is used to identify the end of the record (and of the experiment); data are first stored in the disk file and then used by this program.

It was common practice in the past to analyze bird songs as a stationary sequence of events, assuming that the probabilities of different outcomes do not change with time. The present analysis clearly shows that duetting songs are highly nonstationary processes: the probabilities of outcomes are very much different at the beginning of the song from those in the middle or at the end of the song. In contrast to transition matrices, the tree method stores all observed duet sequences, preserving the relative time-dependent relationships between syllables.

The analysis of bird songs based on associative trees, leads to the model presented in Figure 7.11.

In the beginning of this study, the three classes of syllables, M_{17}, M_{22}, and M_6, were observed and assigned discrete codes. It turned out that the behavior of the female to these three types was indistinguishable. Moreover, the transitions from these to other male elements were identical. Finally, the linear interrelationships between M_6 and M_{22} suggested that both were members of a graded continuum. Since the females apparently failed to discriminate between them, both are assigned to one group, M_6/M_{22}. M_{17} is also a member of this group, but because of its rarity it is not included in the group code.

7.6 SPEECH RECOGNITION SYSTEMS

One of the most difficult tasks in sound-wave analysis is the definition and recognition of basic elements or syllables. In animal communication study, the recognition process is done by the researcher, who looks at the frequency patterns or "sonagrams" and recognizes the basic elements. This procedure is slow and limited to a small amount of data. Engineers have developed computer systems for automatic recognition of speech. Such systems are used not only for research in the area of human communication but also in industries. Some of the applications in which human voice input systems have already become operational are quality control and inspection, automated material handling, parts programming for numerically controlled machine tools, and direct voice input to the computer. The first voice input systems to be used by industry in these various applications were installed in late 1973 and early 1974.

All automatic speech-recognition systems can be classified under two categories: continuous or connected speech systems, and isolated or discrete speech systems. The differences between these two types of systems can become obscure and overlap when we attempt to classify a particular approach as either isolated or

TABLE 7.10

```
 1   REM TREE PATTERN
 2   DIM G(5)
 3   M=1
 4   FILES DUET
 5   DIM F(1Ø)
 6   DIM D(3ØØ)
 8   DIM C (3ØØ)
1Ø   DIM T1(3ØØ)
12   DIM A(15ØØ)
15   FOR I=1 TO 3ØØ
16   D(I)=Ø
17   C(I)=Ø
18   T1(I)=Ø
2Ø   FORK=1 TO 5
22   X=(I-1)*5+K
24   A(K)=Ø
25   NEXT K
26   NEXT I
27   PRINT "ROOT,FILE ?"
29   INPUT R,Z
3Ø   FOR J=1 TO 1Ø
31   INPUT #1,F(J)
32   IF F (J)=99 GO TO 92
35   IF F(J)=98 GO TO 37
36   NEXT J
37   IF F (1)< >RGO TO 3Ø
45   N=1
5Ø   FOR T=1 TO 1Ø
51   IF F(T)=ØGO TO 3Ø
52   IF F(T)=98 GO TO 3Ø
53   FOR K=1 TO 5
55   X=(N-1)*5+K
56   B=A(X)
58   IF B>=3ØØ GO TO 99
62   IF B=ØGO TO 68
63   IF F(T)=D(B)GO TO 8Ø
65   NEXT K
66   PRINT "OVFL.ROOT=",N
67   GO TO 69
68   A(X)=M+1
69   M=M+1
7Ø   IF M>=3ØØ GO TO 99
71   B=M
72   D(B)=F(T)
73   T1(B)=T
8Ø   C(B)=C(B)+1
82   N=B
```

TABLE 7.10 (cont.)

```
84    NEXT T
90    GO TO 30
92    PRINT"OUT=0,MORE=2"
93    INPUT W
94    IF W=2 GO TO 27
95    GO TO 100
99    PRINTS"300 NODES"
```

TABLE 7.11

```
100    PRINT
101    FOR T=1 TO 10
102    PRINT
103    PRINT "TIME POSITION=",T
106    FOR N=2 TO 300
108    IF T1(N)<>TGO TO 200
109    IF D(N)=0GO TO 200
115    PRINT
116    PRINT "ROOT/CO/ADR"
117    PRINT D(N)
118    PRINT C(N)
120    PRINT N
126    PRINT
130    PRINT "BR/CO/ADR"
131    J=0
150    FOR K=1 TO 5
152    X=(N-1)*5+K
153    IF A(X)=0GO TO 160
154    J=J+1
155    G(K)=A(X)
160    NEXT K
165    FOR K=1 TO J
168    Z=G(K)
170    PRINT D(Z),
171    NEXT K
172    PRINT
173    FOR K=1 TO J
174    Z=G(K)
175    PRINT C(Z),
177    NEXT K
178    PRINT
180    FOR K=1 TO J
184    PRINT G(K),
185    NEXT K
186    PRINT
200    NEXT N
205    NEXT T
300    END
```

continuous. Isolated speech systems can be defined as those systems that require a short pause before and after utterances that are to be recognized as entities. The minimum duration of a pause that separates independent utterances is on the order of 100 msec.

A number of techniques have been developed for automatic recognition of isolated, single-word-length utterances. In fact, until recently the vast majority of recognition work in the field has been at the presegmented level, and only recently has there been widespread interest in the continuous speech problem.

It is customary to capture the acoustic speech signal, convert it to frequency, and quantize it into a form that is usable by subsequent processing. There are at least three major candidates for this task: filter-bank analysis, discrete Fourier transformation, and linear predictive coding. It is not clear at this point which of these is superior in application to the speech-analysis problem.

A practical, limited-vocabulary system achieves recognition processing by comparing an unknown utterance with a set of stored samples of the vocabulary words obtained from the user of the system. These reference data must be stable over long periods of time for practical applications. Once the reference data have been obtained, the operator should be able to use the voice-input system with little or no retraining over time.

Frequency-domain representation of the speech signal is particularly advantageous for two reasons:

1. The human auditory system performs a crude frequency analysis at the periphery of auditory sensation (preprocessing of the signal).
2. An exact description of the speech sound can be obtained with a natural frequency concept model of speech production.

Time-domain representation of the speech signal has also been used recently for speech analysis based on the linear predictability of speech waveforms.

Each pattern-recognition system must define the key processing function as the feature extractor. The feature-extraction processes frequently used are the spectral shape of the speech signal and the time derivative of the spectral envelope function. The spectral shape and its changes with time are continuously sampled over the frequency range of interest. Combinations and sequences of these samples are processed to produce a set of significant acoustic features. This segmentation process is performed using both special hardware and computer software. The feature-extraction system has two modes of operation: training and recognition.

During the training mode, the system automatically extracts a time-normalized feature for each repetition of a given speech signal (word). A consistent matrix of feature occurrences is required before the features are stored in the reference pattern memory.

During the recognition mode, each speech signal entering the system is processed: the features are extracted, digitized, and time-normalized. The result is then compared digitally to each stored reference matrix. The stored reference producing the highest overall correlation is selected as the test signal.

Today, limited-vocabulary systems exist and are used in both research labo-

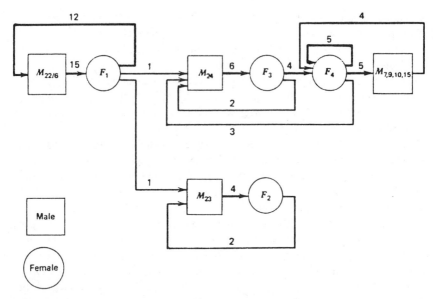

Figure 7.11 *Bird duetting program. Diagrammatic representation of the structure of male (boxes) and female (circles) sequences, based on transitional data from tables. Values shown above the lines are probabilities representing the utilization of sequence pathways.*

ratories and industry. Advances in microcomputer technology promise that practical systems capable of handling 1000 to 5000-word vocabularies will become available. In animal communication study, even today's systems with limited vocabulary can be successfully used for feature extraction and recognition.

Speech perception integrates multiple sources of information. This fact suggests a highly parallel distributed model, such as the TRACE model developed by McClelland and Elman[11]. In TRACE processing takes place through the excitatory and inhibitory interactions of a large number of simple units. The units are organized into three levels: feature, phoneme, and word. The pattern of activation left by a spoken input is a trace of analysis of the input at each of the three processing levels. TRACE is related to the adaptive learning systems and artificial neural systems described in Chapters 11 and 12.

The analysis of bird songs based on associative trees, leads to the model presented in Figure 7.11.

In the beginning of this study, the three classes of syllables, M_{17}, M_{22}, and M_6, were observed and assigned discrete codes. It turned out that the behavior of the female to these three types was indistinguishable. Moreover, the transitions from these to other male elements were identical. Finally, the linear interrelationships between M_6 and M_{22} suggested that both were members of a graded continuum. Since the females apparently failed to discriminate between them, both are assigned to one group, M_6/M_{22}. M_{17} is also a member of this group, but because of its rarity it is not included in the group code.

It would be interesting to combine associative trees with parallel distributed models, such as TRACE.

REFERENCES

1. B. Souček and F. Vencl: Bird communication study using digital computer. *J. Theor. Biol.* **49**, 147–172 (1975).

2. C. G. Beer: On the responses of laughing gull chicks to the calls of adults. I. Recognition of the voices of parents. *Anim. Behav.* **18** (1970).

3. B. Bertram: The vocal behaviour of the Indian Hill, Mynah *Gracula religiosa, Anim. Behav. Monogr.* **3**, (1970).

4. R. Evans: Imprinting and mobility in young ring-billed gulls, *Larus delawarensis. Anim. Behav. Monogr.* **3** (Part 3), 193–248 (1970).

5. R. Lemon and C. Chatfield: Organization of song in cardinals. *Anim. Behav.* **19**, 1–17 (1971).

6. W. Thorpe, II: *Bird-Song.* Cambridge Univ. Press, London and New York, 1961.

7. B. Souček and A. D. Carlson, Flash pattern recognition in firefly. J. Theor. Biol. **55**, 339 (1975).

8. B. Souček: Model of alternating and aggressive communication with the example of katydid chirping. *J. Theor. Biol.* **52**, 399–417 (1975).

9. F. Vencl and B. Souček: Structure and control of duet singing in the white-crested jay thrush. *Behaviour* **57**, 20–33 (1976).

10. B. Souček: *Minicomputers in Data Processing and Simulation.* Wiley, New York, 1972.

11. J.L. McClelland and J.L. Elman, Interactive processes in speech perception: The TRACE model. In McClelland et al (ed.), *Parallel Distributed Processing,* The MIT Press, Cambridge, Vol. 2. 58–121 (1986).

CHAPTER 8

Quantized Information Transmission on Neural Terminals

INTRODUCTION AND SURVEY

A large number of systems are under development, based on self-adaptable learning networks. Learning networks are influenced by research in the adaptable neural networks. The neural networks are connected through the synaptic neural terminals. Here we present the model of information transmission on neural terminals.

Action potential carries information over an axon until it reaches the neural terminal. The chemical transmitter is contained in vesicles in the presynaptic knot and, on the arrival of the action potential at the neural terminal, some of the vesicles are discharged into the synaptic cleft. An integral number of vesicles are discharged each time. Hence, the potential on the other side of the junction is built up from an integral number of contributions, or quanta. It is believed that many central synapses mediated by chemical transmitters operate in this way. Quantal transmission was first discovered at the neuromuscular junction (end-plate). This chapter explains the computer model developed by Souček.[1]

A statistical model of the composition of end-plate potentials has been designed and used for detailed study of an end-plate potential's amplitude distribution function. The model is based on the present knowledge of synaptic functions and takes into account the miniature end-plate potential's amplitude distribution, pulse shape, and latency fluctuation, as well as the residual potential difference across the membrane, nonlinear summation of unit quanta, and the mean quantum content. The build-up of end-plate potentials is a stochastic process in which all of the above factors have significant influence. The computer model for statistical building of end-plate potentials is designed on the basis of the Monte Carlo technique. The end-plate potentials' distribution is not calculated, but is built up in the same way as in a living neuromuscular junction, through the addition of miniature end-plate potentials, which have random amplitudes and random times of arrival.

Large numbers of experiments have been performed with the model with the mean quantum content in the range from 2 to 200, mean amplitudes of miniature end-plate potentials in the range of 0.2 to 0.8 mv, coefficients of variation of miniature end-plate potentials in the range of 0.1 to 0.2, and the number of depolarizations per experiment up to 25,000. Latency fluctuation and pulse shape have been taken according to the measurements by Katz and Miledi.[2]

Very close agreement between results produced by the theoretical model and real experiments was obtained. Coefficients of variation of end-plate potentials produced by the model are in good agreement with experimental results for all values of mean quantum content. This is due partly to the fact that not only nonlinear summation but also the latency fluctuation diminishes the coefficient of variation.

8.1 EXAMPLE OF END-PLATE POTENTIAL

8.1.1 Problem

Del Castillo and Katz[3,4] have shown that the end-plate potentials (e.p.p.) at myoneural junctions of frog muscle is built up of small all-or-none units ("quanta") which are identical in size and shape with the spontaneously occurring miniature e.p.p.s (m.e.p.p.). Similar results have been obtained by Boyd and Martin[5] on mammalian muscle and have been proven on a number of other preparations. It was found that when the average "quantum content," m, of the e.p.p. was small ($m < 5$), the value of m could be obtained from the ratio

$$\frac{[\text{mean amplitude of e.p.p.}]}{[\text{mean amplitude of m.e.p.p.}]}$$

The amplitude of the e.p.p. fluctuated in a manner described by Poisson law, suggesting that there is a latent population of excitable units at the junction, each with a small probability of responding to a nerve stimulus. However, at higher and more nearly normal levels ($m > 10$) the fluctuations were much less than expected on this basis.

Martin[6] has shown that for e.p.p.s exceeding a few millivolts in size, m cannot be calculated as stated above, but a correction must be applied because, unlike quantal conductance changes, miniature potentials do not add linearly beyond a limited range. When the correction factor was applied to the e.p.p. measurements, the discrepancy between the observed and theoretical values was diminished. The coefficient of variation was in more satisfactory agreement with $m^{-0.5}$, as would be expected according to the Poisson law. (Actually, m.e.p.p.s add more linearly than indicated by the above correction because of the effect of membrane capacity.)

In a resting terminal, transmitter packets are released at random intervals with a low probability. When the terminal is depolarized by an action potential, the release rate rapidly increases to a high value and then returns to the resting level. Synaptic delays and the time course of acetycholine release at the neuromuscular junction have been measured by Katz and Miledi.[2] This measurement shows that the quantal release at the neuromuscular junction is not instantaneous with the arrival of the action potential, but rather it fluctuates in a random way.

E.p.p.s are built up of m.e.p.p.s, which are added together in a random fashion. Souček[7] developed a general equation for e.p.p. amplitude probability distribution function, and showed that statistical composition of e.p.p.s can be treated as a transient in a stochastic process. The e.p.p.s' probability distribution is a function of the latency distribution, the m.e.p.p.s' pulse shape, the m.e.p.p.s' amplitude distribution, and mean quantal content.

From all the knowledge accumulated up to now, many aspects of neural information transfer are well understood, and many of the remaining problems are clearly defined. Two things are, however, obvious:

1. Experimental investigations of the statistical nature of e.p.p.s give results for a limited number of cases determined by parameters of measurements. Also, experimental results are smeared by measurement errors, the most serious of which are noise, rough quantization, and large statistical inaccuracies due to the small number of data analyzed.
2. Analytical investigations of e.p.p.s ask for the use of sophisticated stochastic-process theory. Obtained equations describe the statistical nature of e.p.p.s in mathematical language, which is not easy for everyday laboratory usage.

To overcome these difficulties, a computer model[1] for statistical building of e.p.p.s has been designed. The model simulates m.e.p.p.s with random amplitudes and random times of arrival. The m.e.p.p.s are added in nonlinear fashion, producing the e.p.p. Large numbers of simulated "experiments" have been performed for various sets of parameters. The model enables one to make "measurements" of e.p.p.s' distribution functions, analyzing thousands of e.p.p.s and controlling quantization steps and noise level. The parameters of simulated experiments have been chosen according to the most important real experiments published up to now.

Very close agreements between results produced by theoretical models and real experiments have been obtained. Different models have been investigated. The best results are obtained from the model[1] which takes into account mean quantum content, m, the m.e.p.p.s' pulse shape, the m.e.p.p.s' amplitude distribution, latency distribution, and nonlinear summation. Coefficients of variation of the e.p.p.'s distributions produced by such a model are in very good agreement with experimental results for all values of m. This is explained through the fact that not only nonlinear summation but also the latency fluctuation have an influence on the e.p.p.'s distribution function and on the coefficient of variation.

8.1.2 Method

The model for statistical building of e.p.p.s has been designed on the basis of the Monte Carlo technique. The e.p.p.'s distribution is not calculated but is built in the same way as in living neuromuscular junctions. The simulation programs have been written in FORTRAN language for Control Data 6600 computer and can be applied on other FORTRAN-oriented computers. Before simulating an experiment, the program reads experimental data describing the m.e.p.p.s' pulse shape, the m.e.p.p.s' amplitude distribution, latency distribution, and mean quantum content. The experimenter can choose the number of amplitude-channels for the e.p.p.'s distribution (quantization step). The experimenter can also choose the noise level or perform an ideal, noiseless experiment. The experimenter also decides on the number of depolarizations during one experiment. The experiments, with a few thousand depolarizations, can be simulated, eliminating statistical fluctuations, which are very large in real experiments because it is difficult to collect thousands of data values and get a preparation to remain absolutely stable for many hours.

The experimental, nonsimulated data used for computer statistical analysis were obtained from the work of Martin[6]; his paper should be consulted for a complete description of the experimental method used. In summary, the usual techniques of intracellular recording of e.p.p.s and m.e.p.p.s were employed.[8] The median extensor longusdigitorium IV muscle of the frog (*Rana temporaria*) was used. It was immersed in an isotonic solution containing $CaCl_2$ and $MgCl_2$, adjusted to reduce the end-plate response to just below threshold for the initiation of a propagated muscle action potential. Prostigmine, an anticholinesterase, was included in the solution to increase the amplitude of the spontaneous m.e.p.p.s. Special attention has been given to investigate the coefficient of variation as a function of mean quantum content.

8.2 COMPUTER MODEL

In describing the model and results obtained, the following notations will be used:

m	mean quantum content
s	amplitude of e.p.p.
$f(s)$	probability distribution of e.p.p.s' amplitudes
A	amplitude of m.e.p.p.
$P(A)$	probability distribution of m.e.p.p.s' amplitudes
v	mean amplitude of m.e.p.p.s
$h(t)$	pulse shape of m.e.p.p.s
$\alpha(t)$	the release rate of m.e.p.p.s after depolarization
x	fraction of m.e.p.p.s which is used in summation to form e.p.p.
$g(x)$	distribution function of x
V_0	residual potential difference across the membrane
N	number of depolarizations during one experiment

Figure 8.1 explains the model for statistical building of e.p.p.s, taking into account facts known up to now.

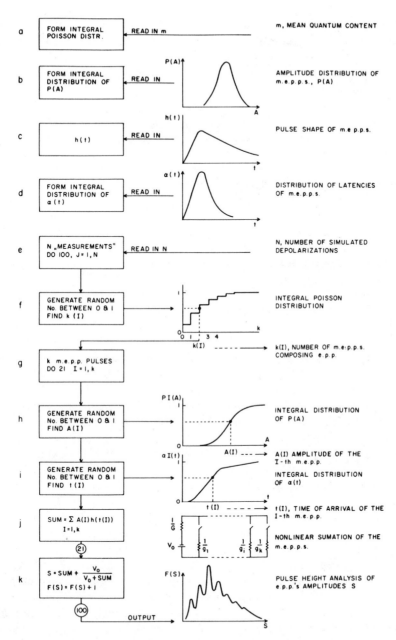

Figure 8.1 *Computer model for the statistical composition of the end-plate potential. Steps (a), (b), (c), (d), and (e) present set-up of the experiment. Steps (f), (g), (h), (i), (j), and (k) present buildings of one e.p.p.*

The e.p.p.s, on the basis of quantal theory, are composed of a sum of m.e.p.p.s. It has been shown, experimentally, that the number of m.e.p.p. units composing an e.p.p. is Poisson-distributed with the mean quantum content, m (for $m < 10$). Hence, the probability that e.p.p. amplitude, s, is composed of 1, 2, 3, k m.e.p.p.s will be

$$p(k) = \frac{e^{-m}}{k!} m^k \tag{8.1}$$

The mean quantum content, m, or the average rate of unit release depends upon membrane potential, ion concentrations (particularly calcium) in the bathing medium, the quantity of transmitter available for release, and the history of synaptic use. Here we shall consider only depolarizations applied on a resting terminal.

To simulate an experiment, the experimenter must first decide the value of m. The program reads m, calculates the Poisson distribution (Equation 8.1), and calculates the integral Poisson distribution (Figure 8.1a),

$$pi(k) = \sum_{i=0}^{k} \frac{e^{-m}}{i!} m^i \tag{8.2}$$

The distribution, $pi(k)$, gives the number of cases when the e.p.p. is composed of less than (or equal to) k m.e.p.p.s. The distribution is shown in Figure 8.1f.

In the next step, Figure 8.1b, the program reads in the m.e.p.p.s' amplitude distribution function $P(A)$. This distribution has been measured in many experiments. Usually, $P(A)$ can be presented as a gaussian distribution. The experimenter can choose mean values between 0.2 and 1.0 mv, with the coefficient of variation (i.e., standard deviation divided by the mean) between 0 and 0.3. This value depends largely on the experimental conditions and the noise level in the system. The program converts the distribution $P(A)$ into integral form $PI(A)$, which is shown in Figure 8.1h.

In the next step, Figure 8.1c, the program reads in the m.e.p.p.s' pulse shape $h(t)$. Its amplitude, rise time, and half-fall time depend on the distance from the end-plate focus on the temperature and on the preparation.

In the next step, Figure 8.1d, the program reads the time course of the release rate, or latency distribution $\alpha(t)$. In a resting terminal, transmitter packets are released at random intervals with a low probability. When the terminal is depolarized by an action potential, the release rate, $\alpha(t)$, rapidly increases to a high value and then returns to the resting level. The program converts the distribution, $\alpha(t)$, into integral form, $\alpha I(t)$, which is shown in Figure 8.1i.

In the next step, Figure 8.1e, the program asks for a number of depolarizations, N, during one experiment. For highly accurate statistical analysis, an experiment composed of a few thousand depolarizations should be simulated.

Steps a, b, c, d, and e present the set-up of the basic experimental conditions. Steps f, g, h, i, j, and k simulate one depolarization and are repeated N times (loop number 100).

In the first of the simulation steps, Figure 8.1f, an integral Poisson distribution is used to determine the number of m.e.p.p.s composing an e.p.p.. A random number generator generates a number between 0 and 1. This number is compared with the integral Poisson distribution. K, for which the match is found, represents the number of m.e.p.p.s. If the random number generator generates all the values between 0 and 1 with equal probability, k will be governed by the Poisson distribution. (For a detailed explanation see Chapter 5.) For each m.e.p.p., steps g, h, i, and j are repeated (k repetitions of loop number 21).

In the next step, Figure 8.1h, the integral distribution, $PI(A)$, is used to determine the random amplitude of one m.e.p.p.. The technique is the same as in the previous case, with the use of the random number generator.

In the next step, Figure 8.1i, the integral latency distribution, $\alpha I(t)$, is used to find the random time of arrival of m.e.p.p.s, relative to the action potential.

In the next step, Figure 8.1j, the sum of k m.e.p.p.s is performed, each having random amplitude and random time of arrival, which are not correlated. Figure 8.1j also represents the end-plate membrane during an e.p.p. consisting of k units. To allow for the residual potential difference across a completely short-circuited membrane (the liquid junction potential between myoplasm and the external solution), V_0, which represents the maximum e.m.f. of the e.p.p., is taken to be equal to the recorded resting potential minus 15 mV (see Del Castillo and Katz[4]). At the height of the e.p.p., the potential across the membrane will be $V_0 - s$, where s is the e.p.p. amplitude. The potential across the resistances, $1/G$, $1/g_1, \ldots, 1/g_k$ will be s, $A_1, \ldots, A_k$, respectively, where A_1, and A_k are the m.e.p.p.s' amplitudes.

$$\frac{A_1}{V_0 - A_1} = \frac{g_1}{G} \tag{8.3}$$

$$\frac{A_1}{V_0} \approx \frac{g_1}{G} \tag{8.4}$$

and, in general,

$$\frac{A_i}{V_0} \approx \frac{g_i}{G} \tag{8.5}$$

For k m.e.p.p.s, we then have

$$\frac{s}{V_0 - s} = \frac{g_1}{G} + \cdots + \frac{g_k}{G} = \frac{A_1}{V_0} + \cdots + \frac{A_k}{V_0} = \frac{1}{V_0} \cdot \sum_{i=1}^{k} A_i \tag{8.6}$$

$$s = \frac{\displaystyle\sum_{i=1}^{k} A_i}{1 + (1/V_o)\displaystyle\sum_{i=1}^{k} A_i} = \sum_{i=1}^{k} A_i \cdot \frac{V_0}{V_0 + \displaystyle\sum_{i=1}^{k} A_i} \tag{8.7}$$

The nonlinear summation given by equation (8.7) is shown in Figure 8.1*k*. If we take the average of *s*, $\bar{s}$, and the average of the sum

$$\sum_{i=1}^{k} A_i = m \cdot v$$

where *v* is the mean value of m.e.p.p.s, we get

$$\bar{s} = \frac{m \cdot v}{1 + (mv/V_0)}$$

and

$$m = \frac{\bar{s}}{v} \cdot \frac{1}{1 - (\bar{s}/V_0)} \tag{8.8}$$

Equation (8.8) presents a correction factor, as introduced first by Martin.[6]

In the next step, Figure 8.1*k*, one count is added to the amplitude channel, *s*, and the analysis of one e.p.p. is finished. This procedure is repeated *N* times, and the distribution function, *f*(*s*), is formed. After *N* loops, the program plots the curve, *f*(*s*), as a result of the experiment.

Next we show the results of a number of simulated experiments. In all of the experiments, the latency distribution, $\alpha(t)$, and m.e.p.p. pulse shape, *h*(*t*), are taken on the basis of measurements by Katz and Miledi[2] (Figure 8).

Figure 8.2 presents the distribution *f*(*s*) of e.p.p.s for the following conditions: *P*(*A*) gaussian distribution, *v* = 0.5 mv; coefficient of variation 0.1; number of depolarizations, *N* = 25,000; number of amplitude channels in each measurement is 200; mean quantum content, *m* is 10.

In Figure 8.2, we notice that the distribution *f*(*s*) is composed of asymmetrical peaks. For example, the fourth peak has the maximum for *s*/*v* = 3.6 rather than 4.0. This is explained as a result of imperfect summation of m.e.p.p.s based on their different times of arrival. Due to the latency fluctuation, four m.e.p.p.s are not added with full amplitudes; rather, they are piling up on the tails of each other.

In Figure 8.2 one can see, going from left to right, that subsequent peaks are broader; after the tenth peak we cannot recognize separate peaks anymore. The experiments shown in Figure 8.2 are purposely performed with a fine quantization, low noise level, and a large number of depolarizations. In this way, a fine structure of the distribution, *f*(*s*), is shown.

In Figure 8.3, we can see distortions introduced through imperfect measurement. Experimental conditions are the same as in Figure 8.2, except that the total number of amplitude channels is reduced from 200 to 80. Due to the rough quantization, all the fine peaks on the distribution function, *f*(*s*), are smeared out and lost. Notice the difference between distributions in Figure 8.2 and 8.3. In real experiments, the number of amplitude channels is often less than 80, producing significant errors in results.

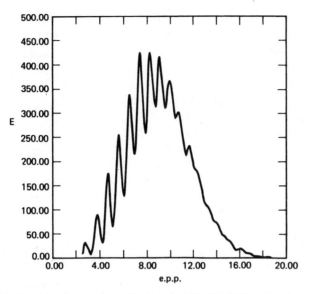

Figure 8.2 *Fine structure of e.p.p.s' amplitude probability distribution. Mean quantum content m is 10. The distribution is composed of asymmetrical peaks. Abscissa is normalized e.p.p. amplitude s/v, where v is mean amplitude of m.e.p.p.s.*

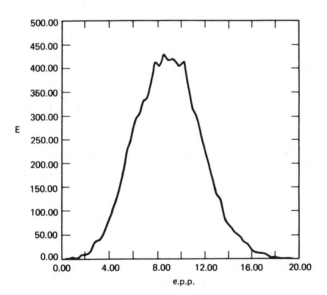

Figure 8.3 *Distortions introduced through rough quantizations and noise. Experimental conditions are the same as in Figure 8.2, except that the total number of amplitude channels is reduced from 200 to 80 and coefficient of variation of m.e.p.p.s increased from 0.1 to 0.2. Abscissa is s/v. All fine peaks are lost.*

In Figure 8.4, three different theories for the statistical composition of e.p.p.s are compared: Poisson, nonlinear summation, and latency fluctuation. Experimental conditions are as follows: $P(A)$, gaussian distribution; $v = 0.5$ mv; coefficient of variation is 0.2; mean quantum content, m, is 40; number of depolarizations is $N = 5000$; number of amplitude channels is 80.

Three curves for $f(s)$ are presented: in curve A, the e.p.p. is composed through linear summation of m.e.p.p.s. All m.e.p.p.s are arriving at the same moment (steps i and k from Figure 8.1 are avoided); in curve B, the e.p.p. is composed through nonlinear summation of m.e.p.p.s. All m.e.p.p.s are arriving at the same moment (step i from Figure 8.1 is avoided); in curve C, the e.p.p. is composed through nonlinear summation of m.e.p.p.s. M.e.p.p.s' times of arrival are random (the most complete model).

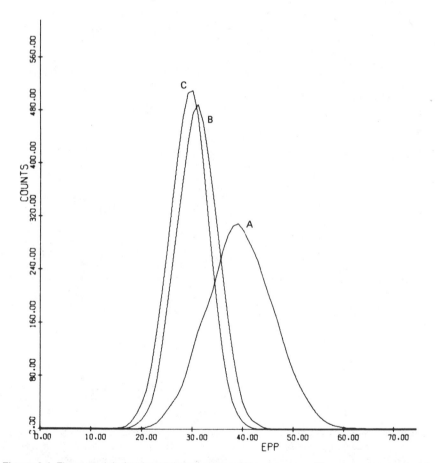

Figure 8.4 *Three models for the statistical composition of e.p.p.s. Mean quantum content is 40. Curve A, linear summation; curve B, non-linear summation; curve C, nonlinear summation and influence of latency fluctuation.*

It is important to compare the three different models with experimental results. It is well known, up to now, that the first model (curve *A*) is only in approximate agreement with experimental results for $m < 10$. Hence, we shall concentrate on the other two models, taking into account nonlinear summation and latency fluctuation.

Figure 8.5 presents results of five simulated experiments. The number of depolarizations for each experiment is 2000; the number of amplitude channels is 80. The coefficient of variation of m.e.p.p.s' distribution is 0.2.

The parameters of five simulated experiments are chosen to be the same as in five measurements by Martin;[6] see Table 8.1. Each experiment is simulated two times: *FL*, taking into account nonlinear summations, but with "fixed latency"; and *VL*, taking into account both nonlinear summation and "variable latency." In Figure 8.5 we can see five pairs of curves for five experiments. The left curve of each pair is the VL curve.

In Table 8.2, coefficients of variation and mean values of e.p.p.s' distributions are presented. We can make a comparison between observed values in five experiments and simulated results for models *FL* and *VL*.

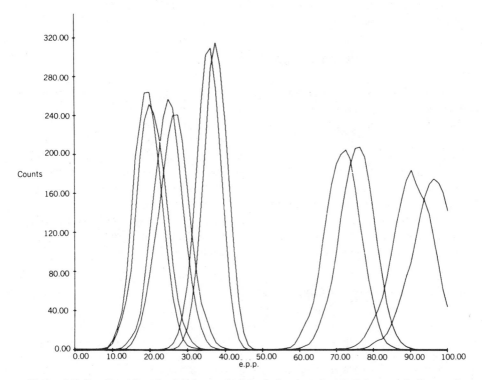

Figure 8.5 *Results of five simulated experiments. Left curve of each pair presents the result of model VL (variable latencies and non-linear summation). Right curve presents the result of model FL (fixed latencies and nonlinear summation).*

TABLE 8.1   Parameters of Five Experiments

Experiment	ν(mv)	m
I	0.48	24.8
II	0.44	32.3
III	0.76	62.3
IV	0.34	117.0
V	0.25	143.0

In Figure 8.6, coefficients of variation are plotted as a function of mean e.p.p. amplitude $\bar{s}/v$. We can examine five groups of results for five experiments. In all experiments, model *VL* (variable latency) is in better agreement with observed data than model *FL* (fixed latency).

The five experiments just described have different mean values of m.e.p.p.'s, v; therefore, it is difficult to compare results between experiments. Figure 8.7 presents results of the same group of experiments, but with $v = 0.5$ mv in all five experiments. Figure 8.8 presents coefficients of variation and mean quantum contents plotted as a function of mean e.p.p. amplitude, $\bar{s}/v$, for the above cases.

For small values of $\bar{s}/v$, the two models produce similar values for *m* but rather different coefficients of variation. For large values of $\bar{s}/v$, the two models produce similar coefficients of variation but rather different values for *m*.

8.3   FIXED AND VARIABLE LATENCY

A model for the statistical composition of end-plate potentials has been designed and used for detailed study of e.p.p.s' amplitude distribution function. The model is based on present knowledge of synaptic functions and takes into account m.e.p.p.s' amplitude distribution, m.e.p.p.s' pulse shape, m.e.p.p.s' latency fluctuation, residual potential differences across the membrane, nonlinear summation, and mean quantum content. It is shown here that the statistical building up of e.p.p.s is a stochastic process in which all of the above factors have significant influence.

The results provide further support for the view that transmission at a nerve-muscle junction takes place in all-or-none quanta whose sizes are identical with those of spontaneously occurring miniature potentials. The amplitude of the e.p.p. fluctuates in a manner predictable on this basis by Poisson's law.

TABLE 8.2   Results of Five Experiments

Experiment	Observed C.V.	$\bar{s}/v$	Model *FL* C.V.	$\bar{s}/v$	Model *VL* C.V.	$\bar{s}/v$
I	0.148 ± 0.009	20.8	0.189	20.6	0.189	19.5
II	0.127 ± 0.007	26.4	0.159	26.4	0.158	24.9
III	0.093 ± 0.004	37.8	0.085	37.5	0.091	35.6
VI	0.071 ± 0.003	74.0	0.064	75.5	0.067	71.6
V	0.058 ± 0.003	96.4	0.057	96.4	0.061	91.0

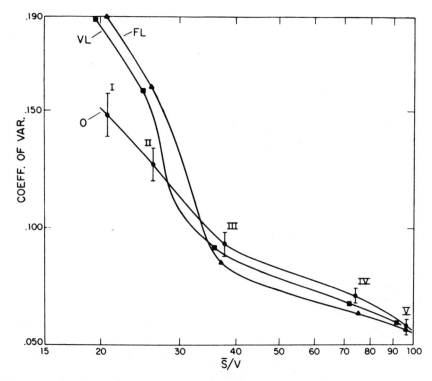

Figure 8.6 *Coefficient of variation as a function of normalized mean value s/v for five exper-iments O, observed data[6]; FL, simulated experiment (nonlinear summation); VL, simulated experiment (nonlinear summation and variable latencies).*

Unit potential of, say, 0.25 msec rise time and 0.5 mv size can appear as early as 0.5 msec and as late as 2.6 msec after the arrival of the nerve impulse. This indicates that the nerve impulse is followed by a period of a few milliseconds, during which the probability of quantal release is increased. Due to this latency fluctuation, m.e.p.p.s are not added with full amplitudes but rather are piled up on the tails of each other. As a result, the distribution of e.p.p.s, $f(s)$, is composed of asymmetrical peaks.

If a noiseless experiment is performed with fine quantization and large numbers of depolarizations, we can distinguish separate peaks in the distribution, $f(s)$, up to $m = 10$. For $m > 10$, the $f(s)$ distribution has a bell-like shape, and its coefficient of variation and mean value can be explained through the influence of the latency fluctuation and nonlinear summation of unit components.

In Figure 8.6, comparison is shown between experimentally observed data and data simulated by the "fixed latency" and "variable latency" models. The coefficient of variation is plotted as a function of a mean e.p.p. amplitude, $\bar{s}/v$. Five experiments are presented, as in Table 8.2. In experiment I, observed data give values for the coefficient of variation which are too small. Experiment I has

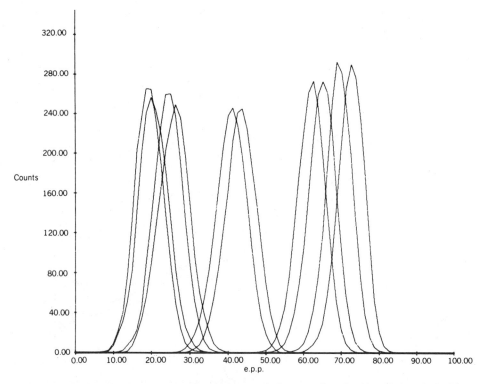

Figure 8.7 *Results of the simulated experiments. Left curve of each pair presents the result of model VL, right curve of model FL. Mean quantal contents in five experiments are 24.8, 32.3, 62.3, 117 and 143, respectively.*

a mean e.p.p. amplitude $\bar{s}/v = 20.8$. According to Equation 8.8, we obtain the correction factor, $m/(\bar{s}/v) = 0.864$, giving $m = 24.8$. Poisson distribution with $m = 24.8$ should have a coefficient of variation of 0.201. Due to the nonlinear summation, this value should be multiplied by the above correction factor, giving the value 0.175. Allowance must be made for the fact that the m.e.p.p.s themselves are not of uniform size. This should increase the observed coefficient of variation by a factor of $\sqrt{1 + \delta^2}$, where δ is the coefficient of variation of the m.e.p.p.s' amplitudes (in this case $\delta = 0.2$, $\sqrt{1 + \delta^2} = 1.04$). Thus, the observed coefficient of variation should be $1.04 \times 0.175 = 0.183$. (The simulated experiment gives the value 0.189). The observed value, 0.148, is too small and does not agree with either model *FL* or model *VL*.

Experiment II shows better agreement. In experiments III, VI, and V, curves O and VL are within experimental error. In all experiments, model *VL* is in better agreement with experimental data than model *FL*.

Figure 8.8 shows that for a given mean e.p.p. amplitude, $\bar{s}/v$, model *VL* always gives a smaller value for coefficient of variation and a larger value of m than model *FL*. The claim that latency fluctuation reduces the coefficient of variation of the

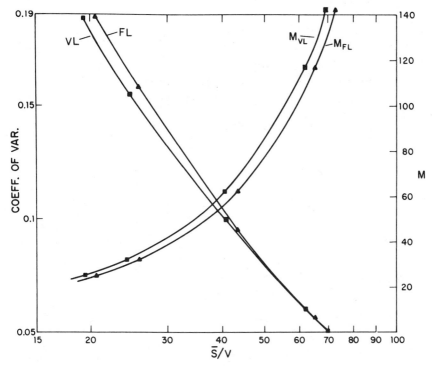

Figure 8.8 *Coefficient of variation and mean quantum content for the distributions of e.p.p.s presented in Figure 8.7. Abscissa is normalized mean amplitude of e.p.p., $\bar{s}/v$. VL and FL curves present coefficient of variation, M_{VL} and M_{FL} present the mean quantum contents for VL and FL models, respectively.*

e.p.p.s ought to be carefully qualified. If latency fluctuation is introduced into the model, while mean quantum content, m, is kept constant, the coefficient of variation is probably slightly increased (Table 8.2; sometimes the coefficient of variation is decreased, probably by an amount less than random error). The mean e.p.p. amplitude is decreased by latency fluctuation, however, and so, on a model with latency fluctuation, a larger mean quantum content must be taken to arrive at the same e.p.p. amplitude. Consequently, there is a decrease in the coefficient of variation for a given mean e.p.p. amplitude $\bar{s}/v$.

Computer modeling can be especially useful in cases where the m.e.p.p.s' amplitudes have skewed distribution.

REFERENCES

1. B. Souček, *J. Theor. Biol.* **30**, 631 (1971).
2. B. Katz and R. Miledi, *Proc. R. Soc. London, Ser. B* **161**, 483 (1965).
3. J. Del Castillo and B. Katz, *J. Physiol. (London)* **124**, 560 (1950).

4. J. Del Castillo and B. Katz, *J. Physiol. (London)* **125**, 546 (1952).

5. I. A. Boyd and A. R. Martin, *J. Physiol. (London)* **132**, 74 (1950).

6. A. R. Martin, *J. Physiol. (London)* **130**, 114 (1955).

7. B. Souček, *Biophys. J.* **11**, 127 (1971).

8. P. Fatt and B. Katz, *J. Physiol. (London)* **115**, 320 (1951).

9. B. Souček, *Minicomputers in Data Processing and Simulation.* Wiley, New York, 1972.

CHAPTER 9 ───────────────────────────

Brain-Window Logic

INTRODUCTION AND SURVEY

This chapter presents an example of logic based on fuzzy, adjustable sets called "brain windows." The logic is supported by a network of coupled nonlinear oscillators. This kind of logic has many features that would be desirable in brain-like computers; it was first observed in computer-based analysis of the brain of the firefly.[1] A quantitative model has been developed that explains numerous communication patterns in female fireflies (*Photuris versicolor*). This chapter is adapted from Souček and Carlson[1].

Upon receiving a flash stimulus, the firefly brain generates a sequence of time windows of different widths. Receiving and sending windows are interleaved in the sequence. Each receive window recognizes a particular subgroup of flash intervals. These flash intervals may represent courtship flashes of the female's conspecific male or courtship flashes of heterospecific males. Each sending window determines the latency of the response flash from the female. The windows are arrayed in priorities and controlled by the fireflies' memory. Memory stores the past history of flash stimulation.

Brain windows are generated through mutual coupling of the primary oscillator, answer oscillator, and window generator. Hence, the brain windows are directly related to the inherent biological oscillators and to the memory.

The brain window model has been programmed into the computer. Computer-simulated response patterns are in excellent agreement with hundreds of experimental response patterns produced by female fireflies when tested with artificial flashes. A single model explains all the communication-behavior patterns observed in the female firefly. Brain windows can explain communication and behavior in other species as well. The brain-window concept could also be used for new computer architectures.

9.1 EXAMPLE OF FIREFLY COMMUNICATION

A firefly flash is a brilliant burst of light which serves as a signal in a dynamic courtship/communication system between males and females. Each species of firefly uses a unique courtship code, in which the males of one species emit their flashes in particular timing patterns and their conspecific females recognize the male patterns; the females respond with flashes of appropriate latency.[2] The flash is triggered by a neural burst in the firefly's brain,[3] and the flash patterns and responses are thereby activated by central pattern generators and timing circuits in the brain. Because it is possible to observe and record firefly flashes from a distance and to communicate with fireflies using artificial flashes, these animals provide ideal material for the analysis of insect brain functions. Furthermore, the flash communication system uses a pulse-time code in which the information is not coded by flash amplitude, but rather by the time interval between flashes. As the time interval can vary continuously, it presents information in analog form. Hence, we are dealing with a pulse-code (digital), analog information processing system. This system lends itself to analysis using computer techniques.[4,5]

The *Photinus* fireflies compose a genus of several dozen species.[2,6] They communicate by one of two basic codes: (1) a string of consecutive flashes emitted by the searching male, and a single flash response appropriately timed after each male flash by the female; and (2) courtship flashes emitted in pairs by the male, and a single flash after the second flash of the male pair by the female.

In another genus, the firefly *Photuris versicolor*, the male emits strings of twinkling flashes, each flash of which is composed of three or four pulses. The female responds after each twinkling male flash. Within three days after mating, the female of this species converts to predatory behavior and will no longer respond to her own male's twinkling flashes. Instead, she responds to the flash patterns of *Photinus* males, capturing and eating them.[7] These aggressive mimics will entrain to a very wide range of flash patterns with flashes of fixed latency.

Using a wide variety of artificial flash patterns, we have used a computer to analyze the responses of a large number of *femmes fatales*. From this analysis we have developed a quantitative model to explain how the female firefly brain is programmed to respond to the courtship flash patterns of conspecific and heterospecific male fireflies. The model is in excellent agreement with the measured data. It explains the response patterns of both virgin and mated females (FF) and therefore covers all basic communication behaviors of these fireflies. The model is based upon the following "computer-like" elements: memory, self-adjustment, feedback and oscillation, and pattern recognition. The core of the model involves brain windows: a sequence of adjustable receive-send brain windows can readily explain numerous communication and behavior patterns.

Photuris versicolor femmes fatales (FF) were captured and maintained in the field in glass terraria of approximately one-cubic-foot volume. Each evening a particular female was courted using artificial flashes provided by a flashlight. The flashlight was driven with a relay controlled by a Grass S4 stimulator which allowed us to vary the flash interval. The duration of the flashlight flashes varied between

0.1 and 0.2 seconds. The artificial flashes and female responses were recorded using a hand-held photomultiplier (RCA 931A), the output of which was fed into a Hewlett-Packard four-channel FM Instrumentation Tape Recorder. The stimulator output and a voice commentary were recorded on two other channels. The tape recorder output was transferred to a Beckman Dynagraph Type RM four-channel Direct Writing Recorder and measurements of flash intervals were made from the recorder records. The recorded light intensity of both artificial and firefly flashes is greatly affected by the relative positions of both light source and photomultiplier, and therefore the absolute light intensities are not comparable. Field temperatures varied from 20° to 25°C.

The FF was stimulated with flashes of different intervals—single flashes separated by long pauses, paired flashes of different interflash interval, long trains of consecutive flashes, or short trains of flashes. The females responded for up to one hour to flash trains repeated every few seconds. They respond to some stimulus patterns and do not respond to others; the latency of their responses depends on the stimulus pattern. The absolute latencies of FFs depend on the temperature during the experimental session and also are somewhat different from one firefly to the next.

9.2 RECEIVING AND SENDING WINDOWS

Upon receiving one flash stimulus, the *femmes fatales* (FF) generate a sequence of time windows—receive windows $R1$, $R2$, and $R3$, (Figure 9.1).

$R1$: This time window is the highest-priority window. It is open for the values $0.1 < R1 < 0.3$ sec. This is the expected courtship pulse interval range of the conspecific male flash (IC). If the virgin female receives a stimulation interval at this window, she will respond with a flash of approximately 1 sec latency. In this way, courtship communication is established. She does not open windows $R2$ and $R3$ in this sequence. In the FF, however, this receive window appears to be missing. If she receives flashes with intervals within this window, she answers with a long latency of more than 2 sec.

$R2$: The time window $R2$ is a second-priority window. It is open for the values $1.1 < R2 < 2.0$ sec. This is the range of double intervals of a number of *Photinus* species in which the males produce courtship flashes in pairs. If the FF receives the second stimulus through the open window, $R2$, she will respond with a flash. In this way, she appears to mimic the female of the prey species. By answering appropriately, she establishes communication with the prey male and may attract, capture, and devour him.

$R3$: The time window $R3$ is the lowest-priority window. It is open for the values $3.0 < R3 < 4.0$ sec. This is a broad range of intervals that separate the regular patterns. We call it a separation interval, IS. It could be the first flash of a regular pattern or a single flash. If the FF receives the stimulus flash through the open window $R3$, she will respond with a flash. If the second stimulus arrives at such a time that it does not match either of the

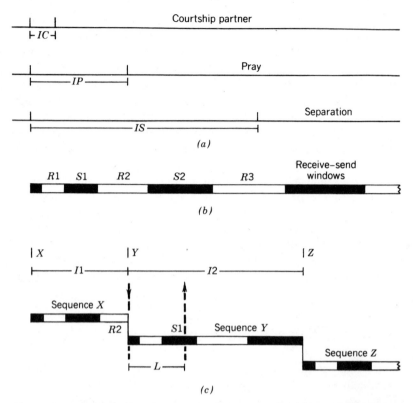

Figure 9.1 *Receive-send brain-window sequence: (a) courtship, prey, and separation intervals; (b) receive-send brain-window sequence: each window is responsible for recognizing or screening a particular subgroup of stimuli and responses; (c) brain-window sequences X, Y, and Z, triggered by the stimuli X, Y, and Z. Note that stimulus Y is received through the window R2 and it causes the response flash with latency L through the window S1. Each stimulus initiates a new brain-window sequence.*

windows, the FF will consider it an unexpected stimulus and will not flash back. In other words, such a second stimulus finds the windows closed.

The receiving windows $R1$, $R2$, and $R3$ are interleaved with sending windows $S1$, $S2$, and $S3$. The firefly uses sending windows to define the time during which it is proper to send the answer in the form of a response flash. Each stimulus will start a new sequence of receiving-sending windows. In Figure 9.1, three sequences are shown. Stimuli X, Y, and Z start the sequences X, Y, and Z respectively.

Upon receiving a flash, the firefly matches the stimulus interval I with the R-window sequence that is in progress. If a match is found, the internal logic generates the proper response latency L. The latency is matched with the sequence of sending windows, $S1$, $S2$, $S3$. If the match is found, the firefly produces the response flash. Hence, the stimulus interval I will produce the response flash with the latency L only if:

There is a match between the stimulus interval I and one of the receive windows, and

There is a match between the internally produced latency L and one of the sending windows.

In Figure 9.1, the stimulus interval I_1 will produce the answering flash, because I_1 matches with the receive window $R2$, and the latency matches with the sending window $S1$. The stimulus interval I_2 will not produce the flash, because it does not match any of the R windows.

The firefly generates the sequence of brain windows with the help of the primary oscillator and window generator.

9.3 PRIMARY OSCILLATOR

The communication features of the firefly are controlled by an oscillator which defines the basic timing of behavior and communication. Hence, it can be called the primary oscillator. The output of the primary oscillator is a primary waveform, $P(t)$, of a sinusoidal shape.

Upon receiving a stimulus, the firefly modifies the operation of the primary oscillator: a sinusidal waveform of constant period is changed into a waveform with variable period (Figure 9.2a). This entrainment lasts for three or four cycles, after which time the period of oscillations is back to the original, constant period.

The variability of the cycles of the primary oscillator can be described with the phase-response curve (PRC). The PRC or "Zeitgeber" notation is used for biological clocks and their entrainments.[9,10] Each stimulus starts the phase-response curve and in this way modulates the oscillations of the oscillator.

An alternative way to explain the entrainment is to associate a memory with the primary oscillator. The memory accepts the stimulus and modulates the oscillations. However, the memory is not ideal and is slowly erased. Hence, the modulatory effect of the stimulus is strong immediately after the stimulation and slowly vanishes with time: the oscillations return to normal.

The memory in the oscillator is similar to a resistor-capacitor integrating filter in electrical circuits. It stores the initial charge in the capacitor (inertia). The capacitor is then slowly discharged through the resistor (energy dissipation, leakage). In this way the filtering network produces an exponentially shaped memory voltage. The memory voltage is introduced in the oscillator's feedback mechanism and modulates the oscillations. When the memory voltage reaches zero the modulation is stopped, and the oscillator again operates at constant period: the stimulation is forgotten.

The modulated primary waveform is shown in Figure 9.2a. The primary waveform is responsible for an inherent timing program that controls the communication and behavior of the firefly. The primary waveform also controls the relationship between the stimulus and the response. Hence, the primary waveform presents the basic, precise, and quantitative description of a part of the firefly's brain. It

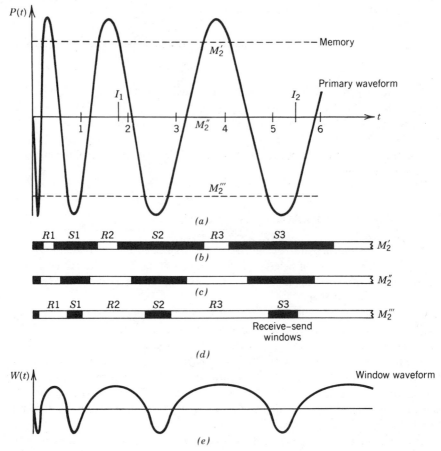

Figure 9.2 *Primary waveform defines the basic timing of behavior and of communication:* (a) *primary waveform-memory interaction defines the receive-send windows:* I_1 *and* I_2 *represent two stimuli which arrive during different phases of the primary waveform and have different effects on memory level;* (b, c, d) *three window sequences corresponding to memory levels* M_2', M_2'', *and* M_2'''; (e) *window waveform corresponding to the sequence shown in* (d).

could be expected that the primary waveforms can describe the brain-behavior functions in other species as well. In the case of the firefly, the primary waveform is responsible for the generation of the send-receive window sequences. The primary waveform produces the sequences in cooperation with the window generator.

9.4 THE WINDOW GENERATOR

Window generator operation is similar to that of an electronic differential amplifier. It receives control signals from two sides and produces the output that is proportional to the difference between the two signals.

The window generator has a memory of its own. Each stimulus received by the firefly will contribute to the voltage stored in the window memory. The window memory has only a small leakage, so the voltage in the memory will keep accumulating. The discharge between stimuli is small.

Two signals control the window generator: the primary waveform and the voltage from the window memory (Figure 9.3). Hence, the output $W(t)$ of the window generator is proportional to the difference between the primary waveform and the window memory voltage (Figure 9.2e). Positive, negative, and zero differences will produce positive, negative, and zero outputs from the window generator.

In other words, the primary waveform is compared with an internal voltage or bias stored in window memory. The portion of the primary waveform above the memory produces a positive window waveform $W(t)$ and opens an R window. The position of the primary waveform below the memory produces a negative window waveform and opens an S window.

Figure 9.2a shows the primary waveform, $P(t)$, and three window memory voltages, M_2', M_2'' and M_2'''. Figures 9.2b, c, and d show the generated receive-send sequences for memory voltages M_2', M_2'', and M_2''', respectively. Figure 9.2e shows the window waveform $W(t)$ for memory voltage M_2'''. This window waveform $W(t)$ generates the receive-send sequence shown in Figure 9.2d.

Notice the difference between the three receive-send sequences. If the memory is highly positive, such as M_2' in Figure 9.2, the receive windows are narrow and

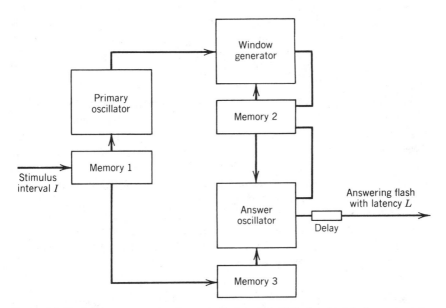

Figure 9.3 *Model of sensory and motor control in female firefly brain, simulated on a computer. The model is divided into 3 blocks with separate memories: the primary oscillator, which is entrained by the stimulus through the memory M_1; the window generator, which defines the receive-send windows through the interaction between the primary waveform and the memory M_2; and the answer oscillator, which defines the latency of the answering flash. Its initial phase is determined by the contents of memories M_2 and M_3.*

the sending windows are wide open. Oppositely, if the memory is highly negative, such as M_2''' in Figure 9.2, the receive windows are wide open and the sending windows are narrow.

The firefly keeps track of the past history of stimulation in the window memory, M_2. Based on the previous flash history, the memory—in cooperation with the primary oscillator—generates the proper sequence of receive-send windows. Each stimulus contributes to the window memory. The contribution of the stimulus interval I is proportional to the value taken from the primary waveform $P(I)$. Hence, stimulus I_1 in Figure 9.2a will produce a positive contribution, and stimulus I_2 will produce a negative contribution to the window memory (M_2). The stimulation pattern I_1, I_2 produces the contribution $P(I_1), P(I_2)$. If $P(I_1) = -P(I_2)$, the contribution to the memory is zero and memory stays unchanged during the stimulation. This is a typical situation in good courtship communication.

The stimulation pattern I_1, I_1 will keep pushing the memory up, closing the R windows. This is typical for non-perfect courtship communication. The pattern I_2, I_2 will keep pushing the memory down, opening the R windows. This is typical for communication mimicry.

9.5 ANSWER OSCILLATOR

For each stimulation pattern, the female firefly generates a flash response. The latency of the answering flash contains the message sent back to the male. If the stimulation pattern is not acceptable, the female firefly does not respond at all.

The generation of a flash response of fixed latency is produced by a special oscillator. We can call this oscillator the answer oscillator (Figure 9.3) and its waveform, $A(t)$, the answer waveform.

The answer oscillator also has a memory, M_3. In addition, the window generator and the answer oscillator are mutually coupled through the common memory, M_2. In this way, they entrain each other. The answer oscillator is connected to the primary oscillator's memory, M_1, for the short instant when the stimulus arrives. In this way, the phase of the entrainment from the primary memory, M_1, is transferred into the memory M_3 of the answer oscillator. The phase of the answer oscillator is therefore controlled by the memories M_1, M_2, and M_3.

When the answer waveform crosses the zero level (Figure 9.4), it produces the trigger for the lantern. The trigger travels through the internal delays. When it reaches the lantern, the answering flash is produced. It can be shown that the latency of the flash is composed of five parts:[1]

- Part is controlled by the primary memory M_1 and is proportional to the stimulation interval I.
- Part is controlled by the memories M_2 and M_3, which keep the past history of stimulation.
- Part is equal to $\frac{1}{2}T_1$, where T_1 is a period of the answer oscillator.

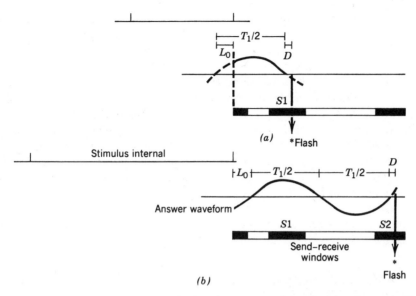

Figure 9.4 *Answer waveform and production of responses of short and long latencies. The answer waveform's initial phase is determined by the content of memories M_2 and M_3. This initial phase defines the fraction L_o of the cycle. Zero crossing of the answer waveform plus delay D are matched against the sending windows. $1/2T_1$ equals one half the answer oscillator cycle. (a) The match is in the window S1; a response flash with short latency is produced. (b) The match is in the window S2; a response flash with long latency is produced.*

- Part is equal to D, where D is internal fixed delay, composed of the time for the flash triggering a neural burst to travel from the brain to the lantern and the neuroluminescence coupling time.
- Part is random fluctuations, producing the noise (jitter) in the latency.

We see that, unlike what is commonly believed, the answering latency is not a function of the last stimulation interval only. This is due to the memories M_2 and M_3. As the memories are erased, the more recent stimuli produce the largest contributions to latency. The contributions of the stimuli that occurred a long time ago are slowly forgotten.

The content of the memories is a weighted sum of the contributions of all stimuli. Hence, part of the latency is a function of this weighted sum. We conclude that the latency is a function of the last stimulus interval, of an internal delay of the primary cycle, and of the past history of stimulation.

If two experiments are performed with the same last stimulation intervals, they might produce two different latencies. This variation in latencies was associated in the past only with random factors. In fact, this model shows that latencies are mostly deterministic and predictable. Yet the latencies depend on past history, and not on the last stimulation interval alone. This fact should also be kept in mind in models which try to explain communication behavior with one single phase-response curve, relating the response only to the last stimulus. These kinds of models are only approximations, neglecting the memories and the effects of the past history of stimulation. In the case of *Photuris femmes fatales*, the past history contribution could be from zero to fifty percent of the contribution due to the last stimulus interval, and it cannot be neglected.

The generation of the answering flash is controlled by the sequence of brain windows (Figure 9.4). Only if the latency matches one of the sending windows will the flash be generated. Figure 9.4*a* shows the flash produced in the sending window *S*1. Figure 9.4*b* shows the case when the basic latency is outside the *S*1 window. In this case, the next zero-crossing plus delay that coincides with an *S* window will produce the trigger for the lantern. In Figure 9.4*b*, the flash is produced in window *S*2. Note that the value $\frac{1}{2}T_1$ is added to the basic latency.

The receive-send windows explain why a broad region has not been observed in measured latencies. This empty region coincides with the *R* windows during which the generation of the answering flash is not allowed.

9.6 ARCHITECTURE BASED ON COUPLED NONLINEAR OSCILLATORS

Upon receiving the stimulus (male flash), FF starts the following sequence of actions:

1. The stimulus interval *I* is matched with the receiving windows. If the match is found, the stimulus is accepted; if not, the stimulus is rejected. In both cases, the stimulus starts a new entrainment process.
2. The phase of the entrainment process from the previous flash is retained in the answer oscillator. This phase, together with the values stored in memories M_2 and M_3, defines the initial phase and hence the zero-crossing of the answer waveform.
3. Eventually, the answer waveform crosses the zero level and produces the trigger.
4. The motor delay propagates the trigger towards the lantern.
5. The lantern is fired and produces the flash.

The double-interval pattern is frequently observed in experimental data. It is composed of two intervals, I_1 and I_2. The range of the intervals depends on the species. In the case of *Photinus macdermotti* (courtship), and in *Photinus versicolor* (mimicry), the ranges are $1.1 < I_1 < 2.1$ and $2 < I_2 < 5$ sec. The FF readily responds to a stimulus I_1 in the middle of the range, but not so at the edges of the range. She first rejects a number of flashes and then she starts responding.

Figure 9.5 shows the communication pattern with the intervals 2.2 and 2.8, with each interval measured from the initial flash. This particular pattern is rarely observed (see experiment *K* in Figure 9.6 and also in Table 9.1). The pattern is simulated on a computer, and the results are presented in Figure 9.5.

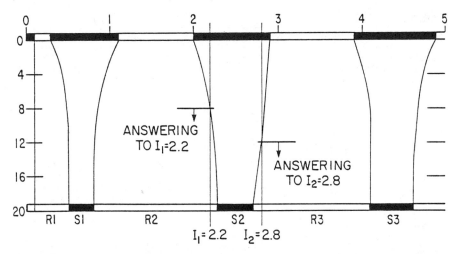

Figure 9.5 *Dynamic adjustment of the receive-send window sequence. Computer simulation of experiment K (see Table 9.1 and Figure 9.6). Interval (I_1) was 2.2 sec, interval (I_2) was 2.8 sec. The firefly did not answer to the first eight pairs of intervals. After the eighth pair, she answered to the interval I_1. After the twelfth pair, she answered to both intervals I_1 and I_2*

Figure 9.5 displays 20 repetitions of the pattern 2.2, 2.8. In each repetition stimuli contribute to the memories, and in this way they modify the receive-send windows. The contributions to the memories are proportional to the values taken from the primary waveform, $P(2.2)$ and $P(2.8)$. Both values are negative (Figure 9.6) and they push the memory into the negative region. In this way, S windows are narrowing and R windows are widening. After eight repetitions, the $R2$ window is

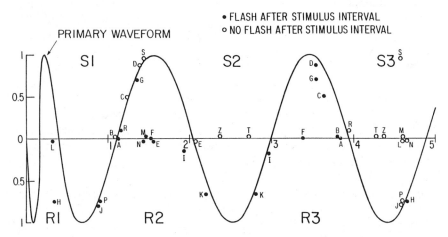

Figure 9.6 *Results of experiments A to Z and a theoretically calculated waveform for Photuris mated female firefly. Each pair of letters represents one sequence of two intervals. Note that all stimulus intervals that match an R window produce a response flash. All stimulus intervals that match an S window produce no flash.*

TABLE 9.1

Experiment	First Interval I_1	First Latency L_1	Second Interval I_2	Second Latency L_2
A	3840	1080	1080	910
B	3840	1080	1264	
C	3640	1264	1264	
D	3558	1290	1384	
E	2080		1540	1200
F	3380	1112	1520	840
G	3560	1320	1360	784
H	4620	1180	340	1000
I	2968	1100	1940	968
J	4640		840	840
K	2800	1356	2180	1100
L	4620		340	1040
M	4580		1480	980
N	4640		1440	940
P	4640		840	860
R	3872		1080	848
S	4580		1480	
T	2600		4300	
Z	2400		4500	

wide enough to accept the stimulus interval I_1, and the FF responds with a flash. After twelve repetitions, the $R3$ window is wide enough to accept the stimulus interval I_2, and the FF responds with a flash.

We see in this experiment three modes of communication. In repetitions 0 through 8, the double interval pattern receives no response. In repetitions 8 through 12, the FF responds after the first interval $I_1 = 2.2$, but not after the second. This is the flash pattern of *Photinus macdermotti* males which induces mimicry responses from the FF. In repetitions 12 through 20, the FF responds to both intervals. This is double-interval communication with a double response, but it can also apply to flash patterns composed of a series of rhythmically repeated flashes.

Notice that the windows are quite "plastic" at the beginning of the sequence, and that they readily adjust. However, when the windows are pushed far away from the normal width, they resist further change.

In double-interval patterns, experiments usually concentrate on the effects of the shorter interval. This model shows that both intervals carry the information. In particular, for a stable double-interval pattern that will not modify the memory, the condition $P(I_1) = -P(I_2)$ is necessary. Both intervals also contribute to the response latency.

A large number of experiments have been performed on *Photuris* FFs. Experiments A to Z on FFs are summarized in Table 9.1. Each experiment presents a long repetition of double-interval patterns. Table 9.1 lists the intervals I_1 and I_2 and typical corresponding latencies L_1 and L_2 observed in experimental data. All kinds of responses are found: no response, response only to one interval, response to both intervals.

For these double-interval patterns, memory is modified only by a small amount from one interval to the next. We use this fact to plot the experimental results over the computer-calculated primary waveform (Figure 9.6). If the theory matches the experimental data, three conditions must be fulfilled:

1. The memory levels for two intervals of the same pattern (experiment) must be approximately the same.
2. An interval which produces a flash must be received in an R window.
3. An interval which produces no flash must be received outside R windows, that is, during an S window.

For example, in experiment labeled R in Table 9.1, with intervals of 1.080 and 3.872 seconds, both intervals are placed in Figure 9.6 on the same memory level. Only if the memory level is 0.1 will stimulus 3.872 be outside an R window (no flash) and stimulus 1.080 be inside an R window (flash), as observed in experiment.

Typical balanced double-interval patterns are those found in experiments F, M, and N: the first interval is near the middle of the R2 window, and the second interval is in the middle of the S3 window; memory is not changed. It is easy to find large numbers of such sequences in experimental data. More critical are sequences at the edge of the range, and their explanations. These sequences are plotted in Figure 9.6:

- No response: experiments S, T, and Z
- Response to the long interval, but no response to the shorter interval: experiments B, C, and D
- Response to the short interval, but no response to the longer interval: experiments E, J, L, M, N, P, and R
- Response to both intervals: experiments A, F, H, I, K, and G

We see that in all experiments, A to Z, conditions 1, 2, and 3 are fulfilled. Also, the experimentally observed latencies correspond to the latencies calculated from the theory. Hence, the brain-window model readily explains the patterns observed in experimental data.

9.7 COMPUTER MODEL

The communication behavior of *Photuris versicolor* female fireflies is explained with three elements: primary oscillator, window generator, and answer oscillator. The primary oscillator dictates the basic frequency of oscillations and is entrained by the flash stimulus. The window generator produces a sequence of receive-send windows. This sequence presents an inherent program that controls the acceptance and recognition of stimuli as well as the generation of the proper answer (the latency of the flash). The answer oscillator defines the instant of the answering flash.

All three elements have memories. These memories can be explained by chemical, physical, or electrical processes with inertia. The memories are similar to electrical low-pass filters or integrators. The memory receives the information in the form of amplitude, charge, or phase, and keeps this information for the future. The memories are analog, and they store the continuous information. The process of forgetting is similar to the process of discharging in electrical integrators. Hence, we associate with each memory a forgetting function, $f(t)$. The forgetting function describes how the initial information stored in the memory slowly vanishes with time.

The memories control both the receive-send brain windows and the latencies of the answering flash. The interaction between the brain windows and memories readily explains communication behavior in fireflies. This interaction is described with three groups of equations: memory, latency, and language equations. The equations make firefly communication a predictable system: given the stimulation pattern, the equations calculate the response.

The equations explain the communication behavior in both virgin and mated (*femmes fatale* or FF) *Photuris versicolor* fireflies. Virgin and mated females differ in sensory delay, which is introduced after the mating. Due to the introduced sensory delay, the receiving window responsible for courtship ($R1$) is moved towards longer intervals. As a result, the mated *Photuris* female does not respond any more to the courtship flashes of the male of her species: she switches into mimicry behavior instead.

9.7.1 Primary Oscillator and Memory M_1

The basic features of memory are remembering and forgetting. All forgetting functions are described with the equation

$$f(t) = ze^{-g(t-d)} + (1 - z)e^{-q(t-d)} \tag{9.1}$$

Equation 9.1 breaks the forgetting function into two processes with time constants g and q and with the delay d. The parameter z defines the contributions of the two processes. All memories will be described in the same way, based on equation 9.1.

Matching computer-simulated data with experimental data, we find the parameters of the forgetting function $f_1(t)$ of the primary memory M_1:

$$z_1 = 0.15, \ g_1 = 0.1, \ q_1 = 1, \ \text{and} \ d_1 = 0.2$$

We see that the process of forgetting starts after the delay d_1. At the beginning, the process of forgetting is fast (g_1), and then it slows down (q_1).

Memory M_1 receives the stimulus through the sensory input. This stimulus is the amplitude of the received flash. Memory M_1 converts the amplitude information into the phase information. It also normalizes the amplitude: regardless of the initial information stored in the memory M_1, and regardless of the intensity of the stimulus, the initial stored information is always the same (in our normalized notation it is one). The content of M_1 is

$$M_1(t) = -f_1(t) \tag{9.2}$$

The memory M_1 is connected into the feedback loop of the primary oscillator. In this way, $M_1(t)$ presents the modulation phase of the primary waveform $P(t)$:

$$P(t) = \sin\left\{2\pi\left[\frac{t}{T_1} + M_1(t)\right]\right\} = \sin\left\{2\pi\left[\frac{t}{T_1} - f_1(t)\right]\right\} \tag{9.3}$$

T_1 is the period of the primary waveform. A good match with experimental data is obtained for $T_1 = 1.95$ sec. The stimulus is remembered in the memory M_1 and changes the period of oscillation of the primary waveform. As M_1 discharges towards zero, the primary oscillator approaches the normal period of oscillations, T_1.

9.7.2   Window Generator and Memory M_2

The parameters of the forgetting function $f_2(t)$ are as follows:

$$z_2 = 1, \ g_2 = 100, \ q_2 = 30, \ \text{and} \ d_2 = 0$$

In $f_2(t)$, the delay and the fast forgetting processes are not present. The forgetting time constant g_2 is longer than the typical interval between the stimuli. As a result, the memory M_2 retains the fraction of received information from previous stimuli.

Memory M_2 receives information from the window generator and from the answer oscillator (Figure 9.3). The memory M_2 is a coupling circuit between the window generator and the answer oscillator. Memory M_2 continuously integrates (accumulates) the received information. The stored information slowly vanishes, due to forgetting. This process is described in equation 9.4:

$$M_2(t) = [M_2(I) + C_{22}P(I) - C_{23}f_1(I)]f_2(t) \tag{9.4}$$

In equation 9.4, the continuous integration processes are concentrated into one instant, $t = I$, where I is the stimulation interval.

When the stimulus arrives, it stops the primary waveform $P(I)$ and the primary forgetting function $f_1(I)$. The fraction $C_{22}P(I)$ is added to the window memory through the window generator. The coupling coefficient C_{22} defines the contribution to the memory M_2, obtained through the window generator. When the stimulus arrives, the value of the primary forgetting function $f_1(I)$ is transferred into the answer memory M_3.

The fraction $C_{23}f_1(I)$ is added to the window memory through the answer oscillator. The coupling coefficient C_{23} defines the contribution to the memory M_2, obtained through the answer oscillator. The forgetting process is described by $f_2(t)$. The time t is measured relative to the stimulus.

Let us consider stimulation with the train of identical intervals I. The first stimulus contributes to the memory. The contribution still remembered when the second stimulus arrives is

$$x = [C_{22}P(I) - C_{23}f_1(I)]f_2(I)$$

The contribution of the first stimulus at the time of arrival of the third stimulus is $xf_2(I)$. We see that contributions of n intervals form a geometrical series, with the sum S:

$$S = [C_{22}P(I) - C_{23}f_1(I)\sum_{n=0}^{\infty}[f_2(I)]^n \tag{9.5}$$

$$S = [C_{22}P(I) - C_{23}f_1(I)]\frac{f_2(I)}{1 - f_2(I)}) \tag{9.6}$$

Example 1: $C_{22} = 0.2, P(t) = 0.5, C_{23} = 0.5, f_1(I) = 0.1, f_2(I) = 0.2$. The memory M_2 will gradually approach the value of the sum $S = 0.5$.

Example 2: $C_{22} = 0.2, P(I) = -0.5, C_{23} = 0.5, f_1(I) = 0.1, f_2(I) = 0.2$. The memory M_2 will gradually approach the value of the sum $S = -0.75$.

Example 3: $C_{22} = 0.1, P(I) = 0.5, C_{23} = 0.5, f_1(I) = 0.1, f_2(I) = 0.9$. The memory M_2 will gradually approach the value of the sum $S = 0$.

Example 4: $C_{22} = 0.1, P(I) = 1, C_{23} = 0.5, f_1(I) = 0.1, f_2(I) = 0.9$. The memory M_2 will gradually approach the value of the sum $S = 0.45$.

Each stimulus contributes to the memory M_2. As the contributions of past stimuli are slowly forgotten, the memory M_2 stores the weighted sum of the past history of stimulation. The dominant effect is that of the last stimulus, because its contribution is fully remembered.

The window generator produces the window waveform that is proportional to the difference between the driving signal $P(t)$ and the memory $M_2(t)$:

$$W(t) = P(t) - M_2(t) \tag{9.7}$$

The window waveform defines the sequence of the receive-send brain windows. If the window waveform is positive, a receive R window is open. If the window waveform is negative, a send S window is open. Hence, the R-S sequence depends on the memory M_2. Highly positive M_2 will result in narrow R windows and in wide S windows. Oppositely, highly negative memory will result in wide R windows and narrow S windows.

9.7.3 Answer Oscillator and Memory M_3

The parameters of the forgetting function $f_3(t)$ are as follows:

$$z_3 = 1, \ g_3 = 100, \ q_3 = 100, \ \text{and} \ d_3 = 0$$

The forgetting function $f_3(t)$ is ideal: it does not forget. Hence, the information stored into the answer memory M_3 is retained unchanged from the instant of the arrival of the stimulus until the response flash. The memory M_3 receives the information from the memory M_1'. When the stimulus arrives, the instant value $M_1(I)$ is transferred into M_3:

$$M_3(t) = M_1(I) = -f_1(t) \tag{9.8}$$

The memory $M_3(t)$ is connected into the feedback loop of the answer oscillator. The answer oscillator is also connected to the memory M_2 of the window generator. Hence, both M_3 and M_2 modulate the answer waveform:

$$A(t) = \sin\left\{2\pi\left[\frac{t}{T_1} - M_3(t) - C_{32}M_2(t) + C\right]\right\} \tag{9.9}$$

C is the initial phase of the answer oscillator. The coupling coefficient C_{32} describes the coupling between the window memory M_2 and the answer oscillator. Both $M_2(t)$ and $M_3(t)$ are almost at a constant level during a short time. Hence, they do not modulate the period of the answer waveform $A(t)$. They only produce the constant phase shift in $A(t)$. Equation 9.9 can be written in this form:

$$A(t) = \sin\left\{2\pi\left[\frac{t}{T_1} - M_3(I) - C_{32}M_2(I) + C\right]\right\} \tag{9.10}$$

When the waveform $A(t)$ crosses the zero level, it produces the trigger. After passing the motor delay d, the trigger produces the answering flash. Hence, the latency is obtained from equation 9.10, when the argument of the sine is equal to π:

$$t = T_1\left[M_3(I) + C_{32}M_2(I) + \frac{1}{2} - C\right] \tag{9.11}$$

The latency is composed of t, of the delay d, and of a random component responsible for the flash jitter j.

$$L = t + d + j = T_1\left[M_3(I)\right] + T_1\left[C_{32}M_2(I)\right] + d + j + \frac{T_1}{2} - T_1C \tag{9.12}$$

Matching the computer-simulated data with experimental data, we find that $T_1 = 1.95$ sec, $C_{23} = C_{32} = 0.45$; $C_{22} = 0.15$; $d = 0.3$ sec, and $C = d/T_1$. We first calculate the basic latencies without the random jitter and without the contribution of the past history of stimulation. The basic latency is then

$$L = T_1M_3(I) + \frac{T_1}{2} = -T_1f_1(I) + \frac{T_1}{2} \tag{9.13}$$

The results are presented in Figure 9.7c.

Now we can concentrate on a more realistic case of a double-interval pattern. The pattern is composed of communication interval I and separation interval I_s. This pattern is repeated n times.

Figure 9.7*a* shows the results for $I_s = 4.4$ sec and $n = 10$. It shows the influence of the past history of stimulation. The separation interval $I_s = 4.4$ sec is in the middle of the *S3* window, and the primary waveform is $P(I_s) = -1$ (see Figure 9.2). As a result, interval I_s will contribute negative values to the memory M_2. If the flash interval is in the *S* window, it also gives a negative contribution to the memory. This explains the low values on curve *a* in the *S* windows. If the flash interval *I* is in an *R* window, $P(I)$ is positive and partially compensates the negative contributions of $P(I_s)$.

Fig. 9.7*b* shows the results for $I_s = 3.4$ sec and $n = 10$. This time I_s is in the middle of the *R3* window, hence $P(I_3) = 1$, and the memory receives positive contributions from I_s. If the flash interval *I* is in an *R* window, $P(I)$ is also positive. This explains the high values on the *b* curve inside *R* windows. If the

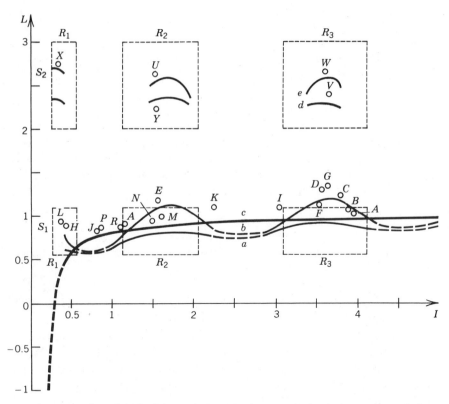

Figure 9.7 *Language of the firefly as an intersection between brain windows and vocabulary. Theoretical computer-calculated latencies plotted over experimental data. Windows S1R1, S1R2, and S1R3 are responsible for responses with short latencies (courtship, mimicry). Windows S2R1, S2R2, and S2R3 are responsible for responses with long latencies (patrolling flashes and separation of flash patterns). Experiments A through T and Z from series 55; V and W from series 57, and U, X, and Y from series 59, each of which represent different Photuris versicolor femmes fatales.*

flash interval I is in an S window, $P(I)$ is negative and partially compensates the positive contributions of $P(I_s)$. We see that for a given communication interval I, the latency can be obtained from curves a, b, or c in Figure 9.7, depending on the past history of stimulation.

In the middle of R windows the latencies can take the values $L > 1.1$ sec; that will bring the answering flash into the $R2$ window. Because the flash can be generated only during an S window, the value T_1 is added to the latency (Figure 9.4). In this way, curves d and e in Figure 9.7 are formed.

9.7.4 Vocabulary-Window-Dialect Sets

Each point on curves a to e in Figure 9.7 presents two "words" of a male-female dialogue: answering latency as a function of a stimulation interval (question). Figure 9.7 presents two sets of possible words, or two sets of vocabularies. Set $V1$ is outlined with curves a and b and presents the vocabulary composed of short latencies. Set $V2$ is outlined with curves d and e and presents the vocabulary composed of long latencies.

Figure 9.7 also shows the brain windows R_iS_j. Each window presents a set of I, L values. All windows together present a family of windows.

The female firefly will produce a flash only if there is an intersection between the vocabulary sets and the window sets. In this way, a family of dialects (dialogues, answers) is formed. Let us use the following notation. The vocabulary is composed of all the elements of the sets V_1 and V_2:

$$V = V_1 \cap V_2 = \phi \qquad (9.14)$$

The symbol $\cap$ represents the intersection. The symbol ϕ represents the null set. In other words, by using the symbol ϕ we show that V_1 and V_2 are disjoint sets.

The family of windows W is composed of all the elements of the window sets S_iR_j:

$$W = S1R1 \cap S1R2 \cap S1R3 \cap S2R1 \cap S2R2 \cap S2R3 = \phi \qquad (9.15)$$

Again the windows present disjoint sets.

The family of dialects D is an intersection between the vocabulary and the family of windows W:

$$D = V \cap W \qquad (9.16)$$

The family of dialects D is composed of sets D_1, D_n, each of which is related to one window SR. For example,

$$D_1 = V_1 \cap (S1R1) \qquad (9.17)$$

is a set of dialogues through the window $S1R1$. We conclude that the family D of all dialects D_1, D_n represents the communication language of the firefly.

Communication behavior in the *Photuris versicolor* female firefly is explained through interaction between brain windows and memory. Each stimulus starts a sequence of receive-send windows in the firefly brain. Each stimulus also contributes to the information stored in the memory.

The memory stores the past history of stimulation in the form of a weighted sum. The last stimulus produces the largest contribution to the memory. The contribution of the stimulus interval I is proportional to the value taken from the primary waveform $P(I)$, and it can be positive, negative, or zero.

The memory controls both the brain windows and the latency formation. Both the brain windows and the latencies fluctuate dynamically. Each combination of receive-send windows presents one set of windows. All windows together present a family of windows.

Each combination of stimulus interval I and the response latency L presents two words (question, answer). All words together present the family of words, or the vocabulary.

The intersection between the family of windows and the vocabulary forms the family of dialects and, therefore, the language of the firefly.

The windows $S1R1$, $S1R2$, and $S1R3$ produce the answers (dialects) with short latencies. This kind of communication is typical in courtship as well as in mimicry.

The windows $S2R1$, $S2R2$, and $S2R3$ produce the answers (dialects) with long latencies. This kind of communication is typical in patrolling flashes. Also, the *Photuris femmes fatale* produces a long answer for intervals $I < 0.3$ sec. If the interval $I > 4$ sec, most of the answers will be long latencies. Due to the random jitter, the intervals in the range $1 < I < 2$ sec sometimes produce latencies that fall out of the window $S1R2$ and into the window $S2R2$.

Figure 9.7 shows the theoretical computer-simulated results, as well as results from a large number of experiments. Each letter describes one experiment (multiple repetition of a double-interval sequence). We see that the latency depends on the last stimulation interval, on the past history of stimulation, and on the vocabulary-window intersection.

Interaction between brain windows and memory forms the language of the firefly and readily explains the hundreds of patterns observed in experimental data.[11] It is possible that the brain window and memory interaction can explain some other features of the brain and behavior as well.

The brain-window principle can be used to design fuzzy hardware (or software) neural or expert system. The basic law of brain windows is:

If there is a match between the stimulus interval I and one of the receive windows, and

If there is a match between the internally induced latency L and one of the sending windows,

Then the response flash with the latency L will be produced.

This law can be translated into production rules of the fuzzy expert system:

If fuzzy sensory condition C_1

And if fuzzy inferred condition C_2

Then fuzzy action A

Note that the windows define fuzzy symbols, and the transfer functions (curves a, b, or c in Figure 9.7) define the action value A as a function of the stimulus C_1.

REFERENCES

1. B. Souček and A.D. Carlson, *J. Theor. Biol.* **119**, 47–65 (1986).
2. J.E. Lloyd *Misc. Publ. Mus. Zool., Univ. Mich.* **130** 1 (1966).
3. J.F. Case and J. Buck, *Biol. Bull. (Woods Hole, Mass.)* **125**, 234 (1963).
4. B. Souček and A.D. Carlson, *J. Theor. Biol.* **55**, 339 (1975).
5. A.D. Carlson and B. Souček, *J. Theor. Biol.* **55**, 353 (1975).
6. J.W. Green, *Proc. Calif. Acad. Sci.* **28**, 561 (1956).
7. S. Nelson, A.D. Carlson, and J. Copeland, *Nature (London)* **255**, 628 (1975).
8. J.E. Lloyd, *Science* **149**, 653 (1965).
9. T. Pavlidis, *Biological Oscillators: Their Mathematical Analysis.* Academic Press, New York, 1973.
10. A.T. Winfree, *The Geometry of Biological Time.* Springer-Verlag, New York, 1980.
11. B. Souček, and A.D. Carlson, *Computers in Neurobiology and Behavior.* Wiley, New York, 1976.

CHAPTER 10 ────────────────────

Brain-Window Language

INTRODUCTION AND SURVEY

This chapter presents an example of the coding and language based on the fuzzy, adjustable sets called "brain windows." These languages have many features that would be desirable in brain-like computers. Brain-window language was first observed in the computer-based analysis of firefly communication patterns. This chapter is adapted from Souček and Carlson[1].

Before mating, female fireflies of the species *Photuris versicolor* respond to the courtship flashes of conspecific males. After mating, they become *femme fatales* (FFs) by answering the courtship flashes of males of other species. By analyzing the responses of females to artificial stimulus flashes, we have identified the language of the firefly, based on brain windows and on biological oscillators with a period of about two seconds.

The response latency of the female is a function of the stimulus interval, and these stimulus-response relationships form six clusters or "dialogues." Each dialogue is composed of a narrow range of stimulus intervals and their associated narrow range of response latencies. These dialogues are related to the three response behaviors of females: responses to the short stimulus intervals of conspecific males, and responses to medium and long stimulus intervals of heterospecific males. These interval classes are named courtship, mimicry, and patrolling, respectively. Each behavior uses one receive brain window and one send brain window. The receive window is a time interval during which a female can only accept the stimulus flash. The send window is a time interval during which the female can only initiate a response.

Similar stimuli can produce different latencies, depending on the context stored in the female's memory. This context or expectation is defined by the past history of stimulation. The context is used to dynamically adjust the brain windows, depending upon the behavior.

The six dialogues together form the brain-window language of the firefly. The language is defined in terms of message quantum, distance, and redundancy. The message quantum is the smallest item used in coding and is a fraction of the biological oscillator period. The coding distance is a measure of how far the receive windows are separated from each other and determines the safety of coding. The coding distance, measured in message quanta, is large for courtship and small for mimicry communication. Language redundancy shows the efficiency of coding and is greater than one.

A computer model[1] has been developed that uses brain-window language and is in excellent agreement with the experimental data. The concept of brain-window language can also be used in brain-like computers.

10.1 MODEL OF THE FIREFLY

Fireflies communicate through the medium of light flashes; the language of communication resides in the time parameters inherent in their flash patterns. To understand how information exchange occurs, it is necessary to establish the link between the language and the operation of the biological system. Because it is possible to observe and record firefly flashes with precision, and to communicate with fireflies using artificial flashes, this system lends itself to analysis by computer techniques. Computer models based on experimental data have been developed to explain the flash behavior of females of *Photuris versicolor*[1] and *Photinus macdermotti*.[2-4]

In *Photuris versicolor* fireflies, the flying male produces a complex flash composed of three or more pulses of 125 msec duration and about 6 Hz frequency, which appear as rapid twinkles to the human eye. The unmated female responds from her stationary perch with a simple flash of approximately 1 sec latency, measured from the end of the male flash. Male and female exchange courtship flashes, eventually locating each other and mating. Within one to three days after mating, the female undergoes a behavioral switch.[5] She no longer responds to the twinkling courtship flash of her conspecific male. Instead, she responds to the simple flashes of males of other species, occasionally attracting, capturing, and devouring them.[6]

The intervals of male flashes represent the language of this communication system and can be classified into three categories. The shortest intervals (less than 300 msec and called courtship intervals) are reserved for the courtship flash of *Photuris versicolor* and are recognized only by unmated females. Flash intervals between 1 and 2.5 sec represent courtship flash phrases of males of prey species (called mimicry intervals); longer intervals represent the separation between flash phrases (called patrolling intervals). The medium and longer intervals are answered by FFs which are mimicking the responses of females of other species. For example, *Photinus macdermotti* males produce courtship flashes in pairs of two-second interpair intervals and longer, variable intervals between the pairs. The conspecific female and the FF both answer about one second after the second courtship flash. *Photinus pyralis* males flash every six seconds; the flashes represent patrolling intervals to the female.

The model which describes the response behavior of both virgin and mated (FF) females is based upon the concept of brain windows (Figure 10.1). The communication process is governed by a biological oscillator. The oscillator generates a primary waveform $P(t)$ with a period T_1 of approximately 2 sec. Upon receiving a flash stimulus, the firefly memory M_1 is charged and slowly discharges back

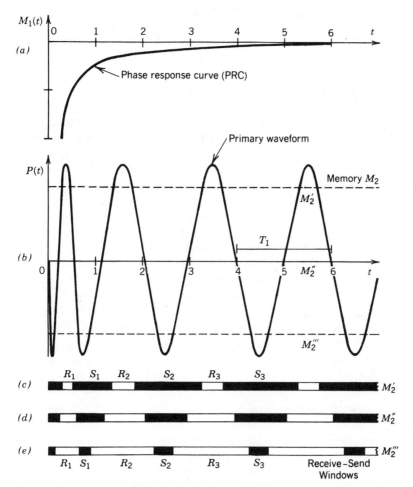

Figure 10.1 *The concept of brain windows in the female firefly. Horizontal axis is time in seconds. (a) Phase-response curve (PRC). The stimulus flash charges the memory (M_1) which decays with time, producing the PRC. (b) Primary waveform defined by the PRC. As the PRC declines toward zero, the period of the primary waveform increases towards the resting value. Memory levels caused by previous flashes (M_2) are shown as horizontal lines intersecting the primary waveform. These memory levels define the receive-send windows. (c,d,e) Receive-send window periods defined by memory levels (M_2): (c) highly positive memory level (M_2); receive windows narrow, send windows wide; (d) memory at zero level (M_2); (e) highly negative memory level (M_2); receive windows wide, send windows narrow.*

toward zero (Figure 10.1a). In this way, M_1 modulates the primary waveform (Figure 10.1b). Hence, $M_1(t)$ is equivalent to a phase-response curve (PRC).

The positive and negative phases of the primary waveform designate receive and send windows. Receive windows, defined by the positive phase of $P(t)$, are periods during which a second stimulus flash can command a female answer. Send windows, during which a response flash can actually be generated by the female, are defined by negative phases of $P(t)$.

A second memory, M_2, recalls the past history of stimulation. Depending on the past history, M_2 can take any value in the range $-1 < M_2 < 1$. The intersection of the memory M_2 and the primary waveform $P(t)$ defines the sequence of the receive-send brain windows. Figures 10.1c, d, and e show three receive-send window sequences for the memory values M_2', M_2'', and M_2''', respectively.

The basic carrier of information is the interval I between two stimulus flashes. The second flash is matched against the train of receive windows. Each receive window recognizes a particular group of intervals (courtship, mimicry, or patrolling). In this way, the firefly receives and analyzes the stimulation interval I. This interval can be considered as a question in the communication.

The logic of the firefly's brain generates the answer to the received question. The answer information is coded in the latency L of the response flash. The latency is matched against the train of send windows. Each send window defines a particular group of latencies as a group of legal answers (answer to a courtship flash, answer to a prey courtship flash, or answer to a patrolling interval). Hence, the receive interval I (question) will produce the answering flash with the latency L only if I matches one of the receive windows and if L matches one of the send windows.

For a detailed description of experimental conditions and of a computer model based on brain windows, see Chapter 9. Brain windows are combined here with context switching and message recognition. In this way, brain window language is defined and verified by experimental data. Message quantum, coding distance, and language redundancy are defined for this communication system.

The sequence of the receive-send windows is used to check both the stimulus interval and the response latency. For this reason, it is convenient to plot receive-send windows over the function $L = L(I)$. Each value of the memory M_2 will result in a specific receive-send window sequence. The computer model, based on Figure 10.1, is used to simulate the latencies derived from the phase-response curve; the windows are defined by the intersection between the primary waveform and the memory.

Figure 10.2 presents a two-dimensional plot of receive-send windows for the memory value $M_2 >> 0$. Note the narrow receive windows and the wide send windows. Figures 10.2b and d present the latencies produced by the computer model. Figure 10.3 presents the windows for the memory value $M_2 << 0$. Note the narrow send windows and wide receive windows. Figures 10.3a and e present the latencies. Curve e is obtained by adding the oscillation period T_1 to curve a. Curve d is obtained by adding the value $\frac{1}{2}T_1$ to curve b.

We have performed a computer analysis of the experimental data from two sets of experiments:

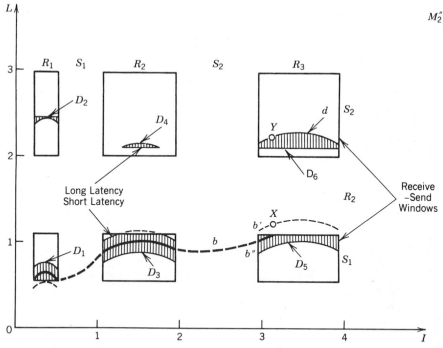

Figure 10.2 *Brain-window language for highly positive memory (M₂). The receive R windows are narrow and the send S windows are wide. Belts b and d represent the vocabulary. Shaded areas represent the dialogues.*

1. The female is stimulated with the double-interval pattern I, I_S, where the separation interval I_S matches the window $R2$. Under these conditions, the memory is charged to the positive value, $M_2 \gg 0$. The results are plotted in Figure 10.2, shaded areas. Note that the experimentally observed stimulus-latency (I, L) points are found only inside the windows.

2. The female is stimulated with the double-interval pattern I, I_S, where the separation interval I_S matches the window $S2$. Under these conditions, the memory is charged to the negative value, $M_2 \ll 0$. The results are plotted in the shaded area of Figure 10.3. Again, the experiments produce the points $L = L(I)$ only inside the windows.

Under the unchanged experimental conditions, the latency is somewhat different from one stimulation to the next. In other words, there is a random component (jitter) in the latency. The effect of the jitter is to smear curve b into a belt $b'b''$. In the same way, other curves are smeared into belts a, b, d, and e. Figures 10.2 and 10.3 show a good match between computer-simulated data (belts) and the data from real experiments (shaded areas). Each point in the belt is a question-answer (I, L) dialogue. Each belt presents a set of possible words or a set of dialogues. All the belts together present a vocabulary.

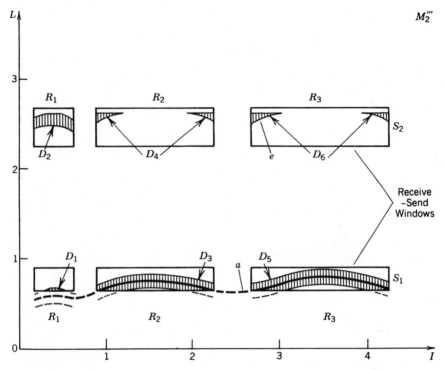

Figure 10.3 *Brain-window language for highly negative memory (M₂). The receive R windows are wide and the send S windows are narrow. Belts a and e represent the vocabulary. Shaded areas represent the dialogues.*

10.2 LANGUAGE

Language involves a set of legal messages used in a particular communication system. The sender and the receiver must agree upon the meaning of the messages. In the case of fireflies, the stimulus interval I and the response latency L present the messages. The intersection between the vocabulary (belts) and the family of windows defines the family of dialogue. Relating the measured data to behavior, we find the following dialogues:

Dialogue D1
This is the dialogue between the virgin female and the conspecific male. It is an intersection between the belt b and the window $S1R1$:

$$D1 = b \cap (S1R1)$$

The stimulus interval is in the range $0.1 < I < 0.3$, and the response latency is $0.6 < I < 0.8$ seconds.

Dialogue D2

This is the dialogue between the mated female (FF) and the conspecific male. It is an intersection between belt d and the window $S2R1$:

$$D1 = d \cap (S2R1)$$

The stimulus interval is in the range $0.1 < I < 0.3$, and the response latency is in the range $2.4 < I < 2.5$.

Dialogue D3

This is a dialogue between the FF and the heterospecific male (*Photinus macdermotti*) producing courtship calls. It is an intersection between the belt b and the window $S1R2$:

$$D3 = b \cap (S1R2)$$

The stimulus interval is in the range $1.3 < I < 1.7$ and the response latency is in the range $0.8 < L < 1.1$ seconds. Dialogue D3 is the case of communication mimicry.

Dialogue D4

This is a dialogue between the FF and the heterospecific male producing courtship calls. For this particular range of calls, the belt b goes outside of the window $S1R2$: the female adds the clock period $\frac{1}{2}T_1$ to the short latency, and in this way the long latency is formed (belt d). The dialogue is an intersection between the belt d and the window $S2R2$:

$$D4 = d \cap S2R2)$$

The stimulus interval is in the range $1.3 < I < 1.7$, and the response latency is $2.1 < I < 2.2$ seconds.

Dialogue D5

This is a dialogue between the FF and the heterospecific male producing flashes at long intervals. It is an intersection between the belt b and the window $S1R3$:

$$D5 = b \cap (S1R3)$$

The stimulus interval is in the range $3.0 < I < 4.0$, and the response latency is in the range $0.8 < I < 1.1$ seconds.

Dialogue D6

This is a dialogue between the FF and the heterospecific male producing flashes at long intervals. For this particular range of calls, the belt b goes outside of the window $S1R3$. As a result, the female adds the clock period $\frac{1}{2}T_1$ to the short latency, and in this way the long latency is formed (belt d). The dialogue is an intersection between the belt d and the window $S2R3$:

$$D6 = d \cap (S2R3)$$

The stimulus interval is in the range $3.0 < I < 4.0$, and the response latency is $2.1 < L < 2.3$ seconds.

Dialogues $D1$ to $D6$ are represented in Figure 10.2 (shaded areas). Both experimental data and computer model-generated data are found only within six isolated islands, described here as dialogues $D1$ to $D6$. The dialogues $D1$ to $D6$ put together form the communication language of the firefly *Photuris versicolor*.

Exact positions of the dialogues and the windows depend on experimental conditions and on the animal used in the experiment. However, the basic findings are always the same: communication is clustered into six islands (dialogues). Each island is related to one specific behavior: courtship, mimicry, or patrolling flashes of long intervals.

In computer and communication theories, language is put into parameters in terms of bit, distance, and redundancy. The bit is the smallest information item used in coding. In computers and in communication systems, the bit is binary one. The distance is the number of bits by which two messages are different. For example, the distance between the messages 101 and 011 is two. The redundancy is defined as $r = n/m$, where n is the number of available bits in the system, and m is the minimum number of binary bits necessary to convey the same message. Digital information systems are based on switching elements, each presenting one bit. If a system is composed of N switching elements (bits), it could produce 2^N different messages. For reasons of redundancy, sometimes only a fraction of these messages is introduced into the definition of language.

The biological communication system of the firefly is not digital. Rather, it is based on the concept of the biological oscillator. Hence, the digital definitions of bit, redundancy, and distance cannot be directly used in this biological system. Here we propose new definitions.

10.3 THE MESSAGE QUANTUM

The modulated primary waveform produces a train of different half-periods. Each half-period defines one receive or one send window. Hence, each half-period presents a message range in the firefly language.

The first (negative) half-period is the shortest one. In the case of the firefly, it is approximately 0.25 sec. This is one-eighth of the period of the nonmodulated primary waveform ($T_1/8$). As this is the smallest information item used in coding, we call it the "message quantum," q:

$$q = T_1/k \text{ (in the case of the firefly, } k = 8) \tag{10.1}$$

We use the message quantum q to measure the windows: For $q < R_1 < 3q$, the window width is $2q$. For $5q < R_2 < 9q$, the window width is $4q$, and so forth.

10.4 REDUNDANCY

Redundancy is proportional to the safety of coding and inversely proportional to the efficiency of usage of the available coding building bricks. Redundancy r can be defined as

$$r = n/m \tag{10.2}$$

where n = number of available message quanta and
       m = minimum number of message quanta necessary to convey the same message.

In the firefly, language is composed of at least three message windows, R_1, R_2, and R_3, for which six message quanta would be enough ($m = 6$). In reality, the first three cycles of the primary waveform take more than $2T_1$; hence, $n = 16$. The resulting redundancy is $r = 16/6$. Firefly language is obviously highly redundant. For example, the stimulation intervals (I) of 1.3, 1.5, or 1.7 sec will be recognized as legal messages with identical meaning, defined by the window R_2.

10.5 DISTANCE

Distance is defined as a minimal separation between the adjacent receive windows. Obviously, the distance is equal to the width of the corresponding send window. Measured in units of message quanta, the distance is

$$d = S/q \tag{10.3}$$

Hence, the distance d_{12} between the window R_1 and R_2 is approximately $3q/q = 3$. Similarly, the distance d_{23} between R_2 and R_3 is 4, and so on. Large distances between messages make the firefly language highly reliable.

The situation becomes more complicated if we consider the cases in which memory M_2 is highly positive (Figure 10.2) or highly negative (Figure 10.3). Figure 10.2 shows the case of courtship communication. The R_1 window is responsible for recognizing the courtship partner. The narrow R_1 window makes the female very selective. She will accept only a very precise stimulation interval I. For the survival of the species, it is important for the female to choose a partner that produces the most precise species-typical courtship flash. Narrow R windows (large distances) define the language with a smaller range of acceptable messages.

Figure 10.3 shows the case of communication mimicry used to attract the male of other firefly species. The attracted male is a source of food, and its features, including the interval I, could belong to a broad class. Hence, the receive window R_2 is wide, increasing the chance to establish dialogue with the potential prey. Wide R windows (smaller distances) define the language with a larger range of acceptable messages.

10.6 THE USE OF CONTEXT

Figures 10.2 and 10.3 show that firefly language is not always the same. The shape of the windows changes from one situation to the next, depending on the past history of stimulation stored in the memory M_2. The past history or recalled experiences can be considered as internal context. In brain-window language, the context is present in several areas: the shape of the windows, the general dependence of the response latency on the past history of stimulation, and the switching from short to long latencies.

1. The shape of the windows depends not only on the past history of stimulation but also on the behavior (courtship, search for food). These dependencies are present in both experimental and computer-simulated data. It is possible that data from other sensory and behavior-generating modalities also contribute to the context.
2. The gradual (analog, continuous) dependence of the latency on the past history of stimulation is related to the change of the window shape in a form of a chase: if M_2 is increasing, both the latency and the S windows will increase, but not at the same rate. Eventually, the latency curve will grow out of the window (point X in Figure 10.2).
3. FFs switch their responses from short to long latencies when the latency grows out of the $S1$ window. The internal logic of the brain adds the value $\frac{k}{2}T_1$ ($k = 1, 2, 3, \ldots$) to the short latency. In this way, a long latency is formed that matches another window (point Y in Figure 10.2). Hence, the context produces the switch from one message window to another message window.

In cases 1 and 2, the context helps in sensory-pattern recognition, matching the stimulation interval I with the receive windows. In case 3, the context helps in decision making, generating the response latency L and matching the latency with the send windows.

10.7 THE LANGUAGE OF FLEXIBLE, FUZZY, ADJUSTABLE WINDOWS

A language has been defined here that can explain the communication behavior of fireflies. The language is based on the concept of brain windows. Brain windows are generated through the interaction between the primary oscillator and the memory. The memory stores the internal context. Memory adjusts the sequence of receive-send windows. The stimulus interval I presenting the sensory pattern is matched against the train of receive windows. The response latency L, presenting the answer or decision, is matched against the train of send windows. The language is directly related to the physiological findings: biological oscillators and pulses (flashes).

Communication behavior in fireflies is explained with one level of oscillator-pulse interaction. This concept can be extended to the hierarchy of oscillator-pulse levels. Each level has its sequence of receive-send windows, and its memory (context). The sensory patterns and the decisions or commands pass through the hierarchy in opposite directions.

Definitions are introduced for bit, redundancy, and distance in biological coding. All of the above are functions of the message quantum. The message quantum is the smallest item used in coding and is a fraction of the biological oscillator period.

Brain-window language is in excellent agreement with experimental data measured on *Photuris versicolor* female fireflies stimulated by artificial flashes. Computer analysis of a large volume of experimental data reveals the fact that data points are clustered into islands of dialogue (shaded areas in Figures 10.2 and 10.3). The dialogue $D1$ was identified in experimental data of the virgin female only. The dialogues $D2$ to $D6$ have been identified in experimental data of mated females.

Similar stimuli can produce different latencies, depending on the context stored in the firefly's memory. The context is used to adjust the brain windows dynamically depending upon behavior. An example of context switching is shown in Figure 10.2, points X and Y. For the stimulus interval in the range $3.1 < I < 3.3$ seconds, the response latency defined by the belt b will be in the range $0.9 < L < 1.1$. However, if the female's internal logic generates a latency only slightly above this range (point X), the value $\frac{1}{2}T_1$ is added to the latency. In this way, a long latency is formed (point Y) producing the flash through the window $S2$. The addition of the context or expectation based on the past history to the sensory input increases the dimensionality of the pattern input space. Thus, as shown in Figure 10.2, the ambiguous stimulation intervals producing the latencies near the upper edge of the $R3S1$ window, too similar to be reliably recognized as in separate classes, can be easily distinguished when accompanied by the context: the flash is produced either through the window $S1$ or through a distant window $S2$.

The experimental data and computer model-generated data show that the latency interacts with the sensory inputs and with behavior in several ways:

1. The latency L is a continuous (analog) function of the stimulus interval I, and of the content of the memory, as shown with belts a, b, d, and e in Figure 10.2 and in Figure 10.3.

2. The latency L is also a discrete (discontinuous) function of the context stored in the memory. In this way, the latency and the answering flash can be switched from one window to another, although the windows are far away.

3. Interaction between belts a, b, d, e, and the windows is equivalent to the process of quantizing. The process of quantizing the information is necessary to form the basic messages of the language.

4. The windows are discrete but flexible. The windows change shape, depending on the behavior of the FF and on external stimulation. By narrowing the window, the female firefly becomes highly selective during courting communication. By widening the window, the firefly increases its chance of catching the prey during aggressive mimicry.

5. The brain-window mechanism of fireflies uses continuous and discrete information, connected through the quantizing process. The experiments presented here show the existence of one layer of continuous/quantizing/discrete (CQD) information. This layer is the easiest to investigate, because it involves the external sensory and motor logic of the firefly.

Further experiments would be necessary to search for a possible existence of additional CQD layers deeper in the neural system. The concept of brain windows may explain the language and behavior of other species as well and it could be used to design a new class of neural and expert systems.

REFERENCES

1. B. Souček and A. D. Carlson, *J. Theor. Biol.* **125**, 93–103 (1987).

2. B. Souček and A. D. Carlson, *J. Theor. Biol.* **55**, 339 (1975).

3. B. Souček and A. D. Carlson, *Computers in Neurobiology and Behavior*. Wiley, New York, 1976.

4. A. D. Carlson and B. Souček, *J. Theor. Biol.* **55**, 353 (1975).

5. S. Nelson, A. D. Carlson, and J. Copeland, *Nature (London)* **255**, 628 (1975).

6. J. E. Lloyd, *Science* **149**, 653 (1965).

PART III ⎯⎯⎯⎯⎯⎯⎯⎯⎯⎯⎯⎯⎯⎯⎯⎯⎯⎯⎯

NEUROCOMPUTERS AND GENETIC SYSTEMS

Adaptive Learning Systems

Artificial Neural Systems or Neurocomputers

Adaptive Rule-Based Expert and Goal-Directed Systems

Event-Train Processing Systems

CHAPTER 11

Adaptive Learning Systems

INTRODUCTION AND SURVEY

Learning is one of the basic features of intelligence. The concept of learning machines comes from biological models. Learning is effective self-modification of the organism that lives in a complex and changing environment. Learning is any directed change in the knowledge structure that improves the performance.

This chapter starts with a description of trainable pattern classifiers. They employ a number of discriminators whose outputs are compared by a maximum selector. The simplest classifier is a linear machine in which the components of the pattern vector are connected to a summary device through a network of weights. The specification of a linear discriminant function is achieved by specifying the weights. The training method is based on error correction. The field of applications for simple linear machines is limited. More elaborate devices are needed for practical applications, with the following features: continuous pattern vectors; nonlinear discriminant functions; elaborate selectors; machines with several layers; and committee machines.

Different learning rules are described. These include simple Hebbian learning without a teacher; the Widrow-Hoff or Delta rule, in which the amount of learning is proportional to the difference between the achieved activation and the activation provided by the teacher; the Grossberg rule; the Hopfield minimum-energy rule; the generalized Delta rule, involving hidden units; the competitive unsupervised learning rule; the Sigma-Pi rule; and the Boltzmann learning algorithm.

For learning systems it is not necessary to write the program. Having been shown the appropriate input-output exemplars specifying some function, the system learns to compute that function in general. Hence, the system programs itself. This is a very useful feature, especially in the case of parallel computers, which are difficult to program.

Concrete examples of adaptive learning systems are presented, including the perceptron model of vision; the neocognitron; NETtalk; bidirectional associative memory BAM; fuzzy cognitive maps FCM; and the traveling salesperson model.

11.1 TRAINABLE PATTERN CLASSIFIERS

Machines with the ability to learn have been investigated and designed for a long time, with limited success. Learning machines can be divided into two categories:

1. Programmed systems specialized for a given application area, and based on recurrent calculations. The goal of learning is to formulate explicit rules and generalizations. This kind of system is out of the scope of this chapter.
2. Adaptive trainable pattern classifiers, directly related to physical models such as connectionist brain theory. These systems use only simple physical components and operate in a highly distributed parallel fashion. The goal of learning is to establish connection strengths, enabling the system to act as though it knew the rules.

Thanks to new technology, some interesting new approaches and applications are under way using adaptive trainable pattern classifiers. These systems will be described here.

Nilsson[1] has developed a mathematical theory of learning machines; we follow Nilsson's definitions and notations here.

Figure 11.1 shows the basic model for a pattern classifier. The pattern is a set of real numbers, $x_1, x_2, \ldots, x_d$, applied to the classifier. The numbers are components of the pattern vector X.

Any device for sorting patterns into categories is called a *pattern classifier*. It will have d input lines and one output line. The d input lines are activated simultaneously by the pattern, and the output line produces a signal i_o that may have one of R distinct values, where R represents the number of categories into which the pattern must be sorted. The example of the pattern might present $d = 1000$ meteorological data (pressure, temperature, wind, or moisture, all measured at several points), and the response might be the weather prediction with $R = 4$ categories (sunny, cloudy, rainy, stormy).

A pattern classifier employs R discriminators, each of which computes the value of a discriminant function for one of R outcomes. The outputs of the discriminators will be called *discriminants*. In classifying a pattern X, the R discriminants are compared by a maximum selector which indicates the largest discriminant.

In many cases, there is little if any knowledge about the patterns to be classified. Also, the relation between the patterns and the response is usually poorly defined. Hence, discriminant functions cannot be selected in advance. The discriminant functions are formed by an adjustment process which has become known as training.

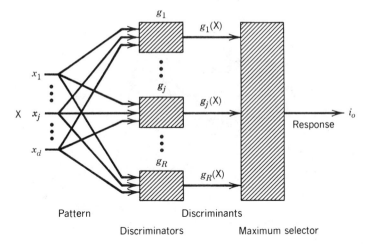

Figure 11.1 *Basic model for a pattern classifier. Reprinted by permission from Nilsson.* [1]

A set of typical patterns, called a *training set*, is used to adjust the machine. For the training set, the responses are assumed to be known. The machine is then adjusted in such a way that it produces the best classification.

11.2 LINEAR MACHINE

Figure 11.2 presents a special case of pattern classifiers called a *linear machine*. In a linear machine, the components x: $x_1, \ldots, x_d$ are connected to the summing devices through the network of weights w. In this way, the family of R discriminant functions is achieved. The form of discriminant functions is linear:

$$g(X) = w_1 x_1 + w_2 x_2 + \ldots + w_d x_d + w_{d+1} \tag{11.1}$$

The specification of the linear discriminant function is achieved by specifying the weights w. In Figure 11.2, the notation w_{ij} represents the coefficient of x_j in the ith linear discriminant function.

A special case of a linear machine is a threshold logic unit TLU, presented in Figure 11.3. The TLU classifies the patterns into only two categories, $R = 2$. The maximum selector makes the decision by evaluating the sign of the discriminant function:

$$g(X) > 0, \; i_o = 1 \qquad \text{if pattern category 1}$$

$$g(X) < 0, \; i_o = -1 \qquad \text{if pattern category 2}$$

The TLU consists of weights, a summing device, and a threshold element.

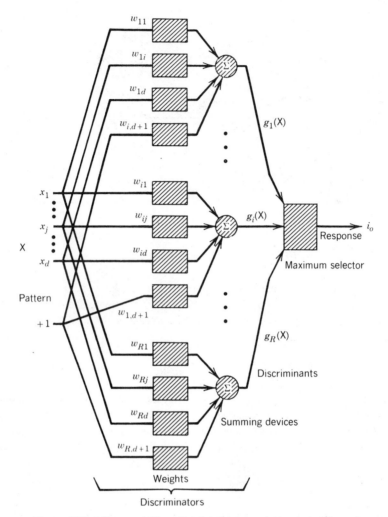

Figure 11.2 *A linear machine. Reprinted by permission from Nilsson.* [1]

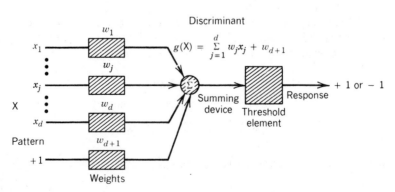

Figure 11.3 *The threshold logic unit, TLU. Reprinted by permission from Nilsson.* [1]

The simplest training method for the TLU is based on error correction. The training patterns are presented to the TLU one at a time for trial. The obtained response of the TLU is compared with the desired response for a given category of the pattern. If the TLU responds correctly to the pattern Y, no adjustment is made. If the TLU responds incorrectly to the pattern Y, adjustments are made to the old weights W in the following way:

$$W' = W + cY \qquad \text{if } Y \text{ belonged to category 1}$$

$$W' = W - cY \qquad \text{if } Y \text{ belonged to category 2} \qquad (11.2)$$

where W' is a new weight vector. Hence, the weight vector W is changed in proportion with the pattern vector Y. The value c is called the *correction increment*. Correction increment c can be formed in several ways, of which the best known are the following:

1. Fixed increment: c can be any fixed number greater than zero
2. Absolute correction: c depends on the quantity WY
3. Fractional correction: c depends on the quantity $(WY - W'Y)$

The training procedure must be convergent: the weight vectors W produced by the training procedure must converge towards a solution weight vector. Mathematical theory and convergence proofs can be found in Nilsson.[1]

The concept of learning machines comes from biological models. McCulloch and Pitts[2] developed the model of the "formal neuron," based on the on-off threshold device. Hebb[3] developed the model of learning through the adaptation of synaptic strengths in neural networks. Rosenblatt[4] combined the concepts of the threshold device, adaptation, and networks, to develop the system called the *perceptron*. Many systems have been developed since then and have been used to explain brain and behavioral functions, as well as for pattern recognition.

11.3 A NUMERICAL EXAMPLE OF TRAINING

Figures 11.4 and 11.5 show a set of eight three-dimensional patterns with binary components in geometrical presentation and in tabular presentation. The patterns should be classified into two categories with the desired responses 1 or -1. A separation plane between two patterns is shown in Figure 11.4. The TLU with fixed-increment $c = 1$ should be used. The TLU has four inputs: x_1, x_2, x_3 and 1 (Figure 11.3). The training history[5] for this example has been followed by a computer and is presented in Table 11.1. Note the following:

- The initial value of the weight vector is W (0 0 0 0).
- The first training pattern is X (0 1 0 1).
- Training is composed of iterations; in each iteration all eight patterns are used for training.

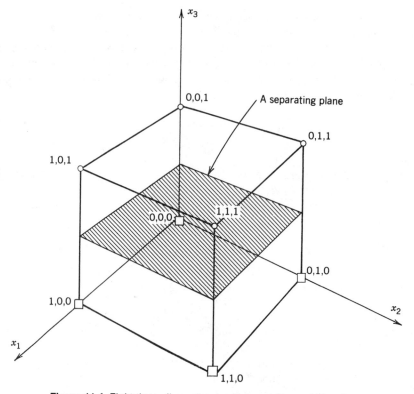

Figure 11.4 *Eight three-dimensional patterns and separating plane.*

- The successful termination occurs during the second iteration after a total of 13 pattern presentations.
- The weights have been adjusted thirteen times.

At the end of training, the TLU responds correctly to any of eight three-dimensional binary patterns.

A computer program was used to learn numerical patterns, such as in Figure 11.5, as well as symbolic patterns (e.g., books or journals). It belongs to the group

x_1	x_2	x_3	x_4	Desired Response
0	1	1	1	−1
0	0	0	1	1
1	0	0	1	1
1	0	1	1	−1
0	0	1	1	−1
1	1	0	1	1
1	1	1	1	−1
0	1	0	1	1

Figure 11.5 *Eight three-dimensional pattern vectors.*

TABLE 11.1

Pattern				Weights				W·X	Desired?	Adjustment?
x_1	x_2	x_3	x_4	w_1	w_2	w_3	w_4			
0	1	0	1	0	0	0	0	0	> 0	Yes
0	1	0	1	0	1	0	1	2	> 0	No
0	0	1	1	0	1	0	1	1	≤ 0	Yes
0	0	1	1	0	1	−1	0	−1	≤ 0	No
1	0	0	1	0	1	−1	0	0	> 0	Yes
1	0	0	1	1	1	−1	1	2	> 0	No
0	1	1	1	1	1	−1	1	1	≤ 0	Yes
0	1	1	1	1	0	−2	0	−2	≤ 0	No
1	1	0	1	1	1	0	0	1	> 0	No
1	0	1	1	1	0	−2	0	−1	≤ 0	No
1	1	1	1	1	0	−2	0	−1	≤ 0	No
0	0	0	1	1	0	−2	0	0	> 0	Yes
0	0	0	1	1	0	−2	1	1	> 0	No
0	1	0	1	1	0	−2	1	1	> 0	No
0	0	1	1	1	0	−2	1	−1	≤ 0	No
1	0	0	1	1	0	−2	1	2	> 0	No
0	1	1	1	1	0	−2	1	−1	≤ 0	No
1	1	0	1	1	0	−2	1	2	> 0	No
1	0	1	1	1	0	−2	1	0	≤ 0	No
1	1	1	1	1	0	−2	1	0	≤ 0	No
0	0	0	1	1	0	−2	1	1	> 0	No

of programs[5] for the "Learning Library" (written in Sperry Univac MCO COBOL REV 4R1.0).

11.4 THE PERCEPTRON

Perceptrons have largely been used to analyze neural networks, notably visual networks. By modeling a visual system based on current neurophysiological knowledge, researchers can compare how a computer simulation compares with other observed behavior of visual systems. In one such project, Rosenblatt[4] compared the ability to distinguish similar letters of the alphabet between a perceptron and the results obtained from preliterate schoolchildren.

A perceptron is a network made up of three types of units: *sensory units*, *associative units*, and *response units* (Figure 11.6). The sensory units correspond to the initial sensory input. The associative units represent points where the flow of information through the network is controlled. The response units represent the output information from the network.

A given perceptron may contain several association layers. A common technique is to connect random and/or constrained elements between the various layers of the perceptron. Typically, several inhibitory and excitatory elements from the previous layer are connected to each element in a given layer. The logic in this layer compares the sum of the inputs with a given threshold value to produce a (typically) binary value of 1 or 0 for the element which is used by the next layer.

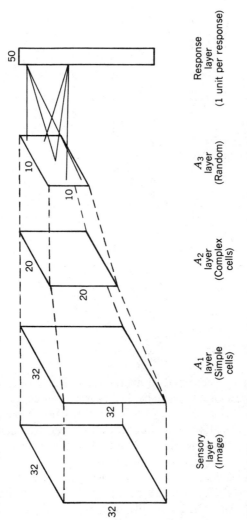

Figure 11.6 *The perceptron model: 32 by 32 element sensory "retina"; three associative layers; 50-element response layer. Adapted from Van Nest.*[6]

The connections between the last association layer and the response layer contain variable weights on each connection.

Figure 11.6 illustrates the perceptron model developed by Van Nest[6] to explore some of the processing of cats' visual systems. The model consists of a 32 by 32 element sensory "retina," followed by an associative layer which makes connections on 3 by 3 groups of cells to mimic simple cells on center cells and off center cells. The next associative layer makes connections with the A–1 layer and models some basic features of complex cells. The A–3 connection connects with random connections to the A–2 layer to implement the basic perceptron concept. The lines between A–3 and A–2 include excitatory and inhibitory connections. The response layer is connected to the A–3 layer by random, variable-weighted connections.

The program[6] to illustrate some perceptron concepts was written in FORTRAN-77 on a VAX 11/780 computer. The visual patterns used to test the computer model were a few simple alphabetic letters, columns of horizontal lines, columns of vertical lines, and a solid triangle. Figure 11.7 demonstrates how the A–1 layer has converted one input image into a simpler image containing only the edges of the original. In this way, the perceptron may be used to study how an animal may develop neural connections that allow it to see.

11.5 HEBB'S LAW

Hebb's law is the fundamental psychophysical law of associative learning. Therefore, it is a basic law of psychology; it is also a basic law of artificial neural systems. Hebb[3] formulated the law as follows:

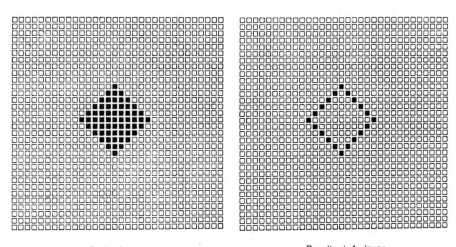

Retina image   Resultant A_1 layer

Figure 11.7 *The A-1 layer converts an input retina image into a contour image. Adapted from Van Nest.*[6]

If neuron A repeatedly contributes to the firing of neuron B, then A's efficiency in firing B increases.

Hestenes[7] combines Hebb's law and Grossberg's neural modeling theory[8,9] to explain learning processes in Pavlovian experiments:

When a dog is presented with food it salivates. When the dog hears a bell it does not salivate initially. But after hearing the bell simultaneously with the presentation of food on several consecutive occasions, the dog is subsequently found to salivate when it hears the bell alone. To describe the experiment in more general terms, when a conditioned stimulus (such as a bell) is repeatedly paired with an unconditioned stimulus (such as food) which evokes an unconditioned response (such as salivation), the CS gradually acquires the ability to evoke the UCR.

To interpret this in the simplest possible neural terms, consider Figure 11.8. Suppose that the firing of neuron B produces the UCR output, and suppose that the UCS input fires neuron C, which is coupled to B with sufficient strength to make B fire. Now if a CS stimulates neuron A to fire simultaneously with neuron B, then, in accordance with Hebb's law, the coupling strength w_{AB} between neurons A and B increases to the point where A has the capacity to fire B without the help of C.

Hestenes concludes that the association strength between stimulus and response that psychologists infer from their experiments is a crude measure of the synaptic coupling strength between neurons in the central nervous system (CNS). The same can be said about all associations among ideas and actions. Thus, the full import of Hebb's law is this:

All associative (long-term) memory resides in synaptic connections of the CNS, and all learning consists of changes in synaptic coupling strengths.

The strengthening of specific synapses within neural circuits is the most accepted theory for learning and memory in the brain. Yet recently another layer of intelligence has attracted attention: the molecular (cytoskeleton) layer. The relation between the neural and molecular layers is described by Hameroff[10] in the following way: Dynamic structural activities of the cytoskeleton are responsible for all cytoplasmic rearrangements including formation and regulation of dendritic spines

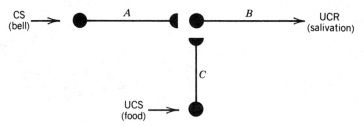

Figure 11.8 *A neural interpretation of Pavlovian learning. Reprinted by permission from Hestenes.*[7]

and synapses. The spines are branchings of dendrites which themselves are branchings of neurons. A further dimension of complexity, these cytoskeletal appendages are prime candidates for synaptic adaptation, the cornerstone for prevalent models of brain and memory. The neuron's complexity may indeed be more like a computer than a single gate. Relatively recently, with perfection of electronic microscopic fixation, immunofluorescence, and other techniques, the interior of living cells has been revealed. It has been shown to possess complex, highly parallel interconnected networks of cytoskeletal protein lattices, which connect to and regulate membranes and all other cellular components. According to Hameroff, the structure of these protein polymers, their dynamic activities, and the lack of a clear alternative understanding of cognition have led to theoretical consideration of dynamic cytoskeletal activities as functional information processing models such as cellular automata and holograms. Complex and highly connected as neuronal branches are (i.e., dendritic trees), the cytoskeleton within all neurons may be a forest within those trees. The intraneuronal cytoskeleton is the nervous system within the nervous system. Hebb's linkage of learning and synaptic efficacy may also operate within cytoskeletal networks.

11.6 LEARNING RULES

Multilevel perceptrons are also called *parallel distributed processing* systems (PDP). In PDP systems, the programs and the data patterns themselves are not stored. Rather, what is stored is the connection strengths between units that allow these patterns to be recreated. PDP systems could serve as a pattern associator between two sets of units. One set could serve as a visual pattern, the other set as an acoustic pattern for the same object. Learning or building the knowledge structure in PDP systems involves modifying the patterns of interconnectivity. Rumelhart et al.[11,12] define the process of learning using the notation of Figure 11.9.

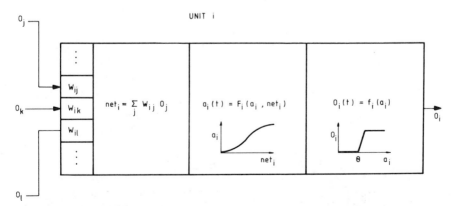

Figure 11.9 *The basic components of a parallel distributed processing system.*

Output from the unit j, O_j is connected to the input of unit i through the weight w_{ij}. The net input is usually the weighted sum of all inputs to the unit. The state of activation a_i is a function F of the old state a_i and of the net input. The useful, frequently used activation function is a sigmoid function, Figure 11.10. The output O_i is a function f of the activation state. The useful, frequently used f function is the threshold function.

Different learning rules to modify the pattern of connectivity as a function of experience have been developed. These include: 11–15 Hebbian learning; the Delta rule; competitive learning; the Hopfield minimum-energy rule; the generalized Delta rule; Sigma-Pi units; and the Boltzmann learning algorithm.

Hebbian Learning Without a Teacher

$$\Delta w_{ij} = \eta a_i o_j \tag{11.3}$$

where η is the constant of proportionality representing the learning rate. A simple version of Equation 11.3 is this: where unit i and unit j are simultaneously excited, the strength of the connection between them increases in proportion to the product of their activations.

The Delta Rule or Widrow-Hoff Rule With a Teacher

$$\Delta w_{ij} = \eta[t_i(t) - a_i(t)] \cdot o_j(t) \tag{11.4}$$

The amount of learning is proportional to the difference between the actual activation achieved and the target activation $t_i(t)$ provided by the teacher.

The Competitive Learning Rule Without a Teacher.
This rule allows the units to compete in some way for the right to respond to a given subset of input. The competitive rules have been developed by von der Marlsburg,[16] Grossberg,[17]

a

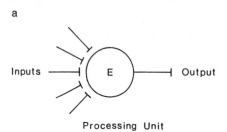

Processing Unit

b

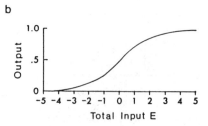

Figure 11.10
(a) *Schematic model of a processing unit receiving inputs from other processing units;* (b) *transformation between summed inputs and output of a processing unit.*

Fukushima,[18] Fukushima and Miyaki,[19] and Kohonen.[20] According to Rumelhart and Zipser,[15] the units in a given layer are broken into a set of nonoverlapping clusters. Each unit within a cluster inhibits every other unit within a cluster. The clusters are winner-take-all, such that the unit receiving the largest input achieves its maximum value (1) while all other units in the cluster are pushed to their minimum value (0). The fixed total amount of weight for unit j is designated $\sum_i w_{ij} = 1$. A unit learns by shifting weight from its inactive to its active input lines:

$$\Delta w_{ij} = 0 \qquad \text{if unit } j \text{ loses on stimulus } k$$

$$\Delta w_{ij} = g \cdot \frac{c_{ik}}{n_k} - g \cdot w_{ij} \qquad \text{if unit } j \text{ wins on stimulus } k \qquad (11.5)$$

where C_{ik} is equal to 1 if in stimulus pattern S_k, unit i in the lower layer is active and zero otherwise, n_k is the number of active units in pattern S_k, and g is a proportionality constant. See Section 11.7.

Grossberg has developed a similar rule, of the form

$$\Delta w_{ij} = \eta a_i(t) \left[o_j(t) - w_{ij} \right] \qquad (11.6)$$

The Hopfield Minimum-Energy Rule. Hopfield's study[21] concentrates on the units that are symmetrically connected (i.e., $w_{ij} = w_{ji}$). The units are always in one of two states: $+1$ or -1. The global "energy" of the system is defined as

$$E = -\sum_{i<j} w_{ij} s_i s_j + \sum \theta_i s_i \qquad (11.7)$$

$$\Delta E_k = \sum_i w_{ki} s_i - \theta_k \qquad (11.8)$$

where s_i is the state of the ith unit (-1 or 1); θ_i is a threshold; and ΔE_k is the difference between the energy of the whole system with the kth hypothesis false and its energy with the kth hypothesis true. See Sections 11.9 and 11.10.

The Generalized Delta Rule. All the rules presented so far have been developed for two-layer networks: input layer + output layer. Three or more layers in networks present special problems: how to modify an inner or hidden layer (associative layers). One response is unsupervised competitive learning, which generates useful hidden-unit connections. The second response is to assume a hidden-unit connection matrix, on some a priori grounds. The third response is the modification of the hidden units through the backward propagation of error. The determination of error starts with the output units, and then propagates to the next hidden layer, until it reaches the input units. This kind of learning is called the *generalized Delta rule*. The rule for changing weights following presentation of input/output pair p is given by[14]

$$\Delta_p w_{ji} = \eta \delta_{pj} o_{pi} \qquad (11.9)$$

where: o_{pj} = the jth element of the actual output pattern produced by the presentation of input pattern p

o_{pi} = the value of the ith element of the input pattern

$\Delta_p w_{ji}$ = the change to be made to the weight from the ith to the jth unit following presentation of the pattern p

The error signal δ_{pj} depends on the derivative of the activation function. The most frequently used function is

$$o_{pj} = \frac{1}{1 + e^{-\sum_i W_{ji} O_{pi} + \theta_j}} = \frac{1}{1 + e^{-E_i}} \tag{11.10}$$

where θ_j is a bias similar in function to the threshold. The function is shown in Figure 11.10. For the above function, the error signal δ_{pj} for an output unit is given by

$$\delta_{pj} = (t_{pj} - o_{pj}) o_{pj} (1 - o_{pj}) \tag{11.11}$$

where t_{pj} is the jth component of the target output pattern. The error signal δ_{pj} for an arbitrary hidden layer j is given by

$$\delta_{pj} = o_{pj} (1 - o_{pj}) \sum_k \delta_{pk} w_{kj} \tag{11.12}$$

where $\sum_k$ is the weighted sum of the deltas to which the unit sends activation via outgoing connections. For mathematical analysis as well as for application examples see Rumelhart et al.[14] Other recent approaches include Barto,[22] Barto and Anandan,[23] Parker,[24] and Le Cun.[25] See section 11.8.

Sigma-Pi Units.   The most common "additive units" form the connections through the addition: $\sum w_{ij} a_i$. More elaborate "Sigma-Pi units" form the connections using both addition and multiplication. The net input is given by

$$\sum w_{ij} \prod a_{i_1} a_{i_2} \ldots a_{i_k}$$

where i indexes the conjuncts impinging on unit j and $u_{i_1}, u_{i_2}, \ldots, u_{i_k}$ are the k units in the conjunct. Sigma-Pi units can be used for elaborate models. These include

- Gates; weighted connections
- Dynamically programmable networks in which the activation value of some units determine what another network can do
- Mimicking different monotonic activation and interconnection functions

Learning rules discussed so far can be modified for application on Sigma-Pi units.

The Boltzmann Learning Algorithm. This algorithm is designed for a machine with symmetrical connections. While the binary threshold in perceptron is deterministic, in a Boltzmann machine it is probabilistic:

$$p_i^{\,\prime} = P(\Delta E_i) = \frac{1}{1 + e^{-\Delta E_i/T}}$$

where p_i is the probability for the ith unit to be in state 1; $P(x)$ is a sigmoidal probability function (Figure 11.10); T is a parameter analogous to temperature and is a measure of the noise introduced into the decision; and the total input to the unit is

$$\Delta E_i = \sum w_{ij} s_j$$

The Boltzmann learning algorithm is closely related to the maximum likelihood methods. It has been designed to solve a class of optimization problems in vision.[26-29]

The learning is supervised: the input units are clamped to a particular pattern, while the network relaxes into a state of low energy in which the output units have the correct values. Due to the symmetry, the energy gradient with respect to W_{ij} depends only on the behavior of the ith and jth units and not on the whole network. This fact helps in updating input, output, and hidden units.

11.7 THE NEOCOGNITRON

Fukushima and Miyaki[19] have developed an algorithm for pattern classification without supervised learning. The algorithm is named the *neocognitron*. The neocognitron recognizes stimulus patterns correctly, without being affected by shifts in position or even by considerable distortion in shape. The algorithm is suggested by the structure of the visual neural system.

The neocognitron is a self-organized multilayer network. The network is based on the principles that only maximum-output cells have their input interconnections reinforced and that no instructions from a teacher are necessary. The neocognitron has a hierarchical structure. Each layer is used to extract some of the features from the pattern, with the cells in deeper layers responding to more complicated features. Hence, the pattern is broken into features. Several patterns contain the same feature.

All the cells employed in the neocognitron are of analog type. The inputs are either excitatory or inhibitory. The input-output relation coincides with the logarithmic relation expressed by Weber-Fechner's law and has a form of an S-shaped saturation (Figure 11.10). The same expression is often used as an empirical formula in neurophysiology and psychology to approximate the nonlinear input-output relations of the sensory systems in living organisms.

The cells in any simple layer are sorted into subgroups according to the optimum stimulus features of their respective fields. In a computer simulation of the neocognitron, five training patterns, 0, 1, 2, 3, and 4 are used. After repeated presentation of these five patterns, the neocognitron gradually acquires the ability to classify these patterns. The neocognitron recognizes these patterns even if they are distorted in shape or contaminated with noise.

Rosenblatt's model[4] was based on research into Hebb's hypothesis, which says that a single neural pathway is reinforced each time it is used. Fukushima modified Hebb's hypothesis by requiring that the connection be reinforced only when the receiving cell alone responds, as compared with its neighbors. In other words, only paths that stimulate individual cells and inhibit the surrounding cells are reinforced. Hence, the neocognitron is based on competitive learning.

The cognitron, developed nearly 10 years ago, performed recognition of symbols from any alphabet after being trained merely by having symbols presented to it. No manual programming was required. But the cognitron had a deficiency—it could not recognize patterns that were shifted in position or distorted. So Fukushima sought a way to recognize things distorted in shape and shifted in position. Enter the neocognitron.

The neocognitron is a multistage pattern-recognizer/feature-extractor that simulates the way visual information feeds forward in the human brain's cortex. It uses successive stages which can recognize patterns, regardless of position or distortion. As it goes deeper through successive stages, the position of the symbol in the input pattern becomes less and less important.

On the highest level, patterns are unique and distinct, but as the successive stages are activated, a pattern tends to stimulate the same cells regardless of how the pattern is shifted or distorted. Eventually a level is reached where a single cell reacts for each training pattern. In the early stages (there are nine stages in the current handwriting recognition system) many cells are activated; in successive stages, however, fewer are activated until only a single cell is activated on level nine for each character in the alphabet.

This method of "reverse reproduction" simplifies training by allowing a deep cell to activate the network backwards, causing the pattern it is trained for to appear in the first layer of the input cells. The column structure of the brain, according to Fukushima,[18] is attributable to each stage recognizing the same pattern, but at different shifted and distorted positions.

11.8 NETtalk: A PARALLEL NETWORK THAT LEARNS TO READ ALOUD

NETtalk is a massively parallel network that converts unrestricted English text into speech. NETtalk is based on the incremental learning that establishes the strength or weight and connections in the system (the connectionist model). The system is composed of three layers and can solve problems that are beyond the capability of networks with a single layer of modifiable weights (perceptrons). Several multilayer architectures have been reported recently.[11-14]

NETtalk has been developed by Sejnowski and Rosenberg.[30,31]

The network is composed of a large number of identical processing units. Each unit receives the input from many other units in the layer below. The output is a function of the net input, (Figure 11.10). Positive connection strength, or weight linking one unit to another represent excitatory influence, while negative weight represents inhibitory influence.

The network is hierarchically arranged into three layers of units: an input layer, an output layer, and an intermediate or "hidden" layer, as illustrated in Figure 11.11.

According to Sejnowski and Rosenberg,[30,31] there are seven groups of units in the input layer, and one group of units in each of the other two layers. Each input group encodes one letter of the input text, so that strings of seven letters are presented to the input units at any one time. The desired output of the network is the correct phoneme, or contrastive speech sound, associated with the center, or fourth, letter of this seven letter "window." The other six letters (three on either side of the center letter) provide a partial context for this decision. The text is stepped through the window letter-by-letter. At each step, the network computes a phoneme, and after each word the weights are adjusted according to how closely the computed pronunciation matches the correct one.

The discrepancy between the desired and actual values of the output is used to adjust the weights. For each phoneme, this discrepancy was "backpropagated" from the output to the input layer using the learning algorithm introduced by

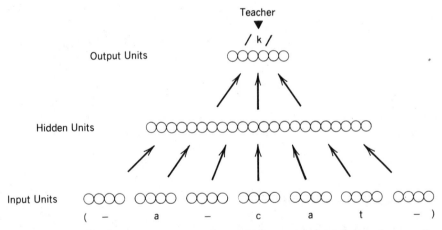

Figure 11.11 *Schematic drawing of the network architecture. Input units are shown on the bottom of the pyramid, with seven groups of 29 units in each group. Each hidden unit in the intermediate layer receives inputs from all of the input units on the bottom layer, and in turn sends its output to all 26 units in the output layer. An example of an input string of letters is shown below the input groups, and the correct output phoneme for the middle letter is shown above the output layer. For 80 hidden units, which were used for the corpus of continuous informal speech, there was a total of 309 units and 18,629 weights in the network, including a variable threshold for each unit. Adapted from Sejnowski and Rosenberg.[30]*

Rumelhart and McClelland.[11] Each weight in the network is adjusted to minimize its contribution to the total mean square error between the desired and actual outputs.

The NETtalk network with 120 hidden units was tested on a randomized dictionary of 20,012 words. [The performance was 90% best guesses and 48% perfect matches.] This level of performance was achieved using a window of only seven letters. It is expected that the network analyzing larger parts of sentences could reach even higher performance levels.

It is interesting to compare the NETtalk with commercial text-to-speech systems, such as DECtalk.[32] Commercial systems use a look-up table of about a million bits to store the phonetic transcription of words. For the words that are not in the table, phonological rules are applied to produce the string of phonemes. The phonemes are converted to sounds with a digital speech synthesizer.

In the NETtalk, a massively parallel network learns how to convert the string of letters into a correct string of phonemes. No look-up table, no phonological rules. The network acquired its competence through practice. The information is distributed in the network in such a way that no single unit or link is essential.

According to Sejnowski and Rosenberg[31] the NETtalk has some similarities with observed human performance:

- Learning follows a power law.
- The more words the network learns, the better it is at generalizing and correctly pronouncing new words.
- The performance of the network degrades very slowly as connections in the network are damaged.
- Relearning after damage is much faster than learning during the original training.

The network could be easily trained on any language with the same set of letters and phonemes. It also could be used as a research tool to explore neural networks, training, coding, and scaling. It also presents a simple model of the process of learning the language and of reading skills in humans. The future promises more elaborate adaptive networks for commercial and for research areas.

11.9   THE TRAVELING SALESPERSON

Hopfield[21] has developed the minimum-energy learning algorithm, and has used it to solve the very tough problem of the traveling Salesperson: given a list of cities, what is the shortest route a salesperson can take and still make a sales call in every city?[33] This problem entails a high level of combinative complexity. A N-city tour, for example, has $N!/2N$ possible tours. It could easily take hours of computational time on a classical computer. By comparison, a neural-network computer finds the answer in a fraction of a second.

Hopfield has arranged a set of connections with neurons in rows and columns. Figure 11.12 shows a case of six cities and a network of $6 \times 6 = 36$ neurons. In general, for N cities a network of N^2 neurons is needed. The rows A, B, C, D, E, and F correspond to the cities on the tour. The columns 1, 2, 3, 4, 5, and 6 indicate the position of the city on the tour. The solution is indicated by the most active neurons (the black nodes in Figure 11.12). Thus the shortest route obtained in Figure 11.12 is this one: first, city D; second, city B; third, city F; fourth, city C; fifth, city A; and last, city E.

Obviously, in each row and in each column there can be only one active neuron. All other neurons in the same row and column are suppressed or inhibited. Necessary inhibitory connections are shown for neurons B2 and D5. Each neuron also has a stimulating connection to all other neurons. Each connection indicates one possible route/phase between two cities. The connection strength represents the distance between two cities.

The network finds the solution through a number of iterations. In each iteration, the network is modified using the minimum-energy learning algorithm, Equations 11.7 and 11.8. Consequently, repeated iterations are guaranteed to find an energy minimum. It is possible, however, that the system gets stuck at local minimums that are not globally optimal. This is avoided by "shaking" or "annealing" processes, which allow the state of the network to escape from local minima.

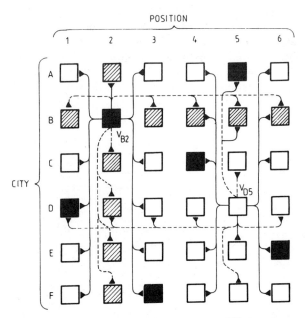

Figure 11.12 *Connective syntax for a salesperson problem.*[33,34] *Partial connectivity for two neurons (B2 and D5) is shown. Dark: active neurons; shaded: neurons inhibited by* V_{B2}.

The neural network doesn't always find the best answer, just a good one, or often several good enough answers. However, the answer is found very quickly and with a minimum of hardware. By comparison, a typical classical computer has about 10^4 times as many devices as a neural net.

11.10 BIDIRECTIONAL ASSOCIATIVE MEMORY AS A PATTERN ASSOCIATOR

Pattern associators are systems in which a pattern of activation over one pool of units can cause a pattern of activation over another pool of units. In this way the system associates responses with sensory stimuli, effect with cause, character with face, voice with image, a set of templates with a set of input patterns. The association is stored in the strengths of interconnections between units. The knowledge about any individual pattern is not stored in the special part of the connection network reserved for that pattern, but is distributed over the network.

Simple pattern associator is bidirectional associative memory BAM. BAM connects two pools or layers of units. Each node in one layer is connected to all the nodes of the opposite layer. The connection is symmetrical: $w_{ij} = w_{ji}$. Here we follow an example with the first layer of six neurons and the second layer of four neurons. The connection matrix has $6 \times 4 = 24$ elements. The two layers and the matrix are shown in Figure 11.13.

The learning in the matrix is based on Grossberg[35] reciprocal outstar coding. It has been found that BAM correlation encoding improves if bipolar vectors and matrices are used instead of binary vectors and matrices. Bipolar vectors and matrices are obtained from binary with -1s replacing Os. Hence the binary pattern $A = (100\ 101)$ becomes bipolar pattern $X = (1 - 1 - 11 - 11)$.

The binary pair of patterns (A_1B_1) is replaced by a bipolar pair (X_1Y_1). Then the bipolar correlation matrix $X_1^T Y_1$ is formed, where the column vector X_1^T is the vector transpose of the row vector X_1. For example, if $X_1 = (-1, 1, -1)$, then

$$X^T = \begin{array}{c} -1 \\ 1 \\ -1 \end{array}$$

	b_1	b_2	b_3	b_4
a_1	1	1	1	1
a_2	1	-3	1	1
a_3	3	-1	-1	3
a_4	-3	1	1	-3
a_5	-1	3	-1	-1
a_6	3	-1	-1	3

Figure 11.13 *Bidirectional Associative Memory as a Pattern Associator.*

Many association pairs can be stored one over another in the same correlation matrix. Example shows the storage of three associations: (A_1B_1) (A_2B_2), and (A_3B_3).

$$A_1 = 101011 \qquad B_1 = (1101)$$
$$A_2 = 111001 \qquad B_2 = (1011)$$
$$A_3 = 100110 \qquad B_3 = (0110)$$

We follow the notation and the algorithm reported by Kosko.[36]

1. Convert binary pairs into bipolar pairs:

$$X_1 = (1 - 11 - 111) \qquad Y_1 = (11 - 11)$$
$$X_2 = (111 - 1 - 11) \qquad Y_2 = (1 - 111)$$
$$X_3 = (1 - 1 - 111 - 1) \qquad Y_3 = (-111 - 1)$$

2. Convert bipolar pairs into bipolar correlation matrices $X_i^T Y_i$.
   The jth column is X multiplied by the jth element of Y. Similarly the jth row is Y multiplied by the jth element of X.

$$X_1^T Y_1 = \begin{array}{rrrr} 1 & 1 & -1 & 1 \\ -1 & -1 & 1 & -1 \\ 1 & 1 & -1 & 1 \\ -1 & -1 & 1 & -1 \\ 1 & 1 & -1 & 1 \\ 1 & 1 & -1 & 1 \end{array}$$

$$X_2^T Y_2 = \begin{array}{rrrr} 1 & -1 & 1 & 1 \\ 1 & -1 & 1 & 1 \\ 1 & -1 & 1 & 1 \\ -1 & 1 & -1 & -1 \\ -1 & 1 & -1 & -1 \\ 1 & -1 & 1 & 1 \end{array}$$

$$X_3^T Y_3 = \begin{array}{rrrr} -1 & 1 & 1 & -1 \\ 1 & -1 & -1 & 1 \\ 1 & -1 & -1 & 1 \\ -1 & 1 & 1 & -1 \\ -1 & 1 & 1 & -1 \\ 1 & -1 & -1 & 1 \end{array}$$

3. Add up the bipolar correlation matrices, $M = X_1^T Y_1 + X_2^T Y_2 + X_3^T Y_3$, Figure 11.13:

$$M = \begin{array}{rrrr} 1 & 1 & 1 & 1 \\ 1 & -3 & 1 & 1 \\ 3 & -1 & -1 & 3 \\ -3 & 1 & 1 & -3 \\ -1 & 3 & -1 & -1 \\ 3 & -1 & -1 & 3 \end{array}$$

This is the end of the encoding procedure. Matrix M stores the three associations: (A_1B_1), (A_2B_2), and (A_3B_3). To prove this, we go into the decoding procedure: if the vector A_1 is presented to the BAM, it should evoke the vector B_1. Similarly A_2 should evoke B_2, A_3 should evoke B_3.

The vector A is composed of six neurons, a_1 to a_6. The vector B is composed of four neurons, b_1 to b_4. Each neuron in A fans out to all the neurons in B. The neuron b_j receives a fan-in of input products

$$a_1w_{1j} + a_2w_{2j} + \cdots + a_nw_{nj}$$

In other words the fan-in input received by B is AM. In case of A_1 (101011) the vector $A_1M = (6 \ 2 - 2 \ 6)$. The threshold converts this fan-in into the binary vector $(1101) = B_1$. This proves that the A_1 evokes B_1. Similarly A_2 evokes B_2 and A_3 evokes B_3:

$$A_1M = (6 \ 2 - 2 \ 6) \qquad \text{or binary } (1101) = B_1$$

$$A_2M = (8 - 4 \ 0 \ 8) \qquad \text{or binary } (1011) = B_2$$

$$A_3M = (- \ 3 \ 5 \ 1 - 3) \qquad \text{or binary } (0110) = B_3$$

The association operates both ways. If vector B is presented to the system, it should evoke the vector A. In this case the fan-in input received by A is BM^T (switching rows and columns). Some examples are:

$$B_1M^T = (3 - 1 \ 5 - 5 \ 1 \ 5) \qquad \text{or binary } (101011) = A_1$$

$$B_2M^T = (3 \ 3 \ 5 - 5 - 3 \ 5) \qquad \text{or binary } (111001) = A_2$$

$$B_3M^T = (2 - 2 - 222 - 2) \qquad \text{or binary } (100110) = A_3$$

BAM does not require a perfect copy of the input to produce the correct output. BAM will recognize incomplete and noisy patterns, and it will operate even if a part of the network is damaged. Thus the system degrades gracefully both under degraded input and under damage.

As an example we examine the input A_4 (001011), which is A_1 perturbed by 1 bit. Then $A_4M = (5 \ 1 - 3 \ 5)$ or binary $(1101) = B_1$. Hence similar but not identical input evokes the correct association. This feature does not exist in the rule-based logic.

The BAM operates on the minimum energy principle. The energy is defined as

$$E(A_iB_i) = -A_iMB_i$$

Hence

$$E(A_1B_1) = -(6\ \ 2 - 2\ \ 6)(1101) = -14$$

In the examples above, the energy is:

$$E(A_1B_1) = -14$$

$$E(A_2B_2) = -16$$

$$E(A_3B_3) = -6$$

$$E(A_4B_1) = -11$$

Note that $E(A_1B_1) = -14 < -11 = E(A_4B_1)$, evidence that the BAM encoding procedure placed (A_1B_1) at a local energy minimum. Figure 11.14 outlines the BAM demonstration program written in BASIC by D. De Sieno, R. Taber, and J. Davis, and reported by Kosko.[36] Figure 11.15 illustrates BAM recall. Field A

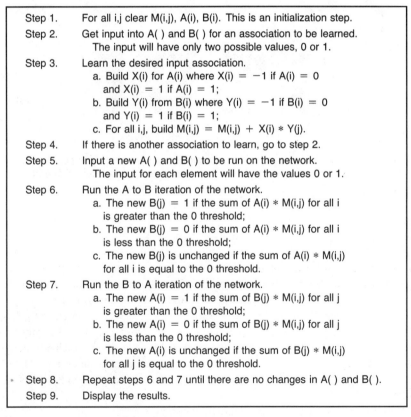

Step 1.	For all i,j clear M(i,j), A(i), B(i). This is an initialization step.
Step 2.	Get input into A( ) and B( ) for an association to be learned. The input will have only two possible values, 0 or 1.
Step 3.	Learn the desired input association. a. Build X(i) for A(i) where X(i) = −1 if A(i) = 0 and X(i) = 1 if A(i) = 1; b. Build Y(i) from B(i) where Y(i) = −1 if B(i) = 0 and Y(i) = 1 if B(i) = 1; c. For all i,j, build M(i,j) = M(i,j) + X(i) ∗ Y(j).
Step 4.	If there is another association to learn, go to step 2.
Step 5.	Input a new A( ) and B( ) to be run on the network. The input for each element will have the values 0 or 1.
Step 6.	Run the A to B iteration of the network. a. The new B(j) = 1 if the sum of A(i) ∗ M(i,j) for all i is greater than the 0 threshold; b. The new B(j) = 0 if the sum of A(i) ∗ M(i,j) for all i is less than the 0 threshold; c. The new B(j) is unchanged if the sum of A(i) ∗ M(i,j) for all i is equal to the 0 threshold.
Step 7.	Run the B to A iteration of the network. a. The new A(i) = 1 if the sum of B(j) ∗ M(i,j) for all j is greater than the 0 threshold; b. The new A(i) = 0 if the sum of B(j) ∗ M(i,j) for all j is less than the 0 threshold; c. The new A(i) is unchanged if the sum of B(j) ∗ M(i,j) for all j is equal to the 0 threshold.
Step 8.	Repeat steps 6 and 7 until there are no changes in A( ) and B( ).
Step 9.	Display the results.

Figure 11.14 *BAM demonstration program written in* BASIC. *Reprinted with permission from Kosko*[36].

Figure 11.15 *Asynchronous recall in a BAM consisting of two fields of neurons, one containing 140 neurons and another containing 108 neurons. Reprinted with permission from Kosko* [36].

contains $n = 10 \times 14 = 140$ neurons. Field B contains $p = 9 \times 12 = 108$ neurons. Both fields are arranged as binary matrices to help the eye detect interesting spatial patterns. The BAM stores the three alphabetic associations: (M, V), (S, E) and (G, N). A 40% noise corrupted version (99 bits randomly flipped) of (S, E) is presented to the BAM. Figure 11.15 shows 11 snapshots of the asynchronous recall process, starting with the local chaos and reaching the global order.

The BAM goes through a series of resonating steps. If a value close to S, say S^{III}, is input into the BAM, an approximation, E^{III}, will appear at the other part on the first iteration. If E^{III} is then returned to the part from which it emerged, then something close to S, say S^{II}, will appear at the original input part. The process is repeated until the BAM resonates and zeros in on the exact values of E and S.

Note that BAM maps data to data. In general:

• Associative memory (AM) maps data to data,

- Random access memory (RAM) maps addresses to data,
- Content addressable memory (CAM) maps data to addresses.

11.11 KOSKO FUZZY COGNITIVE MAPS AND FUZZY ENTROPY

11.11.1 Adaptive Maps

Standard expert systems consist of a collection of condition-action rules or implications with associated uncertainty factors. A powerful application of the present fuzzy knowledge combination theory is to allow several weighted experts, not just one, to determine the uncertainty weights. Different subsets of experts with different credibility weights can be used for different rules. Again the generality obtained from a poset structure tends to increase expert concurrence.

According to Kosko,[37,38] this fuzzy knowledge combination theory is especially useful for combining arbitrary fuzzy cognitive maps. In fact, this theory was initiated by just this application. The idea is to let knowledge sources draw and amend causal pictures, and have them drawn and amended for them, to form huge connected knowledge bases in arbitrary problem domains. A fragment of such a fuzzy causal picture from the soft knowledge domain of international sociology is shown in Figure 11.16.

Here the nodes represent variables causal concept nodes, or simply fuzzy sets. A variable quantity like SOCIAL STABILITY can be a node. Arbitrary data, like newspaper reports, activate all the nodes to different degrees. The directed fuzzy edges represent causality. Fuzzy poset values or weights like *usually* indicate degree of causality. Plus (+) indicates causal increase and minus (−) indicates causal decrease (e.g., if price inflation increases, then social stability usually decreases; if price inflation decreases, then social stability usually increases). On a numeric restriction on the fuzzy causal weights, dynamic (adaptive feedback)

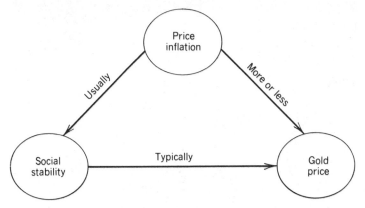

Figure 11.16 *Soft knowledge domain: international society. Courtesy and copyright* ©*1987 by Kosko.*

fuzzy cognitive maps obey a non-Hebbian learning law and further subsume standard rule-set inference engine and neural net models.[37,38] Dynamic fuzzy cognitive maps also exhibit many associative memory properties.

If many arbitrary knowledge sources, suitably weighted, are queried about the strengths of arbitrary causal connections, then the present fuzzy knowledge combination theory can be applied to quickly produce a single fuzzy cognitive map. Such maps can easily possess millions, even billions, of causal concept nodes and orders of magnitude more causal connections. They can further be augmented and modified as more knowledge sources respond, as they change their responses in light of evidence or other responses, or as they are dynamically reweighted. At this point, fuzzy poset versions of many *artificial neural system*[39-41] properties— adaptive, resonance, avalanche activation, rapid spatiotemporal pattern classification—can occur, often without any one mind (or computer) perceiving their occurrence. In principle the knowledge of the ages could be stored in such huge fuzzy cognitive maps (FCM). Indeed such knowledge would only initiate, not culminate, the dynamic map learning process.

Kosko[37,38] considers a simple example. Suppose four unweighted experts provide simple FCMs as shown in Figure 11.17. There are six distinct concept nodes. Each expert uses only four concepts. We can represent these FCMs by four 6-by-6 augmented connection matrices:

$$\mathbf{F}_1 = \begin{pmatrix} 0 & 1 & -1 & 1 & 0 & 0 \\ 0 & 0 & 0 & -1 & 0 & 0 \\ -1 & 1 & 0 & -1 & 0 & 0 \\ 0 & 0 & 1 & 0 & 0 & 0 \\ 0 & 0 & 0 & 0 & 0 & 0 \\ 0 & 0 & 0 & 0 & 0 & 0 \end{pmatrix} \qquad \mathbf{F}_2 = \begin{pmatrix} 0 & 1 & -1 & 0 & 1 & 0 \\ 1 & 0 & -1 & 0 & 1 & 0 \\ -1 & -1 & 0 & 0 & 1 & 0 \\ 0 & 0 & 0 & 0 & 0 & 0 \\ 0 & 1 & -1 & 0 & 0 & 0 \\ 0 & 0 & 0 & 0 & 0 & 0 \end{pmatrix}$$

$$\mathbf{F}_3 = \begin{pmatrix} 0 & 1 & -1 & 0 & 0 & 0 \\ 1 & 0 & 1 & 0 & 0 & -1 \\ -1 & -1 & 0 & 0 & 0 & 1 \\ 0 & 0 & 0 & 0 & 0 & 0 \\ 0 & 0 & 0 & 0 & 0 & 0 \\ 1 & -1 & -1 & 0 & 0 & 0 \end{pmatrix} \qquad \mathbf{F}_4 = \begin{pmatrix} 0 & 1 & 0 & 0 & 1 & -1 \\ -1 & 0 & 0 & 0 & 1 & 1 \\ 0 & 0 & 0 & 0 & 0 & 0 \\ 0 & 0 & 0 & 0 & 0 & 0 \\ 1 & 0 & 0 & 0 & 0 & -1 \\ 1 & -1 & 0 & 0 & -1 & 0 \end{pmatrix}$$

which combine to yield FCM connection matrix F,

$$\begin{pmatrix} 0 & 4 & -3 & 1 & 2 & -1 \\ 1 & 0 & 0 & -1 & 2 & 0 \\ -3 & -1 & 0 & -1 & 1 & 1 \\ 0 & 0 & 1 & 0 & 0 & 0 \\ 1 & 1 & -1 & 0 & 0 & -1 \\ 2 & -2 & -1 & 0 & -1 & 0 \end{pmatrix}$$

Inference occurs on a FCM as data-driven activation flows through FCM edges and nodes. The causal edge structure is the logical structure that represents empiri-

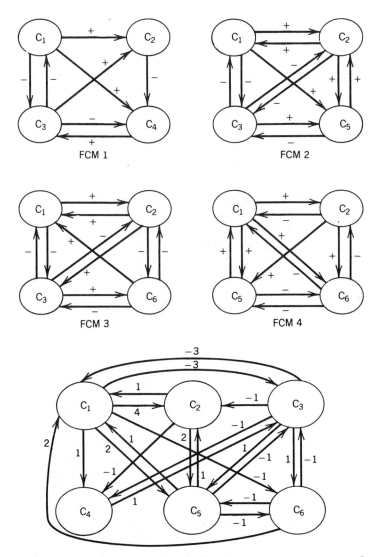

Figure 11.17 *Partial and combined fuzzy cognitive maps. Courtesy and copyright ©1987 by Kosko.*

cal hypotheses. This is clear when causal edges are viewed as fuzzy logical implications (or conditional probabilities). *Adaptive* inference occurs when this logical
structure itself is modified by data. Persistent activation of FCM concepts gradually
shapes the inferential mechanisms housed by the FCM connection matrix.

The FCM combination technique described by Kosko is a simple form of
adaptive inferencing. It represents a recursive "learning" procedure for gradually
modifying connection strengths as new causal information becomes available in the
form of weighted expert opinion. A new FCM can always be added to the current

combined FCM by suitably augmenting the new FCM matrix or the combined FCM matrix, or both. Once several FCMs have been combined in a problem domain, new FCMs are less likely to contain new concepts. More important, since each new FCM matrix contains weighted elements in $[-1, 1]$ and the unnormalized strength of a combined edge is in $[-k, k]$, the addition of a new FCM matrix is not likely to significantly change the magnitude of an arbitrary combined edge and is even less likely to change its sign.

The problem of adaptive inference can be stated as a question. How can the causal structure of an environment be inferred? Which things are connected to which things and how? One answer is to ask an expert. To the extent that such information is available it should be incorporated in the inferential structure. But how did the expert obtain this knowledge? Surely it came directly or indirectly from observation, from sensing and perhaps measuring the flux of experience. Experience enters the FCM model by additively entering the equation for a concept node's activation. If the activation of the ith node C_i is some real number x_i, then the simplest model for causal activation is equivalent to the additive short-term memory model of a neuron's activation:

$$\dot{x}_i = -x_i + \sum_j C_j(x_j)\, e_{ji} + I_i,$$

where C_j is a sigmoid function. The first term is passive causal decay. Something happens only if something causally makes it happen. The second term is path-weighted internal feedback. The third term is external input, raw observation.

11.11.2 Fuzzy Entropy

Fuzzy logic deals with intuitive constructs such as "small," "medium," or "tall." For example, a 5-foot man would have partial or fuzzy membership in the set of "medium," and also in the set of "small." This partial membership may be expressed through a unit on a scale of 0 to 1. This fuzzy unit, or *fit*, replaces bit in normal, "crisp" logic.

A fuzzy message is a vector composed of several fits. Examples of 3-fit messages would be:

$$A = (0.4,\ 0,\ 0.8)$$

$$B = (1,\ 0.3,\ 0.8)$$

$$\overline{\rule{4cm}{0.4pt}}$$

$$l = 0.6 + 0.3 + 0 = 0.9$$

The value l is the fuzzy Hamming distance between the messages A and B.

The nonfuzzy message nearest to A is obtained by adjusting each fit to the nearest bit:

$$\overline{A} = (0,\ 0,\ 1)$$

Conversely, Kosko[37] introduces the nonfuzzy message farthest from A:

$$\underline{A} = (1, 1, 0)$$

Kosko[37] defines the fuzzy entropy, to measure the information content of fuzzy sets, as shown in Figure 11.18. Consider two distances:

The distance a between A and $\overline{A}$
The distance b between A and $\underline{A}$

Note that if $\underline{A}$ is nonfuzzy, then $\overline{A} = A$, and hence $a = 0$. Now suppose $A = P = (0.5, 0.5, 0.5)$. Then A is equidistant to all nonfuzzy sets. Hence $a = b$. Finally, note for the complement A^c, that the distance $(A^c, A) = a$, and the distance $(A^c, \overline{A}) = b$. These intuitions suggest taking the ratio a/b as the fuzzy entropy:

$$R(A) = \frac{a}{b}$$

In the extreme case in which the fuzzy message becomes crisp, fuzzy entropy is zero. An opposite case is the message $A = P = (0.5, 0.5, 0.5)$, with fuzzy entropy becoming 1. Thus, fuzzy entropy is defined over the range (0,1).

Combined research[11-42] in BAM, FCM, fuzzy entropy, and fuzzy-set theory opens a new avenue toward brain-like devices and systems.

The entropy is the opposite of the information. It is related to unpredictable situations and to rare, informative events. According to Ostojić,[43] our time is determined by movement toward the increased entropy of the system. When a system has achieved maximum entropy, its state no longer changes and time stops. When a system reduces its entropy, the time of the system moves in the opposite direction. The system grows younger as it increases its information. The creation of new information depends on chance. Fleming discovered penicillin only because the right bit of mold accidentally fell into the Petri dish in which he was examining completely different micro-organisms.

The chance brings us to the mutation, and to genetic computers (see Chapter 13).

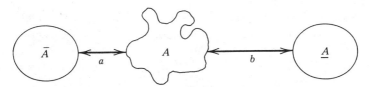

Figure 11.18 *Fuzzy message A, farthest nonfuzzy message $\underline{A}$, and nearest nonfuzzy message $\overline{A}$. Courtesy and copyright ©1987 by Kosko.*

11.12 STORAGE CAPACITY OF BAM AND FCM

Neural associative memory stores the data by super imposing them on the same memory medium.

The network in Figure 11.13 is called bidirectional associative memory, BAM. It is a two-layer feedback network of interconnected neurons. Each neuron, X_i of the layer X is connected to every neuron Y_j of the layer Y and vice versa. There are no connections within one layer. The learning procedure fixes the connecting weights w_{ij}. All connection information is contained in an n-by-p matrix M, where n and p are the numbers of nodes (neurons) in the layer Y and X respectively. The storage capacity is defined as $m < \min(n,p)$. In other words, m is the number of patterns that could be stored (encoded) and recalled (decoded) in the n by p system. The number of neurons or connections limits the storage capacity. The encoding procedure places the association between two patterns at or near system energy minima. An input pattern rolls down the energy surface into a particular local minimum. Convergion to the nearest minimum is immediate, regardless of the number of nodes or neurons in the system.

Each association pattern stores a basin of attraction in the BAM state space. A small number of association patterns result in a small number of large and deep basins, which are easy to identify. Large number of association patterns result in a large number of small and shallow basins, which are more difficult to identify. Spurious basins can emerge, causing misclassification.

REFERENCES

1. N.Y. Nilsson, *Learning Machines*. McGraw-Hill, New York, 1965.

2. W. McCulloch and W. Pitts, A logical calculus of the ideas immanent in nervous activity. *Bull. Math. Biophys.* **5**, 115–133 (1943).

3. D. Hebb, *Organization of Behavior*. Science Editions, New York, 1961.

4. F. Rosenblatt, *The Perceptron: A Perceiving and Recognizing Automation*, Proj. PARA, Cornell Aeronaut. Lab. Rep. 85-460-1. Cornell University, Ithaca, NY, 1957.

5. M. Souček, Dialogue-based learning library. *Proc. Int. Conf. Automaton Robots*, 61-67, Belgrade, 1987.

6. W.D. Van Nest, Term paper for the course 695BX. University of Arizona, Tucson, 1985.

7. D. Hestenes, How the brain works. In C.R. Smith (ed.), *Maximum Entropy*. Reidel Publ., Boston, MA, 1987.

8. S. Grossberg, *Studies of Mind and Brain*. Reidel Publ., Boston, MA, 1982.

9. S. Grossberg and M. Kuperstein, *Neural Dynamics of Adaptive Sensory Motor Control*. North-Holland Publ., New York, 1986.

10. R.S. Hameroff, *Ultimate Computing: Biomolecular Consciousness and Nanotechnology*. Am. Elsevier, New York, 1987.

11. D.E. Rumelhart and J.L. McClelland (ed.), *Parallel Distributed Processing. Explorations in the Microstructure of Cognition*. MIT Press, Cambridge, MA. 1986.

12. D.E. Rumelhart, G.E. Hinton, and J.L. McClelland, *A General Framework for Parallel Distributed Processing*. In Ref. 11, MIT Press, Cambridge, MA, pp. 45–46, (1986).

13. G.E. Hinton and T.J. Sejnowski, *Learning and Relearning in Boltzmann Machines*. MIT Press, Cambridge, MA, pp. 282–317, (1986).

14. D.E. Rumelhart, G.E. Hinton, and R.J. Williams, *Learning Internal Representations by Error Propagation*. In Ref. 11, MIT Press, Cambridge, MA, pp. 318–362, (1986).

15. D.E. Rumelhart and D. Zipser, *Feature Discovery by Competitive Learning*. In Ref. 11, MIT Press, Cambridge, MA, pp. 151–193, (1986).

16. C. von der Marlsburg, Self-organizing of orientation sensitive cells in the striated cortex. *Kybernetic* **14**, 85–100 (1973).

17. S. Grossberg, Adaptive pattern classification and universal recording. *Biol. Cybernet.* **23**, 121–134 (1976).

18. K. Fukushima, Cognitron: A self-organizing multilayered neural network. *Biol. Cybernet.* **20**, 121–136 (1975).

19. K. Fukushima and S. Miyaki, Neocognitron: A new algorithm for pattern recognition tolerant of deformations and shifts in position. *Pattern Recognition* **15**, (6), 455–469 (1982).

20. T. Kohonen, Clustering, taxonomy and topological maps of patterns. In M. Lang (ed.), *Pattern Recognition*. IEEE Computer Society Press, Silver Spring, MD, 1982.

21. J.J. Hopfield, Neural networks and physical systems with emergent collective computational abilities. *Proc. Natl. Acad. Sci. U.S.A.* **79**, 2554–2558 (1982).

22. A.G. Barto, *Learning by Statistical Cooperation of Self-Interested Neuron-Like Computing Elements*, COINS Tech. Rep. 85-11. University of Massachusetts, Amherst, 1985.

23. A.G. Barto and P. Anandan, Pattern recognizing stochastic learning automata. *IEEE Trans. Syst., Man, Cybernet.* **15**, 360–375 (1985).

24. D.B. Parker, *Learning Logic*, TR 47. Center for Computational Research in Economics and Management Science, MIT, Cambridge, MA, 1985.

25. Y. Le Cun, Une procédure d'apprentissage pour reseau à senil assymetrique. *Proc. Cognitiva* **85**, 599–604 (1985).

26. G.E. Hinton and T.J. Sejnowski, Optimal perceptual inference. *Proc. IEEE Comput. Soc. Conf. Comput. Vision Pattern Recognition*, 448–453 (1983).

27. S.E. Fahlman, G.E. Hinton, and T.J. Sejnowski, Massively parallel architectures for AI. *Proc. Natl. Conf. Artif. Intell.*, 109–113 (1983).

28. D.H. Ackley, G.E. Hinton, and T.J. Sejnowski, A learning algorithm for Boltzmann machines. *Cogn. Sci.* **9**, 147–169 (1985).

29. T.J. Sejnowski, P.K. Kienker, and G.E. Hinton, Learning symmetry groups with hidden units: Beyond the perceptron. *Physica D (Amsterdam)* **22D**, 260–275 (1986).

30. T.J. Sejnowski and C.R. Rosenberg, *NETtalk: A Parallel Network that Learns to Read Aloud*, Tech. Ref. THU/EECS-86/01. Johns Hopkins University, Baltimore, MD, 1986.

31. T.J. Sejnowski and C.R. Rosenberg, Parallel networks that learn to pronounce English text. *Complex Syst.* **1**, 145–168 (1987).

32. *DECtalk DTC01 Owner's Manual*, Doc. No. EK-DTC01-OM-002. Digital Equipment Corporation, Maynard, MA.

33. J.J. Hopfield and D. Tank, Neural computation of decisions in optimization problems. *Biol. Cybernet.*, **52**, 141–152 (1985).

34. Modified from T. Williams, *Comput. Des.* Mar. 1 (1987).

35. S. Grossberg, *The Adaptive Brain*, Vols. I and II. North-Holland Publ., Amsterdam, 1987.

36. B. Kosko, Constracting an associative memory. *Byte* **12** (10), 137–144 (1987).

37. B. Kosko, Fuzzy entropy and conditioning. *Inf. Sci.* **40**, 1–10 (1987).

38. B. Kosko, Fuzzy knowledge combination. *Int. Intell. Syst.* **1**, 293–320 (1986).

39. B. Kosko, Adaptive inference in fuzzy knowledge networks. *Proc. IEEE Int. Conf. Neural Networks, 1987.*

40. B. Kosko, Competitive adaptive bidirectional associative memories. *Proc. IEEE Int. Conf. Neural Networks, 1987.*

41. B. Kosko, Fuzzy associative memories. *Fuzzy Expert Syst.* (1987).

42. B. Kosko, Adaptive bidirectional associative memories. *Appl. Opt.* (1987).

43. B. Ostojić. *The Great Change, Book on Mind and Life* (to be published).

CHAPTER 12 ———————————————

Artificial Neural Systems or Neurocomputers

INTRODUCTION AND SURVEY

Large-scale adaptive learning systems are called *artificial neural systems* (ANS) or *neural computers*. An ANS mimics the brain's vast web of interconnected neurons. When a neuron fires in the brain, it broadcasts a signal to thousands of other neurons, which in turn alert millions more. The human brain has about 10^{10} neurons and 10^{13} interconnections, all of them operating in parallel. Presently available artificial neural systems have up to 1,000,000 processing elements and up to 10 million connections. Systems with 100 million processing elements are the next goal.

Each of many thousands of processing elements in an ANS is governed by the two difference equations: transfer function equation, and the learning equation. These equations follow processing principles of neural modeling formulated by neuroscientists. Hence, ANS systems differ from numerical computers and from symbolic processors such as LISP machines.

This chapter starts with the description of the commercially available ANS MARK III/IV developed by TRW for DARPA, as a part of the project ADAPT. The ANZA and DELTA neurocomputing coprocessors for IBM PC/AT compatible computers are described next.

The chapter describes the basic structures of ANS: instar, outstar, avalanche, associative memory. These structures are responsible for learning, near match recognition, and memory.

As an example of an application of ANS, a spatio temporal pattern classifier is presented. The chapter ends with the comparison table displaying features of both neural computers and digital computers. These machines are so different that they do not compete with each other. Together, the two technologies promise a new age in computers.

12.1 TERMINOLOGY

12.1.1 General

The terminology used here is adapted from Hecht-Nielsen.[1,2]

> *Artificial Neural Systems* (ANS) is the engineering discipline concerned with the design, implementation, and application of dynamical systems, typically possessing adaptive energy functions that can carry out useful information processing by means of their state response to initial or continuous input.
>
> *Processing elements*, PE, emulate the operation of neurons in living organisms. They are interconnected via information channels called *interconnects*.
>
> *Processing element inputs* are PEs that can have multiple input signals, which are mostly just copies of output signals from other PEs. Some inputs also come from outside world.
>
> *Processing element outputs* are PEs that have only one output signal (each neuron has only one axon).
>
> *Transfer function* defines the relation between the inputs and the output of a PE.
>
> *Weight* is an adaptive coefficent or weight associated with each PE input or weight.
>
> *Learning* is the process of adjusting the PE weights in response to external inputs.
>
> *Learning function*, first order, ordinary differential, or difference equation governing the state of PE.
>
> *Slab* is a collection of processing elements that use the same transfer and learning functions. PEs could be interconnected within the slab, as well as between the slabs.
>
> *Self-organization* is the autonomous modification of the dynamics of a complete network (via learning in some or all of its PEs) to achieve a specified end capability or result.
>
> *Training* is the exposure of a neural network to a specified data set or to a specified information source environment for the purpose of achieving a specified self-organization goal.

Connections to processing elements and to slabs is shown in Figures 12.1 and 12.2.

12.1.2 Instar

Instar is the most basic functional structure in biological as well as in artificial neural systems. Figure 12.1 shows typical instar structure. It has multiple inputs

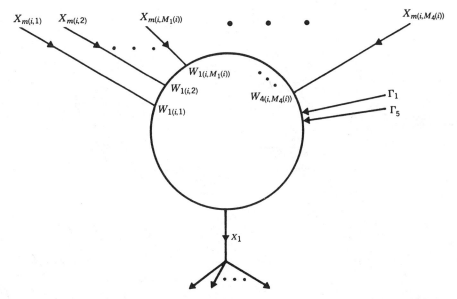

Figure 12.1 *ANS processing element. Reprinted by permission from Hecht-Nielsen.* [1,2] *Courtesy and copyright SPIE.*

and one single output. The inputs are simply copies of other processing element outputs, or they may be filtered or direct sensor data.

The operation of the instar processing element is fully described by equations 1 and 2 in section 12.3. The instar functions as the neuron of artificial neural systems. When input signals exceed a certain threshold value, the instar fires, sending an output signal to other instars. The instars comprising a slab compete with one another to exhibit the highest level of response to each input pattern. The winning instar becomes a detector for that input pattern. The instars which learn the features they respond to are called feature detectors.

12.1.3 Outstar

Outstar is a network of instars linked as shown in Figure 12.3a. Each outstar has one control processing element, labeled X_0, and the number of target processing elements, labeled X_1 through X_n.

The outstar is the simplest network that can learn and reproduce a single spatial pattern. Consider the outstar composed of nodes 1 through n, to which an image vector $I = (I_1, I_2, ..., I_n)$ is connected. The image vector drives the nodes above thresholds. The associative learning is performed if image vector I is presented to the outstar simultaneously with the signal X_o. Simultaneous arrival of I and X_o produces output signals X_i, which are proportional to the respective components of I (e.g., if I_2 is very large, the X_2 will also be very large).

The signal X_o is called the sampling signal. The rate of learning is proportional to the sampling signal X_o. With a stronger signal, learning will occur faster. If the

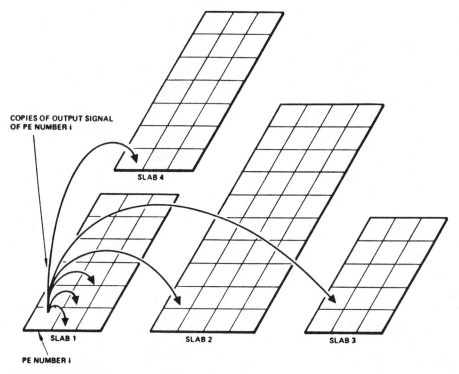

COPIES OF OUTPUT SIGNAL
OF PE NUMBER i

SLAB 4

SLAB 1

SLAB 2

SLAB 3

PE NUMBER i

Figure 12.2 *ANS architecture example. Reprinted by permission from Hecht-Nielsen.* [1,2] *Courtesy and copyright SPIE.*

simultaneous input of both I and X_o occurs a large number of times, the weighting vectors of each node will approach the value of I.

The outstar has truly learned the image pattern I in the sense that it can recall the pattern exactly in the following way. Suppose that, at some time after learning, the external pattern I vanishes. If now the signal X_o goes to a high level, it will read out of the nodes an activity pattern which is proportional to the weights, and hence to the pattern I.

Outstar's learning is an instance of Pavlovian learning and is based on Hebb's law. The output of nodes can be interpreted as the unconditional response controlled by unconditional stimulus I. When the conditional stimulus X_o is synchronized with the unconditional stimulus I, the outstar gradually gains control over the unconditional response.

If two different image vectors I' and I'' are sampled by the outstar at different times, the pattern stored in the outstar will be a weighted average of sampled patterns.

12.1.4 Avalanche

Outstar can only learn time-stable patterns. To store a time-varying pattern, a cascade of outstars is needed. Such a cascade is called an avalanche, Figure 12.3*b*.

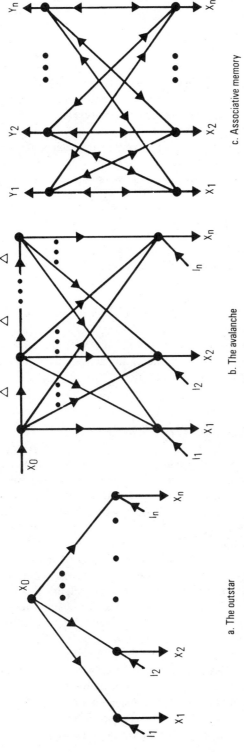

a. The outstar

b. The avalanche

c. Associative memory

Figure 12.3 *Outstar, avalanche, and associative memory. Reprinted by permission from TRW manuals. Courtesy and copyright TRW.*

A time-varying pattern is composed of a succession of still spacial patterns. In Figure 12.3*b*, time is represented as moving from left to right.

A horizontal chain at the top of the avalanche presents primary nodes. An initial signal X_o enters the system at time t_o and activates the first primary node. An interval of time later, the next primary node becomes highly active as X_o diminishes. One interval later, the third primary node becomes active as the previous signal diminishes, and so on.

If the same sequence of events occurs many times, each outstar learns its spacial time slice of the pattern. The outstar can recall the learned spatio-termoral pattern at a later time. It is enough to introduce the sampling signal X_o to cause a replay.

12.1.5 Associative Memory

Associative memory is a structure composed of reciprocal outstars, as shown in Figure 12.3*c*. In this way an analog or fuzzy associative memory could be created. It could be used to recognize similar as well as identical patterns using the approach of nearest matching.

In associative memory, each node is both a control (primary) and a target node. In essence, if the patterns $X(X_1, X_2, \ldots, X_n)$ and $Y(Y_1, Y_2, \ldots, Y_n)$ are frequently paired, the network associates them. Introducing X on the bottom row of nodes (with no pre-existing activities) reproduces the activity pattern Y on the top row. Conversely, Y can reproduce X. See Section 11.10.

12.2 VIRTUAL ELECTRONIC NEUROCOMPUTERS

Neurocomputers can be divided into two groups: fully implemented and virtual. Fully implemented systems face the problem of very complex interconnection networks. Hence virtual systems are more interesting. As a result most neural network implementations currently in use are based on the virtual processing element architecture. This architecture implements a large number of *virtual* processing elements by time-division multiplexing them among a small number of physical processing elements. The advantage of this approach is that it provides the most efficient use of presently available processing resources. Virtual neurocomputers follow a particular pipelined structure, as shown in Figure 12.4.

According to Hecht-Nielsen,[1] the basic idea is to have a number of physical processing elements (one per module) that each update a subset of the total collection of virtual processing elements in the network. The modules shown in Figure 12.4 are numbered from 1 to R. Each module updates the virtual PEs it is responsible for in a continuous cycle; starting with the first, going to the last, and then starting again with the first. The ultimate result is that the whole network gets marched forward in time, one discrete step after another. Such a machine can also be viewed as a highly specialized difference equation solver.

Each module contains a single digital physical processing element. This element

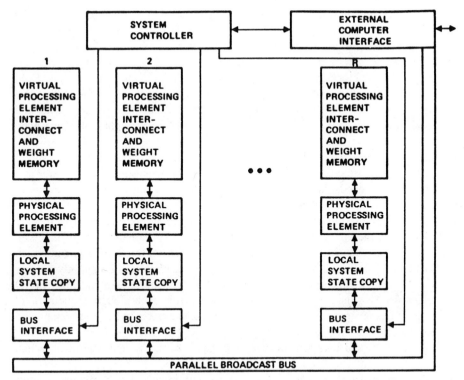

Figure 12.4 *General virtual electronic neurocomputer design. Reprinted by permission from Hecht-Nielsen.*[1,2] *Courtesy and copyright SPIE.*

takes care of weight change equations and of transfer function update. The weight information the interconnect information and the input type information are part of the module. Each module is an independent unit, with the data stored in local table: local system state copy. The traffic within one module is shown in Figure 12.5.

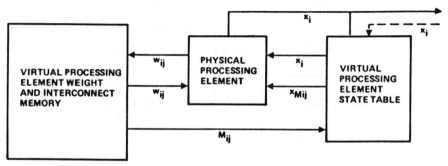

Figure 12.5 *Data flow in virtual processor module. Reprinted by permission from Hecht-Nielsen.*[1,2] *Courtesy and copyright SPIE.*

The complete network is defined through two tables: one for the updates currently being performed and one for those made during the last update cycle (this holds true for the weight tables also). After a module completes a virtual PE update the new output signal X_i and PE number i are broadcast by the bus interface on one clock cycle as a wide word over the parallel broadcast bus. Each bus interface (including the one that transmitted it) receives the update at the same time. This update is added to the state table currently being updated. At the end of each update cycle the "old" and "new" state tables and weight tables ping pong (exchange places), shown in Figure 12.6.

According to Hecht-Nielsen,[1] each module usually only needs access to a subset of the complete state table. By carefully partitioning the system, the PE states that each module's needs can be determined swiftly by testing the high-order bits of the PE number i to see if they lie in one of the desired ranges. If so, the update is accepted by the bus interface and added to the local copy of the system state table. If not, the update is ignored. By this technique the bandwidth of inputs to the state table from the broadcast bus can be kept fairly low. Similarly, since each PE update typically takes many bus clock cycles (a physical PE can only process one input per machine cycle, which itself may involve more than one clock cycle) the bandwidth of the bus interface transmissions from each module to the parallel broadcast bus is also rather low. The net result is that the broadcast bus can handle the traffic from a large number of modules.

The sequence of data transmission is in hands of the system controller, which tells each bus interface when to transmit.

The transmissions take place in sequence, with module 1 transmitting its latest update (if any) and then module 2, and so forth. After module R transmits then

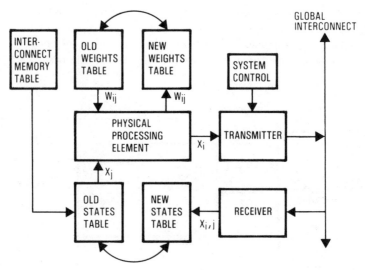

Figure 12.6 *Virtual processor table update. Reprinted by permission from TRW manuals. Courtesy and copyright TRW.*

module 1 starts the cycle over again. If an electronic bus is used it is better to count down from R to 1 and then start the cycle over.

In the future, the parallel broadcast bus will be constructed out of electro-optical components. In general, the neurocomputer design will move from virtual systems toward fully implemented systems.

Recently commercial versions of neural-net machines have been introduced to the market. The first machines had been MARK III/IV, originally developed for Defense Advanced Research Project Agency (DARPA). DARPA and TRW have inaugurated the program called Adaptive Distributed Analog Processor Technology (ADAPT). Other interesting products are the ANZA and DELTA neurocomputer coprocessors. The primary rationale for developing these products stems from following facts:

- Classical computers cannot efficiently implement neural networks. It takes hours or days to simulate or train neural-like networks. These slow responses make it impossible to conduct a reasonable experimental program.
- In real-time applications such as radar image analysis, speech recognition, expert systems, and so on, the neurocomputers will operate hundreds or thousands of times faster than the computers of the VAX class for a fraction of the cost.
- Artificial neural systems open many new application areas: intelligent robots flying planes or working in mines, new medical instruments, brain-like machines.

Artificial neural systems build largely on the information processing principles of neural modeling formulated by neuroscientists, particularly by Grossberg.[3,4]

12.3 MARK III NEURAL NETWORK*

12.3.1 Mark II, III, and IV

The Mark II, III, and IV neurocomputers share a common set of design principles. These principles are embodied in each of the neurocomputer architectures themselves. They all implement locally dependent difference equations using a virtual processing element technique. They also share a common design environment which emphasizes flexibility. These design principles are described in the following paragraphs.

A fundamental characteristic of neural networks is the principle of local processing based on the inputs transmitted through single connections. The Mark II, III, and IV all enforce this principle by restricting the network definition to those configurations which obey locality of processing.

Another fundamental characteristic of most neurocomputers is an ability to

*Section 12.3 is adapted from TRW manuals.[15–18] Courtesy and copyright ©1986, 1987 by TRW, Military Electronics and Avionics Division.

implement a large set of coupled differential equations. Because the Mark II, III, and IV are digital neurocomputers, these differential equations are implemented as a set of difference equations. The speed at which the network runs is determined by the processing required to update these difference equations.

The Mark II, III, and IV neurocomputers are based on a virtual Processing Element (PE) architecture. A virtual PE architecture is analogous to the virtual memory systems found in many Von Neumann computers. The virtual memory Von Neumann machine presents the user with a large memory model, while the virtual PE neurocomputer presents the user with a large PE and interconnect model. In both cases, the machine physically contains only a small fraction of the user model. The trade-off is simply between cost and speed. The difference between virtual memory and virtual PE architectures is really the same as the difference between the Von Neumann model and the neural-net model. While the Von Neumann model defines one processor interacting with large amounts of memory, the neural-net model defines large amounts of processors each with one memory (which may be a simple integrative element). The virtual PE architecture must store the entire state of each virtual PE when it is not being processed. In both systems, the physical to virtual ratio is driven by the cost of the physical quantity (where cost includes price, power consumption, physical size, etc.) and the demand for processing speed.

All three (and future TRW neurocomputers) share the same design environment known as the Artificial Neural System Environment (ANSE). This design environment supports the neural network designer in the areas of network definition, network editing, network storage and retrieval, and network implementation. The last item, network implementation, is achieved by cross-compiling the network description into load data targeted for a specific machine. Because the ANSE is machine independent, networks designed under ANSE will be upward-compatible with future members of the TRW neurocomputer family. Real-time hardware implementations include plans for a silicon compiler to convert an ANSE network description into an integrated circuit for fieldable units.

A neural network is a specific example of a parallel computational structure.[1-20] It is characterized by the many input connections to each of the many processing elements. The efficient implementation of any computational structure is achieved by applying the bulk of the available processing power to the processing bottleneck of the structure. The neural network's bottleneck is the processing of all of the input connections. Efficient neural network implementation must focus on rapid processing of these *inter*connections. This will be pointed out in each of the following neurocomputer descriptions.

Mark II Neurocomputer. The Mark II is a software simulation which is functionally equivalent to the Mark III and Mark IV. The Mark II processes its interconnections using a tight software loop to maximize neural network throughput. Because it is a software simulation, the speed and size of Mark II networks is dependent on the speed and memory of the host computer (typically a member of the VAX family).

Mark III Neurocomputer. The Mark III Neurocomputer is a parallel processor family using a virtual PE and interconnect structure. The physical processing elements (up to 15 physical processors may be used) are actually Motorola 68020 microprocessors coupled with 68881 floating point co-processors. Figure 12.7 shows a block diagram of the Mark III hardware. The diagram shows several slave processors which perform the bulk of the network processing. In this type of parallel architecture, the interconnection speed is maximized by localizing (to each board) the information required to perform each connection. This minimizes the amount of bus traffic which in turn allows a large number of processors to share a common bus. This parallel structure is combined with a software package that ensures full utilization of all processors (within the network constraints). This architecture is very attractive for low-risk, near-term applications of neural networks. The current Mark III supports 65,000 processing elements with over 1,000,000 trainable interconnections and can process up to 450,000 interconnections per second.

Mark IV Neurocomputer. The Mark IV Neurocomputer (funded by DARPA) is a single high-speed, pipelined processor using a virtual PE and interconnect structure. This architecture provides dedicated hardware for performing the large number of virtual interconnects required by neural networks. The Mark IV's principle of dedicating the bulk of the hardware to the task of forming interconnections will surely be the cornerstone of future electronic neurocomputer design. The Mark IV, which supports 256,000 processing elements with over 5,500,000 trainable

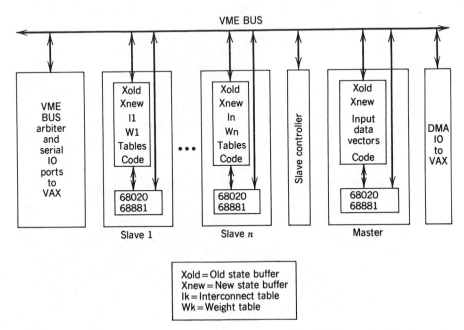

Figure 12.7 *Mark III Architecture. Reprinted by permission from TRW manuals. Courtesy and copyright TRW.*

interconnections, is capable of processing 5,000,000 interconnections per second (including the preweighting function and learning law). The Mark family growth is outlined in Figure 12.8.

12.3.2 Mark III-1 Overview

The Mark III-1 Artificial Neural System (ANS) processors is first in a family of expandable sixth-generation computer emulators. The Mark III-1 is designed to support ANS research in industry, university, and government laboratories. Its main function is to accelerate the programming and running of ANS networks. The Mark III-1 is a general-purpose ANS processor which can accommodate a broad range of research using trainable topological processing to sample, filter, organize,

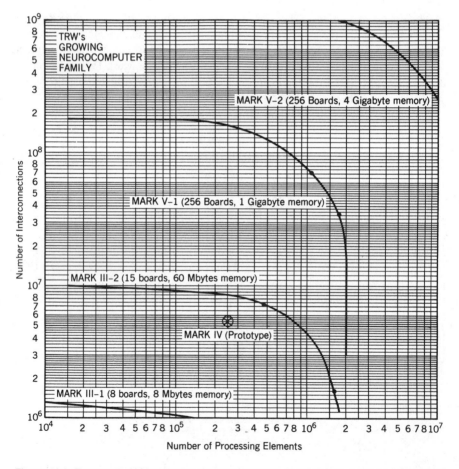

Figure 12.8 *The growth of Mark family of neurocomputer. Reprinted by permission from TRW manuals. Courtesy and copyright TRW.*

learn, and respond to its environment. TRW has already demonstrated Mark III applications to spatiotemporal pattern learning and classification of time varying spectograms, and image processing and understanding of images using multiple hierarchical transforms. Much remains to be done to exploit this exciting research tool in areas of pattern recognition, data/sensor fusion, speech, vision, fuzzy knowledge processing, and coordination and control of robot motion, just to name a few. The user friendly environment software ANSE enormously simplifies experimentation and allows the rapid evaluation of trial networks on real or simulated data, and frees the experimenter from the task of software design.

The expectation is that, for most researchers currently running on minicomputers, the Mark III-1 will speed up their experiments by an order of magnitude. In fact, the current Mark III-1 which runs as a peripheral to a VAX has just been benchmarked at 29 times the speed of the Microvax implementing the same networks in Pascal. Researchers currently using supercomputers will most likely experience a slowdown with the Mark III-1. However, they will be able to run experiments 24 hours per day, which few can afford to do on a $10 million supercomputer. In all cases, it is expected that the speed and efficiency of the Mark III-1 will have a profound impact on the productivity of scientists and engineers engaged in ANS research.

Beyond its speed of network implementation, the Mark III-1 has two other important features that aid research productivity:

1. It has a complete ANS Environment (ANSE) software package that facilitates rapid NETWARE design, that is, network specification, editing, archiving, and experimental run control

2. It runs as a coprocessor to any Digital Equipment Corporation VAX computer with the VMS operating system (from the Microvax II to the 8600)

The Mark III-1 ANSE is a DEC VAX/VMS-compatible software package that allows the user to rapidly specify a network, archive a network, and later edit that network. It also has provisions for controlling experimental runs on the Mark III-1, if the user wishes to run experiments in this manner (the other option is to treat the Mark III-1 as a procedure call—in which case it can be simply embedded in other user software on the VAX). The ANSE is run from a color graphics terminal that is connected to the VAX and is provided as part of the Mark III-1 hardware/software package.

Input data for network experiments (and outputs of user-selected system states, processing element—PE, values) are in terms of VAX/VMS files or arrays, depending on whether the Mark III-1 is being run from the ANSE or is acting as a software procedure. If the user simply wants to run networks, then this can be done directly from the ANSE. The user gives the name of the file containing the input data (at each time step of the experiment the user can specify the values of the inputs that are to be made to the user-selected processing elements of the network being run) and the name of the file to which user-selected PE outputs are to be sent (at user-selected time steps).

Alternatively, if the Mark III-1 is being used as a software procedure that is called by other user software, then the user puts the input data to be used into the procedure as an array. The user-selected PE outputs are then returned as an array to the calling routine when the Mark III-1 has finished executing the time steps specified in the procedure call. This facility makes the Mark III-1 completely general in terms of how it can be embedded into user-defined systems. With this capability, the user can easily connect sensors (spectrum analyzer, video camera, LPC speech encoder, etc.) and effectors (LPC speech synthesizer, robot arm, color graphics display, etc.) to their network by means of standard DEC VAX peripheral interfaces and software drivers. This capability also allows the user to carry out preprocessing and postprocessing algorithms in software on the VAX— which allows the user's ANS network to be used as part of a complete system.

The Mark III-1 processor can implement general ANS networks comprised of N Processing Elements (PEs), numbered from 1 to N. In general, the index i will be used to denote PE numbers. The ith PE receives a number of nonnegative input signals and produces a single nonnegative output signal x_i that varies with time. With the exception of input signals that arrive from outside the system (which is how information inputs to the system occur), all input signals to a PE are simply fanned out copies of the output signals of other processing elements. By sending extra copies of selected PE output signals outside of the system, the state of the system can be monitored externally. This is how information output from the system is accomplished.

The Mark III-1 implements differential equations by numerically integrating the first order difference equations given below (see Figures 12.1 and 12.2).

$$x_i^{new} = x_i^{old} - F_1(x_i^{old}, I_i^1, I_i^2, I_i^3, I_i^4, \Gamma_1, \Gamma_2) = F(x_i^{old}, I_i^1, I_i^2, I_i^3, I_i^4, \Gamma_1, \Gamma_2) \quad (12.1)$$

$$w_k(i,j)^{new} = w_k(i,j)^{old} + G_k(w_k(i,j), x_i, x_{m(i,j)}) \quad (12.2)$$

with

$$I_i^k = \sum_{j=M_{k-1}(i)+1}^{M_k(i)} w_k(i,j) f_k(x_{m(i,j)}), \quad k = 1, 2, 3, 4 \quad (12.3)$$

where: $x_i(t) = $ Output Signal from PE number i, $i = 1, 2, ..., N$.

$x_i(t) = $ External Signal Input i to System, $i = N + 1, N + 2, ..., N'$.
$\quad\quad\quad$ $x_i(t) \geq 0, i = 1, 2, ..., N'$.

$m(i,j) = $ PE input identifier giving the number of the PE output signal
$\quad\quad\quad$ or external signal that forms the jth input to PE i.
$\quad\quad\quad$ Clearly $1 \leq m(i,j) \leq N'$.

$w_k(i,j) = $ Weight (Adaptive Coefficient) associated with j^{th} input of type k
$\quad\quad\quad$ to PE i.

$M_k(i) = $ Number of inputs of "type k" to PE i.

$f_k =$ Preweighting function for inputs of type k.

$\Gamma_1, \ldots \Gamma_5 =$ Global signals 1 thru 5 (that are recalculated by a user-defined procedure).

$F =$ PE update function.

$G_k =$ Weight update function.

Note that the function F incorporates the addition of x_i and F_1. This allows the user full control over the new value of x_i. However, explicit control of the new value of $w_k(i,j)$ is not provided. The difference in the handling of these two variables results form the level of resolution each requires. This will be discussed below. Also, note that the time increment (Δt) has been absorbed into the F and G_k functions. Using these difference equations, the entire system is marched forward in time, step by step. It is important to realize that these difference equations are in general not very good numerical approximations to the continuous time differential equations. However, accurate quantitative results are not required for implementing neural networks. Rather, it is the qualitative behave of the network that must be maintained, and the difference Equations 12.1 and 12.2 perform this task quite well. They are called Transfer and Learning Equations.

During each time step, the state of each PE in the network (the x_i and $w_k(i,j)$ values) is updated using the PE states from the previous time step. All PEs are updated every time step in a pre-determined sequence (that sequence need not be 1,2, . . . , N; however, it often is). Thus, the Mark III-1 implements a synchronous form of PE updating rather than an asynchronous form.

The PEs of the system are arranged into disjoint subsets calles *slabs*. The PEs of each slab have the same F, f_k, and G_k functions and the same global signals Γ_1 thru Γ_5. Different slabs can have different functions and global signals.

During each time step, the state of the system (the x_i and $w_k(i,j)$ values) are updated, based upon the state from the previous time step.

Each of the arguments and function values used in the above equations is stored, used, and transmitted as a binary word. Some of these words are described in the following list:

x_i: The signal value is implemented as a 8 bit unsigned integer.
This means that x takes on integer values in the range 0 to 255.

$w_k(i,j)$: The weight is implemented as a 21 bit integer.

$m(i,j)$: The PE input identifier is implemented as a 16 bit unsigned integer.
The value of m ranges between 1 and 65,000.

$\Gamma_1 \ldots \Gamma_5$: The global signals are implemented as 8 bit unsigned integers,
and thus can take on values in the range of 0 to 255.
These signals can depend only upon the x_i values of the system at the end of each time increment. They are calculated by calling a user-supplied procedure at the end of each time step.

The constraints on M_k and N' are:

$$\sum_{i=1}^{N}\sum_{k=1}^{4} M_k(i) \leq 1,130,000/1,700,000 \tag{12.4}$$

and

$$N' \leq 65,000 \tag{12.5}$$

Note that the total number of interconnects is 1,130,000 if weight modification is used, and 1,700,000 if the weights are fixed. The Mark III-1 can implement up to eight slabs. On each of these slabs the user can define functions f_k, F, and G_k arbitrarily.

$f_k(x_i)$:   This function determines an 8 bit unsigned value based upon the 8 bit unsigned argument.

F: This function determines an 8 bit unsigned value calculated by a user-defined algorithm. Floating point arithmetic may be used internal to the F function. All of the I_i^k are non-negative 16 bit 2's complement values.

$G_k(w_k(i,j),$
$x_i, x_{m(i,j)})$:   This function determines a 22 bit 2's complement value based upon the most significant 8 bits of $w_k(i,j)$, the 8 bits of x_i and 8 bits of $x_{m(i,j)}$.

The Mark III-1 can implement networks with as many as 65,000 PEs and 1,130,000 interconnects (1,700,000 if the weights are fixed) subdivided into from one to eight slabs. Neural elements can be designed with from 1 to 1,130,000 trainable weights, with up to four separate types of data (to allow complex arithmetic) and with floating point processing embedded in the neural node transfer F function. The Mark III-1 has been benchmarked at 29 times the speed of the Microvax with the experiment programmed in Pascal. In many typical cases, where full connectivity is not required, network update rates of several time per second are realized. The graphical display used with the Mark III-1 is a powerful visual aid in analyzing and understanding the processing in the experiments, and experience at TRW has proven the great power of the visual in helping cut through very complex problems.

12.3.3 Applications

Most neurocomputer users fall into one of three broad groups: education, design, and end-use application. The educational group includes students and researchers. This group often deals with novel, example-scale networks. The design group contains engineers and technicians involved in government or commercial applications of neural networks. This group is highly concerned with the productivity per incremental cost provided by neurocomputer design stations. The final area of neurocomputer use is the end-use application itself. These neurocomputer systems must be complete, fieldable solutions to specific problems. The education and design groups also require a high degree of flexibility/user-friendliness. Because the Mark II, III, and IV share the same user environment ANSE, they are all highly flexible and user friendly. In the size/speed/cost arena, the Mark II is typically an educational machine, the Mark III is a design workstation, and the Mark IV is a low-end applications machine. Note that these categories overlap. The Mark IV could be considered a high-end research (educational) machine, while the Mark III could be used for some low-end applications.

The best measure of a neurocomputer workstation's performance is the level of productivity achieved by its users. We present a varied selection of experiments and applications performed at the TRW Rancho Carmel ANS Center. Note that although the examples shown are taken from particular machines, all of the examples could have been run on any of the machines. All of the processing (including preprocessing) occurred using neural network paradigms. Each different example is a representative result from that series of runs. Each collection of processing elements within the figures which performs a specific function is a single slab.

Figure 12.9 shows Mark III implementation of the Digital Fourier Transform (DFT) using a neural network. Although the DFT may be implemented algorithmically, this network implementation provides an easy method of performing top-level system design totally within the ANS Environment. The DFT (or any other preprocessing structure) is simply invoked as a mapping function as needed. In true parallel hardware, this would provide a single cycle DFT. This network has also been used as a training example for new users.

Figure 12.10 shows Mark III demonstration of spatio-temporal pattern classification. The original time-varying doppler spectra is delayed through a cascade of PEs to convert temporal variation to a shifting-window spatial pattern. This pattern is then passed through a DFT to produce a stable representation. The following slab is trained on the representations of several waveforms using Heb-

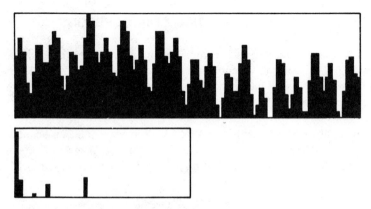

Figure 12.9 *Digital Fourier Transformer (DFT). From the TRW manual.*

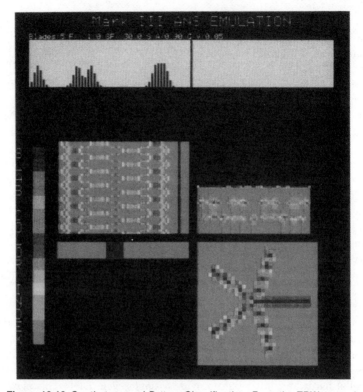

Figure 12.10 *Spatio-temporal Pattern Classification. From the TRW manual.*

bian learning. These elements are then trained to associate the input pattern with a display pattern using an instar-outstar mechanism.

Figure 12.11 shows a Mark III neurocomputer workstation.

12.4 THE ANZA NEUROCOMPUTING COPROCESSOR*

The ANZA is a general purpose neurocomputing coprocessor that is installed in an IBM PC/AT or compatible computer to speed execution of neural networks. Operating in parallel with the host computer system, it off-loads from the host all neural network processing, thereby allowing the host more time to carry out its other activities.

The processing performance of the ANZA is derived from the on-board 20 MHz Motorola MC68020 microprocessor with access to four megabytes of one-wait state dynamic RAM. To improve floating point performance, a 20 MHz Motorola

---

*Section 12.4 is adapted from ANZA User's Guide. [19] Courtesy and Copyright Hecht-Nielsen Neurocomputer Corporation, ©1987. All rights reserved.

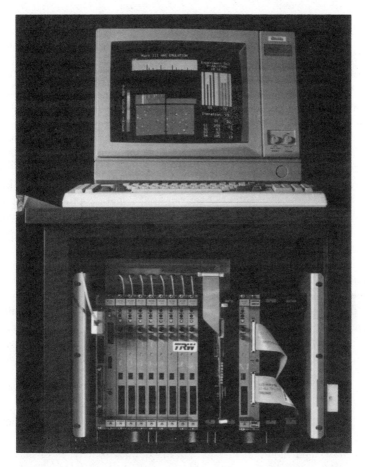

Figure 12.11 *Mark III-1, Neurocomputer Workstation. Courtesy of TRW.*

MC68881 floating point coprocessor is also included. With these resources and customized proprietary software, the ANZA is able to process 25,000 interconnects per second, with learning. This benchmark is based on a back propagation network using double-precision floating point calculations. With learning disabled, the performance figure rises to 45,000 interconnects per second. Performance figures for other netware packages are provided in their accompanying documentation.

The ANZA was designed to make easy neurocomputing integration into existing software environments. Interaction between user software an the ANZA is accomplished through a set of callable subroutines that comprise the User Interface Subroutine Library (UISL™, pronounced "wee sil"). The UISL provides access to all of the ANZA's network data structures and functions. This allows the user to quickly and easily add neural network capability to new or existing software.

As a general purpose neurocomputing coprocessor, the ANZA can implement any of the known network paradigms. To execute a network, the user must provide a description of that network. Such a description is called netware. Netware can be obtained in one of two ways. First, it can be purchased as a complete package. The ANZA comes with five standard netware packages. Each package can be tailored to satisfy individual user requirements. The second source of netware is the AXON™ network description language being developed by HNC™. AXON will allow the user to completely define a network and then compile it into netware suitable for execution on the ANZA.

The ANZA coprocessor will operate in any PC/AT or compatible computer with a hard disk drive and a minimum of 512k of memory. No other hardware is required. However, an Enhanced Graphics Adapter (EGA) board and monitor is required for executing the netware package demonstration programs since they use the EGA for graphics output. Also, an 80287 math coprocessor is useful for preparing data that is sent to the ANZA since data preparation is often computationally intensive.

In the previous section, a neural network was defined as a collection of highly interconnected, simple processing elements. To implement such a network with the virtual architecture requires a representation of a processing element that can be stored in digital memory and periodically updated by some kind of processor. The representation used by the ANZA partitions the PE into its output state value, its interconnect specification, and its input weights. These data items combined with a specification of the transfer and learning functions completely describe the processing element. Of this data, only the state and weight values change during the execution of the network.

The interconnect specification and the form of the transfer and learning functions are fully determined by the network paradigm that is being implemented. The final piece of data that is needed is a set of tuning parameters or *constants* which allow the user to adjust the transfer and learning functions.

From these data requirements, the ANZA defines four types of network data elements: states, weights, constants, and a network description. The function of the first three of these data elements is obvious. The final element consists of all of the static network information such as interconnect specifications, transfer and learning functions, and initialization values.

In order to use the ANZA to carry out neural network processing, the user must be able to select a network paradigm and instantiate that paradigm according to the needs of a particular problem. After instantiating the network, the user must be able to load data into the network, iterate the network, and retrieve the results of processing. Further, the state of the network (i.e. the processing element state and weight values) must be captured or saved periodically so that subsequent network execution can build on previous results. All of these tasks are handled by the user interface. This interface was designed and implemented around four specific goals: generality, flexibility, simplicity, and extensibility.

Generality requires that the ANZA be able to implement any known neural network. Thus, the ANZA and its user interface cannot take advantage of any characteristic of a particular type of network. Rather, they must depend only on those features common to all networks. This implies that the user interface must operate as a "data mover" only. That is, it transfers data between the PC and the ANZA, but it does not interpret the data. All network processing is external to the interface.

Flexibility requires that the user interface provide access to all network data structures. This requirement ties in closely with that of generality since the data needed to determine network performance varies significantly from network to network. The most important implication of the flexibility requirement is that the interface command set be complete.

Simplicity requires that the interface be easy to use and simple to integrate into the existing software development process. Simplicity and ease of use are characteristics that are desirable in any user interface. However, in the case of the ANZA, the need for ease of integration into existing software is of equal, if not greater, importance. The reason for this is that neural network processing is a technology that in many cases simply augments existing information processing techniques. Therefore, it must build on top of a large base of existing software. This requirement implies that the user interface must take the form of a library of subroutines. Further, these subroutines must be callable from a number of popular programming languages.

Extensibility requires that the interface allow user software to migrate to future products with minimal change. Thus, as their need for network processing increases, users can extend their network capabilities to new products with very little effort. This implies that the interface should not depend on any ANZA specific characteristics. Rather it must target a specific model of network processing that is independent of hardware implementation.

From these design goals and their implications, the ANZA user interface has been developed. The relationship of this interface, called the User Interface Subroutine Library to the other elements of a complete network application is shown in Figure 12.12. The remainder of this chapter focuses on the various components of the UISL and how the UISL is used with the ANZA to carry out network processing.

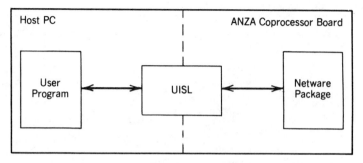

Figure 12.12 *Functional Role of UISL. Reprinted by permission of the Hecht-Nielsen Neuro-computer Corporation, all rights reserved.*

12.5 THE ANZA USER INTERFACE SUBROUTINE LIBRARY, UISL*

12.5.1 UISL Data Types

Any discussion of UISL data types must begin with processing element states, weights, and constants. However, these three data elements pose a difficult problem for the UISL: states, weights, and constants vary in their data types from one network paradigm to another. Thus, the UISL should be flexible enough to handle any data format defined for a particular network implementation. A detailed discussion of these data types is deferred until the end of this section. First, a set of auxiliary data types are defined to support the UISL's primary tasks.

The data types used by the UISL were selected to aid the user in developing software for the ANZA and to satisfy the extensibility requirement. Most of the data types are derived from a noun that specifies the particular network entity, such as slab or weight, and a tag that describes a particular category of data, such as a pointer or count. Table 12.1 lists the defined noun and tag specifiers. Not all combinations of nouns and tags are valid. For example a pointer to a network, **net_prt**, is not defined. Only those combinations required for implementation of the UISL subroutines have been defined. Table 12.2 lists the defined UISL data types. Note that the data types are lower case with an underscore separating the noun and the tag.

It is important to note that all of these data types are network independent. All references to network data are via pointers, leaving the format of the underlying data unspecified. The only exception is the interconnect data type **inc_val**. The format of an interconnect is independent of the specific network. It specifies only the connectivity of the network. Note, the **icn_ptr** data type is not a pointer to an **icn_val** data element. This is due to UISL implementation problems associated with using multiple memory models on the PC.

*Section 12.5 is adapted from ANZA User's Guide. [19] Courtesy and copyright Hecht-Nielsen Neurocomputer Corporation, ©1987. All rights reserved.

TABLE 12.1 UISL Data Type Noun and Tag Specifiers

	Nouns		Tags
ncp	Neurocomputer	id	Identifier
net	Network	val	Value
slab	Slab	cnt	Count
sts	State values	ptr	Pointer
wts	Weight values		
icn	Interconnects		
pe	Processing element		
cts	Function constants		
itr	Iterations		
type	Interconnection types		
str	Character string		
flg	Flag		

TABLE 12.2 UISL Data Types

Identifier types	ncp_id	slab_id	type_id
	net_id	pe_id	
Count types	sts_cnt	icn_cnt	
	wts_cnt	itr_cnt	
Pointer types	sts_ptr	cts_ptr	str_ptr
	wts_ptr	icn_ptr	
Value types	flg_val	icn_val	
Miscellaneous types	bool		

The data type names used for netware specific data are also constructed from the nouns in Table 12.1. However, these nouns are prefixed with the name of the network. For example, the counter propagation network defines **cpn_sts, cpn_wts**, and **cpn_cts** as data types. In general, the network specific data types only use the nouns **sts, wts**, and **cts**.

Some networks require different data types for weight values on different slabs. If this is the case, the data type names will simply have a number added to them to indicate which slab it refers to. For example, a weight data type named **cpn_wts1** refers to a weight value on slab 1 of a counter propagation network. If a slab does not have a special weight data type, it is assumed to use the network default (i.e., the network name followed by **wts** with no number). The following example illustrates this for a generic network, **net**, having four slabs:

> net_wts   Default data type for weights
> net_wts1   Data type for weights on slab 1
> net_wts4   Data type for weights on slab 4

In this example, weights on slabs 1 and 4 would be of type **net_wts1** and **net_wts4** respectively and on slabs 2 and 3 would be of type **net_wts**.

The constants data type is a structured type meaning it is a collection of individual data elements or fields. This allows all the constants data to be collected into one data structure. The definition of each field in this structure is given in the documentation for each netware package.

12.5.2 UISL Subroutine Names

As with the data types, the UISL subroutines adhere to a naming convention that is designed to aid the user in developing software for the ANZA. The details of these subroutines and their usage in developing neural network applications is described in the ANZA manual. The current section is intended to describe the concept behind the names that have been chosen for the subroutines.

UISL subroutine names use the same set of nouns as the data types, but are prefaced by one of a set of verbs that describe an action on that noun. Table 12.3

TABLE 12.3   UISL Verbs and Their Actions

Verb	Action
Alloc	Allocates item
Dealloc	Deallocates item
Load	Moves item from a disk file to Ncp memory
Save	Moves item from Ncp memory to a disk file
Free	Releases item
Get	Moves item from Ncp memory to PC memory
Put	Moves item from PC memory to Ncp memory
Read	Moves item from disk file to PC memory
Set	Modifies item flags
Iter	Iterates item
Chk	Checks item

lists the verbs that are defined and their actions. As with data types, not all verb/noun combinations are implemented as subroutines. Table 12.4 indicates which combinations are valid.

12.5.3   UISL Data Files

The data required to implement neural networks on the ANZA was shown in a previous section to be divided into four classes: state data, weight data, constants data, and network description data. The UISL defines four types of data files to store this information. Each file type is identified by a specific file extension. The file extension in the MS-DOS operating system consists of up to three characters separated from the file name by a period. The file extensions used by the UISL are "sts" for state data, "wts" for weight data, "cts" for constants data, and "net" for network description data. The next paragraphs will briefly discuss the contents of each data file type. Details on the use of each file and how the files are manipulated by the UISL subroutines is presented in the following section.

The network description file, referred to as the net file, forms the core of each netware package. It contains information required to instantitate the network. This

TABLE 12.4   Defined UISL Subroutines

Noun	Subroutine	
Ncp	AllocNcp	DeallocNcp
Net	LoadNet	SaveNet
	IterNet	Freenet
	SetNet	
Sts	GetSts	PutSts
Wts	GetWts	PutWts
Icn	GetIcn	
Cts	PutCts	ReadCts
Slab	SetSlab	
Itr	ChkItr	
Misc.	PrintErr	

includes a description of the overall organization of the network into processing slabs, the interconnect geometry between processing elements, and the transfer and learning functions for each slab.

Each netware package has one net file that is used for all network instantiations. The net file resides in the ANZA subdirectory under the installation base directory.

The state and weight data files contain all processing element state and weight values respectively for the entire network. Together they comprise a snapshot of the state of the network at some given point in its execution. Typically, they reflect the state of the network at the end of execution. This data can then serve as a starting point for the next execution. These files generally reside in a user's working directory.

The constants data file is used to store the current values of the network constants. These constants provide the user with a means of customizing the netware package to meet the needs of a particular problem. Like the state and weight files, the constants file resides in the user's working directory. The state, weight and constant files that constitute a particular network instantiation all share a common file name. However, the network description file may or may not have the same file name as the other three. In most cases it will not. The constants file contains a link to the network description file.

The division of the network data into four separate files allows the information in the net file to remain static. Therefore it should not be modified by the user. On the other hand, the state, weight, and constants files contain highly dynamic information that serves to specialize the network to a particular problem. The data in these files reflects the current state of network execution.

12.5.4 User Software Components

This section describes the general components of the user's software that are required to carry out neural network processing with the ANZA. Certainly each user will have varying needs. However, certain general software components must be present. Figure 12.13 illustrates these components in a block diagram showing the relationships between them. Note that any element of the user's software can communicate directly with the UISL subroutines. This is indicated in the diagram by the two arrows that terminate at the border of the user software box.

From Figure 12.13 it can be seen that there are three primary tasks that the user software must perform:

1. Generate input data for the network to operate on;
2. Call the user interface subroutine library to control neurocomputer operation; and
3. Generate an output response based on the results of network execution.

Input data is needed to drive the network during execution. To provide this input data, the user must create software to generate it. The two most common methods for accomplishing this are reading the data from a previously created data file or collecting it in real-time (or near real-time) from a set of input devices (i.e., video

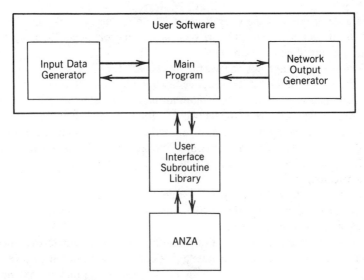

Figure 12.13 *User software components. Reprinted by permission of the Hecht-Nielsen Neurocomputer Corporation, all rights reserved.*

camera, speech I/O, etc.). The input data is grouped to form an input pattern. The size of the input pattern is determined by the user in conjunction with the requirements of the netware package and the pattern to be solved. When transferred to the ANZA, the netware package treats the input pattern as a collection of processing element state values. The input pattern can be inserted in part or as a whole into any slab or set of slabs in the network. The specific procedure for loading data into the network is defined in the documentation for each netware package.

Regardless of how the data of the input pattern is loaded, each data element must be formatted as a processing element state value. Therefore, the input pattern must be defined to be of type **net_sts** where **net** refers to any particular netware package. The definition of state value data types is provided in the netware package definition file. The user should carefully read the section discussing input data in the netware package documentation before beginning to write the input data portions of the software.

The second task required of the user's software is simply to call the UISL subroutines required to control the ANZA operation. The proper sequence of these library calls will be discussed in the next section.

The final software component is the generation of an output response based on the results of network execution. This may take the form of a graphics display that shows the processing element state or weight values. Alternatively, it may involve selecting and implementing an action in response to the network's classification of an input or some other back-end processing such as the calculation of various statistics for use in evaluating the network's performance. The exact nature of this component depends strongly on the user's application.

12.5.5   Using the UISL

This section describes the sequence of UISL subroutine calls that are typically used to control ANZA operation. The emphasis is on the order of the calls not the detailed functionality of the subroutines or the complete definition of the call arguments.

The first UISL subroutine called is usually **AllocNcp**. **AllocNcp** allocates and initializes the ANZA coprocessor. It must be executed prior to any other subroutine that accesses the ANZA. Some UISL subroutines such as **ReadCts** do not access the ANZA and may therefore be called without previously executing **AllocNcp**.

Once the ANZA has been allocated, networks can be loaded and executed. ANZA supports the execution of multiple networks. In this case each network is treated as an independent entity and the following discussion would apply to each individually.

To begin network processing, the ANZA must be loaded with a network. The **LoadNet** subroutine is used to perform this operation. **LoadNet** is passed a file name that specifies a constants file (a file extension of "cts" is assumed) in the users default directory. A full path name not longer than 64 characters including the ".cts" extension may be used. The file header of the constants file contains information that associates it with a particular netware package. In this way **LoadNet** can identify the correct network description file to be loaded with a particular constants file.

In addition to the constants file, the file name passed to **LoadNet** may also specify a state and/or weight file (the file extensions "sts" and "wts" are assumed) to be loaded when the network is instantiated. A flag passed to **LoadNet** determines which combination of these two files are required for the load operation to be successful. This allows the user to control the initialization of the state and weight values.

LoadNet also allows the user to pass a network constants structure to override the values contained in the constants file. This provides the user the ability to modify the constants at run-time. The **ReadCts** subroutine can be used to read a constants structure from a constants file so that the values can be modified prior to executing **LoadNet**.

After the network is loaded, the user can call the SetSlab and SetNet subroutines to modify the state of the slab and network flags. Currently, only one flag, LEARN, is defined for both slabs and networks. Setting the learn flag to TRUE enables the learning function for that slab or network. Setting the learn flag to FALSE disables learning for the slab or network. The network learn flag acts as an override and does not modify the state of each individual slab flag.

During the execution of **LoadNet**, the processing element weights are assigned initial values either from a previously generated data file or by an initialization function defined in the network description file. If other values are required for the initial weight values, the **PutWts** subroutine can be used to load user specified values into the weight tables.

These operations complete the intialization functions of the network. The network is now ready to begin processing input patterns. Input patterns are loaded into the network using the **PutSts** subroutine. This subroutine transfers a buffer of data from PC memory to the network state tables.

With the input pattern loaded, **InterNet** is called to iterate the network. **InterNet** is passed a count specifying the number of iterations to perform. All of the iterations will be performed with the same input pattern. For this reason, the count is usually one. However, some networks, particularly those that use inhibitory interconnects to mediate competition, require multiple iterations of the same input pattern. When multiple iterations are used, the **ChkItr** subroutine can be used to determine how many iterations have been completed since the last call to **InterNet**.

When the network has finished updating, the user can examine the results by calling **GetSts** or **GetWts**. These subroutines transfer network state or weight data respectively from the ANZA memory to PC memory. **GetSts** will return all states for a specified slab. **GetWts** will return a specified number of weights from a particular slab and is often used in conjunction with the **GetIcn** subroutine which retrieves interconnect information.

At this point, another input pattern can be loaded and the network iterated. This cycle continues as long as the user requires. If the user discovers that the network is not executing properly, the **PutCts** subroutine can be used to adjust any of the transfer or learning function constants. **PutCts** can be called at any time during network execution. However, it is important to note that **PutCts** cannot modify any of the network size constants. These can only be adjusted prior to loading the network. The documentation for each netware package describes the constants that can be changed with **PutCts**.

At any time, the user can save the state of the network using the **SaveNet** subroutine. This subroutine will create a file containing the current values of constants, states, and weights for the entire network. These files can later be used by **LoadNet** to begin network processing at the point the **SaveNet** was performed.

SaveNet may overwrite existing data files. However, before doing so, it will rename the existing files from extensions cts, sts, and wts to extensions cbk, sbk, and wbk respectively. This provides one layer of backup protection. A second **SaveNet** operation will result in the original data files being lost.

When network execution is complete and the network has been saved (if desired), the **FreeNet** subroutine can be used to remove the network from the ANZA. This frees space in the ANZA that can then be used to load new networks.

The **DeallocNcp** subroutine is called after all network processing is complete. This subroutine performs an implicit **FreeNet** for each network that is currently loaded. However, it does not save any network data. All network save operations should be completed prior to calling **DeallocNcp**.

The following summarizes the sequence of subroutine calls described in the preceding paragraphs:

1. **AllocNcp**
2. **ReadCts** if modification of size constants is required
3. **LoadNet**
4. **PutSts** and **PutWts** as desired

5. **SetSlab** and **SetNet** as desired
6. **InterNet** (use **ChkItr** if desired)
7. **GetSts, GetWts**, and **GetIcn** as desired
8. **PutCts** as desired
9. **SaveNet** if desired
10. Repeat steps 4–9 until execution is complete
11. **FreeNet**
12. Repeat steps 2–11 to execute another network
13. **DeallocNcp**

The preceding sequence is for one network only. If multiple networks are used, the steps may be repeated multiple times and in any order that is appropriate for the specific network execution. ANZA will support as many simultaneous networks as its memory size will allow. Figure 12.14 presents the ANZA coprocessor.

12.6 THE DELTA-SIGMA NEUROCOMPUTER

The DELTA[20] Floating Point Processor produced by SAIC is a 12-M Byte accelerator board installable in an IBM-PC chassis, that takes two slots. The SIGMA is a neurocomputer workstation PC/AT operating at 16 MHz and is based on 80386 + 80387. Both the DELTA board and the SIGMA workstation come with software packages ANSim and ANSpec. The ANSim package allows configuration and operation of neural models. ANSim can store up to 25,000 processing elements, 100,000 connections, and can process 40,000 connection updates per second, on a suitable machine. Combined with the DELTA accelerator board, ANSim simulates 1,000,000 processing elements, 10,000,000 connections, and updates 1,000,000 connections per second.

Figure 12.14
ANZA neurocoprocessor. New ANZA-Plus, based on the Weitek XL family of processors can implement up to 2,500,000 processing elements and updates up to 10,000,000 interconnections per second. Reprinted by permission of the Hecht-Nielsen Neurocomputer Corporation, all rights reserved.

ANSpec is an object-oriented neural system description language suitable for implementation of complex neural networks, beyond ANSim. The system uses EGA color and a mouse.

12.7 NEURAL COMPUTERS VERSUS DIGITAL COMPUTERS

Artificial neural systems gradually became more and more sophisticated. Advanced systems could be called neural computers. Neural computers and digital computers are so different that they do not compete. Together, the two technologies promise a new age in computers, with digital machines doing calculations and neural machines serving as eyes and ears, able to match, listen, and talk back.

Table 12.5 compares the features of digital and neural computers, Smith.[21]

The hallmark of the *neural net* is massive parallelism and high interconnectivity between a large number of relatively simple processors. The information in a neural processor is stored in the inteconnection pattern rather than at specific spatial locations uniquely defined by a memory address.

Instead of a program of rules, which controls the operation of standard computers, these new systems work by actually learning a series of facts and instantaneously bringing those facts to bear upon a problem.

Instead of a central processor that acts on a few bits of information at a given time, as is found in standard computers, a neural network recruits its entire force of processors or "neurons" to work on a given problem all at once.

In this manner, the devices seemingly mimic the brain, in which a signal fired from a one neuron can trigger a cascade of thousands of other signals from one region to another and back.

TABLE 12.5 How Digital and Neural Computers Differ

Digital Computers	Neural Networks
Process digital data that are written in 1s 0s for mathematical precision	Process analog signals that fluctuate continuously, providing a range from, say, black through all shades of gray to white
Make yes/no decisions, using mathematical and logical functions	Make weighted decisions on the basis of fuzzy, incomplete, and contradictory data
Handle data in a rigidly structured sequence so that operations are always under control and results are predictable	Independently formulate methods of processing data, often with surprising results
Find precise answers to any problem, given enough time	Find good, quick—but approximate— answers to highly complex problems
Sort through large data bases to find exact matches	Sort through large data bases to find close matches
Store information so that specific data can be retrieved easily	Store information so that retrieving any piece of information automatically calls up all related facts

Source: C.T. Smith, "Computers That Come Awfully Close to Thinking," *Business Weekly*, June 1986.

Commercial applications for the technology will be vision systems, continuous speech between man and machine, adaptive learning by robots, and extraction of knowledge from large amounts of data.

Continuous speech would be an improvement over present speech recognition programs run on conventional computers because a pause must be included after every word spoken to the machine. Neurocomputers will be able to make sense of normal conversation, respond in kind and teach themselves how to speak by listening. A researcher at Johns Hopkins University recently developed a system that taught itself how to speak in 16 hours.

Robots are currently programmed to perform a certain set of motions with no room for error. Neurocomputers can run a robot that will be able to pick up a part, see that it is oriented properly, insert it, and be able to identify and adapt to any malfunction in the assembly process.

Extracting knowledge from data has been applied to medical diagnosis and financial analysis. The computer is able to look at seemingly unrelated masses of data and identify patterns from it, by using processes similar to human thinking. The process is not the same as artificial intelligence on "expert systems."

In this way, neurocomputers have another advantage over traditional computers in that they don't need exact input to search and find data. They are able to get past misspellings or incomplete input by recognizing what the user intended.

Two major benefits of artificial neural systems (ANS) are storage capacity and classification speed.

ANS can store large number of complex patterns: visual scenes, speech templates, robot movements. It can classify new patterns to store patterns quickly. The classification speed is independent of the number of patterns stored. These features promise new fields of applications, such as real-time pattern recognition, sensory processors, real-time fuzzy expert systems, robot control, and others.

REFERENCES

1. R. Hecht-Nielsen, *Performance Limits of Optical, Electro-Optical and Electronic Neurocomputers,* TRW Rancho AI Center, Carmel, CA, 1985.
2. R. Hecht-Nielsen, Neural analog processing. *Proc. SPIE–Int. Soc. Opt. Eng.* **360**, 180–189 (1982).
3. S. Grossberg, *Studies of Mind and Brain.* Reidel Publ., Dordrecht, Netherlands, 1982.
4. S. Grossberg, and M. Kuperstein, *Neural Dynamics of Adaptive Sensory-Motor Control,* North-Holland Publ., Amsterdam, 1986.
5. S. Grossberg, Some networks that can learn, remember, and reproduce any number of complicated space-time patterns. *J. Math. Mech.* **19**, 53–91 (1969).
6. W. Reber, Ph.D. dissertation, University of California, Los Angeles (to be published).
7. C. Smith, M. Myers, and R. Kuczewski, *Avionics Artificial Intelligence, TRW Independent Research and Development Program,* Proj. 87143001, 1987.
8. J.J. Hopfield, and D.W. Tank, 'Neural' computation of decisions in optimization problems. *Biol. Cybernet.* **52**. 141–152 (1985).

9. T. Kohonen, *Self-Organizational and Associative Memory*. Springer-Verlag, New York, 1984.

10. D.E. Rumelhart, G.E. Hinton, and R.J. Williams, *Parallel Distributed Processing*. MIT Press, Cambridge, MA, 1986.

11. G.W. Cottrell, P. Munro, and D. Zipser, *Image Compression by Back Propagation: An Example of Extensional Programming*, ICS Rep. 8702. 1987.

12. M. Myers, R. Kuczewski, and W. Crawford, *Applications of New Artificial Neural System Information Processing Principles to Pattern Classification*, Final Report. Contract DAAG-29-85-C-0025. U.S. Army Research Office, Washington, DC, 1987.

13. R. Kuczewski, Neural network approaches to multi-target tracking. *IEEE ICNN Conf. Proc. 1987.*

14. S. Grossberg, and E. Mingolla, Neural dynamics of perceptual grouping: Textures, boundaries, and emergent segmentations. *Percept. Psychophy.* **38**(2). 141–171 (1985).

15. *The TRW Mark III-1 Artificial Neural System Processor. Product Description.* TRW MEAD AI Center, San Diego, CA, 1987.

16. R.M. Kuczewski, M.H. Myers, and W.J. Crawford, Neurocomputer workstations and processors: Approaches and applications. *IEEE ICNN Conf. Proc. , 1987*; also TRW report.

17. J. Prichett, The new cybernetics: ADAPTing to AI. *TRW Messages* **4** (1) (1986).

18. R. Hecht-Nielsen, and C.A. Smith, *DARPA ADAPT Program MARK IV ADAPT Processor*. TRW Rancho AI Center, Carmel, CA, 1985.

19. *ANZA User's Guide*, Hecht-Nielsen Corporation, Release 1.00, 1987.

20. DELTA/SIGMA/ANSim, Editorial; *Neurocomputers*, **2** (1), (1988).

21. E.T. Smith, Computers that come awfully close to thinking. *Business Week* June 2, pp. 92–95 (1986).

CHAPTER 13

Adaptive Rule-Based Expert and Goal-Directed Systems

INTRODUCTION AND SURVEY

Knowledge-based expert systems are artificial intelligence problem-solving programs designed to operate in narrow domains, performing tasks with the same competence as a skilled human expert. The heart of these systems is a knowledge base. Most well-known expert systems make use of the rule-based representation of knowledge.

Adaptive expert systems change or modify the rule set over time, in order to improve their ability to perform a task. Given a set of rules to start with, the adaptive system applies various genetic algorithms to generate and test new rules. The genetic algorithms resemble the process of chromosome recombination, when DNA strands from parent cells combine to form new offspring cells.

This chapter examines the genetic algorithms used to generate new rules. It then presents a concrete example of an adaptive expert system. Each solution reached by the system is evaluated, and credit is assigned to each rule and the rule set. The current rule set has a weeding criteria applied to it; low performers are removed and new rules are placed into the rule set.

As an example, a navigation system is shown. The system must find the path between the initial and the goal position. The distance between the positions is used to compute the credit given to the rule set for its solution. This system is an expert system as well as a goal-directed system.

13.1 RULE-BASED REPRESENTATION OF KNOWLEDGE

Expert systems can usually be viewed as composed of two modules, as shown in Figure 13.1: a knowledge base and an inference machine. This structure nicely

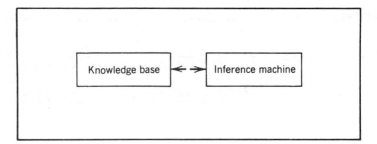

Figure 13.1 *Structure of expert systems.*

reflects the two main tasks of knowledge engineering: representing and storing large amounts of problem-domain knowledge in the computer and actively using the problem-domain knowledge for solving problems and answering user queries.

The knowledge base contains facts, relations between facts, and possible methods for solving problems in the domain of application. The inference machine implements algorithms which solve problems and answer user queries by either simply retrieving facts from the knowledge base or by inferring new facts from the facts that are explicitly stored in the knowledge base. Inferring new facts involves the use of general relations, or principles, which can also be stored in the knowledge base.

A production system[1-3] is defined by a set of rules, or productions, which form the production memory (PM), together with a database of assertions called the working memory (WM). Each production consists of a conjunction of pattern elements, called the left-hand side (LHS) of the rule, along with a set of actions called the right-hand side (RHS). The RHS specifies information that is to be added to (asserted) or removed from WM when the LHS successfully matches against the contents of WM. In operation, the production system repeatedly executes the following cycle of operations:

1. Match: For each rule, it determines whether the LHS matches the current environment of WM. All matching instances of the rules are collected in the conflict set of rules.
2. Select: It chooses exactly one of the matching rules according to some predefined criterion.
3. Act: It adds to or deletes from WM all assertions specified in the RHS of the selected rule, or it performs some operation.

During the selection phase of production system execution, a typical interpreter provides conflict-resolution strategies based on how recent the matched data in WM are as well as on syntactic discrimination. Rules matching data elements that were more recently inserted in WM are preferred, with ties decided in favor of rules that are more specific (i.e., have more constants) than others.

In general, rules are of the "if-then" form, but they can have different interpretations. Some examples:

If precondition *P*, *then* conclusion *C*.
If situation *S*, *then* action *A*.
If conditions C_1 and C_2 hold, *then* condition *C* does not hold.

A more concise notation is often used:

$$P \rightarrow C$$

The meaning of this depends on interpretation, that is "if precondition *P*, then conclusion *C*."

In the rest of this text we shall use the general forms

$$< \text{condition/action} > \qquad (13.1)$$

$$< \text{condition } 1 \wedge \text{condition 2/action 1, action 2} > \qquad (13.2)$$

Equation 13.1 presents a "first-order" rule. Similarly, Equation 13.2 presents a "second-order" rule. In general, the system will reward rules for becoming higher order, since higher-order rules encapsulate more specific knowledge; hence, they probably apply more "power" towards solving a problem once they become active.

13.2 GENETIC ALGORITHMS

An adaptive system is organized as a shell consisting of an inference engine, adaptive rules, and assorted other functions which handle various interfaces. This shell accepts a set of condition/action rules. Through continued operation of the system, new rules are created by the system and integrated into the existing rule set. The new rules are usually higher-order rules. Here we list several algorithms suitable to create higher-order rules.

13.2.1 AND Algorithm for Independent Rules

The AND algorithm combines two rules into a new higher-order rule. From the two conditions, a new condition is made which is the AND of the two. From two actions, a new action is formed, as a sequence of the two. Here is an example:

$$\left. \begin{array}{l} [C_1/A_1] \\ \\ {[C_2/A_2]} \end{array} \right\rangle \qquad \text{First-order rules}$$

$$C_1, C_2/A_1, A_2 \qquad (13.3)$$

Equation 13.3 presents the new, second-order rule.

Combining the rules in the above fashion is reasonable only if the two rules are independent. If one rule depends on the other one, it would be impossible to formulate the resulting action.

13.2.2 Crossover Genetic Algorithm

The crossover genetic algorithm was originally proposed by Holland[4,5]; it follows the process observed during recombination of chromosomes. Crossover may occur in nature whenever DNA strands from parent cells combine to form new offspring cells. Crossover then becomes the rather obvious operation of taking two strings and making two new different strings from them. In rule-based systems the crossover point is chosen as the point between the condition and action. Here is an example taken from the system designed by Stackhouse[6] and Zeigler[7]. Given two rules,

$$C_{a1}, C_{a2}, \cdots, C_{an}/A_{a1}, A_{a2}, \cdots, A_{am} \qquad (13.4)$$

and

$$C_{b1}, C_{b2}, \cdots, C_{bn}/A_{b1}, A_{b2}, \cdots, A_{bm}$$

the two rules obtained from crossover are given by

$$C_{a1}, C_{a2}, \cdots, C_{an}/A_{b1}A_{b2}, \cdots, A_{bm}$$

and (13.5)

$$C_{b1}, C_{b2}, \cdots, C_{bn}/A_{a1}, A_{a2}, \cdots, A_{am}$$

13.2.3 Scaling Algorithm for Linear Systems

In the linear system, the condition C repeated N times should produce the sequence of N identical actions A. Hence, from the rule

$$C/A$$

we can generate a new file:

$$N*C/N*A \qquad (13.6)$$

13.2.4 Complement Algorithm for Symmetrical Rules

Two rules are symmetrical if they produce exactly opposite actions. As an example we consider a navigation system. Given a set of rules for local motion, a starting location, and a goal location, the system must find a sequence of motion rules which brings the object from the initial position to the goal position. Arbitrarily, the goal state is chosen to be at the origin. For the x, y planes, the pair of rules might be of the form

$$\text{IF } X \text{ coordinate } < 0$$
$$\text{THEN } X: = X + 1 \tag{13.7}$$

and

$$\text{IF } X \text{ coordinate } > 0$$
$$\text{THEN } X: = X - 1 \tag{13.8}$$

If the X coordinate coincides with the north-south notation, Equations 13.7 and 13.8 can be written using a more semantic notation:

$$\text{NORTH-OF/SOUTH} \tag{13.9}$$

$$\text{SOUTH-OF/NORTH} \tag{13.10}$$

Equation 13.9 reads as follows: if the point is north of the origin, then go south. Similarly, Equation 13.10 reads, if the point is south of the origin, then go north. Obviously, Rules 13.9 and 13.10 are symmetrical. In the case of symmetry, the rules are related in the form of a complement. Knowing Rule 13.9, we can generate a new rule:

$$\overline{\text{NORTH-OF}}/\overline{\text{SOUTH}} \tag{13.11}$$

which leads directly into Equation 13.10. For three-dimensional space, the symmetrical pairs are

$$\text{NORTH} - \text{SOUTH}$$
$$\text{EAST} - \text{WEST}$$
$$\text{UP} - \text{DOWN}$$

The system can start with only three rules. The complement algorithm can be used to generate the additional three rules.

The critical point in an adaptive expert system is the choice and modification of the rule set. If the best rule set is being used all the time, a system is not risking enough in order to improve its performance. A rather elegant solution was developed by Zeigler[7,8], in which the system alternates between two different rule-selection strategies from one generation to the next. Specifically, during the first generation the best rules are selected to attempt a solution to the problem. During the next generation, an "experimental" rule set is selected. In both cases, the generation algorithms are applied to the selected rule set.

The two modes were introduced into the system because the small amount of randomness used in generating new rules from the best-so-far rule set did not allow enough variation in the generation of new rules. The system was implemented by both Zeigler[7,8] and Stackhouse[6] on a Texas Instruments PC, using Scheme development language (a dialect of LISP). We call it here Zeigler Adaptive System.

13.3 ZEIGLER ADAPTIVE SYSTEM *

The material in this section has been adapted from Stackhouse[6] and Zeigler[7,8]

The system time is broken into generations. The system operates in a loop consisting of the following steps which are performed each generation.

1. A solution to all problems in P is attempted using a subset of the current rule set.
2. Each solution reached is evaluated and credit is assigned to each rule and the rule set.
3. The current rule set has the "weeding" criteria applied to it. Low performers are removed.
4. A few new rules are generated from, and placed into the current rule set.

These will be discussed in more detail now.

At a fairly high level, the system can be described using the block diagram in Figure 13.2.

The problem space is loaded with a rule set which is selected from the rule operator's section by the selection-generation process. The rule operator section attempts to solve the problem within its own environment (the problem space),

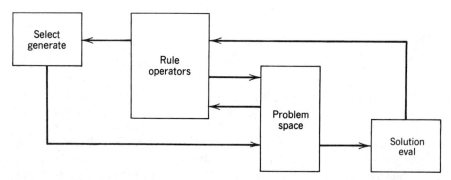

Figure 13.2 *High-level diagram of adaptive system. Reprinted with permission from Stackhouse[6] and Zeigler[7,8]*

using the selected rules. The solution reached is evaluated, the results being saved by the rule manager within its internal structures, which include rules and rule sets. This is repeated *ad infinitum*.

Figure 13.3 affords a more detailed view of the system.

Note that here the rule operator section has been broken up into the rule manager, the rule history, the inference engine, and the master rule set. Also, solution evaluation has become performance evaluation and credit allocation.

When the system is started, the master rule set, the rule history and problem space are initialized to contain the basic rules. These are the only data areas. There are also a handful of parameters which are initialized from a disk file (for easy editing).

The inference engine is used to forward chain on the rules in the problem space until the termination criterion (domain dependent) becomes true. This condition will usually test the current state for equality to the goal state of the current problem.

At that point, the solution obtained is evaluated by the performance evaluation component (note that this is also domain dependent as previously above). The credit resulting from the performance evaluation is distributed among the rules in the rule history using the algorithms described in the previous section. The same rule set is then used to solve the next problem in the problem set.

When the termination condition of all the problems in the problem set has been reached, the rule set itself is evaluated, ie., average performance is calculated and compared with that of the best-so-far rule set. If it is higher, it is appended to the rule history list and becomes the new best-so-far rule set. In any case, the rules in the master rule set are now updated to reflect the new credit values of the rules just used.

The weeding criterion is then applied to see if the rule manager is ready for weeding. This is a simple fixed rate (i,e., every *w* times through the top level loop, the rule manager is "weeded"). Finally, a subset of the rules are selected from the rule manager's current rule set and used to generate new rules (using the

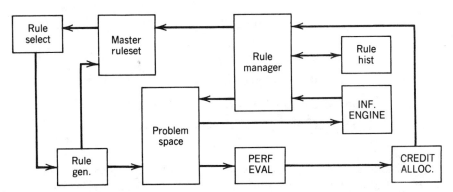

Figure 13.3 *Detailed diagram of adaptive rule-based system. Reprinted with permission from Stackhouse[6] and Zeigler[7,8]*

rule combination algorithms) for the next generation. These new rules are added to the current rule manager rule set as well as the master rule set and the problem space. The next generation then begins, using the selected subset and any new rules generated from them. The weeding and selection algorithms will be discussed in detail in the following section.

Payoff Allocation. An extremely important component of the system at the production level is the payoff allocation scheme. The algorithms used in this system are examples of genetic credit allocation schemes, discussed earlier. That is, rather than the bucket brigade which uses a subgoal reward strategy, rules are only rewarded for being in a set of profitable rules which lead directly to payoff.

The payoff enters the system upon reaching the termination condition which is domain dependent. For example, in one domain, the termination condition was either solving the given problem or reaching a fixed number of rule firings, whichever came first. Note that credit enters the system every time a problem is attempted.

To describe the credit algorithms, the system must be described generally and some difinitions given. First, the system operates upon a set of problems P, given a starting rule set R_O. It is expected that R_O will be complete in the following sense. R_O must contain enough conditions and actions (state operations) to allow all state transitions necessary for a solution to all the problems in P.

This state allows the system to start. Time is divided into an infinite number of generations, during each of which, the following steps take place:

1. A solution to all problems in P is attempted using a subset of the current rule set.
2. The current rule set is "weeded[*]" (low performers are removed).
3. The next rule set is created.

A master set of rules is kept, from which each generaton's rule set is selected. Hence the master rule set during generation g is given by

$$R_g = [R_o \cup (\cup_{i=1}^{g} RG_i)] - \cup_{i=1}^{g} RW_i \tag{13.12}$$

where: $U =$ union of sets.

$R_o =$ the initial rule set (generation o).

$RG_i =$ the set of rules generated at generation i.

$RW_i =$ the set of rules weeded at generation i.

---

[*] In practice, the rule set is only rarely weeded down (rather than every generation). One of the parameters of study is how often to "weed" the rule set. For the purposes of discussion here, suffice it to say that the weeding *criteria* is applied at the end of each generation.

The rule set used during generation g to attempt solving the problem set is given by

$$r_g = \{r_i \mid r_i \in \text{select } (R_g)\} \tag{13.13}$$

where: $\mid$ = "such that"

"select" = the selection function.

Note that weeding takes place before selection, hence R_g is taken as the set obtained after weeding.

The credit entering the system while attempting problem p is domain dependent and will simply be called c_p for now. We may now compute the credit assigned to a rule during generation g. First the utilization of r_i is calculated:

$$u_{ip} = \frac{f_{ip}}{tf_p} \tag{13.14}$$

where f_{ip} = the number of times r_i fires while rule set.

r_g is solving problem p.

tf_p = total number of rule firings which occurred while rule set

r_g is solving problem p.

Now we can compute the credit assigned to rule $r_i(\epsilon r_g)$ for each problem attempted during generation g:

$$c_{ip} = \{3 * c_p - 0.1 * \text{complexity}(r_i)\} * u_{ip} \tag{13.15}$$

where f_{ip} = the number of times r_i fires while rule set r_g is solving problem p. This leads to the total credit assigned to rule i during generation g:

$$c_{ig} = \sum_{p=1}^{|P|} c_{ip} \tag{13.16}$$

In addition, the total number of firings of r_i is saved:

$$f_{ig} = \sum_{p=1}^{|P|} f_{ip} \tag{13.17}$$

Since these two values are saved for all generations in which r_i exists in the system, their values after generation g are

$$c_i = \sum_{g \in s} c_{ig} \tag{13.18}$$

$$f_i = \sum_{g \in s} f_{ig} \tag{13.19}$$

where s is the set of generations in which r_i is selected.

A figure of merit for rules which is often used is its "rating." This is easily computed whenever necessary, from the above two values. Semantically, the rating is the "net credit per firing," and is computed as:

$$\text{rating}_i = c_i / f_i \tag{13.20}$$

Information is also saved about rule sets. In particular, each rule set is evaluated after attempting a solution to a problem set. The value of the best performing rule set is saved as well as the rule set itself. The performance of a rule set is calculated as follows:

$$CR_i = \frac{1}{|P|} * \sum_{p=1}^{|P|} c_p \tag{13.21}$$

Note that this is just the average performance of the rule set over the problem set.

Weeding Algorithms. A parameter to the system is the weeding period, W, which is an integer. It specifies the number of generations which elapse between weedings of the rule set (i.e., every W generations, the rule set is weeded). When a rule set is weeded, the following steps take place:

1. All rules which have never fired are removed.
2. Low performing rules are removed.

Selection Algorithms. Currently, the system operates in two modes, "best" and "experimental" which alternate with each generation (i.e., on odd numbered generations it is "best" and on even, it is "experimental"). The only difference between the two modes is the algorithm which was used for selection of the generation's rule set. To select a "best" rule set, the following algorithm is used.

1. Select the $M + P_m$ best rules, where M is the number of rules in the best-so-far rule set, and P_m is a parameter (order of M).
2. Randomly reduce the above list to length M.

The resulting list is the selected "best" rule set, which is used for the next generation.

An experimental rule set is obtained using the following algorithm:

1. Calculate the "cutoff" point of rule performance, using the formula

$$C = (7/8) * \text{best} + (1/8) * \text{worst}$$

   where best and worst are respectively the highest and lowest ratings in the rule set.
2. Select all rules with rating greater than C.
3. Select P_c rules randomly (P_c is a parameter).
4. Take the union of the above two lists, and randomly reduce it to length M (length of the best-so-far rule set).

In this way, the system will favor rules with high ratings, but will also favor sets of rules which perform well. During development of the system, it became apparent that the two modes would be necessary, since when only the best rules were selected, not enough of the rules were being used (in spite of the small amount of random selection). With the addition of the experimental mode, all rules have decent odds of being selected. This gives "down and out" rules the chance to get back lost credit any time before the weeding takes place.

Problem Description. The prototype problem can probably be best described as a navigation problem. In particular, given a set of rules for local motion, a starting location and a goal location, the [production level] system must find a path (or a sequence of motion rules) which goes from the initial to the goal position. The universe is N-dimensional Cartesian space (the current implementation uses 3 for N). For an interesting system which learns the navigation task, see Kampfner and Conrad.[9] For the navigation problem, the formula

$$c_g = \Delta \text{ dist } - w * f_g$$

where $\quad \Delta \text{ dist } = \text{dist}_{\text{final}} - \text{dist}_{\text{initial}}$

$\qquad \text{dist} = \text{the [Cartesian] distance from the current location to the goal location}$

$\qquad w = \text{parameter less than 1}$

$\qquad f_g = \text{the total number of rule firings used to reach the termination condition}$

is used to compute the credit given to the rule set for its solution. Note that Δ dist is maximum in the case where $\text{dist}_{\text{final}} = 0$, that is the system reaches the goal state.

Other types of problems which might benefit from this type of learning include: rule based control systems, planning, classification, diagnosis, and game-playing.

Table 13.1 shows an experiment in the navigation domain. At each generation

TABLE 13.1

Generation	1
Performance	5.0

[U/D]
[E/W]
[S/N]
[D/U]
[W/E]
[N/S]

Generation	20
Performance	13.0

[U/D]
[U^E]/[D:D]
[U^U]/[D:D]
[E/W]
[E/D]
[D/U]
[S^S]/[N:N]
[W^W]/[E:E]

Generation	760
Performance	66.125

[W^W^W^D^D]/[E:E:E:U:U]
[E^E^E^S^S]/[W:W:N:N:N]
[N^N^W^N^N]/[S:S:E:S:S]
[E/W]
[U^E^U^U^E^S^S^S^S]/[D:D:D:W:W:N:N:N:N]
[S^S^S^S]/[N:N:N:N]
[U/D]
[N^N^N^N^N^N^N^N]/[S:S:S:S:S:S:S:S]
[N^N^W^N^N^N^N^W^N^N]/[S:S:E:S:S:S:S:E:S:S]
[D^S^S^D^D^D^D]/[U:N:N:U:U:U:U]

the old rule set was replaced with a new one. Table 13.1 shows the rule sets in generations 1, 20, and 760. This rule set has been weeded about 30 times from the start of the experiment.

REFERENCES

1. A. Newell, Production systems models of control structures. In W. Chase (ed.), *Visual Information Processing*, Academic Press, New York, 1973.

2. M. Rychener, Production systems as a programming language for artificial intelligence research. Ph. D. dissertation, Carnegie-Mellon University, 1976.

3. J. McDermott, R1: The formative years *AI Mag.* 2, 21–29(1981).

4. J. H. Holland, *Adaptation in Natural and Artificial Systems: An Introductory Analysis with Applications to Biology, Control and Artificial Intelligence.* Univ. of Michigan Press, Ann Arbor, 1975.

5. J. H. Holland, Properties of the bucket brigade algorithm. *Proc. Int. Conf. Genet. Algorithms Appl.*, Carnegie-Mellon Univ., Pittsburgh 1985.

6. C. P. Stackhouse, An adaptive rule-based system. M. Sc. Thesis, University of Arizona, Tucson, 1987.

7. B. P. Zeigler, Expert systems: A modeling framework (unpublished).

8. B. P. Zeigler and C. P. Stackhouse, An adaptive expert system. *Proc. Int. Symp. Model. Simul. Methodol., 4th, University of Arizona 1987.*

9. R. Kampfner and M. Conrad, Computational modeling of evolutionary learning processes in the brain. *Bull. Math. Biol.* 45 (6), 931–968(1983).

CHAPTER 14 ————————————————

Event-Train Processing Systems

INTRODUCTION AND SURVEY

Event-train logic explains basic information processing in neural networks. There is a variety of event-train codes: in "labeled line" codes, the information is embodied in the particular fiber it traverses; in "rate coding," the stimulus intensity is coded by means of the rate of nerve impulses in a particular group of fibers; in "time coding," the length of each interspike interval carries information.

This chapter describes the operation of on-line microcomputer systems, correlators, feature extractors, and pulse generators, based on event-train processing. Real-time data acquisition systems, control systems, and transaction processing systems range from fairly simple units to complex networks. Numerous trains of events occur simultaneously at different points in the system. We show how these trains of events can be measured and analyzed, and what kind of effects they can produce in the system.

The event train presents a point process with events occurring randomly or regularly in time. In our discussion, we are not interested in the amplitude of an event, nor in the information that this event carries. The time of occurrence of the event and its relation to previous events are all that matter. In a real-time system, the "event" could be an electrical pulse, a switching instant, a transaction, an instant when an algorithm ends; or an interrupt. Examples of event-trains in other fields include pulses along a nerve fiber, breakdowns of equipment, pulses from radiation detectors, natural and artificial communication sequences, and behavioral sequences.

An event-train correlator measures the distribution of intervals between two events, regardless of the number of intervening events. The correlation is used here to analyze and compare event-trains in mini- and microcomputer real-time systems, in neural networks and in behavioral systems.

It is shown that multiplexors and synapses, through the superposition of fairly periodic event-trains, produce on the output almost random train. On the other hand, processing algorithms and buffer memories smooth the random train into almost periodic sequence. Examples of detection of hidden patterns in experimental data, as well as detection of dependences between two event trains, are shown, explaining neural and behavioral models.

A simple assembly language algorithm makes it possible to build an on-line correlator. Implemented on VAX, algorithm provides for data acquisition rates of 30 kHz (on an 8-bit microcomputer the rate is 10 kHz.) The system is based on the use of interval-sum storage with circular organization, and of memory for a correlation histogram.

We also describe a system that transforms the random (Poisson) event train into the event train with uniform distribution. The future will see more computing, measurement, and control systems using event trains.

14.1 EVENT-TRAIN AUTOCORRELATION AND CROSS-CORRELATION

A variety of statistical measures have been reported in the literature on event-train analysis.[1] These theories have been summarized by Cox and Lewis,[1] and also by Moore et al.[2] The early processing of neural event-trains has been performed with smaller electronic aids or modified pulse height analyzers.[3-7] More advanced processing is performed for the most part with large digital computers in scientific laboratories, especially for problems in neurobiology.

A simple assembly language algorithm makes it possible to build a microcomputer-based, on-line correlator. This will take event-correlation analysis into new and field-oriented applications, including real-time systems.

Event correlation is based on the measurement of the distribution of intervals between random events. The events can represent the flow of data in a real-time computer system, or the time series of experimental pulses.

The autocorrelation $C(t)$ specifies the probability of encountering an event as a function of time after a given event, irrespective of the number of intervening events, if any; i.e.,

$$C(t)dt = \text{prob(an event in } (t, t + dt)/\text{an event at 0)} \tag{14.1}$$

The crosscorrelation $C(t)$ is used in case of two trains of events, A and B. The crosscorrelation specifies the probability of observing an event in B as a function of time after a given event in A, irrespective of the number of intervening events, if any; i.e.,

$$C(t)dt = \text{prob(an event in } B \text{ in } (t, t + dt)/\text{an event in } A \text{ at 0)} \tag{14.2}$$

So defined, autocorrelation and crosscorrelation are used to explain the behavior of real-time measuring and control systems, neural networks, and behavioral patterns.

Event correlation is used to find out the dependences in the event-trains; to provide the measure of the dependences; to detect the hidden patterns in random sequences; and to suggest the proper probabilistic model of the system under investigation.

14.2 SOME PROPERTIES OF THE EVENT-TRAIN CORRELATION FUNCTION[*]

We shall apply the Poisson process to different systems and look for the output event trains. Event correlation will then be used to recognize the system and to detect its basic properties. Cases of practical interest are

- Systems with built-in generators of repetitive events
- Systems with delay
- Systems with dead time
- Periodic events displaced by random deviation
- Systems with buffer memory for one or more events
- Superposed series of events
- Doubly stochastic Poisson processes
- Branching stochastic processes

Poisson Process.   The Poisson process describes the probability of a number of events, r, in an arbitrary interval of length t:

$$P(r, t) = [(\lambda t)^r / r!] \quad \exp(-\lambda t) \quad (r = 0, 1, \ldots) \tag{14.3}$$

The Poisson process also gives the probability distribution of intervals t between events:

$$f(t) = P(r = 0, t) = e^{-\lambda t} \tag{14.4}$$

The event correlation based on Equation (14.1) for the Poisson process is then equal to the average number of events in dt:

$$C(t) = \lambda, C(0) = 1 \tag{14.5}$$

The result is shown in Figure 14.1a.

* Sections 14.2–14.5 have been adapted from Souček and Prohorov.[8] Courtesy of *Microprocessing and Microprogramming*.

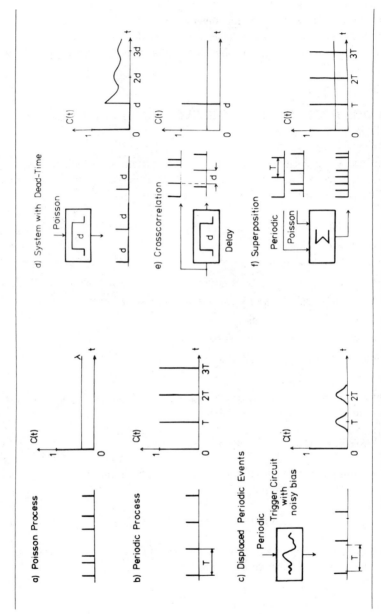

Figure 14.1 Event trains of practical interest (left) and their autocorrelations (right).

Periodic Events. For the periodic events, Equation (14.1) leads to

$$C(t) = 1 \text{ for } t = kT$$

$$C(t) = 0 \text{ for } t \neq kT. \tag{14.6}$$

The result is show in Figure 14.1b.

Periodic Events Displaced by Random Deviation. In this model, events are scheduled to appear at regular intervals (periodically) but are displaced from their scheduled points of appearance by a random amount.

An example is a circuit with inherent noise, or jitter, triggered by periodic events. Each event meets conditions which may delay or advance the firing of the circuit relative to the periodic time.

From Equation (14.1), it follows that

$$C(t + kT) = g(t) * g(t) \tag{14.7}$$

where $g(t)$ is the distribution of the jitter, and * represents the convolution operator. The result is shown in Figure 14.1c.

Systems with Dead Time. The model has inherent dead time. When it receives an input event, the system passes this event to the output and then is closed for a fixed dead time T (e.g., computer processing time). The event-correlation function of the output process can be found in the following way (Figure 14.2).

For $d < t < 2d$, using Equation (14.4) and (14.5) follows:

$$C(t)dt = \text{prob}(1, dt)\text{prob}(0, t - d) = f(t)P[0, t - d] \tag{14.8}$$

For $2d < t < 3d$, the interval t can be formed in two ways, as shown in Figure 14.2a and 14.2b respectively:

In the first way,

$$t = d + t_1$$

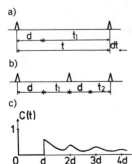

Figure 14.2

Process with dead-time: (a) interval having only one random part; (b) interval having two random parts; (c) autocorrelation function of process with dead time.

with density

$$\phi_1(t - d) = f(t) \tag{14.9}$$

The probability of this way of forming t is $P(0, t - d)$.

In the second way,

$$t = 2d + t_1 + t_2$$

with density

$$\phi_2(t - 2d) = f(t) * f(t) \tag{14.10}$$

The probability of this way of forming t is $P(1, t - 2d)$. Hence,

$$C(t)dt = P(0, t - d)f(t) + P(1, t - 2d)f(t) * f(t) \tag{14.11}$$

Generalization of Equation 14.11 for n exclusive ways gives

$$C(t)dt = \sum_{k=0}^{n-1} P[k, t - (k + 1)d] \cdot [f(t) * \underbrace{\ldots}_{k} * f(t)] \tag{14.12}$$

The multifold convolution of Poisson distribution gives Erlang's distribution. The result is present in Figure 14.2c and in Figure 14.1d.

In a similar way one can extend Figure 14.1 for additional combinations of interactions between random sequences and systems.

14.3   MORE THAN ONE EVENT TRAIN

The most obvious application of event correlation analysis is in cases with more than one event train in the system. The event trains could each be at a different point in the system, in which case the crosscorrelation will give the degree of interdependence; or the event trains could be mixed together (superposed).

Crosscorrelation.   This is an obvious application. In Figure 14.1e, a system with a delay d is shown. In cases like this, the crosscorrelation shows if the output series depends on the input series. Equation (14.2) gives

$$C(t) = 1 \text{ for } t = d$$
$$C(t) = \lambda \text{ for } t \neq d \tag{14.13}$$

Superposition.   In many physical and engineering situations, the event-trains are the superposition of a number of other event trains, such as random interrupts arriving at a processor from many sources, or nerve pulses arriving at synapse from many fibers. If the event train is composed of two or more other event trains, its correlation function will be the sum of the correlation functions of each individual train.

Figure 14.1f shows Poisson and periodic processes superposed, together with the resulting event-correlation function. If a similar correlation function is measured in an experiment, one can compare it with Figure 14.1f and conclude that a periodic process is buried in the random process.

Processes such as those shown in cases a to d, or others, can be superposed in a variety of combinations. The correlation will help to distinguish the participating processes, their intensities, and their speeds. It can also be used in simulation and measurement of random data.[7,8]

14.4 EXAMPLES: REAL-TIME SYSTEMS, NEURAL NETWORKS, AND BEHAVIORAL SYSTEMS

Here we show a few examples from real-time computer systems, neural networks, and behavioral systems.

Scanning.   In real-time computer systems based on scanning, the computer program determines both the timing of operations and the scheduling. Because a variety of algorithms can be used for processing, the scanning might present a process in which events are scheduled at regular intervals but, due to different processing times, are displaced from those scheduled times. Hence, the scanning process and its autocorrelation function will be similar to the one shown in Figure 14.1c. This autocorrelation function presents the measure of irregularity in the scanning operation.

Multiplexing.   If many outputs are connected to the multiplexor, the number of event-trains will be superposed. The resulting correlation function will be the sum of component correlation functions, as in the example of Figure 14.1f. Even if the component event trains are fairly periodic, the sum train might be a random process. An interesting observation has been made on synapses, with nerve pulses arriving from many fibres.[9] A series of nerve pulses may have been formed by superposing a number of fairly regular sequences, yet the result is a random sequence. This fact presents the warning in the design of real-time systems based on multiplexing, because it is more complicated to deal with random than with regular sequences. The event-correlation function gives the degree of regularity.

Dead Time.   If the event-processing time T is of the same order of magnitude as the average interval between events, $1/\lambda$, a substantial percentage of output events will be lost. The dead-time losses can be found for cases of practical interest.[10,11]

For the constant dead time T, the losses are

$$g(T) = \lambda T \qquad (14.14)$$

The output process and its correlation are shown in Figure 14.1*d*.

In real-time measurement systems such as pulse-height analyzers, dead-time losses will not produce the histogram distortion. The information is coded in pulse amplitude, and the pulses arrive at random. The situation is different in real-time systems for measuring the interval histograms (e.g., neuron time of flight analyzers or neural latency analyzers). For such systems, the dead time should be much shorter than the average interval between events.

Buffer Memory.   If the interval between two events is shorter than the processing time T, the buffer memory will store the second event. This results in a smaller percentage of lost events[10]:

$$g_1(T) = \lambda T - [1 - \exp(-\lambda T)] \qquad (14.15)$$

The event stored in the buffer memory is processed immediately after the dead time. Hence, the buffer memory moves events along the time axes, forming more regular intervals. The described autocorrelation function should be used to measure the degree of regularity of intervals.

Neural Spikes.   The train of neural spikes has been recorded by a microelectrode. The intervals between spikes have been analyzed, resulting in the correlation histogram. (For experimental conditions and results see Figure 4.5.) The experimental results have been compared with correlation histograms in Figure 14.1. The most appropriate model for this case seems to be the superposition (Figure 14.1*f*) of the Poisson process (Figure 14.1*a*) and of displaced regular events (Figure 14.1*d*). In this case, the described event correlation has helped to find the proper model of the system.

Insect Calls.   The sequence of insect calls has been analyzed. Insect calls present communication between two insects. The intervals between calls have been analyzed in the correlation histogram (for experimental conditions and results see Figure 4.9). The experimental results have been compared with correlation histograms in Figure 14.1. The most appropriate model for this case seems to be the superposition (Figure 14.1*f*) of the Poisson process (Figure 14.1*a*) and of a system with fixed processing time or dead time (Figure 14.1*d*). Again, the event-correlation function is used to find the model of the system.

In a complex real-time computer system, numerous trains of events occur simultaneously at different points in the system. The measurement, analysis, and proper identification of processes becomes an important part of system design and testing. A high-speed, microcomputer-based correlator presents a simple yet efficient tool for these goals. The applications of an on-line correlator include real-time computer systems, neurobiology, behavior, instrumentation, and communication.

14.5 A SMALL COMPUTER AS AN ON-LINE CORRELATOR

Figure 14.3 shows the block diagram of a small computer event correlator. For each random event, the following sequence of operations is performed.

Step 1. The time interval t_i is digitized. This is done outside of the computer, using the counter connected to the constant frequency clock generator. Each random event interrupts the computer. The computer reads the count into an interval register A, and then it resets the counter. The count presents the digital equivalent of the interval t_i, between the last two events used to reset the counter.

Step 2. Forming the sum-intervals. To calculate the contribution of a new event to the correlation function, the sum intervals are needed:

$$\Sigma_i = t_i$$

$$\Sigma_{i-1} = t_i + t_{i-1}$$

$$\Sigma_{i-2} = t_i + t_{i-1} + t_{i-2}$$

$$\Sigma_{i-N} = t_i + \ldots + t_{i-N}$$

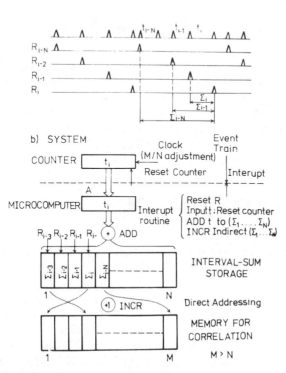

Figure 14.3 *Block diagram of an event correlator: (a) event train and sequence of resets; (b) system organization.*

A storage is reserved to store all the partial sums. We call it the *interval sum storage*. It keeps N partial sums of the preceding event; N is the upper limit of the number of intervals to be added.

The Σ_i will be stored in the ith position in the sum storage. For this reason, the interrupt program will first reset the ith position (R_i). The new set of partial sums is then formed by adding t_i to the old set of partial sums. The partial sums are stored in the sum storage in the circular way: Σ_{i-1} is to the left of Σ_i . . . and Σ_{i-N} is to the right of Σ_i. (The bank of registers can also be used to form and store the partial sums. In this case, adding t_i is performed automatically, if all the registers are connected to the common clock.)

Step 3. Add one to all addressed positions of correlation function. A field in the memory is reserved to store the histogram of the correlation function. Each partial sum will address one location of the correlation field. N addressed correlation locations are incremented by one. Note that the correlation field is composed of M locations, $M > N$. The ratio M/N depends on the interval quantizing step that can be adjusted with the choice of clock frequency.

To explain the above algorithm in another way, let us compare Equation (14.1) for event-correlation function with the well-known equation for autocorrelation function:

$$C_{xx}(t) = \lim \frac{1}{T} \int_0^T x(\tau) \cdot x(\tau + t) d\tau \tag{14.16}$$

In the case of event-train analyses, the event amplitudes $x(\tau)$ carry no information and can be normalized, $x(\tau) = 1$. For a given time lag t, the product from Equation (14.16) can have only one of two values: $x(\tau) \cdot x(\tau + t) = 1$, if the second spike is found at a distance t, or $x(\tau) \cdot x(\tau + t) = 0$, if there is no second spike at the distance t from the first spike. To calculate the correlation function for a given lag t, the above procedure should be applied on all spikes in the train. By adding together so-formed partial products, the correlation function is obtained.

14.6   AN EVENT-TRAIN GENERATOR

A simple event-train generator can be built using standard monostable devices. A monostable system (univibrator, one-shot, electromechanical, and biological monostable systems, etc.), triggered periodically, has a constant duration of quasistable period, T_0.

A monostable system, after being triggered, is in the quasistable state, whose duration T_0 is given by the system time constant τ_1. Usually the systems have resistance-capacitance time constants, whose capacitors change their charge during the quasistable period. When the capacitor voltage reaches some critical value, the system is switched back to the stable state by its own cumulative action. Now the capacitor starts changing its voltage, from a value which it has at the end of the quasistable period, to the stationary value of the stable state. The time constant τ_2 of this recovery period is different from the time constant τ_1, because the capacitor is charged through different paths in the stable and in the quasistable states. Usually the triggering of the system is repeated when the capacitor voltage reaches its stationary value. But if triggered at random, the system can receive the triggering signal during the recovery period, when the capacitor voltage is different from the stationary value.

The duration of the quasistable period T is now different from the characteristic value T_0. The period T becomes a stochastic variable, whose statistical distribution is to be found. To find this distribution, we must know the dependence of the duration on the trigger arrival instant t taken from the end of the last quasistable period.[11]

In most systems, the dependence of the normalized quasistable period T/T_0 on the normalized trigger arrival instant t/τ_2 is given by

$$x(t) = \frac{T}{T_0} = 1 - e^{-a\frac{t}{\tau_2}} \tag{14.17}$$

where the parameter a is determined by the structure of a particular system.

If triggering pulses are coming at random, the monostable circuit may be triggered before the end of the recovery period. Because of that, the duration of the quasistable period will vary from pulse to pulse. This period becomes a stochastic variable, whose statistical distribution is to be found.[11] We suppose that triggering pulses come at random with a rate λ, and that the first pulse which comes after the end of a quasistable period will trigger the circuit.

The probability that the first pulse will come in the interval t, $t + dt$ is equal to the probability $P_0(t)$ that there are no pulses in the interval $0 - t$, and the probability λdt of a pulse in the interval dt. According to the Poisson distribution for random events, we obtain

$$P_0(t)\lambda dt = e^{-\lambda t}\lambda dt \tag{14.18}$$

The probability density function of the arrival instant of the first pulse is then

$$f(t) = \lambda e^{-\lambda t}$$

The quasistable period T and its dimensionless form $x = T/T_0$ are functions of the arrival instant t, $x = x(t)$ (Equation 14.17). The stochastic variable x will have a probability density function g(x), which we can obtain by transformation of the function $f(t)$:

$$g(x) = f[t(x)] \cdot \left| \frac{dt(x)}{dx} \right| \tag{14.19}$$

where $t(x)$ is the inverse function of the function $x(t)$ and, according to Equation (14.17), is

$$t = \frac{\tau_2}{a}\left[\ln 1 - \ln\left(1 - \frac{T}{T_0}\right)\right] = \frac{\tau_2}{a}[\ln 1 - \ln(1 - x)] \qquad (14.20)$$

$$\frac{dt(x)}{dx} = \frac{\tau_2}{a}\frac{1}{1 - T/T_0} = \frac{\tau_2}{a}\frac{1}{1 - x} \qquad (14.21)$$

Substituting Equations (14.18), (14.20), and (14.21) into (14.19) we obtain

$$g(x) = \lambda\exp\left\{-\frac{\lambda\tau_2}{a}[\ln 1 - \ln(1 - x)]\right\}\frac{\tau_2}{a}\frac{1}{1 - x}$$

$$g(x) = \frac{\lambda\tau_2}{a}(1 - x)^{\lambda\tau_2/a-1} = \frac{\lambda\tau_2}{a}\left(1 - \frac{T}{T_0}\right)^{\lambda\tau_2/a-1} \qquad (14.22)$$

Theoretically obtained distributions (Equation 14.22) are shown in Figure 14.4, for parameters $\lambda\tau_2/a$ in the range $0 < \lambda\tau_2/a < 4$, which is of practical interest. These distributions are valid for all types of monostable circuits considered. The curves are normalized by the circuit parameters T_0 and a. The same set of curves has been obtained from experimental data.

This effect has been used to design the generator of random pulses with uniform distribution.[11,12] By selecting the parameters $\lambda\tau_2/a$, a large variety of distributions can be easily generated, as shown in Figure 14.4. This effect is also important in the analyses of event trains in neural networks and in artificial neural systems.

14.7 OSTOJIĆ COINCIDENT REDUNDANT MULTIPLEX

Ostojić[13] has investigated a multiplex network that mixes the event-trains from many sources. He calls the network-coincident redundant multiplex, CRM. The principle of the CRM is shown in Figure 14.5. The event-trains from every activated information source are conducted by many lines (redundancy), but at the same time every line is conducting signals from many information sources (multiplexing). The event-trains are uncorrelated. At the end of the information transmission (the right side) many combinations of the connections of the transmission lines are performed. Every such combination which represents the connection of the lines conducting the event-trains from the same information source (i.e., gemini, redundant signals) represents the point of interference for all the redundant impulses that have originated from the same information source. The coincidence between identical event-trains produces an output. The impulses that reach this point by the different lines but belong to different information sources have mutually different and casual phases, and they will not necessarily coincide. The probability of coincidence (and interference) of nonredundant impulses (which belong

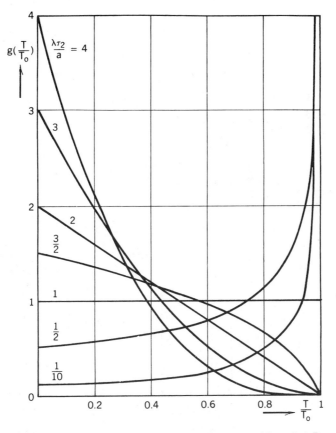

Figure 14.4 *Distribution function of the duration of the quasistable period. From Souček.*

to the different information sources) on the connection points of the information receivers is very small.

The coincidence of the redundant (i.e., gemini) signals that belong to the same information sources results in interference on the connection points and mapping of every information source on the point of coincidence. Figure 14.5 represents the mapping of six impulse information sources by using five connection lines. This shows a very clear representation and a comprehensive scheme. By using the greater number of information sources, the number of the spared connection lines for mapping increases very rapidly but the connection diagram is much more complicated.

Ostojić[13] suggests that the information transmission from the human eye to the visual cortex and human visual memory, is based on CRM, Figure 14.6. The process of CRM makes it possible to map the impulse sources of the information associated to a specific image in the set of the impulse exit elements. This set is different from the image but represents the map or the impulse memory associated with the specific image.

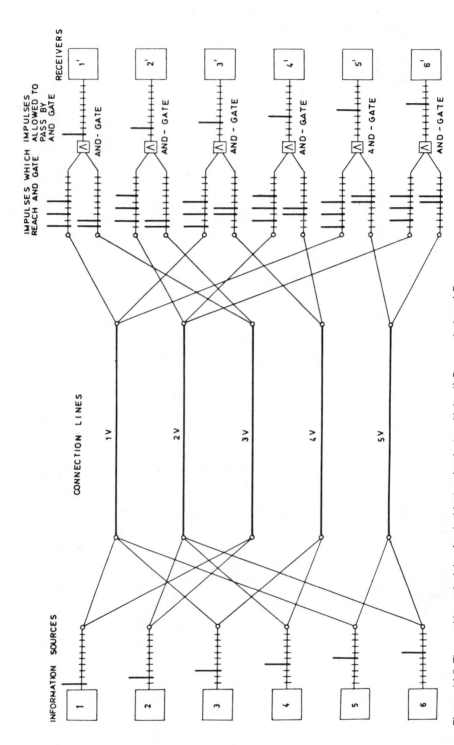

Figure 14.5 The working principle of coincident redundant multiplex. [13] By permission of B. Ostojić.

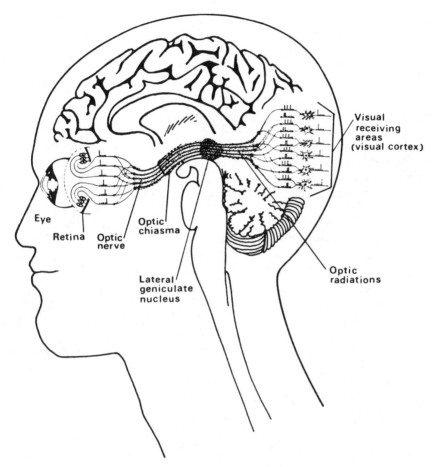

Figure 14.6 *Transmission of information from the human eye to visual cortex by means of coincident redundant multiplex process.*[13] *By permission of B. Ostojić.*

Possible application of CRM is very wide and ranges from the artificial sight, artificial hearing, and artificial command to the human muscles to the memories capable of converting an analog input to an impulse—type of representation and memorization, active memories (with the systems in which the memory is no longer a passive element as it is in present day computers but an active element capable of doing logical processing itself), associative computers, computers with deductive and inductive logic, and stochastic automata. CRM saves the needed number of connections in complex systems.

REFERENCES

1. D.R. Cox and P.A.W. Lewis, *The Statistical Analysis of Series of Events*. Methuen, London, 1966.

2. G.P. Moore, D.H. Perkel, and J.P. Segundo, Statistical analysis and functional interpretation of neural spike data. *Annu. Rev. Physiol.* **28**, 493–522 (1966).

3. W.R. Lewick, Modification of a 256-channel scaler for neurophysiological time analysis. *Rev. Sci. Instrum.* **33**, 1314–1315 (1964).

4. J.H. Schulman and J. Thorson, On-line analog generation of joint-interval histogram. *Rev. Sci. Instrum.* **35**, 1314–1315 (1964).

5. F.F. Hiltz and C.T. Pardoe, A correlator of time intervals between pulses. *IEEE Trans. Biomed. Eng.* **BME-12**, 113–120 (1965).

6. W.R. Lewick, P.O. Bishop, W.O. Williams, and D.G. Lampard, Probability distribution analyzer programmed for neurophysiological research. *Nature (London)* **192**, 629–630 (1961).

7. G.A. Korn, *Random Data Simulation and Measurement*. McGraw-Hill, New York, 1966.

8. B. Souček, S. Prohorov, Event-train correlation and real-time systems, *Microprocessing and Microprogramming*, **11**, 23–29 (1983).

9. P. Fatt and B. Katz, Spontaneous subthreshold activity at motor nerve endings. *J. Physiol. (London)* **117**, 105–128 (1952).

10. B. Souček, Losses in systems with variable dead-time. *Nucl. Instrum. Methods* **27**, 306–309 (1964).

11. B. Souček, Monostable systems triggered at random. *Nucl. Instrum. Methods* **29**, 109–114 (1964).

12. J. Descham, A. Hrisoho, and B. Souček, Generators of uniform distributed pulses for the nuclear laboratory. *Nucl. Instrum. Methods* **84**, 253–261 (1970).

13. B. Ostojić, Laser memory and coincident redundant multiplex memory. *Proc. Int. Symp. Ispra, 1975*, pp. 289–294.

ASSOCIATIVE AND PARALLEL COMPUTERS, CONCURRENT SYSTEMS

Tree Structures and Digital Transformations

INTRODUCTION AND SURVEY

The main purpose of this chapter is to review the techniques that will be needed to explain the software and hardware in brain-like systems. Two groups of techniques are found in many systems: trees and digital transformations.

Tree structures are used in both search algorithms and hardware hierarchical architectures. Single and multiple trees show the way to the descriptor or to the processor/memory element.

Digital transformations are typically used to map data from the sensory field into the memory field. Different digital transformation methods are described. High-speed pseudorandom key-to-address hardware units are shown. Combining these units with random access memory, a pseudoassociative memory is obtained. The Hough transform in computer vision is explained; it is used to detect and isolate straight lines and curves.

It is well known that the human brain preprocesses sensory data into compact units, increasing the information content per unit. The data is then memorized in the form of associative units with common denominators. Human-built brain-like systems should follow the same idea. Digital, analog, fuzzy, deterministic, pseudo-random, and statistical transformations will play an important part in these systems.

15.1 LISTS

15.1.1 Definitions

Information handling and processing problems are present in many experiments. Before we discuss specific problems and their solutions, some definitions and distinctions should be established. These distinctions often govern the selection of equipment and procedures to be used.

First, let us distinguish between data processing, and data storage and retrieval. Both may involve very large files or lists of information. Data-processing systems have as their main goal the manipulation, replacement, alteration, or addition of various items in the file or list. Data storage and retrieval systems have a different main goal: to store the list items for later reuse, rather than for modification, and to maintain the list items unaltered.

A list consists of a number of records. The record can consist of a single word or of several words; the words on the list will be called *descriptors*.

The list can be ordered or unordered.[1-8] The following example shows the difference between an ordered and an unordered list:

Unordered: . . . , 12, 18, 1, 4, 5, 29, . . .
Ordered: . . . , 2, 5, 11, 25, 31, 45, . . .

The list can be dense or loose. When the list is stored in memory, so that few, if any, blank records occur in this portion of the memory, the list is said to be dense. If many holes occur among the list members, the list is said to be loose.

In data measurement, the lists are used for various purposes: to store the results of the experiment; to compare the results with previous values; to count the frequency of occurrence of a given result; to control the experiment; and to lead it according to the stored set of data.

15.1.2   Key, Descriptor, and Associated Information

Each member of the list is specified in general by three quantities: key, descriptor, and associated information. For example, in the list of employees, we can have the following: key ≡ department; descriptor ≡ the name of an employee; associated information ≡ salary.

The *key* is used to find the item on the list. One can search for an item on the list even without the key, but for large lists such a procedure would be inefficient and time-consuming. Organization of the list on the basis of keys can be an obvious one, as in the above example. On the other side, when dealing with laboratory data it is sometimes difficult to decide on the right keys. Some key techniques, suitable for on-line laboratory list processing, are described in the next section.

A *descriptor* is the basic information describing the member of the list. In laboratory application, the task can be to search for a descriptor on a list; to erase an old descriptor; or to modify information associated with the descriptor. A typical example is data-amplitude analysis. The measured amplitude is the descriptor. Each new measurement is compared with the data already on the list. In this way, one can find out if such an amplitude has already occurred.

Associated information keeps all the other information that is of interest in connection to the descriptor. The associated information can be modified many times as the experiment proceeds. A typical example is amplitude-distribution measurement. The descriptor is the amplitude of incoming events. The associated information is the frequency of the occurrence of a given amplitude. Each new event searches the list, until it finds its descriptor. Then one is added to the associated information, which in this case presents the count. In this way, amplitude distribution is formed.

Now we shall consider the basic methods for searching the lists, following Hooton.[9] With these systems, no unusual facilities are required in the storage medium, and conventional computers may be used to implement the techniques described.

15.1.3 Sequential Method

An obvious routine for searching and processing a list (the search algorithm) is to compare the descriptor for a new event with the descriptor in each location in turn, starting at the first. When a "match" is found, that is, when the two descriptors are identical, the associated information is appropriately modified or used for the job, as requested by the program. If, after examining all used locations, no match is obtained, the new descriptor is stored in the next location. Many comparisons, up to the number of locations in the list, may be necessary, but the statistically most probable descriptors will tend to be allocated to early positions in the list. This tendency may be enhanced by periodically rearranging the descriptors in descending order of frequency of occurrence. Nevertheless, a large input buffer must be provided and considerable programs involved to achieve a dead time for a given experiment that is substantially independent of the input descriptor sequence. The mean dead time will be, in any case, a function of the descriptor distribution.

15.2 A TREE METHOD

A marked reduction in access time to the required location may be achieved by the use of a tree-search algorithm.[10] This algorithm depends on a comparison of two descriptors which yields one of three answers: (1) they match, (2) the first is greater than the second, or (3) the first is less than the second. The actual basis of comparison is unimportant, provided that it has a unique and repeatable answer for any given pair of descriptors. In nuclear physics or neurophysiology, a comparison of the numerical value of the descriptors will generally be suitable.

The underlying principle of this algorithm is as follows. The first descriptor A received is inserted in the first location of the list and may be regarded as the first node (p) or the root of a notational binary tree (see Figure 15.1). The second descriptor B is compared with A; if they are identical, associated information is modified or used for processing. If not identical, B is inserted in the next list location and forms a new node (q), supposing $B > A$; if $B < A$, the new node will be (r). A third descriptor C is compared with A and, if matched, the search is finished with A. If C is less than A, C will be inserted in the third location and form node (r); if greater, C will be compared with B. This comparison is acted upon as before. If matched, the search is finished with B; if not matched,

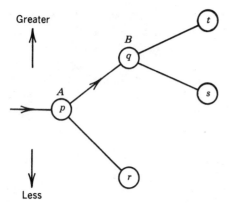

FIGURE 15.1
The tree method for list processing.[9]

C will take the next list location, and a new node will be formed at (s), $C < B$, or (t) $C > B$.

Each node generates two branches, but these are not terminated with nodes, nor are locations specified until an appropriate descriptor is received. Routing through the tree is established by storing in each location the addresses of the two nodes branching from it as they are allocated. The stored word at each location must therefore have space for two further location addresses, in addition to a descriptor and its associated information. Figure 15.2 shows the contents of the store and the corresponding notional tree after seven descriptors *ABCDEFG* have been applied. The magnitudes of the descriptors are assumed to be *GFBEDAC* in descending order, with *E* identical to *B*.

Compared with the sequential search algorithm, the storage space per word required will be increased by $2 \log_2 N$ bits, where N is the number of locations in the store; for example, 24 bits per word are required for 4000 locations. The access time to the nth location will, however, tend towards $\log_2 n$ instead of n.

15.2.1 A Multiple-Tree Method

A further reduction in the number of comparisons required may be achieved by having more than one tree growing simultaneously in the store. Since each location is unspecified until an appropriate descriptor is received and the path to that location is uniquely defined from its root, the tree will not waste storage space or interfere with another tree. The roots must be selected to enable any descriptor to be processed, and they should divide the incoming data evenly for the most efficient operation. It has been suggested by Cooke-Yarborough[11] that, since in scientific experiments events tend to cluster about peaks, several of the less-significant binary digits of descriptors may have approximately equal probability of being 1 or 0 and may, therefore, be used directly as addresses for the roots of a number of trees. The remaining digits alone serve as descriptors within the tree structure. This technique not only improves access time but also reduces the bit capacity required at each store location. A sequential search may also use a store

Location	Descriptor	Counts	Address of higher node	Address of lower node
1	A	1	2	3
2	B, E	2	5	4
3	C	1		
4	D	1		
5	F	1	6	
6	G	1		

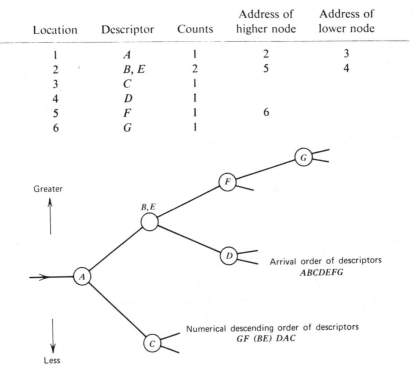

Figure 15.2 *An example of the tree method.* [9]

divided equally, with each section identified by these roots. The bits per location are reduced, but the access time is larger than for the simple tree; some storage space will be lost due to unequal filling of the sections.

With a nonuniform spectrum of descriptors, the multiple tree will show a more marked improvement on the simple tree.

All these methods have an access time to a particular location which is dependent on the history of the list up to the time of specifying the location. This may be an advantage, in that the most probable events will tend to have the shorter access times. However, a tree has been suggested by Landauer[12] in which the number of nodes to any location does not differ by more than one, and hence the access time is approximately constant and independent of both the distribution of descriptors and their arrival order. Access time is also reduced by having more than two branches per node.

15.2.2 Binary Search for Ordered Lists

The ordered list is more difficult to construct and to modify, but it is very easy to reference and search. Descriptors can be ordered in descending order. A search for an item is begun when we enter the list somewhere near the middle. The new descriptor is compared with the one in the middle of the list. If equal, the search is finished. If smaller, only the lower half of the list will be examined. If larger, only the upper half of the list will be examined. The second comparison cuts half of the list into two quarters. The next comparison will cut the quarter into two eighths. The average number of comparisons will tend towards $\log_2 n$, where n is the number of items on the list.

15.3   TRANSFORMATION METHODS

The methods so far discussed use an associative list in the sense that the program finds a location by the descriptor stored. Transformation methods are not truly associative at all but instead endeavour to make the list appear much larger than it actually is. The list is divided into a number of sections, known as buckets, and each bucket is then allotted many more descriptors out of the whole possible range than there are locations available. Provided that the descriptors which actually occur are spread evenly over all buckets, the discrepancy will not be apparent.

Essentially, the descriptor is transformed mathematically to give a location such that any distribution of descriptors will produce a uniform distribution of locations throughout the list. Part of the transformed descriptor is used as the bucket address or key, and the remainder is used to tag a location within the bucket at which the associated information is stored. To retrieve the information for a given descriptor, it is now necessary to search for the tag in the bucket identified from the descriptor. If the required uniform distribution over buckets is to be obtained, the transformation must disperse descriptors which form clusters, that is, have many digits in common. In short, the transformation must have a randomizing effect.

It will be noted that the suggestion described above of selection by least-significant digits[11] constitutes the simplest possible key for bucket identification. More complex transformations have been suggested for the general case when such straightforward methods are inapplicable. One such transformation[13] takes the digits of the descriptor, expressed in radix p, and computes the magnitude in radix q to give the location address, where p is relatively prime to q (preferably $p = (q + 1)$). The least-significant digits are used to identify the bucket.

As an example, let us suppose the descriptors relate to a 1000×1000 xy spectrum and are formed by writing the digits for x after the digits for y. The possible clusters are illustrated in Figure 15.3. We will identify buckets by the two least-significant digits in the location address; that is, the store is divided into 100 buckets. Table 15.1 shows that if the location address is identical with the descriptor, the first cluster is spread over five buckets, while all the members of the second cluster are directed to a single bucket. If, however, we treat the digits of the descriptor as if they were not decimal but based on radix 11, and we then compute the equivalent decimal (radix 10) magnitudes, a new set of locations is obtained. Specifying bucket addresses as before by the two least-significant digits in the location distributes both clusters.

In the example chosen, a uniform distribution for both clusters could have been

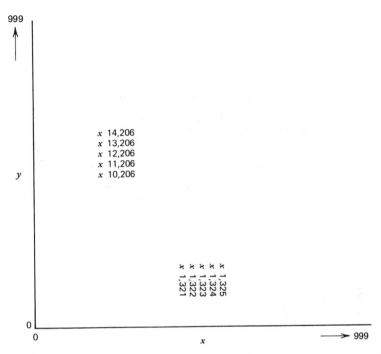

Figure 15.3 *Transformation of decimal descriptors[9] by expressing them on the bases of radix 11.*

obtained by taking the least significant digit of x and of y to form the bucket addresses, that is, 11, 12, 13, 14, and 15 for cluster 1 and 06, 16, 26, 36, and 46 for cluster 2. Such a technique is always preferable to the more complex radix transformation, but it demands an a priori knowledge of the descriptor distribution.

With a fixed bucket capacity, translation methods can only be based on probability which, with an undetermined applied distribution, may lead to unused stor-

TABLE 15.1

Cluster	Descriptor	Without Transformation		After Radix Transformation	
		Location Descriptor	Bucket Address	Location Descriptor	Bucket Address
1	1,321	1,321	21	1717	17
	1,322	1,322	22	1718	18
	1,323	1,322	23	1719	19
	1,324	1,324	24	1720	20
	1,325	1,325	25	1721	21
2	10,206	10,206	06	13558	58
	11,206	11,206	06	14889	89
	12,206	12,206	06	16220	20
	13,206	13,206	06	17551	51
	14,206	14,206	06	18882	82

age space. Overflow routines are required to deal with this problem. Alternatively, the bucket addresses may be used as roots for a forest of trees, as described above.

Transformations suitable for list processing must have the following features:

- The distribution of descriptors must be uniform over memory addresses, for practically any size or shape of the physical spectra.
- The cluster of descriptors in a physical field must be spread over the whole range of possible addresses, and adjacent descriptors must go to addresses far away from each other.
- Transformation must be fast, so that it can be applied on-line for high-data rate experiments.
- Transformation must be simple, so that one can realize it with a small investment in hardware or in software.

An unlimited number of different methods can achieve digital transformation, but most of them will not obey all of these requirements. Methods are usually similar to the generation of pseudorandom numbers. One of the best known is the method which uses residues.[14]

The sequence of pseudorandom numbers can be generated from the recurrence equation

$$a_{n+1} = k \cdot a_n \quad (\text{modulo } M) \tag{15.1a}$$

where k is a large prime number. Equation 15.1a can be modified to the form

$$A = k \cdot D \quad (\text{modulo } M) \tag{15.1b}$$

where $k = 2^{19} - 1$, D is the descriptor, and A is the pseudorandom address into which the descriptor can be stored.

Experiments with this method show results not acceptable for experimental data processing; spectral shape is a parameter of Equation 15.1b, and for some shapes the transformation produces groupings of descriptors instead of uniform distribution.

A number of different arithmetic operations have been tried, but results have always depended on the spectral shape. Now we shall consider logical operations for the key to address transformation, following Bonačić, Souček, and Čuljat.[15] Logical operations produce much better results than arithmetic operations.

15.3.1 Hamming's Codes

One of the simplest logical operations is parity generation,[16] which is used for the following experiment. The generation of sindrom by Hamming's technique[17] is also used. Sindrom corresponds to the address.

The experiment is performed for two-dimensional spectra of 1024 × 1024 ·

channels, described by 20-bit descriptors. Bits have been arbitrarily mixed and then selected by five different masks (1, 2, 4, 8, 16) as shown in Table 15.2.

Each mask selects bits on which the parity test is done. The result of the parity test gives a value (0 or 1) of a 1-bit pseudorandom address. With five masks one can generate a 5-bit pseudorandom address. By using this procedure, descriptors belonging to the 20-bit field can produce 2^5 different addresses. The relationship between descriptors and addresses is pseudorandom and obeys the requirements necessary for transformation.

The problem is that from a large descriptor field (20 bits) one can obtain only a very limited number of addresses (5 bits). For practical purposes in scientific experiments, a 20-bit descriptor field would have to generate about 2^{10} to 2^{14} different addresses, asking for 10 to 14 different masks. Since Hamming's coding allows a maximum of 5 masks for 20 bits, one has to generate more than 1 address bit out of each mask. All the bits selected by a given mask are added together, and the least-significant 2 (or 3) bits of a sum are used as address bit. Digital transformation using such a procedure has been simulated by a computer program. It is possible to realize such a transformation by relatively simple hardware for a given size of memory, if the size of the descriptor field is known in advance. It is not easy to adapt such a transformation to another memory or field size.

15.3.2 Coding Theory in Solving Addressing Problems

The problem of transformation is similar to the file-address problem based on key-to-address transformation.[18-20] The Bose-Chaudhuri method has been used for the construction of such transformations.[21-23]

Bose-Chaudhuri codes are cyclic codes that are best defined in terms of the roots of the generator polynomial. The symbols are assumed to be elements of a Galois field $GF(q)$. The polynomial $T(x)$ over $GF(2)$ generates a code with a minimum distance of at least w if $a, a^2, a^3, \ldots, a^{w-1}$ are roots of $T(x)$. Let a be a primitive element of $GF(2^t)$ that is $a^{2t} - 1 = 1$, but $a^i \neq 1$ for $0 < i < 2^t - 1$; then the code generated by

$$T(x) = (x - a)(x - a^2) \cdots (x - a^{w-1}) \tag{15.2}$$

has a minimum distance w.

The implementation of the Bose-Chaudhuri method to a file-address problem is simple. The keys and addresses have to be represented in it as polynomials. The Bose-Chaudhuri theorem states that if $R(x)$ is the remainder of the division of $K(x)$ by $T(x)$, that is $K(x) = Q(x) \cdot T(x)$, and the degree of $R(x) < w - 1$, then the minimum distance between two keys $K_1(x)$ and $K_2(x)$ giving the same address, which corresponds to $R(x)$, is at least w.

Schay and Raver[18] have used this method for the key-to-address transformation. They define the set of all possible keys as the set K, which is generally very large (10^{36} possible keys). The actual keys appearing in a particular file form a small subset S of the set K. Schay and Raver further assume that the memory has M

TABLE 15.2

	01	02	03	04	05	06	07	08	09	10	11	12	13	14	15	16	17	18	19	20	21	22	23	24	25
20-bit field of descriptor	01	02	03	04	05	06	07	08	09	10	11	12	13	14	15	16	17	18	19	20					
Mixed 20-bit field of descriptor	10	05	18	16	06	01	09	11	20	17	04	12	08	19	02	13	14	07	15	03					
Mask 01 *	X		X		X		X		X		X		X		X		X		X		X		X		X
Mask 02 *		Y	Y			Y	Y			Y	Y			Y	Y			Y	Y			Y	Y		
Mask 04 *				Z	Z	Z	Z					Z	Z	Z	Z					Z	Z	Z	Z		
Mask 08 *								W	W	W	W	W	W	W	W									W	W
Mask 16 *																Q	Q	Q	Q	Q	Q	Q	Q	Q	Q
	01	02	03	04	05	06	07	08	09	10	11	12	13	14	15	16	17	18	19	20	21	22	23	24	25

addresses, and that the number of elements of any set S must not exceed M. The cluster of diameter w is defined as any set of keys in which the maximum distance between pairs is $w = W$. They assume that the only restriction in any input set S is that no cluster will exceed diameter W.

15.4   PSEUDORANDOM TRANSFORMATION

Each signal describing an event can be expressed as a digital number, which we call a descriptor. Any descriptor D may be presented as a polynomial

$$D(x) = a_d x^d + a_{d-1} \cdot x^{d-1} + \cdots + a_2 x^2 + a_1 x + a_0 \qquad (15.3)$$

where $a_0, a_1, \ldots, a_d$ are elements of the Galois field $GF(2)$ and can be either zero or one. For example, the descriptor $D_5 = 000 \cdots 0101$, whose decimal equivalent is 5, will have coefficients

$$a_0 = a_2 = 1$$

$$a_1 = a_3 = a_4 = \cdots = a_d = 0$$

By multiplying the polynomial $D(x)$ of the degree d by the polynomial $S(x)$ of the degree s, we obtain the polynomial $M(x)$ of the degree $d + s$. If all the coefficients $b_0, b_1, \ldots, b_{s-2}, b_{s-1}$ of the polynomial $S(x)$ are equal to zero, and only $b_s = 1$, the polynomial $M(x)$ will be

$$M(x) = c_d x^{s+d} + \cdots + c_2 x^{s+2} + c_1 x^{s+1} + c_0 x^s \qquad (15.4)$$

where $c_0, c_1, \ldots, c_d$ are also elements of a field $GF(2)$ and can be either zero or one.

The polynomial $M(x)$ is in fact the descriptor D, shifted to the left for s places. By dividing the polynomial $M(x)$ by the polynomial $T(x)$, where $s \geq t$,

$$M(x) = Q(x) \cdot T(x) + R(x) \qquad (15.5)$$

The remainder $R(x)$ will be of a degree less than t. Experimentation with different spectra and different polynomials $T(x)$ has shown that the remainder $R(x)$ might be used as a descriptor address on the list. Two adjacent descriptors of any size in the physical field will give two remainders far away from each other for almost any possible polynomials of degree t. The descriptor may come from any point of the physical field, and its remainder will always present one of 2^t different memory addresses. If the original descriptor $D(x)$ has a degree less than t, after dividing it by $T(x)$ its remainder will be $R(x) = D(x)$. On such descriptors, the transformation will not produce the randomizing effect. That is one reason why all descriptors which have a degree less than t have to be first multiplied by $S(x)$. All descriptors have to be multiplied by the same polynomial because of the increase of the physical field and the distance between adjacent descriptors.

One example of transformation is presented in Figure 15.4. In this example, the descriptor $D(x)$ corresponds to decimal 7, and $T(x)$ is of the fourth degree. The first four shifts represent the multiplication by $S(x)$, and the shifts from the fourth to the seventh represent division by the polynomial $T(x)$ with the action through appropriate feedbacks (determined by the polynomial $T(x)$). The remainder $R(x)$, which is a polynomial of a degree less than or equal to $t-1$, represents the t tuple of the address of the descriptor $D(x)$. In this example, $R(x)$ presents the address 1101, which corresponds to the decimal number 13. The total number of different addresses is $2^t = 2^4 = 16$.

The number of different addresses depends on the degree of the polynomial t. The polynomials useful for transformation must have $a_t = a_0 = 1$. Hence, there are 2^{t-1} different polynomials of the degree t. In the example shown, one can have $2^{t-1} = 2^3 = 8$ different polynomials:

$$T_0(x) = x^4 + 0 + 0 + 0 + 1$$
$$T_4(x) = x^4 + x^3 + 0 + 0 + 1 \tag{15.6}$$
$$T_7(x) = x^4 + x^3 + x^2 + x + 1$$

15.5 PROPERTIES OF PSEUDORANDOM TRANSFORMATION THROUGH THE DIVISION OF POLYNOMIALS

The properties of transformation have been thoroughly investigated through simulation by a digital computer.[15] Figure 15.5 shows the field of addresses produced

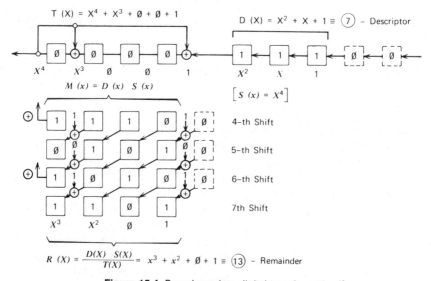

Figure 15.4 *Pseudorandom digital transformation.* [15]

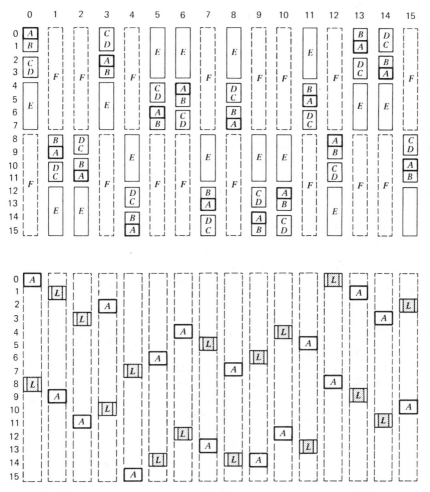

Figure 15.5 *Position of the descriptors which are producing the same address* A *(or* L*).* [15]

by descriptors 0–256 (field of descriptors 16 × 16). Figure 15.5 shows the position of descriptors which are producing the same address A (or L). Those descriptors are congruent modulo $T(x)$, and they form the same residue class.[24]

There are 2^t different residue classes. The descriptors which belong to the same residue class are pseudorandomly distributed between 0 and 256. Their pattern presents the spectrum for which the method will not work. Fortunately such a spectrum is improbable for experimental data.

Changing the structure of the polynomial by changing the coefficients a_{t-1}, $a_{t-2}, \ldots, a_1$, the number of possible different addresses will not change; it is always 2^t. However, some structures might produce a pattern resembling the shape of spectra. The selection of polynomials has been done to avoid even this little probable case. Through computer simulation, we can obtain the polynomials of the degree t having the maximum period 2^t by using a circuit for counting in a Galois field code.[23] Such a circuit is shown in Figure 15.4 and consists in this example of a four-stage shift register with a proper feedback through exclusive OR gates (denoted by a + sign). For the best feedback, a four-stage shift register can have a maximum period of 16, producing 16 different addresses, which are elements of the Galois field $GF(2^4)$.

In general, the Galois field of 2^t elements $GF(2^t)$ may be formed as the field of polynomials over $GF(2)$ modulo $a_t x^t + a_{t-1} x^{t-1} + \cdots + a_1 x + a_0$. This field corresponds to the 2^t different addresses.

The polynomial $T(x)$, giving the maximum period with a circuit for counting in a Galois field code, produces a pseudorandom pattern. Hence, descriptors corresponding to the same residue class are distributed pseudorandomly on the number line.

Table 15.3 shows the pattern of 1024 addresses generated through division from the descriptor field 32×32. The polynomial has the form $T(x) = x^5 + x^4 + 0 + x^2 + x + 1$. In the first column is a "first-degree pattern" produced by descriptors 0 through 31. There are $2^t = 32$ different first-degree patterns, forming the "second-degree pattern," which covers the whole of Table 15.3. The R denotes a few descriptors belonging to the same residue class, producing addresses 0 and 27, which correspond to those classes.

A similar experiment has been repeated using Hamming's masks. The field of 32×32 descriptors (XY), using five Hamming's masks, produced $2^5 = 32$ different addresses with the pattern shown in Table 15.4. Masks have been chosen according to Table 15.2. It was necessary to mix X and Y bits to obtain 32 different columns. M denotes a few descriptors producing the same address. Tables 15.3 and 15.4 show similar patterns for this example, although the transformations used are different.

It would be of interest to find a transformation which would break all regularities. An experiment in this direction has been performed in the following way. Different polynomials $T(x)$ of degree t produce different combinations of pseudorandom addresses inside a pattern. Hence, it would be of interest to change $T(x)$ for each descriptor. The polynomial must have coefficient $a_t = a_0 = 1$, while the other coefficient can be chosen arbitrarily.

For a given descriptor, Hamming's masking was used to produce coefficients $a_{t-1}, a_{t-2}, \ldots, a_2, a_1$, and the same descriptor was then divided by the so-formed polynomial $T(x)$. The results are shown in Table 15.5 for 1024 descriptors (32×32 field). Using masks (1, 2, 4, 8) from Table 15.2, one can generate coefficients $a_4, a_3, a_2,$ and a_1 and produce 16 different polynomials of the same degree t.

The pattern of addresses in Table 15.5 has no more regularities than in the previous two methods. One can follow, for example, two addresses, marked N and E in the first columns. The properties of this transformation and further extension of transformations through division and Hamming's masking have to be investigated in more detail.

TABLE 15.3

```
      00 01 02 03 04 05 06 07 08 09 10 11 12 13 14 15 16 17 18 19 20 21 22 23 24 25 26 27 28 29 30 31
   0|R  7 14  9 28 27|R18 21  3  4 13 10 17 31 24 17 22  1  6 15  8 20 26 29 20 19  5  2 11 12 25 30 23 16
     27 28 18  4 17|R 9 21 24 31 10 17  3 24 10 13 27 12  5 19 25  2  6 15  8 30  8 15 16  6  2  5 12 11  6
     13 10  4 31 10 23  7 14 28  0 18 27 23 14  7  0 28 23  5 30 25 12 11  2  5 20  6 29 26  1 19 26  1 29
     22 17 31 10  6  4  3 21 25 27 28  9 14  2 11  0 16 27 18 21 12  7 14  9 31 24 17 22  3 24 13 22 24 10
     26 29 19 18  1  8 19 14 15 30 16 28  9  5  2 23 28  9 18 21  0  7 14  6 19 24 17 10 13 24 31 22 17 17
      1  6 15 25 11 15 26 29  2 16 29 12 11 30  7  1 17  7 31 24 13 28  9 18 21  3 10 13 24 31  4  9  0  7
     23 16 25  2 19 23 29 17 20  6 23 26  0 25 20 22 10 13 24  1  3 22 17 28  9 10 28  7 18 21  1 18 21 28
     12 11  2  5 12  3  1 22 19 26  8  2  5 16 29 10 13 24  3 30 22 17  8 21  4 28  9  4 31 24  9  6 27 28
     15  8  1  6 24 30  6 19 31 12  2  5 16  1 18 25 24  9  4  7 11 30  3  0 13 21  0 21 18 27 14 29  9  7
     20 19 26 19 20 29 19  4  7  0 11 12 25  6 21  9  0 21 18 27 11 30  3 14  7 14  3  8 15 16  9 23 17 28
      2  5 12 11  8 15 24  3  9 14 25 30  7 20 18 27  4 21 22  3 24 17 10 31  0 28  9  6 19 20 21 17 24 31
     25 30 23 16  5  2 11 30  6 31  8 15 10  5  8 17 31 24 17 22  3 28  7 10 28  9  6 19 14 27  7  1 14  4
     21 18 27  28 2 11 26 29 12 25 20 19  6 19 15  8 20  3 10 23 16  4 13 10  3  8 21 14  3 22  2 11  2  5
     14  9  7 18 21  3 13 10 31 24 17 18  7 22  0  2 30 27 28  6  1 26 29 11 29 19 20  5 16  6  0  7 21 30
     24 31 22 17  4  3 27 28 10 21 18  4 18 31  9 14 30 25 16  1 20  2  5 29 11 26 19  1 20 15  7 14  2  5

     18 21 28 27 14  9  0  7 17 22 31 24 13 18 21  2 20 19 26 29  8 15 23 16  1 25 30 11 12  5 20 19 30 19
     17 22 31 24 13 10  3  4 18 21 28 27 14 15  8 31 19 25 30  4 11 12 10 13 27 26 29  8 15  6  9 14 14  3
     10 13  4  3 22 17 24 31  9 14  7  0 21 28 27 12 16  2  5 31 23 30 25  7 18 21  6 19 20 29 27 18 21 24
     28 27 18 17  7  4 31 24  7 22  0 21  3  4 13 10 26 29 20  9 30  1  8 24 31 10  1 28  9 11  2 11  4  3
      9 14  7  0 21 18 27 28 10 17 22 31 28  4 13 10 29 20 19  6  1  8 15 25 26  2  5 16 23  6 15 20 24
      7  0 21 18 28 27 14  7 17 22  9 14  1  6 15  8  1 22 31 24 29 26 31 20  2  5 12 11 30 25 16 25 29 14
     11 12  5  2 23 16 25 30  6  1 20 29  0 19 29 13 10 17 24 31  8 31 24 14 14  9  0  7 18 21 24 17  7  0
     16 23 30 25 12 11  2  5 19 20 29 26 29 23 16  0 22  3  4 31  6 20 19  8 21  4  3 28  9 14 17 24 22 13
      6  1  8 15 26 29 20 19  5  2 11 12  2  5 11 26 13 21 18 27 19  9 14 24  3 31 22 17 31 10  3 10  3 13
     29 26 19 20  1  6 15  8 30 25 16 23 23 16  8 20 11  0  7  7 28 21 18  9 14 24 17  4 28  4 31 25  5  2
```

TABLE 15.4

00	01	02	03	04	05	06	07	08	09	10	11	12	13	14	15	16	17	18	19	20	21	22	23	24	25	26	27	28	29	30	31
0	24	22	14	21	13	3	27	17	9	7	31	4	28	18	10	12	20	26	2	25	1	15	23	29	5	11	19	8	16	30	6
13	21	27	3	24	0	14	28	2	4	10	18	9	23	31	1	25	26	23	15	20	12	2	26	16	8	6	24	5	29	19	11
19	11	5	29	6	30	16	20	26	26	23	23	25	1	17	7	31	9	17	23	18	28	4	14	3	22	30	0	27	3	13	21
30	6	8	16	11	19	29	5	23	23	15	15	20	2	28	14	17	31	9	10	10	4	17	3	27	24	13	27	22	14	0	24
6	30	16	19	5	11	8	8	29	15	23	25	2	12	26	28	4	18	18	28	17	7	28	13	13	21	22	21	14	3	27	0
11	19	30	6	8	16	5	29	5	2	25	23	26	20	2	4	28	10	10	5	9	9	11	21	21	3	15	23	21	5	11	13
21	13	6	30	16	8	27	3	8	24	26	20	2	18	15	22	2	4	7	11	7	17	31	27	27	13	3	7	6	30	16	19
24	0	14	22	13	21	18	9	10	18	23	15	1	10	9	26	26	29	31	26	28	9	17	3	13	17	3	22	11	19	29	5
14	22	24	0	27	3	31	7	20	7	9	5	25	18	4	2	20	11	7	2	10	17	1	13	21	5	14	8	16	6	30	8
3	27	21	13	22	14	0	24	18	10	4	28	7	17	31	9	15	23	25	1	26	2	12	20	30	6	8	16	11	19	29	5
29	5	11	19	13	21	6	30	12	20	26	2	25	1	23	17	9	7	31	4	28	28	18	10	0	24	22	14	16	3	3	27
16	8	6	30	29	5	11	19	23	15	23	15	20	2	26	28	4	10	18	9	17	31	7	7	13	21	27	3	24	0	14	22
8	16	30	6	5	11	19	29	16	23	15	23	12	26	2	2	28	18	10	17	9	9	31	31	21	13	3	27	0	24	22	14
5	29	19	11	8	16	7	11	16	6	2	26	1	20	15	25	18	10	7	28	28	4	4	18	24	30	14	22	13	21	27	3
27	3	13	21	17	9	31	7	20	12	26	4	25	1	17	23	15	1	25	2	2	26	10	18	6	30	16	8	19	11	5	29
22	14	0	24	3	27	21	18	9	17	31	9	18	10	4	28	26	25	20	15	23	25	1	1	11	19	29	5	30	6	8	16
7	31	17	9	18	10	4	31	14	7	13	11	3	27	21	13	2	9	5	30	6	8	16	26	26	2	1	20	15	23	25	1
10	18	28	4	17	9	31	7	31	3	21	16	14	22	24	0	29	11	8	19	19	5	29	29	23	15	31	12	2	26	20	12
20	12	2	26	10	18	27	27	15	19	11	16	22	24	0	24	6	29	11	13	13	21	7	3	9	17	7	23	4	10	18	18
25	1	15	23	7	31	15	5	2	11	6	29	30	8	30	16	22	3	22	27	0	24	14	14	4	28	28	9	31	7	10	18
1	25	23	15	12	20	2	8	16	6	30	6	8	5	11	19	14	27	3	3	24	0	22	22	28	18	18	10	26	2	12	20
12	20	26	2	25	1	16	16	8	30	6	8	22	19	19	11	28	7	27	21	21	13	24	27	18	10	10	18	4	10	4	28
18	10	4	28	2	26	20	29	6	5	11	19	14	11	11	29	8	21	13	13	21	19	22	5	17	7	7	31	31	7	9	17
31	7	10	18	7	31	30	16	8	29	19	11	16	27	27	3	5	13	21	11	13	29	14	15	9	1	9	1	7	31	17	9
9	17	31	7	9	17	7	31	5	11	8	16	6	3	3	5	29	27	19	16	16	6	22	29	25	25	23	26	26	2	10	2
4	28	7	10	17	9	28	18	29	5	16	11	30	21	14	8	19	21	11	29	8	5	24	3	7	31	17	12	1	12	4	26
26	2	12	20	28	4	16	31	11	29	6	6	6	27	22	14	11	9	9	11	3	11	10	27	10	7	23	23	26	26	2	2
23	15	25	1	15	23	2	26	19	11	8	16	11	22	16	22	21	11	11	21	14	21	24	14	18	10	18	9	18	10	4	28
15	23	1	25	2	26	30	30	6	6	16	11	19	14	8	5	27	7	31	14	22	14	0	21	10	7	4	17	7	31	17	9
2	26	20	12	23	15	12	19	11	5	29	6	6	22	22	8	21	31	7	0	27	3	13	11	7	10	9	15	10	18	28	4
28	4	10	18	9	17	31	13	27	29	3	30	16	16	16	22	11	19	30	30	5	29	19	11	1	25	23	15	20	12	2	26
17	9	7	31	4	28	18	10	24	22	14	21	13	3	27	29	5	11	19	8	16	30	6	6	12	20	26	2	25	1	15	23

324

Table 15.5

00	01	02	03	04	05	06	07	08	09	10	11	12	13	14	15	16	17	18	19	20	21	22	23	24	25	26	27	28	29	30	31
0|N	30	22	30	26	27|E	23	4	11	23	16	13	11	13	21	24	1	16	20	11	5	7	26	18	5	25	11	10	21	29	5	26
27|E	24	30	31	11	4	28	17	5	15	22	15	16	25	3	23	21	2	21	20	20	9	17	26	25	0	29	7	27	5	2	17
14	6	27|E	4	27|E	24	4	26	22	21	8	15	27	18	19	26	5	25	8	31	25	8	3	19	3	23	17	25	9	19	26	24
26	28	15	0|N	28	6	4	25	28	28	29	1	12	7	9	12	18	23	23	11	30	7	13	15	3	19	26	26	16	1	29	4
25	4	6	4	6	8	16	15	21	16	13	6	6	29	28	17	24	9	16	18	7	23	20	1	7	27	17	19	21	15	17	27
18	14	15	18	6	30	17	2	19	28	20	6	29	18	31	16	9	19	18	19	2	31	22	24	18	29	31	26	29	17	5	17
17	16	31	10	2	17	0|N	2	10	30	5	16	21	11	1	25	25	25	24	19	18	17	28	27	11	29	31	24	19	29	17	2
21	6	0|N	19	16	20	20	2	12	7	1	25	22	14	30	21	21	26	1	18	18	30	27	22	11	31	25	31	27	30	31	27
28	20	18	11	24	16	29	23	10	1	26	22	14	30	0	16	26	11	22	18	11	30	22	27	16	14	10	31	7	22	25	2
24	2	8	24	19	29	28	18	9	4	26	28	7	24	13	9	7	19	19	7	5	17	27	1	13	29	10	31	18	5	3	11
2	11	26	9	22	1	25	0|N	14	10	13	23	10	23	25	31	8	8	14	2	2	14	6	18	5	31	21	1	28	20	20	21
11	3	30	24	15	26	26	1	16	8	8	23	15	10	4	6	5	8	9	5	26	19	10	29	18	10	15	28	8	3	3	18
8	13	24	9	0|N	1	1	1	11	27	23	10	12	15	2	17	6	3	14	2	25	0	12	12	3	23	28	27	16	23	1	29
2	9	14	9	29	28	4	11	25	7	7	8	8	6	6	20	8	2	4	4	21	3	0	25	22	20	31	16	23	1	20	20
22	24	22	0|N	22	12	9	15	30	19	16	12	4	10	2	8	19	14	20	21	16	0	25	26	26	27	20	7	5	25	2	8
17	2	13	16	12	3	22	13	10	16	1	4	1	8	27	13	4	14	23	29	0	3	31	3	13	8	20	0	25	29	18	16
18	24	25	20	2	12	5	17	24	26	25	22	10	20	8	5	19	23	19	3	29	15	28	7	10	1	8	23	15	16	28	21
12	14	13	2	21	3	11	5	17	24	16	16	26	22	30	30	13	22	23	7	3	29	7	14	1	7	9	16	16	0	19	1
15	7	23	21	3	25	7	7	21	23	25	1	30	29	8	26	1	3	7	5	5	23	20	22	13	13	7	27	20	19	3	9
4	19	9	30	11	1	1	13	8	26	28	27	23	23	1	22	20	5	16	9	9	8	7	7	16	3	16	13	31	22	28	30
31	31	30	15	20	7	7	7	28	3	28	28	30	18	6	27	9	28	29	28	7	1	23	18	24	1	19	25	13	19	18	21
28	10	9	29	24	11	16	16	28	30	28	22	24	23	25	29	13	21	28	19	8	5	25	19	13	10	11	28	6	16	3	5
4	0|N	13	8	28	7	7	18	24	4	31	9	19	18	7	31	31	27	12	5	31	29	1	25	30	30	0	11	6	26	26	22
20	27|E	21	4	30	1	9	9	6	20	18	28	30	16	24	23	16	30	19	24	24	1	25	19	0	8	18	18	25	3	25	7
3	14	19	8	10	29	15	15	21	17	26	19	21	17	23	7	8	10	25	19	16	30	1	17	8	8	17	17	2	17	4	4
14	0|N	21	28	4	1	29	29	6	14	31	12	21	0	20	16	7	3	3	24	5	31	2	1	16	4	10	3	12	21	31	11
16	12	10	9	8	14	7	6	20	17	17	5	28	14	7	17	8	8	8	24	19	27	6	12	15	26	28	18	18	8	27	6
10	2	9	12	10	13	2	25	6	17	4	23	6	7	17	18	7	7	13	15	4	21	10	4	18	8	14	19	21	8	27	8
14	3	8	8	2	25	8	8	0	28	12	26	2	19	6	14	1	27	21	13	4	16	27	15	2	20	7	1	25	4	0	23
6	22	12	17	4	0|N	26	21	14	0	12	26	27	2	19	26	14	0	17	14	16	2	4	15	6	7	22	26	24	29	23	1
27	11	21	31	16	17	17	8	5	15	24	31	11	19	6	17	14	0	29	29	12	27	2	23	13	10	6	7	10	8	27	25
2	24	15	31	19	5	5	27|E	23	30	22	13	5	23	2	27	14	13	10	21	31	10	26	31	20	23	27	10	14	8	13	

325

15.6   THE HOUGH TRANSFORM IN COMPUTER VISION

The Hough transform[25] is used in shape analysis. The basic concept is to project the elements of the boundary shape with a different domain in which the global characteristics are more clearly manifested.

The Hough transform is explained in Figure 15.6.[26] Four collinear points are displayed on edge element l'. Given any one of these points, say (x', y'), an infinite number of lines can be drawn to pass through that point. Each line may be characterized by two parameters, the angle θ of the normal to line l passing through the origin $(0,0)$, and the length ρ of its normal. Thus any arbitrary point (x, y) on line l is defined by the equation

$$x \cos\theta + y \sin\theta = \rho \qquad (15.7)$$

Equation (15.7) can be discussed in two ways:

- If θ and ρ are fixed, a linear relationship is obtained between x and y.

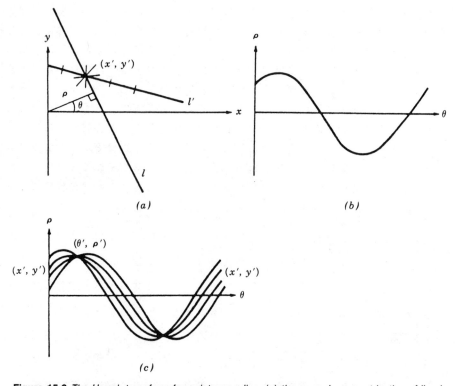

Figure 15.6 *The Hough transform for points on a line: (a) the normal parametrization of line l is given by x cosθ + y sinθ = ρ, where θ and ρ are fixed parameters; (b) ρ as a function of θ, where ρ = x'cosθ + y'sinθ for fixed parameters x' and y'; (c) the Hough transform space representation of the points in (a). (θ', ρ') gives the parameters of the line through the points. Reprinted by permission from Levine.*[26]

- If x and y are fixed, the equation defines the relationship between θ and ρ. This relationship is sinusoidal (Figure 15.6b).

Each (θ, ρ) pair is a transform of one set of straight lines passing through the point (x', y'). Hence the point (x', y') in the image space is projected into the (θ, ρ) space as a sinusoidal curve. Four points in Figure 15.6a are transformed into four curves in Figure 15.6c.

Each point in the (θ, ρ) space is treated as a counter. The point (θ', ρ') will register the count of 4, corresponding to the intersection of four curves. In other words, the peak of four units is formed, while all other counters contain either 0 or 1. The associated value $\theta'\rho'$ indicates the parameters of lines in the image space produced by collinear points. Hence, the Hough transform can be used to isolate the straight lines in the image. Merlin and Forbes[27] and Ballard[28] have developed an extension to the Hough transform which can be used to isolate any arbitrary curve of specific size and orientation. These algorithms are perfectly suited for multiprocessor machines. Parallel visual computation is in a way similar to the cellular organization found throughout the cerebral cortex, from primary sensory to higher associational areas.[29]

REFERENCES

1. L. Alaoughlu and N. N. Smith, *Phys. Rev.* **53**, 832 (1983).

2. M. Blackman and J. L. Michiels, *Proc. Phys. Soc., London.* **60**, 549 (1948).

3. R. Jost, *Helv. Phys. Acta* **20**, 173 (1947).

4. R. L. Chase, *Nuclear Pulse Spectrometry*. McGraw-Hill, New York, 1961.

5. R. W. Schuman and J. P. McMahon, *Rev. Sci. Instrum.* **27**, 675 (1956).

6. G. W. Hutchinson and G. G. Scarrot, **Philos. Mag.** (Ser. 8) **42**, 792 (1951).

7. B. Souček, *Nucl. Instrumen. Methods* **27**, 306 (1964).

8. I. Flores, *Computer Programming*. Prentice-Hall, Englewood Cliffs, NJ, 1966.

9. J. N. Hooton, *Proc. Conf. Autom. Acquis. Reduct. Nucl. Data, 1964* p. 338 (1964).

10. P. F. Windley, *Comput. J.* **3**, 84–88 (1960).

11. E. H. Cooke-Yarborough, *U.K. At. Energy Res. Estab., Memo*, **AERE-M 1411** (1900).

12. W. I. Landauer, *IEEE Trans. Electron. Comput.* **EC-12**(6), 863-811 (1963).

13. A. D. Lin, *AFIPS Conf. Proc.* **23**, 355–366 (1963).

14. Y. A. Shreider, *Method of Statistical Testing–Monte Carlo Method*. Elsevier, Amsterdam, 1964.

15. V. Bonačić, B. Souček, and K. Čuljat, *Nucl. Instrum. Methods* **66**, 213–223 (1968).

16. M. J. Rosenblum, Brookhaven National Laboratory, private communication (1966).

17. R. W. Hamming, *Bell System. Tech. J.* **26** (1950).

18. G. Schay and N. Raver, *IBM J.* April (1963).

19. M. Hanan and F. P. Palermo, *IBM J.* April (1963).

20. G. Schay and W. G. Sprath, *Commun. AC* **19** (1976).

21. R. C. Bose and D. K. Ray Chaudhuri, *Inf. Control* **3**, 68 (1960).

22. R. C. Bose and D. K. Ray Chaudhuri, *Inf. Control* **3**, 279 (1960).

23. W. W. Peterson, *Error Correcting Codes.* MIT Press, Cambridge, MA, 1965.

24. G. Birkhoff and S. MacLane, *A Survey of Modern Algebra.* Macmillan, New York, 1958.

25. P. V. C. Hough, Method and means to recognizing complex patterns. U.S. Patent 3,069,654 (1962).

26. M. D. Levine, *Vision in Man and Machine.* McGraw-Hill, New York, 1985.

27. P. M. Merlin and D. J. Forbes, A parallel mechanism for detecting curves in pictures. *IEEE Trans. Comput.* **C-24**(1), 96–98 (1975).

28. D. H. Ballard, Generalizing the Hough transform to detect arbitrary shapes. *Pattern Recognition* **13**(2), 111–122 (1981).

29. D. H. Ballard, G. E. Hinton, and T. J. Sejnowski, Parallel visual computation. *Nature (London)* **306**, 21–26 (1983).

Pseudoassociative
Memories

INTRODUCTION AND SURVEY

This chapter describes several intelligent instruments based on pseudoassociative memories. The instruments are used to measure multidimensional probability distributions and are called *analyzers:* pulse-height analyzers, time-of-flight analyzers, neuron-activity analyzers, and so forth. They must operate in real time at high data rates of up to a million data per second.

The datum (descriptor) must find its storage location in a very short time. For this reason, the range of descriptors is limited to less than a thousand, if standard random-access memory is used. The solution to this limitation is the use of associative, content-addressable memories; such memories, however, are very expensive.

An alternative solution is pseudoassociative memory. Pseudoassociative memory is a combination of random access memory and a high-speed key-to-address hardware unit. The hardware unit produces pseudorandom addresses in a way similar to that of a software hashing algorithm, but at a high speed. The hardware unit maps a very large (mostly empty) sensory data field into a much smaller pseudoassociative memory field. In this way, a substantial increase in sensitivity is achieved. In the case of nuclear and neural pulse spectroscopy, a sensitivity increase of 1000 times is obtained.

This chapter describes four alternative pseudoassociative memory systems: tree-based, transformation-based, most-active data based and self-adaptable.

16.1 PROGRAMMED PSEUDOASSOCIATIVE ANALYZERS

In a multichannel analyzer, the input signal describing an external event is expressed as a digital number, which we call the descriptor. In a conventional analyzer, the descriptor defines the location in the memory at which the count (number of occurrences of the descriptor) is stored.

With the increasing resolution of physical, biological, and chemical detectors and analog-to-digital convertors, the full range of descriptors may be very large. In certain nuclear physics and biology experiments, particularly those involving coincident spectra, although the possible range of descriptors is very large, the number of different descriptors which actually occur during an experiment is much smaller. A few such two-dimensional spectra displayed in a map form are shown in Figure 16.1. Such spectra in a 1000×1000 resolution have a range of 10^6 possible descriptors, while only thousands of those actually occur in experiments. If we use a conventional analyzer for the measurement of such spectra, we must provide a large memory (10^6 channels), of which only a small percentage of locations will be useful, and all other locations will be empty.

An alternative technique is to allow locations only to those descriptors which actually occur in the experiment. Since the correspondence between the location and the descriptor is lost, it is necessary to store the descriptor as well as the associated count. Hence, the system must be content-addressable or associative. The principle of connections of the physical field of descriptors to memory locations in associative analyzers is shown in Figure 16.2*b*. The numbers show the sequence of arrival of descriptors from the experiment. The first descriptor will take the first available locations in the memory, the next different descriptor the second location, and so on.

When a new datum comes to the associative analyzer input, it must be sorted into its channel on a list; hence, some searching will be required to locate a descriptor. An obvious routine for searching the list is to compare the descriptor for a new event with the descriptor in each location until a match is found. If the list is of length r, the average number of comparisons will be $c = r/2$ (for $r = 4096$, $c = 2048$ comparisons). A marked reduction in access time may be achieved by using a tree-search algorithm, as was actually done in the first associative analyzer reported by Souček.[1,2]

This procedure requires repeated comparisons of pairs of descriptors. Each comparison yields one of the following three answers: (1) they match, (2) the first is greater, or (3) the second is greater. According to the answer, the comparison is either finished or proceeds on to the left or right branch of a "tree" (Figure 16.3). If there are r descriptors on the tree, the average number of comparisons is reduced from $r/2$ to approximately $\log_2 r$ (for $r = 2^{12} = 4096$, $c = \log_2 r = 12$ comparisons). Figure 16.4 shows the high resolution spectra, measured directly on-line with the associative analyzer.

16.2 MOST-ACTIVE ZONE ENCODER FOR MULTIPARAMETER ANALYSIS

Associative mode analyzers ask for a descriptor to be stored in the memory as well as for an associatide count. Hence, about 50 percent of the memory would be accompanied by descriptors. The situation has been improved by the introduction

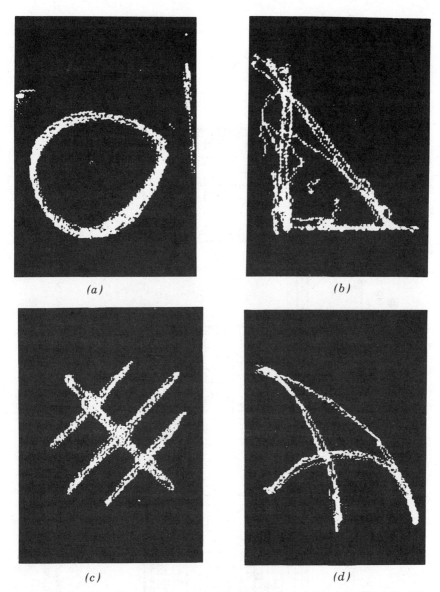

(a)   *(b)*

(c)   *(d)*

Figure 16.1 *Spectra with a great range but limited number of descriptors* [10] *(a) D + P →
P + P + N, 21.1 MeV, 34°, − 34° (b) Van de Graaff experiment 6Li + 3He → P + P + N, 3
MeV, 37.5°, − 37.5° (c) Biological spectra (d) Two-parameter spectrum* $^3He(^3He,2p)^4He$.

of *zone selection*. Here are the basic principles of zone selection, as proposed by
Hooton.[3]

In many experiments information occurs in groups or clusters of channels. The
descriptor field is divided arbitrarily into a number of zones of equal size. Each of
them is a potential digital window. If data occur in any channel within a particular

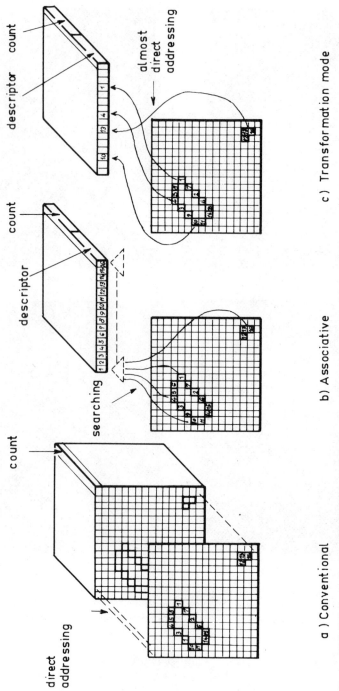

Figure 16.2 *Different principles of direct-accumulating megachannel analyzers.* (a) *conventional analyzer;* (b) *associate analyzer;* (c) *transformation mode analyzer.* [10]

a) Conventional   b) Associative   c) Transformation mode

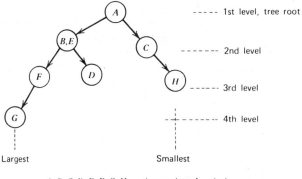

A B C D E F G H — time order of arrival

G F B = E D A C H — amplitude order

Figure 16.3 *Tree-search algorithm used in programmed associative analyzer.* [2]

zone, the location of the zone in the field is held in an associative memory. Hence, for each zone it is necessary to store only one zone descriptor. A group of storage locations is assigned to counts for different channels inside the zone. For example, if the zone is of size $4 \times 4 = 16$ channels, it is necessary to provide one space for storing the descriptor of the zone and 16 spaces for counts, which can be

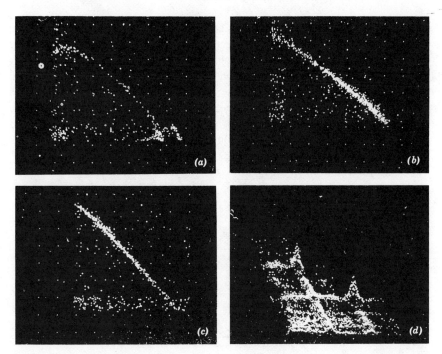

Figure 16.4 *Directly accumulated spectra, using associate analyzers.* (a-c) *present a map display of 3×256× 256 spectrum, using particle identification for grouping (cyclotron experiment); (d) 256×256 bi gamma-gamma spectrum, isometric display.* [2]

addressed inside a zone using two least-significant descriptor digits. In total it is necessary to use $1 + 16 = 17$ spaces, and the fraction of the memory containing the counts will be $u_1 = 16/17 = 94$ percent. In the associative mode without zones, it would be necessary to have 16 spaces for descriptors and 16 for counts, giving $u_2 = 16/32 = 50$ percent. Of course, the high-efficiency u_1 would be achieved only if the clusters of the spectrum were much larger than the size of the zones.

It can be easily shown that the mean utilization of the memory is approximately

$$u = \frac{m + 1}{m + n} \tag{16.1}$$

where m is the number of channels in a cluster and n the number in a zone. It is supposed that the cluster and the zone can be in any relative position; Equation 16.1 gives an average. Equation 16.1 is shown in Figure 16.5.

A hardware zone-selection analyzer was built by Best, Hickman, Hooton, and Prior,[4] using the sophisticated technique of the transfluxor associative memory. At the same time, Best[5] designed a computer-software zone-selection analyzer. Figure 16.6 represents a part of a 256×256 channel spectrum measured by this system. We notice that the spectrum is composed of zones of 4×4 channels each.

16.3 TRANSFORMATION MODE ANALYZERS

Associative and zone/associative analyzers are limited by increased dead time, since a comparison must be made between each input descriptor and the memory content to find the appropriate channel location. To overcome this limitation, Hooton,[6] Rosenblum,[7] and Souček,[8] suggest looking for a randomizing procedure. The problem is similar to the file-address problem by key-to-address transformation. The characteristic of real time spectroscopy is that it does not assume an a priori knowledge of the key set (spectrum or descriptor set) and asks for a procedure suitable for high-speed on-line application.

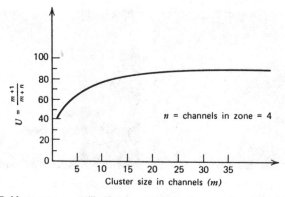

Figure 16.5 Mean memory utilization in zone selection as a function of cluster size. [3]

Souček, Bonačić, and Čuljat[9] have investigated different randomizing transformations and have found that the transformation based on the division of polynomials is the most suitable for real time spectroscopy. The transformation can be realized as a part of a computer data-taking interrupt routine, or as a hardware box between analog-to-digital convertors and a computer.[10,11]

By passing through a transformation box, each descriptor produces a pseudo-random address into which that descriptor is stored (Figure 16.2c). It would be ideal if any distribution of descriptors (spectral shape) would produce a uniform distribution of addresses throughout the memory. For practical spectra there is, however, the possibility of two or more descriptors being transformed to the same address. Because of that, the transformation is used only to generate the address on the list at which to start searching. This method makes almost-direct addressing possible, as in conventional analyzers, and high utilization of the memory space, as in associative systems.

Figure 16.7 shows the principle of transformation through division of polynomials. The descriptor D is shifted to the left through the shift register having feedback through exclusive OR gates. The descriptor and the feedback configuration present polynomials. When the least-significant descriptor bit reaches the top of a shift register, the operation of "polynomial division" is finished, and the shift register

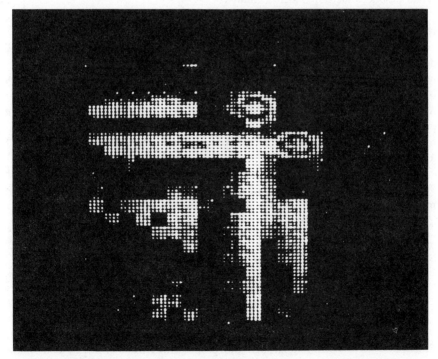

Figure 16.6 *Map display of a two-dimensional spectra measured with zone-selection computer-associative analyzer.*[5]

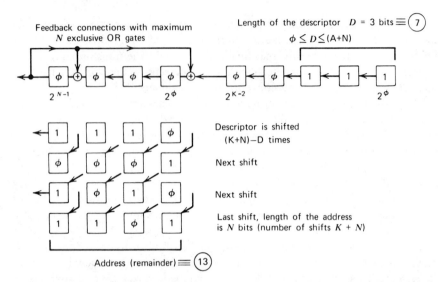

Figure 16.7 *Generation of a pseudorandom address through the division of polynomials.* [10]

will contain the remainder. In a given example, the descriptor presents decimal 7 and produces the remainder decimal 13.

Experimentation with different spectra and different feedbacks shows that the remainder might be used as a descriptor address on the list.

The randomizing feature of such transformations is shown in Table 16.1. The descriptors 0 through 1024 (in 32 × 32 *XY* matrix) are fed through the transformation box, with the feedback over five stages of the register, producing addresses 0 to 31. For example, the descriptor $X = 08$, $Y = 0$ produces address 3: descriptor $X = 21$, $Y = 2$ produces address 16. It is obvious that the produced addresses are pseudorandomly distributed over the field. Over this pattern, one can draw maps of two-dimensional nuclear or neural spectra of arbitrary shapes and see that all addresses are produced with almost equal probability.

The transformation-mode analyzer is specially suitable for spectra such as in Figure 16.1. Those spectra are simulated by a CRT-light pen system, according to the known results of the following experiments:

1. $D + P \rightarrow P + P + N$ 21.1 MeV, 34°, − 34°
2. Van de Graaff experiment: ^{6}Li + ^{3}He→ P + alpha + alpha, 3 MeV, 37.5°, − 37.5°
3. Biological spectra
4. Two-parameter spectrum ^{3}He(^{3}He,2p)^{4}He

Each of those spectra contains 1024 descriptors in the 128 × 128 field. The descriptors have been fed through the programmed transformation box in the computer, always producing practically uniform distributions of 1024 different addresses.

TABLE 16.1

00	01	02	03	04	05	06	07	08	09	10	11	12	13	14	15	16	17	18	19	20	21	22	23	24	25	26	27	28	29	30	31
27	28	9	28	27	18	21	3	0	7	13	10	31	24	17	22	6	1	8	15	26	29	20	19	5	2	11	12	25	30	23	16
13	10	3	7	0	21	24	14	17	13	28	7	4	17	22	6	30	26	19	20	1	16	25	30	8	15	6	23	2	5	12	11
22	17	24	31	10	22	3	21	1	12	11	28	18	24	7	16	23	27	5	25	2	11	2	9	5	20	29	26	15	8	1	6
26	29	20	24	13	17	4	9	23	18	16	14	9	7	11	28	27	0	30	12	23	2	9	31	19	24	17	22	3	4	13	10
1	6	19	6	1	29	8	31	7	26	29	28	5	11	2	21	17	9	14	21	13	24	14	18	4	9	10	3	24	31	22	17
23	16	25	2	6	26	19	18	22	8	11	8	30	12	5	18	22	14	21	30	22	13	27	28	18	14	7	0	21	18	27	28
12	11	2	5	19	12	26	27	5	1	30	19	11	16	19	25	10	7	24	25	0	24	0	10	13	21	4	21	18	17	24	31
15	8	5	16	20	11	12	26	8	23	11	6	30	23	8	30	9	28	0	4	21	13	7	6	10	0	31	22	13	10	3	4
20	19	26	29	8	30	5	12	10	16	8	29	6	16	4	20	14	9	2	18	30	26	24	16	1	7	14	31	24	3	21	18
2	5	1	11	5	23	2	7	3	6	19	14	19	1	3	19	31	27	5	21	25	5	13	28	6	17	18	0	7	14	2	5
25	30	23	12	2	16	11	12	4	29	6	31	10	13	16	6	24	18	30	4	16	2	10	16	23	23	30	25	0	14	9	9
21	18	27	0	22	7	0	17	22	13	10	24	31	10	4	15	20	29	26	8	1	6	1	6	30	12	2	20	12	11	2	5

Figure 16.8 shows the number of lost descriptors *L(s)* which have not found an available place and the average number of comparisons, as a function of the maximum available number of comparisons, for one of the spectra (from Figure 16.1, but for 2048 descriptors). In practice, the number of locations in the memory will be at least a few percent larger than the number of descriptors in a physical field, giving results better than those in Figure 16.8.

16.4 SELF-ADAPTABLE PSEUDOASSOCIATIVE MEMORY

Three, zone, and transformation analyzers have two features in common: they use random access memory and the connection of the sensory field to the memory field is done dynamically during the data acquisition process.

The sensory field is typically much larger than the memory field, but it is mostly empty. In other words, many areas in the sensory field are of low activity. The questions are: how does one assign the available memory locations to highly active areas in the sensory field? How does one make the memory self-adaptable? One way of doing it is to build the systems with two modes of operation: first arrived events and most probable events. An experiment with such a system is shown in Figure 16.9 and 16.10, which show measurement of two dimensional probability distribution. Input parameters *X* and *Y* define the memory address. The content of the addressed location presents the count: how many times a particular *XY* combination has occurred during the experiment.

The system first operates in the first-arrived events mode. As the new *XY* event is generated by the experiment, it takes the location from the memory. Next time when the same *XY* event occurs, it only increases the count associated with that location. The result is presented in Figure 16.9. Some memory locations are associated with highly active areas of sensory field, but some are associated with the areas of very low activity, which are usually of no interest to the user.

To disconnect the low activity areas from the memory, we use the following procedure: divide all the counts stored in memory by two (left shift all memory

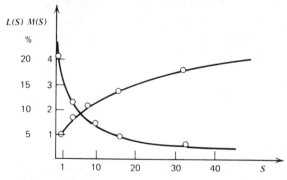

Figure 16.8 *Average number of comparisons* M(S) *and percentage of lost descriptors* L(S), *as a function of maximum permitted number of comparisons* S.

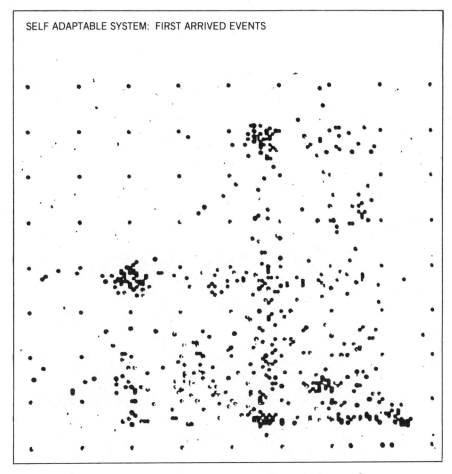

SELF ADAPTABLE SYSTEM: FIRST ARRIVED EVENTS

Figure 16.9 *Self-adaptable system. First arrived events.*[2]

contents). The locations that have received only one count will be cleared to zero. By repeating the procedure several times, we give new chances for highly active events to associate themselves with the memory. The result is shown in Figure 16.10. The measured distribution is composed of horizontal range with the peak in the lefthand end and vertical range with the peak in the upper end. Based on these results, Souček[2] points to the following:

- For Figure 16.9, the data from hills and the low plane are connected to the memory.
- For Figure 16.10, most data is from hills (high activity) and connected to the memory. The low plane is disconnected.

This feature is suitable for learning systems and self-adaptable systems.

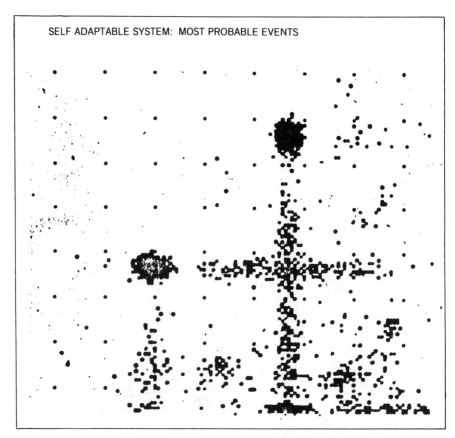

SELF ADAPTABLE SYSTEM: MOST PROBABLE EVENTS

Figure 16.10 *Self-adaptable system. Most probable events.*[2]

16.5 WINDOW PRESELECTION

In a two-parameter experiment, every event is characterized by two parameters, X and Y. The experimental matrix XY might be as big as 4096×256 channels. To store the event in the whole matrix during the experiment requires an expensive data-acquisition system. A cheaper solution is to put constraints on one parameter, say X, and to record Y as a function of these constraints. This is realized by setting windows on the spectrum of one parameter. Window preselections have been designed in different laboratories.[12-16]

A simplified block diagram of a 16-window discriminator[16] is shown in Figure 16.11. The main features are the matrix board and the two 12-bit adders, one adder for the lower threshold and one for the upper. They are connected on one side to the 12-bit lines from the X-address unit. The other side of the adders is connected to 24 horizontal rails on the matrix board, 12 rails per adder set. A 4-bit scaler is, via a decoding matrix, connected to 16 vertical rails on the matrix board, 1 rail per window. To obtain the window settings, the vertical and horizontal rails are

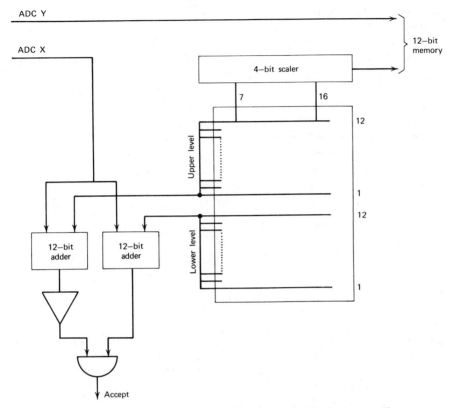

Figure 16.11 *Block scheme of the 16-window digital discriminator.* [16]

connected with diode pins in the binary code in such a way that the combinations on each vertical rail define a lower and an upper threshold. The horizontal rails keep the corresponding side of the adders in 1 state. When the 4-bit scaler is counting, one after the other of the 16 vertical rails are energized via the decoding matrix, and successively all lower and upper thresholds are compared with the binary information on the X-bit lines. The adders sum the binary information on both sides in the standard way. The adders are wired in such a way that if an X event has arrived in one of the selected windows, the output (carry) from the lower-threshold adder, and no output from the other, will result, producing an accept pulse. At this moment bits from the Y ADC and from the scaler are transferred to the memory. Scaler bits determine the window address. In particular instruments, the following number of subgroups or windows can be manually selected: 16 of 256, 8 of 512, 4 of 1024, or 2 of 2048 channels. If one has selected 16 subgroups, then the first 8 bits of the Y ADC (256 channels) and 4 bits of the scaler (16 subgroups) are connected to the memory block (4096 words).

Gamma-gamma coincidence measurements have been performed on the reaction $^{44}Ca(n,gamma)^{45}Ca$ with a 6.5cm^3 Ge(Li) detector and a 12.7 $\times$ 12.7 cm NaI detector, and some of the results are shown in Figure 16.12 (4 windows of 1024 channels each).

The main advantage of the window-selection technique is its simplicity. The main disadvantage is a need to make a preexperiment in order to be able to set the window limits. The data out of the windows are lost.

A hardware window selector shown in Figure 16.11 is built from integrated circuits and could operate at a high speed. Recently 1.25 μ VHSIC (very high speed/scale integrated circuit) has been developed for window selection (WS). The device has been used by TRW to design a general-purpose VME bus component. This WS performs searching and matching operations on n-dimensional data vectors and hyperrectangular windows in an arbitrary n-dimensional Euclidean space. It can carry out search and match operations at up to 7.68 billion arithmetic operations per second. The vector is compared against the window, not against one

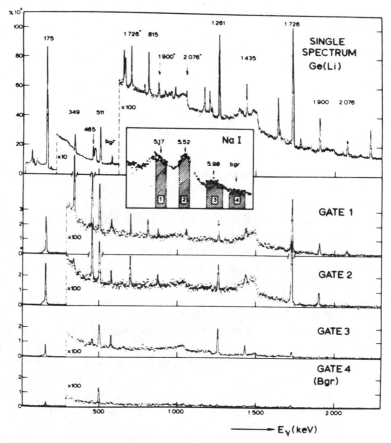

Figure 16.12 *Spectra coincident with four windows in the NaI channel, each is 1024 channels. The window settings are shown in the insert. A Ge(Li) single spectrum is shown in the upper part.*[16]

parameter. Hence the device operates as a fuzzy associative memory. WS functions in one of two search modes: Smith Mode and Nodes Mode (J.L. Smith and T.A. Nodes, inventors of this VHSIC based WS).

16.5.1 Smith Mode

As many as 16 unknown hyperrectangles are compared with as many as 32,768 stored vectors, to check the vectors for inclusion in one or more of the hyperrectangles.

From 1 to 16 hyperrectangles are first loaded into the comparison item memory. After this, the device is given the beginning and ending address of the block of vectors to be searched, and the search process is initiated.

During each 200 ns period of the search, one of the data vectors is checked against all of the hyperrectangles in the comparison item memory for inclusion. If the data vector is included in at least one of the hyperrectangles, the address of the data vector and identification flags of all the hyperrectangles which contained it are recorded in the output buffer. Processing includes two bounds checks (upper and lower) for each dimension of the 16 hyperrectangles in comparison item memory.

16.5.2 Nodes Mode

Instead of storing vectors in the data vector memory, up to 16,384 hyperrectangles are stored. Hyperrectangles are expressed as pairs of vectors, the first vector representing the "upper" corner of the hyperrectangle and the second vector representing the "lower" corner. Up to eight hyperrectangles can be loaded into the comparison item memory for comparison with a block of hyperrectangles in data vector memory. During each 400 ns cycle one hyperrectangle from the data vector memory is checked for intersection with all of the hyperrectangles in the comparison item memory.

For detailed description of this device, consult the TRW documents.[17]

REFERENCES

1. B. Souček, *Rev. Sci. Instrum.* **36**, 750–753 (1965).

2. B. Souček, *Nucl. Instrum. Methods* **36**, 181–191 (1965).

3. I.N. Hooton, *IEEE Trans. Nucl. Sci.* **NS-13** (3), 553 (1966).

4. G.C. Best, S.A. Hickman, I.N. Hooton, and G.M. Prior, *IEEE Trans. Nucl. Sci.* **NS-13** (3), 559 (1966).

5. G.C. Best, *IEEE Trans. Nucl. Sci.* **NS-13** (3), 566 (1966).

6. I.N. Hooton, *Proc. EAUC Conf.*, 1964.

7. M. Rosenblum, Brookhaven National Laboratory, private communication (1966).

8. B. Souček, *IEEE Trans. Nucl. Sci.* **NS-13** (3), 571 (1966).

9. B. Souček, V. Bonačić, K. Čuljat, and I. Radnić, *Nucl. Electron. , Proc. Int. Symp.*, (1968).

10. B. Souček, V. Bonačić, and K. Čuljat, *Nucl. Instrum. Methods,* **66** (2), 202 (1968).

11. V. Bonačić, B. Souček, and K. Čuljat, *Nucl. Instrum. Methods,* **66** (2), 213 (1968).

12. P. Durand and P. Giraud, *Nucl. Electron., Proc. Int. Symp.,* 643 (1964).

13. L. Thenard and G. Victor, *Nucl. Instrum. Methods* **26**, 45 (1964).

14. M.A. Poole, *Brookhaven Natl. Lab., Informal Rep.* **IH-363** (1968).

15. F. Colling and W. Stuber, *Nucl. Instrum. Methods* **64**, 52 (1968).

16. P. Spilling, H. Grappelaar, and P.C. van der Berg, *Nucl. Electron., Proc. Int. Symp.* (1968).

17. J.L. Smith, *VHSIC Fuzzy Associative Memory, Functional Description,* TRW Rep. 1986.

Associative Memories And Processors

INTRODUCTION AND SURVEY

Content-addressable or associative memory searches data on the basis of their contents rather than their location. Ideally, the comparison is done in one single cycle for the whole memory. As a result, associative systems can process a very large volume of data at a high speed. These are the features that we find in the human memory.

The Greek philosopher Aristotle (387–322 B.C.) formed a set of observations on human memory and association. The classical laws of association have been formulated following the ideas of Aristotle's book *On Memory and Reminiscence*. Mental items (ideas, perceptions, sensations, or feelings) are connected in memory under the following conditions:

1. if they occur simultaneously ("spatial contact")
2. if they occur in close succession ("temperal contact")
3. if they are similar
4. if they are contrary

Digital associative memory is a typical brain-like intelligent system. Associative memories as parts of a computer system have been investigated over 20 years. Semiconductor technology has only recently reached the level that enables design of a large-scale associative memory. This chapter starts with a description of the basic structure of associative memory. The word-parallel, bit-serial principle is explained. ASPRO, a high-speed associate processor, is described in detail.

Associative memories and processors present important blocks in many intelligent systems. These include:

- Artificial intelligence machines
- Real-time expert systems
- Airborne surveillance and targeting systems
- Data-base systems
- Intelligent instruments and control systems

This chapter describes intelligent systems built around associative memories. As the price of associative memories and processors goes down, they are becoming standard components in intelligent-system design.

17. 1 CONTENT-ADDRESSABLE OR ASSOCIATIVE MEMORIES

Content-addressable or associative memory searches data on the basis of their contents rather than their location. Accessing data on the basis of their contents always means some comparison of an external search argument with part or all of the information stored in all memory locations. Ideally, the comparison is done in one single cycle for the whole memory.

Figure 17.1 shows a general block diagram of an associative array processor operation.[1] The data to be searched are loaded into the associative array from the auxiliary memory. The search argument is loaded into the comparand register and a mask is set so that only the data of interest will be searched. A search command

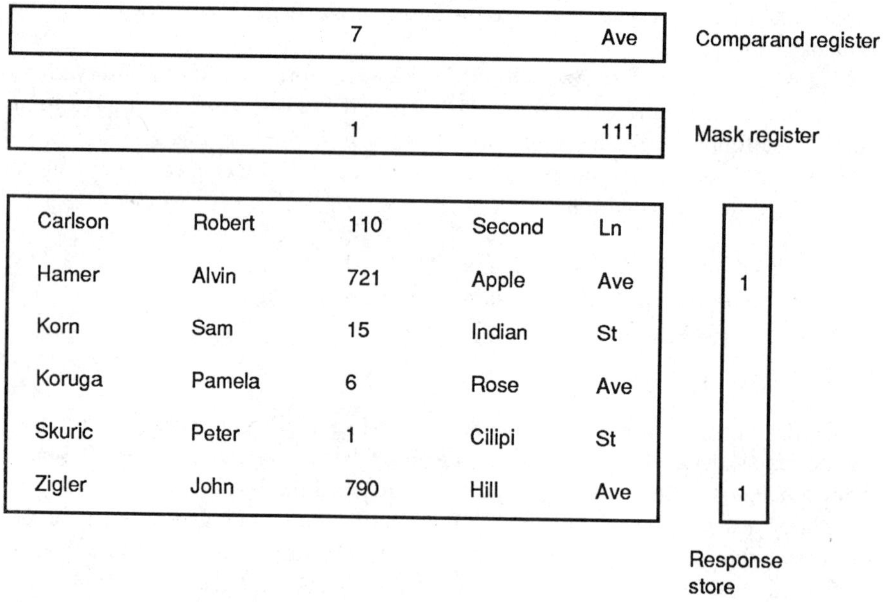

	7		Ave		Comparand register

	1		111		Mask register

Carlson	Robert	110	Second	Ln	
Hamer	Alvin	721	Apple	Ave	1
Korn	Sam	15	Indian	St	
Koruga	Pamela	6	Rose	Ave	
Skuric	Peter	1	Cilipi	St	
Zigler	John	790	Hill	Ave	1

Response store

Figure 17.1 *Associative memory telephone example.*

such as "equal to comparand" is executed; the resulting bits are indicated in the response store. The system then gives these bits to the user or performs further processing if required.

Shown in Figure 17.1 is a telephone example, in which data have been loaded into the associative array. In this search, the object is to obtain the records (tuples) of those persons who live on an avenue (*AVE*) and have a 7 as the first digit of their street number. The values *AVE* and 7 are loaded into the comparand register in the proper places; the mask register is set such that only the fields of interest are searched and then an exact match search is executed. The results appear in the response store. In this example, an AND operation is performed between the responders to the *AVE* argument and the 7 argument. Thus, the records of Hamer and Zigler are responders.

Parallel searching performed in hardware would require the binary-coded search argument to be broadcasted via a set of parallel lines to the respective bit positions of all word locations. A logical equivalence gate at every bit position would be needed. The resulting logic is fairly complex and is used only for associative memories of small size. A large number of alternative ways have been investigated with the goal of building a large-scale associative memory. Extensive reviews on content-addressable or associative memories have been published by Hanlon[2] and Kohonen.[3]

An alternative to all-parallel memory is a word-parallel, bit-serial system. The search is implemented simultaneously and in parallel over all words by reading the bit slices, one at a time, into the output port and comparing the slice with the respective bit of the external search argument.

The word-parallel, bit-serial associative memory principle is shown in Figure 17.2. The memory array is connected to the response store. The response store consists of a set of flip-flops, one for every word location. The flip-flops are set to 1 before the search starts. The bit-slice counter selects one bit slice at a time. The multiplexer picks up the corresponding bit from the comparand argument. The

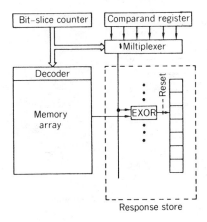

Figure 17.2
Word-parallel, bit-serial associative memory.
Adapted from Kohonen.[3]

selected bit slice is compared with the argument bit. Whenever a bit value read from the bit slice is different from the argument bit, an exclusive OR gate will reset the corresponding flip-flop of the response store. When all bit slices have been read, ones are left only in flip-flops that correspond to completely matching words. For a complete search of an n-bit array, only n reading cycles have to be performed.

New associative memories enable reading and writing by bit slices as well as by words. This is achieved through the use of special methods for permutation of memory arrays. The methods are called *skewed storage techniques*, or *flip networks*.[4,5]

17.2 ASPRO, HIGH-SPEED ASSOCIATIVE PROCESSOR*

ASPRO is a high-speed associative processor developed by Goodyear Aerospace Corporation;[6] it is available as a commercial product.[7,8] The ASPRO consists of five major components, as illustrated in Figure 17.3. It communicates with one or more host processors via two shared-control memory buffers, which can hold data, control words, and status information. When the host processor initiates a task,

*Section 17.2 is adapted from ASPRO manuals. Courtesy and Copyright by Goodyear Aerospace Corporation.

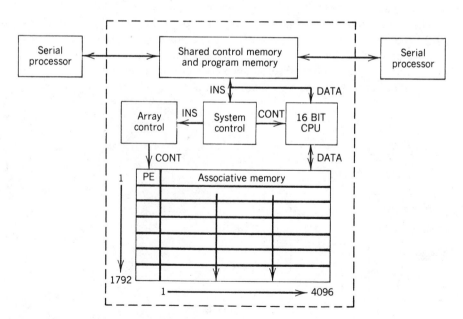

Figure 17.3 *ASPRO architecture. Courtesy and copyright ©1986 by Goodyear Aerospace Corporation.*

it tells the ASPRO what to do via the control word; it also passes any necessary data. When the ASPRO completes a task, it typically uses a shared-control memory buffer to return to host status information, plus the data that are the results of its processing task.

This component also contains a program memory which stores the programs, or series of instructions, for the tasks that the ASPRO executes. It communicates only with the ASPRO. When a task is initiated, the appropriate instructions are activated in the program memory.

The system-control component has overall responsibility for the execution of a task. It retrieves instructions from the program memory and sends them either to the general-purpose processor or to the associative array control unit, as indicated in Figure 17.3. The system control executes program branches and returns and establishes correct timing and coordination of operations to be performed.

The general-purpose 16-bit processor contains standard computer logic and is used for arithmetic and other serial processing. It plays an important auxiliary role in the ASPRO by performing any simple serial processing needed to support or connect parallel operations done by the array unit. Otherwise, all such operations would have to be sent back to the host computer, and the resulting traffic would degrade the overall performance gains achieved by using the ASPRO.

The array-control component controls the processing elements in the array memory itself and the flow of data in and out of the array unit. It identifies the array operation to be performed and supplies correctly synchronized control signals to the array.

The fifth component is the associative-array unit. It performs all parallel operations. There is one processing element for each "word," or data element, of up to 4096 bits, and there can be as many as 2048 processing elements in the current implementation, for a total array size of one megabyte. An operation can be performed in parallel on up to 2048 data elements, which might be track records, sensor reports, or a look-up file of platform characteristics. One unique feature of the array unit is that data can be treated either as individual data elements, or as a slice containing the same bit across all elements (see Figure 17.4).

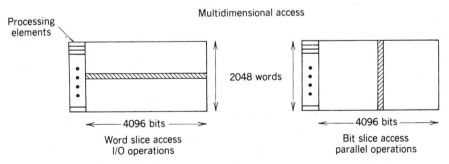

Figure 17.4 *Features of MDA memory. Courtesy and copyright ©1983, 1986 by Goodyear Aerospace Corporation.*

This multi-dimensional access (MDA) memory is the source of the ASPRO's associative capability. It is made feasible, in terms of cost, by the use of a "flip" network that permits either horizontal or vertical access to data. Before the unique MDA technology was discovered and patented by Goodyear, the cost of associative processors was prohibitive because of all the wiring, or interconnections, that were required. MDA technology permits processing the same bit slice across all data elements for parallel operations like searches or correlation; it also permits processing of all bits in a single element for operations such as I/O procedures.

Another important feature of the array memory is that it does not have to be treated monolithically. It can be partitioned into a number of storage areas for different kinds of data, and different operations can be performed on different data sets. An example is shown in Figure 17.5. This provides great flexibility and greatly enhances processing speed, because data do not have to be moved in and out of the array memory as processing requirements change.

One should think of ASPRO as a bit-wise processor, where the bit being processed is at the intersection of a bit column and a bit row. Also think of ASPRO as being able to process a row of bits or a column of bits (or their subsets). Each of 2048 processing elements has three registers, X, Y and M (Figure 17.6).

Register	Function
X	Performs logical operations
Y	Performs logical operations and Specifies responders
M	MDA memory mask

The PE portion of the array consists of 1792 processing elements. The M, X, and Y registers (1792 bits each) can be used as temporary storage of data loaded

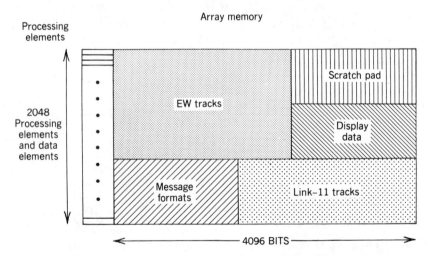

Figure 17.5 *Sample partition of the array memory for a real-time tracking, correlation, and display system. Courtesy and copyright ©1983, 1986 by Goodyear Aerospace Corporation.*

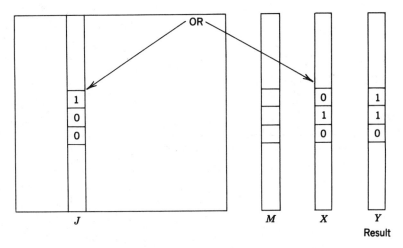

Figure 17.6 *ASPRO column Boolean logic operation.*

from the array memory or may contain the data to be stored. The X and Y registers can also logically combine data simultaneously with the load PE operations. The M (MASK) register is used as a mask to select which words of array memory participate in the store operation. The Y register is used as a responder store in a search-type operation. The X register is used as temporary storage when performing logic operations. Associative array input and output is 32 bits via the common data bus and the common data control.

The common C register of the ALU contains the argument for a search or arithmetic operation performed on the arrays, the input data to be stored into an array, or the output data loaded from an array.

ASPRO is able to process a row of the bits or their subset.

An example of column-wise operation is shown in Figure 17.6. A 2048 words operation is selected by setting J. The processing argument is loaded into the register X. One of the 16 Boolean logical operations is chosen. The example shows *OR* operations. The result of the operation is stored in the Y register.

Note that all the bits of one column are processed in one single step.

An example of row-wise operation is shown in Figure 17.7. A search argument is loaded into the common register C. The argument could be up to 32 bits long. The first active column of the memory is selected. The bit in the selected column is compared with the focus bit in the common register. If no match, a comparison is done. If the match is found, the temporary result equal to 1 is stored in the Y register. Both column address and common register focus bit are advanced by one. In this way the second bit of the common register is compared with the bit in the next column, and so on, until the end of the search argument is reached.

Note that N bits in one column are processed in N steps sequentially, one bit at a time.

ASPRO could search for a match within several rows, Figure 17.8. The focus bit of the argument is compared against all the bits of the active column in the same time. Hence the processing time for the area of N columns by M rows in N.

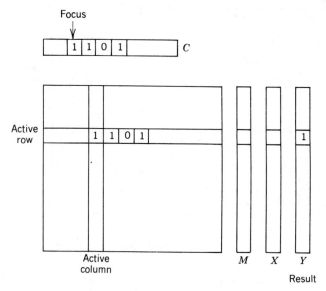

Figure 17.7 ASPRO row-search operation.

Note that processing time for one row and for M rows is the same.

A number of software development tools are available for ASPRO. These include an assembler language, a high-level language, and an ASPRO emulator that runs on the VAX computer. The complete set of tools is listed below:

ASPRO ASSEMBLER
ASPRO COMPOOL
ASPRO LINKER
ASPRO LIBRARIAN
ASPRO DEBUGGER

These run under both the Dec RSX-11 M system and the VMS system for the VAX family of computers.

17.3 REAL-TIME EXPERT SYSTEM

Most of the expert systems communicate with the operator. The response time of the system should be similar to the response time of the human operator, measured in seconds.

A new trend is to connect an expert system to an instrument, robot, or process control systems. Such real-time expert system must have a short response time to match the response of the instrument, robot, or control system.

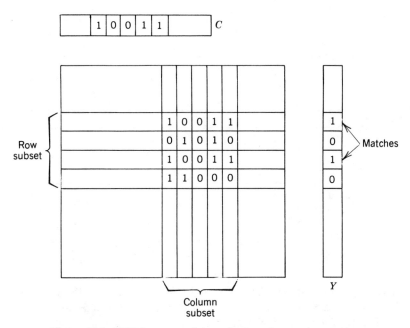

Figure 17.8 *ASPRO row parallel-production rule-search operation.*

The expert system generates the results by using the production rules. The number of rules could run into thousands. On a classical computer it would take a long time to execute a single circle of production system execution. Parallel structure of an associative processor is well suited for high speed, real-time expert system. The number of rules can be easily ANDed or ORed, and executed in one single cycle. Typically disjunctive normal theorem is used to compress or to distribute Boolean expressions used in production rules. Here is an example of two forms of the same rule. Compressed form:

IF (A AND B AND C) OR (D AND E) THEN P

Distributed form:

IF (A AND B AND C) THEN P
IF (D AND E) THEN P

Consider a simple production rule number 23:

IF (OBJECT IS ROUND SHAPED) AND
(IS GREEN)   AND
(HAS 3 INCHES DIAMETER)   THEN
(OBJECT IS AN APPLE)

Figure 17.9 shows a possible representation of a set of production rules in an associative processor.

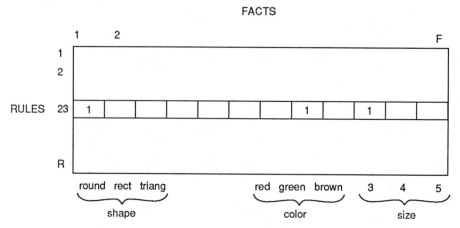

Figure 17.9 *Rule encoding.*

The systems is composed of R rules, and of, F distinct facts. If the fact is true, logical 1 is placed in the proper position in the rule table. Note the bit positions for the IF part of the rule number 23.

The execution time required for the parallel search in an associative processor is independent of the number of rules. Hence thousands of rules could be processed at high speed. In this way a microsecond response time is possible. This fact opens the door for high speed real-time expert system.

Compare Figure 17.9 (facts stored in associative memory) and Figure 11.17 (fuzzy cognitive maps). Both approaches promise short response times, following very different principles of operation. Also the hardware implementations are very different.

17.4 RELATIONAL DATA BASES

Many information systems use some kind of data base, supported by a software for data base management. Ever decreasing cost of very large scale integrated circuits, leads to the movement of software functions into hardware. Data base management also migrates into the hardware, that is called data base machines. A number of data base machines have been reported.[1] They operate as back-end processors connecting the storage devices to the host machine. Flexible and fast solution to the data-base problem is an associative processor.

Relational data bases are noted for their absence of structure; they consist of flat tables, or relations, of data with similar characteristics and contain no indices or directories that point from one item to another. As a result, it is very easy to add new data, delete old data, and change or update current data without having to make a lot of corresponding changes to one or more indicies or directories. Therefore, this approach is well suited to rapidly changing data bases.

An associative processor really shows its usefulness in supporting relational data bases. A lot of searching of relational data bases occurs due to the lack of structure. In fact, this feature makes relational data bases too slow for many real-time applications in the past. Associative processors can compensate by searching a large relation in parallel and rapidly producing the desired match.

Another advantage of a relational data base supported by an associative processor is that any field in a record can be searched just as easily and quickly as any other field. Thus the application is not limited to accessing data via only certain fields in a fixed directory structure, as is true of hierarchical and network organizations.

Figure 17.10 shows the data-base system utilizing several associative memories.[1] Such a system can provide efficient support to managing large data bases under several high-level organizational approaches:

- Hierarchical data bases (e.g., military organizational structure, banking, administration)

- Network data bases (e.g., hierarchical approach that permits two different parts of an index to point to the same item. In other words, a given element

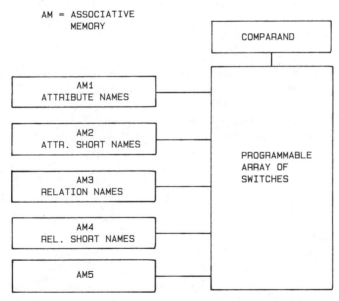

SPECIAL PURPOSE FUNCTION ARCHITECTURES:

DATA BASE FUNCTIONS PERFORMED IN HARDWARE

Figure 17.10 *Data-base functions performed in hardware utilizing several associative memories.*[1]

may have several elements that point to it, several "fathers." Also the element may have multiple elements that it points to, "son" elements.

• Relational data base which uses relations rather than pointers.

Associative processor used in the system shown in Figure 17.10 provides many functions which might not be available in the back-end data base machine. The features include:

• Variety of logical and arithmetic functions.
• Input and output message processing and display.
• Parallel functions like correlation or data-base updates.

These features are crucial for high-speed data delivery, information processing and library systems.

REFERENCES

1. P. B. Berra, Some architecture for database management. In *Supercomputer Systems Technology*, Pergamon Infotech, London, 1982, pp. 171-186.
2. A. C. Hanlon, *IEEE Trans. Electron. Comput.*, **EC-15**, 509-521 (1966).
3. T. Kohonen, *Content-Addressable Memories*. Springer-Verlag, Berlin, 1980.
4. H. S. Stone, *Proc. AFIPS FJCC* p. 949 (1968)
5. K. E. Batcher, U. S. Patent 3,800,289 (1974)
6. *ASPRO Real-Time Expert System Manual*. Goodyear Aerospace Corporation, 1986.
7. N. Anderson Miller and J. W. Law, *ASPRO Technical Introduction*. Goodyear Aerospace Corporation, 1983.
8. R. P. Kirsch, *An Overview and Assessment, Goodyear Aerospace Corporation's ASPRO as an AI Machine*, La Salle Univ. Rep., LaSalle University, Philadelphia, PA, 1985.

Associative Random Access Memory—ARAM

INTRODUCTION AND SURVEY

In classical associative memory, a comparison is made between the search argument and the data field. Due to the elaborate circuitry necessary, only a few associative memories have been designed. An alternative approach is an associative system based on a match-indicating flag, MIF. Instead of being stored in the memory, a descriptor is used as the address to the system. The MIF flag is set, indicating that the location has been selected. The flag is unambiguously correlated with the specific data. A mark MIF = 1 means that the specific data is stored, whereas MIF = 0 shows that the data has not been stored or has already been removed from memory.

This chapter describes an associative random access memory (ARAM) based on the MIF flag. A wordwise supplement with a conventional RAM makes it possible to store additional pieces of information related to the descriptor. Typically, this information can be the frequency of appearance of a particular descriptor.

Associative memory consists of a cascade of ARAM modules. This novel memory includes several associative functions implemented on the hardware level. The whole system is controlled by a specially designed high-speed processor and can be classified as single instruction-multiple data-architecture. The modules have been realized as integrated VLSI circuits. The associative processor serves as coordinator of a modular extensible multi-processor system. Other applications include parallel data management, computer aided design, pattern recognition, artificial intelligence, and intelligent measurement/control systems.

Chapter 18 has been adapted from Roll, Waldschmidt, Strugala and Tavangarian [5–10]. Courtesy and copyright © 1984, 1985, 1986 by Roll, Waldschmidt, Strugala and Tavangarian.

18.1 ARAM MODULE

Early associative memories[1,2] have limited memory space, capable of being applied to special purposes only. In recent times, new microprocessors have been developed comprising fast associative cache memories on the processor chip[3,4]; but these also have only restricted capacity.

The ARAM system, based on the match-indicating flag, presents a new and elegant solution to many associative memory/processor problems.[5-10] For storing of n-bit data, a memory vector consisting of 2^n 1-bit MIF-cells is to be implemented, because any possible data word exactly needs one correlated MIF-cell.[5,6]

With the help of a special decoder circuit, the applied search argument generates an addressing signal for the pertinent MIF-cell. If the search argument is masked, the decoder circuit generates addressing signals in parallel for all MIF-cells that can be addressed by applying the mask to the search argument (Figure 18.1). Matches resulting from search operations are transformed into the interrogated data by encoding the addresses of the matched MIF-cells. Multiple matches are detected in parallel and managed by a multi-match resolver, which renders a sequential computation of the separated matches.

A wordwise supplement with a conventional RAM of k-bit memory words (as shown in Figure 18.1, "data memory") makes it possible to store further information from the associative data (e.g., the frequency of its appearance in the memory). With this memory extension, the ARAM can be used as a parallel associative memory as well as a conventional RAM.

In order to achieve high system performance, the following functions are implemented on the hardware level within the memory modules:

- A search for equality
- A search for matches greater/less than a specified limit
- A search for matches between/outside two specified limits

Each of these functions can be executed with masked or nonmasked search arguments; moreover, each function can be supplemented by a search for a maximum/minimum value in the stored data set, so that all together 47 different functions are available. Since the associative data can be accessed in parallel, the execution of each operation takes only one memory cycle. Figure 18.2 shows the different hardware components within the memory module performing the various functions.

18.2 THE ASSOCIATIVE MEMORY ARRAY

The ability to connect cascades of integrated ARAM modules renders possible the creation of an associative memory array, the capacity of which may be extended by adding further modules (Figure 18.3). Therefore, the memory capacity of this parallel working associative array is no longer restricted and can be varied

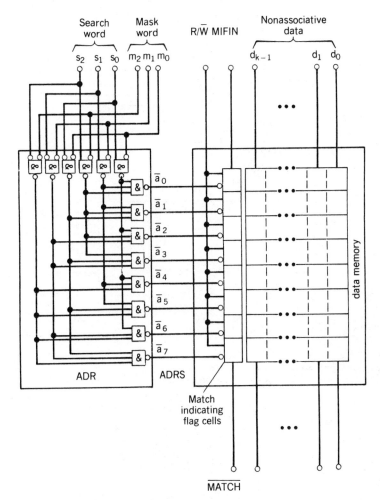

Figure 18.1 *ARAM decoder for an example of a 3-bit ARAM module. Reprinted by permission from Roll, Waldschmidt, Strugala and Tavangarian.* [10]

according to special applications. In the example of Figure 18.3, four *m*-bit ARAM modules are connected, building a memory array with a depth of 2^{m+2} words and a word length of $n = m + 2$ bits. Each module is supplied with the least-significant *m*-bit of the *n*-bit search argument and mask word, with the control signals, the flag bit MIFIN, the non-associative data, and the instruction word. The most significant 2-bit of the search and mask word are applied to activate the appertaining module(s) by chip-select signals generated by a special chip-select circuit (CSG). The memory modules are connected by carry lines holding information about the state of each module (SI0 and S0I).

When executing a masked search operation, the associative memory array has to output the matched words sequentially according to the trigger signals sent by

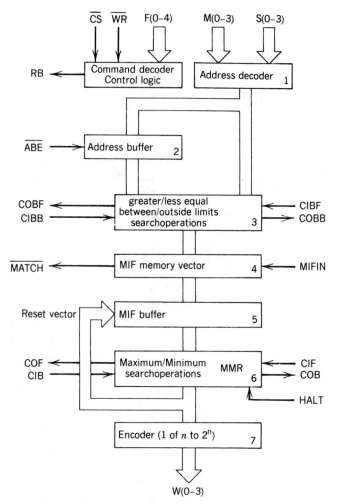

Figure 18.2 *Components of the ARAM memory module. Reprinted by permission from Roll, Waldschmidt, Stugala and Tavangarian.* [10]

the control processor. In order to detect and separate the actual match within the whole memory array during each read cycle, each memory module has to check its input-carry signals. The actual match is located if all input-carries of a module show a logical "0" and at least one match can be detected within this module. The memory module holding the actual match sets all its output-carry lines to logical "1," so that the other modules are kept inactive during the next read cycle.

In order to achieve high performance, a carry look-ahead circuit (CLA) was realized as a VLSI chip based on gate arrays.[8] If a match is located, the appertaining ARAM module sets its remaining-bit (RB) to "1," the MATCH-signal to "0" and, if a read operation is selected, it outputs the matched word to the least-significant m-bit of the W-bus. By encoding the remaining-bits (ENC) of all

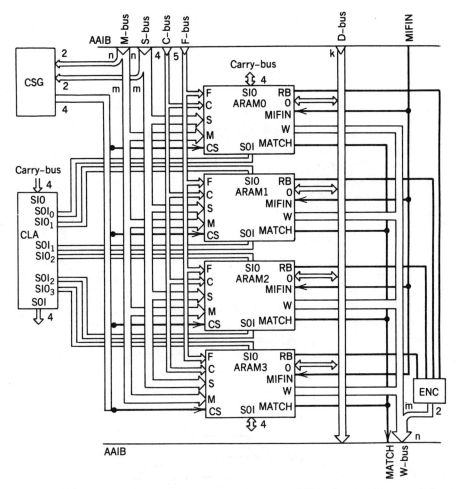

Figure 18.3 *Associative memory array assembled out of 4 ARAMs. Reprinted by permission from Roll, Waldschmidt, Stugala and Tavangarian.*[10]

modules within the array, the most significant 2-bits of the matched word are generated.

The associative memory array is controlled by a processor applying a special bus system (AAIB = associative array interconnection bus), which can be divided into the following components:

5-bit F-bus: instruction bus selecting one of the implemented
                associative functions

n-bit S-bus: for n-bit search words associative data or n-bit limits

n-bit M-bus: for n-bit mask words

n-bit W-bus: for n-bit matched words

k-bit *D*-bus:	for *k*-bit nonassociative data belonging to a search argument or matched word
1-bit MIFIN-signal:	flag bit for storing or removing associative data
1-bit MATCH-signal:	for indicating matches
4-bit *C*-bus:	control bus for handshake and triggers

18.3 THE ASSOCIATIVE PROCESSOR SYSTEM

Figure 18.4 shows a block diagram of the complete processor system, comprising standard components like conventional ROM/RAM memories and I/0 ports. The number of pins required by the control processor chip can be decreased using the system bus twice—for communication with the standard components as well as for controlling the associative memory array. Therefore, the system data bus is directly connected with the *W* and *D* buses of the AAIB. The data and the address bus optionally can be connected with the *S* and the *M* bus by help of latches. In addition, some control lines of the AAIB are usable for conventional components, too.

A hardware diagram of the conceived control processor on the register-transfer level is shown in Figure 18.5 for an example of a 32-bit version. The concept includes the usual standard components of von Neumann computer architecture, such as a control unit (which is not presented in the figure in order to provide more clarity); an arithmetical logical unit (ALU); an address computation unit (ACU); an instruction register; a program counter; and standard register sets (four

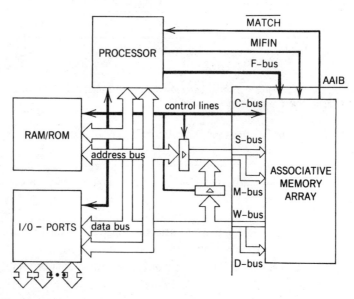

Figure 18.4 *Block diagram of the associative processor system. Reprinted by permission from Roll, Waldschmidt, Strugala and Tavangarian.* [10]

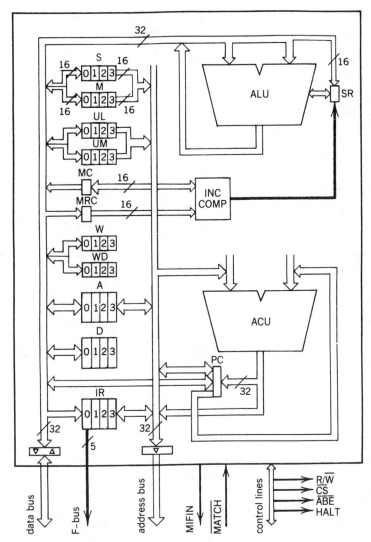

Figure 18.5 *Block diagram of the control processor. Reprinted by permission from Roll, Waldschmidt, Strugala, and Tavangarian.* [10]

32-bit data registers and four 32-bit address registers), enabling the system to be applied as a general-purpose computer with all the additional features of a highly parallel working associative processor. The processor performs codes applying the standard "von Neumann mechanism": sequentially addressed instructions kept in conventional program memory are executed in a sequential manner. However, resulting from its ability to manipulate data sets in parallel according to a single associative instruction, the processor system can be classified as single instruction multiple data architecture.

In order to support associative functions, the processor comprises some sets of

16-bit special-purpose registers for managing associative data words, such as *S* and *M* registers holding often-used search arguments and their mask words, and *UL* and *UM* registers receiving matched data and additional nonassociative data. When using the register-addressing mode, the contents held in a pair of registers (e.g., one *S* and one *M* register) can be applied to the address bus or the data bus in parallel; the search argument is loaded into the most-significant 16-bit of the specified bus; the mask gets admitted to the least-significant 16 bit at the same time. For that purpose, it is not necessary to use the same level of *S* and *M* registers; the register-addressing mode becomes efficient by combining different search arguments with various masks.

Supporting the various usable addressing modes the system bus allows direct data transmission between all system components. This includes the possibility of sending a search argument with its appertaining mask from a I/0 port to the associative memory array. In reverse direction, a matched word read out of the memory can be received by a specified port directly.

Besides the usual state bits known from standard processors, the processor concept described here includes some special-state bits, which create program branches as a result of various events concerning associative operations. For example, during the execution of a search operation, the content of the *MC* register is incremented within each read cycle (INC), so that the *MC* register holds the actual number of matched words. If this number is equal to or greater than the reference value in the *MRC* register, a comparator circuit (COMP) sets two corresponding state bits within the 16-bit state register.

18.4   THE INSTRUCTION SET

The instruction set of the processor is divided into nonassociative and parallel associative instructions. The nonassociative part is a subset of the 68000 instruction set, comprising branch, transmission, and arithmetical-logical instructions, which can be applied to all different register types implemented by this concept. Therefore, often-used search arguments and mask words kept in special-purpose registers may be managed or modified by powerful instructions within short time periods. An important example for the necessity to manipulate associative data by logical operations is given by the problem of pattern recognition, requiring search arguments and mask words to be shifted by various numbers of bit positions in order to find the vertical and horizontal locations of bit patterns within a stored data set. Because of the various logical functions which can be applied to register contents, search and mask words may be constructed by combining partial words, or they can be divided into partial masks or search arguments.

According to the realized ARAM functions, the associative instruction set of the processor comprises 47 different instructions. Table 18.1 shows the assembler mnemonics and the meaning of some typical associative instructions. For example, the WMBL instruction (write match between limits) needs a flag bit *d*, an upper limit *esu*, and a lower limit *esl*. Optionally, the limits may be masked by *emu* and *eml*.

TABLE 18.1 Some Associative Instructions

	Mnemonic	Operands	Function
Write	WMS	\<d\>,\<es\>	Write single match
	WMM	\<d\>,\<es\>,\<em\>	Write multi match
	WMBL	\<d\>,\<esu\>,\<esl\>, {\<emu\>,\<eml\>}	Write match between limits
	WMGE	\<d\>,\<esl\>,\<eml\>	Write match greater equal limit
	WDOL	\<data\>,\<esu\>,\<esl\>, {\<emu\>,\<eml\>}	Write data outside limits
	WDLE ⋮	\<data\>,\<esu\>,\<emu\>	Write data less equal limits
Read	RMR	\<es\>,\<em\>	Read multi-match
	RBML	\<esu\>,\<esl\>, {\<emu\>,\<eml\>},\<ea\>	Read minimum between limits
	ROMR ⋮	\<esu\>,\<esl\>, {\<emu\>,\<eml\>},\<ea\>	Multi read outside limits
Test	TMLE ⋮	\<esu\>,\<emu\>	Test on multi-match less equal limit

d	= 0/1	(flag bit MIFIN)
data	=	effective data (nonassociative data)
es	=	effective search word
em	=	effective mask word
esu	=	effective search word (upper limit)
esl	=	effective search word (lower limit)
emu	=	effective mask word (upper limit)
eml	=	effective mask word (lower limit)
ea	=	effective address

Generally, the conceived 32-bit control processor is capable of performing computer instructions consisting of one to four long words (32-bit words). The first long word is partitioned into the 8-bit operation code, a 6-bit field for holding short constants (e.g., shift factors or flag bits), and an 18-bit field specifying the addressing modes for source and destination operands. The following long words within an instruction are optional and contain addresses and immediate data according to the addressing modes specified by the first instruction long word.

With regard to the standard instruction set, the processor works as a two-address machine, whereas for the associative operations three-address instructions are defined, too. Each instruction using register-addressing modes requires one only long word, increasing operation speed. The most important basic instructions are supported by a number of efficient addressing modes (Figure 18.6), which are well-known from standard processors. In addition, a special "indirect search" addressing mode is implemented using a matched word with nonassociative data as a new search argument and mask word for a second search cycle.

With the help of the short program section shown in Table 18.2, the effect of some basic associative instructions shall be explained. The MOVE instruction

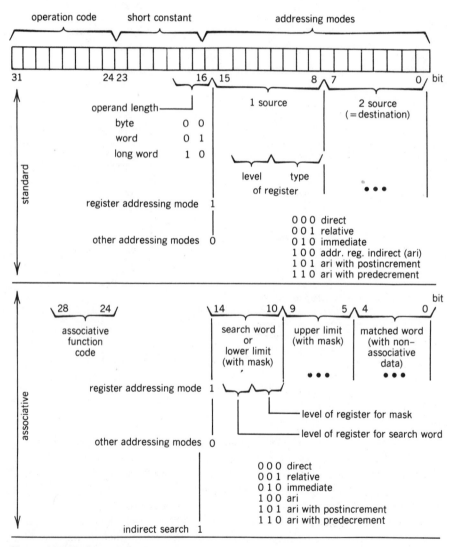

Figure 18.6 *Partition of the first instruction long word. Reprinted by permission from Roll, Waldschmidt, Strugala, and Tavangarian.*[10]

TABLE 18.2   A Short Program Section

	MOVE	#H'10000',A0
	CLR	
	WMM	1,#B'11110000',#B'11001100'
	RBL	#B'10111010',#B'10000000',(A0)+
LOOP	FNM	(A0)+
	BM	LOOP

loads an immediate data (hexadecimal "10000") into address register A0. The following CLR instruction removes all data from the memory array; all of the MIF-cells within the whole associative memory are then reset to 0. Afterwards, the associative write instruction WMM (write multi-match) stores those 16 data words into the memory array, which can be generated by applying the mask (binary "11001100") to the search argument (binary "11110000"), so that according to the ARAM concept a logical "1" is stored into the 16 MIF-cells appertaining to the data set. This parallel write operation requires one memory cycle only. The following associative read instruction RBL (read between limits) initiates a parallel search for all data words, the values of which are equal to or greater than the lower limit (binary "10000000") and are equal to or less than the upper limit (binary "10111010"); the limits are specified as immediate constants within the instruction. In the given example, three matches are detected: "10110000," "10110100," and "10111000." Only the first matched word read out is affected by the RBL instruction and stored into the RAM cell, which is addressed by register *A0*. In order to read out and store the following matched data sequentially, an FNM instruction (fetch next match)—placed within a program loop—is applied as many times as the BM instruction (branch on match) detects a further match. After program execution, the three matched words are stored in RAM memory in the strict order of their values.

REFERENCES

1. S. S. Yau, Associative processor architectures—A survey. *Comput. Surv.* **9** (1) (1977).

2. K. J. Thurber and L. D. Wald, Associative and parallel processors. *Comput. Surv.* **7** (4) (1975).

3. A. J. Weissberger, On-chip cache memory gives μPs a big-system look. *Electron. Des.* (1983).

4. D. Bursky, 32-bit CPU works with 4-Gbyte address. *Electron. Des.* (1983).

5. D. Tavangarian, *A novel modular expandable associative memory*, Euromicro prepr. North-Holland Publ., Amsterdam, 1982.

6. D. Tavangarian, *A general purpose associative processor*, Euromicro prepr. North-Holland Publ., Amsterdam, 1983.

7. K. Waldschmidt, M. Strugala, and D. Tavangarian, Erfahrungen bei dem Standardzellen-entwurf mit dem VENUS-System. In A. Kaesser and K. Woelken (eds.), *Entwurf integrierter Schaltkreise*, GMD-Stud. No. 94. 1984.

8. M. Strugala, G. Roll, and K. Waldschmidt, VLSI-realization of a full parallel associative memory array (to be published).

9. C. Steigner, G. Roll, and K. Waldschmidt, Das Konzept der ASSKO-Datenflus-Architektur. Struktur und Betrieb von Rechensystemen. *NTG-Fachber*. **80** (1982).

10. G. Roll, K. Waldschmidt, M. Strugala, and D. Tavangarian, A universal parallel associative processor. *Proc. Int. Symp. MIMI*, pp. 177–187 (1986).

Massively Parallel Computers

INTRODUCTION AND SURVEY

The human brain has about 10^{11} neurons, each capable of switching no more than a thousand times a second. Hence the brain can perform about 10^{14} switches per second. In contrast, a digital computer may have as many as 10^9 transistors, each capable of switching as often as 10^9 times per second. The total number of switches per second is as high as 10^{18}. If the number of switches is proportional to computational power, the modern computer should be 10,000 times more powerful than the brain. In reality, the computer is far behind the brain.

The classical computer is a single-processor system, while the brain has a very large number of processing units that operate at the same time. Modern semiconductor technology has reached the level at which building a computer with thousands of processors is possible. These systems are called *massively parallel computers.*

This chapter describes the major trends in massively parallel computers. Concrete examples are shown, including the hypercube concurrent computers, the distributed-array processor, the massively parallel processor, and the Connection Machine. Massively parallel computers present an important step towards more brain-like computers. The existence of these machines could also be an important step in brain research. For the first time, it is possible to simulate very large parallel systems such as complex neural networks. Hence, positive feedback is established between brain research and computer science/engineering, each gaining from the other. New discoveries in neural networks, and new massively parallel computers, will emerge from this positive feedback.

19.1 PARALLEL PROCESSING

The two major parts of the classical von Neumann computer are the central processing unit and the memory. Almost all of the hardware is in the memory, and only a small percentage is in the central processing unit. The central processing unit either reads or writes into one memory location at one time. This means that the central processing unit is busy all the time, but that most of the memory is idle. A large percentage of the computer hardware, say 95 percent, sits idle all the time. An obvious way for better utilization of the hardware is an architecture based on a large number of parallel processing units.

Computer architectures are divided into three groups called SISD, SIMD, and MIMD. SISD (single instruction, single data) architecture explains the operation of classical machines. It uses hardware in a very inefficient way; however, this architecture is simple and easy to program, and most of the computer systems presently available follow this architecture. This is especially true in small systems, and in measurement and control systems. In these systems, memories are relatively small and efficiency is not crucial.

SIMD (single instruction, multiple data) architecture offers more efficient use of hardware but also provides a substantially higher speed of operation. SIMD architecture is presented in Figure 19.1. An SIMD system typically consists of identical processing elements (PE), each a processor with its own memory, an interconnection network, and a control unit (CU). The control unit broadcasts instructions to all PEs. Each active PE executes each instruction on the data in its own memory. The instruction is executed simultaneously in all active PEs. The interconnection network enables the data to be transferred among the PEs.

Because the same operation is performed simultaneously on different data items, SIMD systems are particularly well-suited for performing matrix and vector operations. Some application areas, by their nature, call for SIMD architecture. Image processing is such an area. An image is composed of picture elements (pixels); a 1000×1000 point image has a million pixels. It is possible to build an SIMD system with a million processors, one for each pixel.

MIMD (multiple instruction stream, multiple data stream) architecture enables

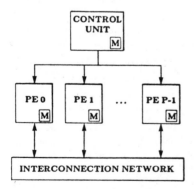

Figure 19.1
Single instruction, multiple data (SIMD) configuration.

a number of independent but related programs to be executed concurrently. Concurrent processing is a single-level or global form of parallelism, denoting independent operation of a collection of simultaneous computing activities. A concurrent machine thus uses loosely coupled multiple processors to perform many operations at once. Figure 19.2 shows MIMD concurrent architecture.

Parallel architectures can be further divided into two categories, based on the way the processors communicate. According to Bell,[1] all of the machines use either bus-based or nonbus-based architectures. Within the bus-based groups are two subcategories: tightly coupled and loosely coupled systems. The tightly coupled systems, sometimes called *multiprocessors*, have multiple processors and common, or global, memory. The processor and memory are connected by one or more high-speed buses. Loosely coupled systems, sometimes called *multicomputers*, have local memories for each processor, although they sometimes have global memory for shared data.

The main architecture in the nonbus-based category is the *hypercube*. Instead of relying on buses, hypercubes rely on direct memory-access channels between neighboring processors and their memories. Each processing unit, called a node, can communicate directly with its nearest neighbors in the *n*-dimensional space in which it was designed and built. Hypercube topology was developed by Seitz[2], following the concept proposed by Sullivan and Brashkow.[3] The hypercube is a binary *n*-cube, also referred to as a *binary hypercube* or *Boolean hypercube* (Figure 19.3).

A two-dimensional hypercube has four nodes, each at a corner of a single square. Each node is able to communicate directly with two other nodes. A three-dimensional hypercube is the familiar cube. This hypercube has eight nodes, each at one corner of a cube; each node communicates directly with three other nodes. Higher-dimensioned cubes are built up from this basic structure.

The cube "dimension" equals the power of two corresponding to the number of nodes in the cube. Thus, a 32-node cube is a five-dimensional system (2^5). Each node is connected to its five nearest neighbors. If the processor needs to communicate with a node that is not one of its nearest neighbors, the data must be routed via intervening processors. If this occurs frequently, it could slow overall processing rates in hypercubes. Each node is a powerful processor operating independently of others. Hence, the hypercube represents a loosely coupled, coarse-grain architecture.

In any parallel computer architecture, there is a trade-off between the numbers and the size of the processors. Possible solutions are single-grain systems, coarse-

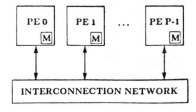

Figure 19.2
Multiple instruction, multiple data (MIMD) configuration.

Dimensions	Nodes	Channels	Topology
0	1	0	
1	2	1	
2	4	4	
3	8	12	
4	16	32	
5	32	80	

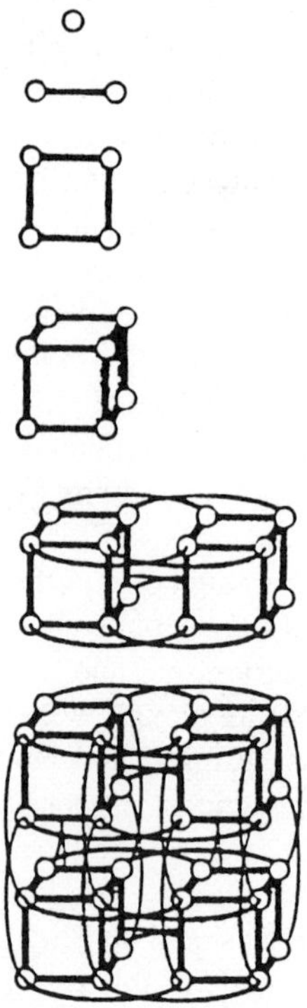

Figure 19.3 *The hypercube topology. The processor nodes have dedicated communication channels to their nearest neighbors. Reprinted by permission from Rattner.* [5]

grain systems, and fine-grain systems. A single-grain system is a classical von Neumann machine with only one processor. A coarse-grain system couples a moderately large number (say hundreds) of powerful processors; hypercubes are typical representatives of this group. A fine-grain system couples a very large number (say thousands) of processors. For example, IBM's GF11 machine contains 576 processing elements, interconnected by a three-stage switching network; the Connection Machine from Thinking Machines Corporation contains 64,000 processing elements, interconnected by a programmable switching network. Each processor is a simple one-bit processing unit.

Parallel systems can be built in many different ways; the choice of architecture depends on the application. Many systems exist in each architecture category. All the categories put together form the computer taxonomy tree suggested by Bell,[1] and shown in Figure 19.4.

19.2 HYPERCUBE CONCURRENT COMPUTERS: iPSC

The iPSC is a course-grain MIMD system with 32, 64, or 128 microcomputers connected into the hypercube. It is a loosely coupled system consisting of inde-

Simplified computer taxonomy

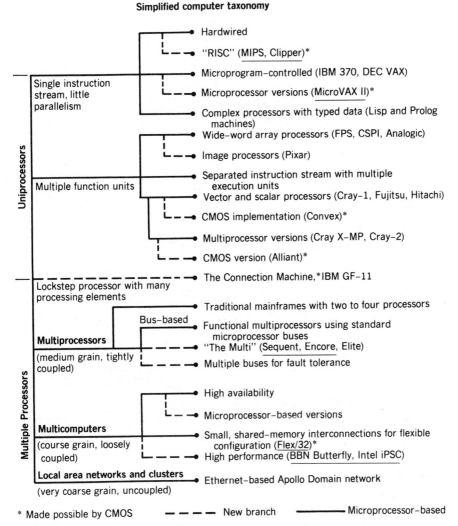

* Hardwired
* "RISC" (MIPS, Clipper)*
* Microprogram-controlled (IBM 370, DEC VAX)
* Microprocessor versions (MicroVAX II)*

Single instruction stream, little parallelism

* Complex processors with typed data (Lisp and Prolog machines)
* Wide-word array processors (FPS, CSPI, Analogic)
* Image processors (Pixar)

Multiple function units

* Separated instruction stream with multiple execution units
* Vector and scalar processors (Cray-1, Fujitsu, Hitachi)
* CMOS implementation (Convex)*
* Multiprocessor versions (Cray X-MP, Cray-2)
* CMOS version (Alliant)*

Uniprocessors

* The Connection Machine,*IBM GF-11

Lockstep processor with many processing elements

* Traditional mainframes with two to four processors

Bus-based

* Functional multiprocessors using standard microprocessor buses

Multiprocessors

(medium grain, tightly coupled)

* "The Multi" (Sequent, Encore, Elite)
* Multiple buses for fault tolerance

* High availability
* Microprocessor-based versions

Multicomputers

(course grain, loosely coupled)

* Small, shared-memory interconnections for flexible configuration (Flex/32)*
* High performance (BBN Butterfly, Intel iPSC)

Local area networks and clusters

(very coarse grain, uncoupled)

* Ethernet-based Apollo Domain network

Multiple Processors

* Made possible by CMOS   — — — New branch   ———— Microprocessor-based

Figure 19.4 *Simplified taxonomy tree, following Bell.* [1]

pendent processors. Each processor executes a portion of a larger program concurrently with other processors. Concurrency is an interactive parallelism that allows asychronous operation of processors in a multiprocessor system.

The hypercube nodes are connected to each other via point-to-point communication channels. Each processor is connected directly to a local host processor—the cube manager—via a global communication channel. This structure is shown in Figure 19.5 for a hypercube with 32 nodes. The cube manager is an Intel System 310 microcomputer running under the XENIX operating system. It serves as a local host for the hypercube and supports program development, application execution, and diagnostics.

Each microcomputer, or processing node, is made up of an 80286 central pro-

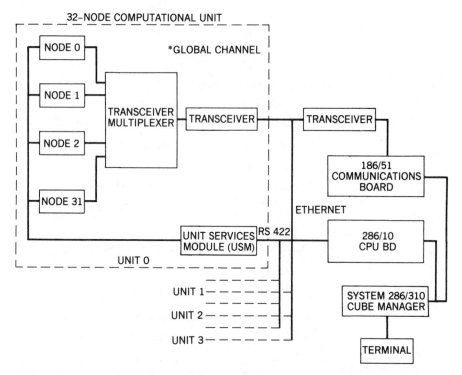

Sporting a cube–managing 286/310 microcomputer and up to four 32–node computational units connected by global and diagnostics channels, the iPSC computer system depend on the Xenix operating system for computer management, and Fortran and C for most of its application programs. An Ethernet network allows local communications.

Figure 19.5 *The iPSC hypercube consists of 32, 64, or 128 microcomputers connected to each other via point-to-point communication channels. Reprinted by permission from Asbury, Frison, and Roth.*[4]

cessing unit (CPU), an 80287 floating-point numeric processing unit, 512 kilobytes of RAM, and 64 kilobytes of PROM. Figure 19.6 shows the node structure. Each node contains seven point-to-point, bidirectional communication channels and a single global channel. Each channel is controlled by a dedicated communication processor, the 82586 local area network coprocessor. These coprocessors move messages between nodes via dedicated bidirectional, point-to-point communication channels with integrated direct memory access to the associated node's RAM. According to Asbury, Frison, and Roth,[4] solving problems on a concurrent machine requires partitioning them into a number of segments that can run independently on more than one processor. Many applications, particularly in scientific computing, lend themselves to this partitioning.

The program to solve a problem that is inherently concurrent in nature can be separated into two components. First, there is a scalar portion called the loop, or problem space, which mathematically describes the problem boundary. Then there is a vector portion (inner loop), which is a software model of the interac-

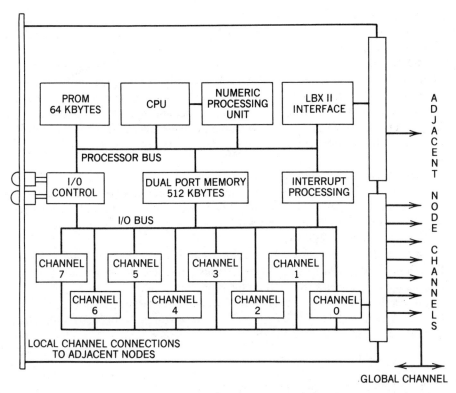

There are $\log_2 N$ channels per node. An actual iPSC node fits on a 9- by 11-in. Eurocard and contains a self-sufficient microcomputer.

Figure 19.6 *The processing node. Reprinted by permission from Asbury, Frison, and Roth.* [4]

tion between the individual problem elements. A common problem in molecular dynamics—the diffusion of one group of molecules through a medium—is a good example of how concurrent processing and vector processing differ in the way they handle similar problems.

A concurrent machine such as the hypercube can also handle nonnumerical problems, such as event-driven simulation, circuit simulation, finite-element analysis, and artificial intelligence. This capability is not found in conventional supercomputers, because their architectures are optimized for handling vector calculations.

Significant work remains to be done to develop software for concurrent architectures. The programming process will have to include application generators based on interactive graphic terminals. In this way the programmers can deal with large parallel programs with the aid of pictures and other tools for automatic programming.

Ashbury, Frison, and Roth[4] present an example of FORTRAN programs that use the hypercube concurrent processing capabilities. These are the programs (processes) STATS and MOMENT shown in Figure 19.7. Running on a one-dimensional hypercube, STATS computes the mean and standard deviation of lists of floating-point numbers on one node.

MOMENT runs concurrently on two nodes, and is used by STATS to do most of its arithmetic concurrently; MOMENT and STATS run concurrently on one node. MOMENT repeatedly receives lists of floating-point numbers, computes a sum of powers of those numbers, and sends the sum back to the host process. The power is equal to the node identification number plus 1, so node 0 computes the sum of the numbers and node 1 computes the sum of the squares of the same numbers.

Data are passed between the processes using CALL SENDW, CALL RECVW, CALL SENDMSG and CALL RECVMSG. When the process STATS needs to do arithmetic, it uses CALL SENDMSG to call MOMENT, and then passes the information to MOMENT. MOMENT is simultaneously awaiting data from STATS, using CALL RECVW.

Once MOMENT processes the data, it issues a CALL SENDW and waits for STATS to issue a CALL RECVMSG. At this point, the program sends the data back to the host process (STATS) on the originating node.

For detailed description of the iPSC hypercube see Rattner,[5] Fox and Otto,[6] Fox, Lyzenga, and Otto,[7] Seitz,[2] and the manufacturer's manuals. For iPSC programming concepts, see Chapter 20.

19.3 DISTRIBUTED-ARRAY PROCESSOR

Today parallel processors are available with over a thousand processing elements. One such computer is that ICL DAP (distributed-array processor) (Figure 19.8).

According to Bowler and Pawley,[8] the basic hardware of the DAP consists of a 64×64 array of connected PEs. Each PE has 4 kbits of storage and a very simple, 1-bit processor with three registers, the most interesting of which is A register. Certain instructions may be made conditional upon the setting of the A register in each processor. Instructions are broadcast to the processor array by a master control unit (MCU), which also handles certain simple scalar functions such as control of DO loop variables in FORTRAN. The processors in array obey each instruction simultaneously, acting on their local data. Thus, the DAP is a single instruction stream, multiple data stream (SIMD) machine.

The DAP is constructed by allocating a processor to each memory chip of a standard 2-Mbyte store module of an ICL 2900 series mainframe. There is thus no overhead associated with loading the DAP as there is with array or vector processors which are attached to mainframes as back-end processors. Data in the DAP store may be processed either by the DAP or by the host computer, but in most calculations it is advisable to do as much of the work in the DAP as possible. This means that serial computations are done in the DAP in a mode which is not the most efficient. This is overcome in the Goodyear Aerospace MPP (massively

```
                        PROGRAM STATS
            INTEGER K,M,N,CID,HOST,BYTES,XLEN,TYPE
            INTEGER COPEN
            DOUBLE PRECISION X(100),SUM,SUMSQS,TEMP,MEAN,STDEV
            DATA XLEN /800/, TYPE /1/, HOST /-1/
   c
   c        Open a channel. Use a process id equal to the node id.
   c
            CID = COPEN(HOST)
   c        Start the main loop. Read the data from the terminal.

       10   WRITE (*,*) 'Enter n, x(1), . . ., x(n)'
            READ(*,*) N, (X(I), I = 1,N)
            IF (N .LE. 0) STOP
            WRITE(*,*) 'N = ',N
   c
   c        Ask node 0 to compute sum of x(i) and
   c        ask node 1 to compute sum of x(i)**2.
   c
            BYTES = 8*N
            CALL SENDMSG (CID,TYPE,X,BYTES,0,0)
            CALL SENDMSG (CID,TYPE,X,BYTES,1,1)
   c
   c        Wait for two replies, which can come in either order.
   c        M is the id of the node originating the reply.
   c
            BYTES = 8
            DO 40 K = 1,2
               CALL RECVMSG (CID,TYPE,TEMP,BYTES,BYTES,M,M)
               IF (M .EQ. 0) SUM = TEMP
               IF (M .EQ. 1) SUMSQS = TEMP
       40   CONTINUE
   c        Compute the statistics and print the results.

            MEAN = SUM/N
            STDEV = DSQRT (SUMSQS/N - MEAN**2)
            WRITE(*,*) 'MEAN = ', MEAN
            WRITE(*,*) 'STDEV = ', STDEV
            WRITE(*,*)
   c
   c        Do it again
   c
            GO TO 10
            END
```

Figure 19.7 *An example of* FORTRAN *programs that uses the hypercube. Reprinted by permission from Asbury, Frison, and Roth.*[4]

```
                        PROGRAM MOMENT
             INTEGER I,M,N,CID,HOST,BYTES,XLEN,TYPE
             INTEGER MYNODE,COPEN
             DOUBLE PRECISION X(100),SUM
             DATA XLEN /800/, TYPE /1/
   c
   c         Find the node id
   c
             M = MYID ( )
   c
   c         Open a channel. Use a process id equal to the node id.
   c
             CID = COPEN(M)
   c
   c         Start the main loop.
   c
      10     CONTINUE
   c
   c         Wait for n and x.
   c
             CALL RECVW (CID,TYPE,X,XLEN,BYTES,HOST,HOST)
             N = BYTES/8
   c
   c         Compute the desired sum.
   c         Note that the node id is involved in the arithmetic.
   c
             SUM = 0.0D0
             DO 20 I = 1,N
               SUM = SUM + X(I)**(M + 1)
      20     CONTINUE
   c
   c         Send the sum back to the host.
   c
             CALL SENDW (CID,TYPE,SUM,8,HOST,HOST)
   c
   c         End of the main loop.
   c
             GO TO 10
             END
```

Figure 19.7 *(continued)*

parallel processor), a 128×128 array computer, by using a dedicated serial computer for this work as well as the basic host computer. The MPP already promises a power increase of nearly 20 over the DAP.

The PEs of the DAP are connected on a 64×64 cyclic array, each PE being joined to its four nearest neighbors. Information is passed between the PEs, achieving any required routing by a sequence of transforms to the appropriate

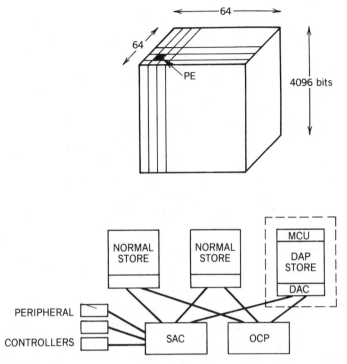

Figure 19.8 *Distributed-array processor. Adapted from Bowler and Pawley.*[8]

neighbor. In order to exploit the parallelism of the DAP, a dialect of FORTRAN (DAP FORTRAN) has been developed.

19.4 THE MASSIVELY PARALLEL PROCESSOR MPP*

The massively parallel processor (MPP) was developed by Goodyear Aerospace to support NASA's need for ultrahigh-speed ground-based image processing.[9] The architecture of MPP, shown in Figure 19.9, includes

- An array unit (ARU) that processes arrays of data. The ARU contains a 128-by-128 array of bit-serial processing elements (PEs). Two-by-four subarrays of PEs are packaged in a custom VLSI HCMOS chip.
- An array control unit (ACU) that controls the operation of the ARU and performs scalar operations.
- A unique staging memory that buffers and permutes data.
- A front-end host computer (DEC VAX 11/780) that controls the flow of data.

*Section 19.4 is adapted from MPP manuals. Courtesy and copyright © 1985 by Goodyear Aerospace Corporation.

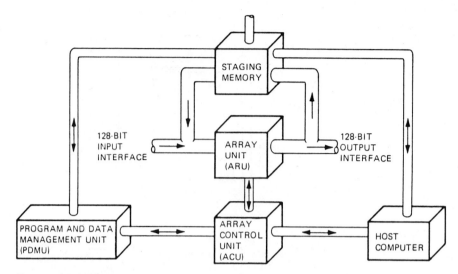

Figure 19.9 *MPP system block diagram. Courtesy and copyright ©1985 by Goodyear Aerospace Corporation.*

The MPP's processing power derives from its SIMD organization; the heart of the MPP is the array unit ARU.

The ARU operates on two-dimensional data in a 128-by-128 array of PEs. Each PE is associated with a 1024-bit RAM (expandable to 65,536 bits); each PE is connected to its north, south, east, and west neighbors. Under program control, cylindrical, toroidal, and spiral connection of PEs can be affected. Four redundant columns of PEs provide enhanced reliability. The basic structure of the ARU is shown in Figure 19.10a.

In the MPP, each PE has direct access to data in its own RAM as shown in Figure 19.10b. Access to other data is by way of inter-PE communication or the staging memory.

The PEs are bit serial elements; their structure is shown in Figure 19.11. Each PE has a full adder and programmable length shift register for arithmetic, six 1-bit registers (A, B, C, G, P, and S), a random access memory (RAM), a data bus (D), and some combinatorial logic. The normal clock rate of the PEs is 10 megahertz. In each clock cycle, all PEs perform the same operations on their respective data streams (except when masked). The basic PE operations are microsteps of the array instruction set. The control signals come from the PE control unit of the array control unit, which reads the microcode from a writable control store. Provided there are no conflicts, many PE operations can be combined into a one-clock cycle.

The PE performs a variety of data-bus source selection, logic and routing, arithmetic, and I/O operations. This discussion expands only on certain routing and I/O operations.

A routing operation reads the state of the P register in a neighboring PE (north, south, east, west) and stores the state in the P register. When routing occurs (a

(A) BASIC ARU STRUCTURE

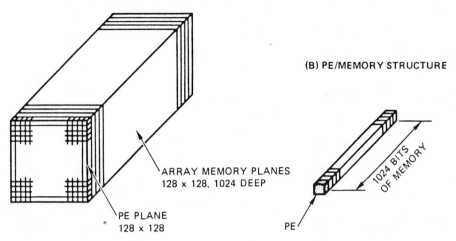

(B) PE/MEMORY STRUCTURE

ARRAY MEMORY PLANES
128 x 128, 1024 DEEP

PE PLANE
128 x 128

PE

1024 BITS OF MEMORY

Figure 19.10 *Array unit. Courtesy and copyright ©1985 by Goodyear Aerospace Corporation.*

routing operation may be masked or unmasked), the 128-by-128 plan of *P* registers is shifted synchronously in any of the four cardinal directions.

The *S* register in all PEs is used for input and output of array data. Columns of input data are shifted into the *S* registers at the west edge of the ARU and shifted across the array until all 16,384 *S* registers are loaded. Then the PE processing

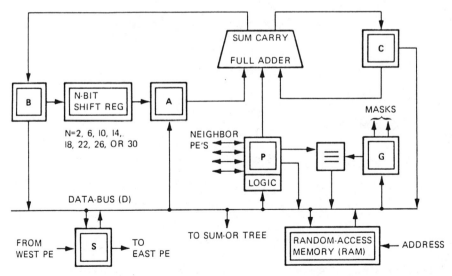

Figure 19.11 *One MPP processing element. Courtesy and copyright ©1985 by Goodyear Aerospace Corporation.*

is interrupted for one machine cycle while the *S* register plan is transferred to a selected plane of the RAMs. Since *S* register shifting can run at 10-megahertz rate, data can be input at a rate of 160 megabytes per second (128 bits every 100 nanoseconds). PE processing is interrupted only once every 128 columns, or less than 1 percent of the time.

Data output is similar and can proceed simultaneously with input.

The PE RAMs use standard RAM integrated circuits. All other components of eight PEs are put on a custom VLSI chip. The use of standard RAMs allows expansion of memory without changing the chip. As delivered to NASA, the MPP had 1024 bits of memory per PE; this can be expanded to 64K bits per PE.

To understand how the ARU is designed to handle two-dimensional problems efficiently, one can view the ARU's organization as a number of two-dimensional processing and memory planes rather than as a number of PEs, words, or bytes; this view of the ARU is shown in Figure 19.12.

Each plane has 128 rows and 128 columns so it can hold 16,384 data bits. Each plane also has four spare columns to bypass faulty hardware; the spare columns

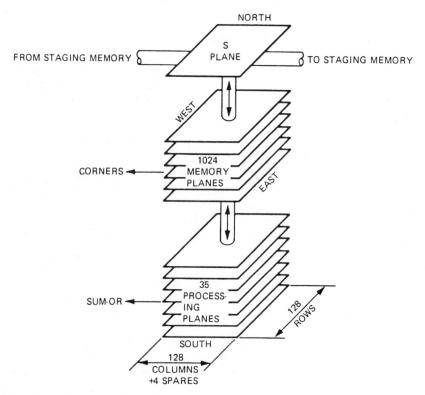

Figure 19.12 *Array unit planar structure. Courtesy and copyright ©1985 by Goodyear Aerospace Corporation.*

are not normally used. The four edges of each plane are called the north, east, south, and west edges. In Figure 19.12, the west edge of any plane is on the left side, the east edge is on the right side, the south edge is out of the page, and the north edge is into the page.

The ARU contains one S plane, 1024 memory planes, and 35 processing planes, for a total of 1060 planes. A plane of data can be transferred en masse between the S plane and a memory plane or en masse between a processing plane and a memory plane in one machine cycle. The nominal machine cycle time in the MPP is 100 nanoseconds (10 million machine cycles per second).

As with conventional computers, the ARU can be programmed at different levels:

- Low-level program modules contain instructions that specify how each data plane is transferred to and from memory, between processing planes, etc. These modules are analogous to assembly language routines in a conventional computer.
- High-level programs contain instructions that specify how memory planes or arrays of memory planes are to be combined and processed. These programs are analogous to high-level language routines in a conventional computer (e.g., FORTRAN).

High-level programs make calls to low-level modules to perform the micro-steps of each high-level operation. The complexities of S plane and processing plane manipulations are not programmed in a high-level program.

The S plane handles data input and output for the ARU. The S plane can handle input and output simultaneously.

The ARU has 1024 memory planes. Like every other plane in the ARU, each memory plane has 128 rows and 128 columns, and it can store 16,384 data bits. Thus, the 1024 memory planes can store 16,777,216 data bits (over 2 megabytes).

Any memory plane can be randomly accessed and sent to the S plane or to one or more processing planes in one machine cycle. A plane of 16,384 data bits can be transferred en masse from the S plane or a processing plane to any memory plant in one machine cycle.

The 35 ARU processing planes provide the logic and routing required for arithmetic and associative operations; they derive from the structure of the PEs.

The MPP includes a complete set of program development and debugging tools that can be used to create application programs for the computer system. NASA is supporting development of Parallel Pascal,[10] which allows direct use of MPP array architecture with the convenience of programming in a high-level language.

The MPP's rectangular array structure with near-neighbor communication is ideal for image processing. Other applications of MPP include weather forecasting, associative processing, simulation of complex digital systems, and parallel high-speed processing.

19.5 THE CONNECTION MACHINE

The Connection Machine[11] is a fine-grain SIMD system with 64,000 process/memory elements. This architecture has very little in common with the von Neumann machine. The Connection Machine computes through the interaction of many simple identical processing/memory cells. Because the processing takes place concurrently, the Connection Machine computer can be much faster than a traditional computer. The prototype is built with 64,000 processor/memory elements, but the same principle could be extended into a million-element machine.

For the first time, computer architecture follows at least roughly the architecture of the brain. In the brain a large number of neurons, maybe 10 billion, operate in parallel. The architects of the Connection Machine claim that they would like to make a thinking machine that would be able to perform the functions of a human mind. The existence of the Connection Machine could be an important step in brain research. For the first time, it will be possible to simulate very large parallel systems such as complex neural networks. Hence, positive feedback is established between brain research and computer science/engineering, each gaining from the other.

The processing elements in the Connection Machine are interconnected through a programmable network. The pattern of connections depends on the application; the structure of the machine matches the structure of the problem. For example, in the VLSI simulation application, a separate processor/memory cell is used to simulate each transistor. The processors are connected in the pattern of the circuit, in the same way as in the simulation on an analog computer. The processors are synchronized, following the behavior of different parts of a simulated circuit from one time interval to the next. The calculation is done concurrently, because the transistors of the circuit operate concurrently. A hundred thousand transistors can be simulated by a hundred thousand processors. Each processor simulates a single transistor and communicates directly with processors simulating connected transistors.

The Connection Machine will be a very strong tool in the field of artificial intelligence. Many artificial-intelligence programs represent data in the form of semantic networks. Because related concepts in the network must communicate in order to perform deduction, the topology of processors should correspond to the topology of the semantic network. Actually, retrieving common-sense knowledge from a semantic network was one of the primary motivations for the design of the Connection Machine.

In solving a problem such as simulation and semantic networks, two requirements have been identified[11]:

Requirement I: There are enough processing elements to be allocated as needed, in proportion to the size of the problem.

Requirement II: The processing elements can be connected by software.

The Connection Machine's architecture follows directly from these two requirements. It provides large numbers of tiny processor/memory cells connected by a programmable communication network. The prototype machine contains 65,536 processor/memory cells, each with 4096 bits of memory.

The block diagram of the Connection Machine is shown in Figure 19.13. The control of the machine exhibits the hierarchical structure: host, microcontroller, active data structures, processor/memory cells.

The Host communicates with the Connection Machine through the high-speed memory bus. This host computer stores the data structure of the Connection Machine. Also, the control of the individual processor/memory cells is orchestrated by the host computer. The host specifies high-level macroinstructions.

The Microcontroller is an intermediary through which the host talks to the processor/memory cells. It interprets the macroinstruction received from the host and executes the next level of instructions, called microinstructions. Each microinstruction is further broken into nanoinstructions. The nanoinstructions are executed directly by the processor/memory cells.

The Active Data Structure is a data-dependent pattern into which multiple cells are connected, as dictated by the host computer. This is necessary because

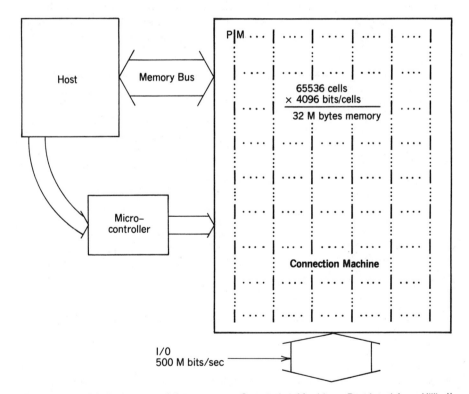

Figure 19.13 *Block diagram of the prototype Connection Machine. Reprinted from Hillis.* [11] *Courtesy and copyright ©1985 by MIT Press.*

each cell is so small that it is incapable of performing meaningful computation on its own. Instead, multiple cells are interconnected into active data structures.

The Processor/Memory Cell is the ultimate node of the machine. The key component from which the connection machine is constructed is a custom design VLSI chip. The chip contains three principal sections: the control unit, the processor array, and the router unit for the packet switch communications network.

The control unit communicates with the microcontroller. It receives and decodes nanoinstructions delivered by the microcontroller. It generates signals necessary to control the processor and the router synchronized to an externally supplied clock.

The processor array contains 16 processor cells. Each processing cell is a simple serial computer, as shown in Figure 19.14. The individual processing cell has only eight bits of internal state information (flags). The data are processed one bit at a time. Under the direction of the control unit the processing element takes data from external memory, performs arithmetic and logical operations on the data, and stores the result into the external memory and sets the proper internal flag.

On the chip, the processors are connected in a 4 x 4 grid. Each processor can directly communicate with its north, east, west, and south neighbors. This local communication does not involve the router. This two-dimensional pattern can be extended across multiple chips by connecting the NEWS pins of adjacent chips.

The router is responsible for routing messages between chips and delivering them to the destination specified by the address. The router has three sections: the

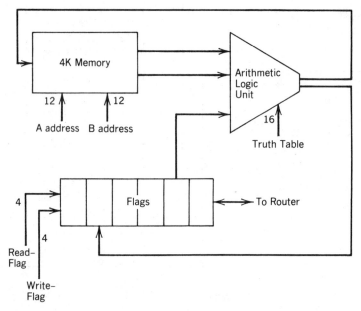

Figure 19.14 *Block diagram of a single Connection Machine processing element. Reprinted from Hillis.[11] Courtesy and copyright ©1985 by MIT Press.*

injector which transmits new messages into the network, the heart which forwards messages between chips, and the ejector which receives and delivers messages to the appropriate processing element. The router is also directly connected to the off-chip memory through the memory pins for buffering messages. All operations of the router are controlled by the control unit. The connecting network within and between chips follows the hypercube structure.

19.6 CONNECTION MACHINE PROGRAMMING

The parallel operations of the Connection Machine are supported by a new language called Connection Machine Lisp.[11,12] Actually the Connection Machine Lisp models the Connection Machine structure. Here is an example that outlines the CM programming concept, following Hillis:[11]

Finding the shortest length path between two vertices in a large graph serves as the example. The algorithm is appropriate because, besides being simple and useful, it is similar in character to the many "spreading activation" computations in artificial intelligence. The problem to be solved is this:

Given a graph with vertices V and edges $E \subset V \times V$, with an arbitrary pair of vertices a, b, ϵ, V, find the length k of the shortest sequence of connected vertices a, v_1, v_2, . . ., b such that all the edges (a, v_1), (v_1, v_2), . . ., $(v_k - 1, b) \epsilon E$ are in the graph.

For concreteness, consider a graph with 10^4 vertices and an average of 10^2 randomly connected edges per vertex. In such a graph, almost any randomly chosen pair of vertices will be connected by a path of not more than three edges.

The algorithm for finding the shortest path from vertex A to vertex B begins by labeling every vertex with its distance from A. This is accomplished by labeling vertex A with 0, labeling all vertices connected to A with 1, labeling all unlabeled vertices connected to those vertices with 2, and so on (see Figure 19.15). The process terminates as soon as vertex B is labeled. The label of B is then the length of the shortest connecting path. Any path with monotonically decreasing labels originating from B will lead to A in this number of steps. A common optimization of this algorithm is to propagate the labels from A and B simultaneously until they meet.

Ideally, we should be able to describe the algorithm to the computer as something like this:

Algorithm I: "Finding the length of shortest path from A to B"

1. Label all vertices with $+\infty$.
2. Label vertex A with 0.
3. Label every vertex, except A, with 1 plus the minimum of its neighbor's labels and itself. Repeat this step until the label of vertex B is finite.
4. Terminate. The label of B is the answer.

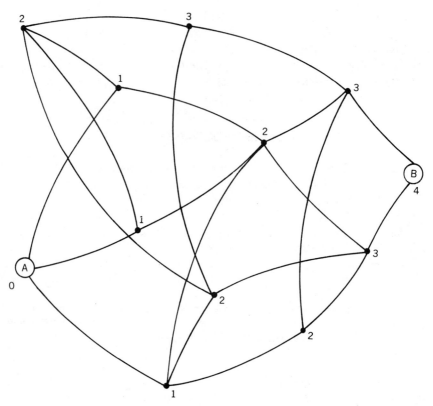

Figure 19.15 *Algorithm I finds the length of the shortest path from vertex A to vertex B by labeling each point with its distance from A. Reprinted from Hillis.[11] Courtesy and copyright ©1985 by MIT Press.*

Algorithms of this type are slow on a conventional computer. Assuming that each step written above takes unit time, Algorithm I will terminate in a time proportional to the length of the connecting path. For the 10^4 vertex random graph mentioned above, Step 3 will be repeated two or three times, so about six steps will be required to find the path length. Unfortunately, the steps given above do not correspond well with the kinds of steps that can be executed on a von Neumann machine. Direct translation of the algorithm into Lisp gives this an inefficient program. The program runs in a time proportional to the number of vertices times the length of the path times the average degree of each vertex. For example, the graph mentioned above would require several million executions of the inner loop. Finding a path in a test graph required about an hour of CPU time on a VAX-11/750 Computer.

A special programming language has been developed to program the Connection Machine. It is called Connection Machine Lisp (CmLisp) and is an extension of Common Lisp. The language expresses the essential character of the architecture; the structure of the language follows the structure of the hardware.

The path-length algorithm expressed in CmLisp is the following[11]:

```
(DEFUN PATH-LENGTH (A B C)
  α(SETF (LABEL ·G)  + INF)
    (SETF (LABEL A) O)
    (LOOP UNTIL (< (LABEL B)  + INF)
         DO α(SETF (LABEL · (REMOVE A G))
         (1 +  (βMIN α(LABEL · (NEIGHBORS · G))))))
  (LABEL B))
```

Hillis[11] points out the following:

1. There is one expression in the program corresponding to each line in Algorithm I that finds the length of path from vertex *A* to vertex *B* in graph *G*.

2. The Greek letter alpha (α) is used to represent the conversion of a value into a constant "Xector" that maps everything onto that value. In implementation terms, this is equivalent to loading a value into every processor. In other words, a xector corresponds roughly to a set of processors, with a value stored in each processor. Because a xector is distributed across many processors, it is possible to operate on all its elements simultaneously. This requires only a single operation cycle, even though the xector may have hundreds of thousands of elements.

3. The Greek letter beta (β) is used to represent the reduction: elements of the xector are reduced into a single value. This reduction is performed in parallel in logarithmic time. In the program example, the final line returns the label of *B*, which is the answer.

4. Alpha notation takes a single thing and makes many copies of it. Beta notation takes many things and combines them into one.

This example shows only the flavor of Cmlisp. For details see Hillis and Steele.[12]

REFERENCES

1. C.G. Bell, Expert opinion. *IEEE Spectrum* Jan., pp. 36-38, (1986).

2. C.L. Seitz, The cosmic cube. *Commun. ACM* **28** (1), pp. 23-33 (1985).

3. H. Sullivan and T.R. Brashkow, A large scale homogeneous machine I and II. *Proc. 4th Annu./Symp. Comput. Archit.* pp. 107-124 (1977).

4. R. Asbury, S.G. Frison, and T. Roth, Concurrent computers ideal for inherently parallel problems. *Comput. Des.* **1** (Sept.) (1985).

5. J. Rattner, Concurrent processing: A new direction in scientific computing. *Proc. Natl. Comput. Conf., AFIPS* **54** (1985).

6. G. Fox and S. Otto, Algorithm for concurrent processor. *Phys. Today* May, pp. 50-59 (1984).

7. G. Fox, G. Lyzenga, and S. Otto, Solving problems on concurrent processors. Book in preparation, 1985.

8. K.C. Bowler and G.S. Pawley, Molecular dynamics and Monte Carlo simulations in solid-state and elementary particle physics. *Proc. IEEE* Jan., pp. 42-55 (1984).

9. P.A. Gilmore, *The Massively Parallel Processor*, GER-17272. North-Holland Publ., Amsterdam 1985; also in S. Fernback (ed.), *The Book of Supercomputers*. North-Holland Publ., Amsterdam, 1986.

10. A.P. Reeves, Parallel pascal: An extended pascal for parallel computers. *J. of Parallel Distributed Comput.* **1** (1984).

11. W.D. Hillis, *The Connection Machine*. MIT press, Cambridge, MA, 1985.

12. W.D. Hillis and Steele, *The Connection Machine Lisp Manual*, Thinking Machine Co., 1985.

iPSC Programming Concepts

INTRODUCTION AND SURVEY

This chapter introduces you to the general programming concepts of the iPSC in order to aid in writing applications for this concurrent machine. It is assumed that you already understand either C or FORTRAN programming, and also have a working knowledge of XENIX.

Although you may already be familiar with concurrent programming, the purpose of this chapter is to provide you with information that will help you write programs for the iPSC.

The iPSC™ is the first family of expandable concurrent *"personal supercomputers."* It is designed to provide the research community with a system upon which to develop parallel programming techniques, tools, and application programs. More information can be found in the iPSC manual set.

The basic system has two main elements:

Cube   The complete ensemble of microcomputers connected in a parallel architecture. Each high-performance microcomputer, along with its own numeric processing unit and local memory, is referred to as a "node." Nodes are connected together by high-speed communication channels to form a self-contained "cube" in a free-standing enclosure.

                The individual nodes are connected in a hypercube interconnect topology. This design eliminates the need for global or shared system resources.

This chapter is adapted from Intel Manual *iPSC Technical Description* 175278-003-86. Courtesy and copyright © 1986 by INTEL and iPSC.

Each node is completely independent. The resident node operating system, in conjunction with communication coprocessors, allows each node to communicate with its neighbors by queued "message passing." This means that each node can execute its own computational task. . .on its own data set. . .without the processor interaction collisions encountered in systems using shared resources. Because a hypercube architecture has multiple independent processors. . .all working on different segments of the same problem. . .the iPSC is classified as a multiple instruction, multiple data (MIMD) machine.

Cube Manager Intel's Multibus-based System 310AP microcomputer connected to each node by an Ethernet communication channel. The System 310AP provides the user interface to the cube as well as hosting the programming tools and system diagnostics. This station allows you to use the iPSC as either a stand-alone concurrent computer system or as a computational server within a distributed processing environment. In the latter case, the iPSC communicates with other systems through an optional Ethernet interface.

System software includes those elements residing in the nodes of the cube; other elements residing in the cube manager.

Node-Resident Software A message-based operating system which supports message passing, input/output services, and process creation/destruction and a *PROM*-based node confidence test which initializes the board at system powerup.

Cube Manager Software Includes the XENIX operating system, program development tools, and commands to manage the cube and monitor its status.

Various models and options are available. A system has one, two, or four computational units. In the standard system, each unit contains 32 nodes. In a Large Memory system, each unit contains 16 nodes and 16 LBX memory boards (name derived from the fact that the memory board is accessed through its companion node's LBX port). In a Vector Processing system, each unit contains 16 nodes and 16 vector processor boards.

The following pages provide more detailed information on both the hardware and software components of the iPSC system.

When using the iPSC, you are basically implementing an application (the problem to be solved) as a set of sequential processes that operate in parallel on this common problem. These processes may be either "node" processes, "cube manager" processes, or. . .more typically. . .a combination of both. A process can be defined as a C or FORTRAN program that includes system routines that cause messages to be sent and received.

Commonly, a parallel processing application requires distributing the input data to the node processes. . .and collecting the results. This function is performed by a host process. . .or processes. . .running on the cube manager. In a simple application, each node process initializes, then waits for its initial data from the cube manager. When the data is received, the node process begins its computation. . .exchanging intermediate data with other node processes as necessary. When the computation is complete, each process returns its results to the host. Although applications usually are composed of a combination of host and node processes, there is no rule that excludes having only node processes if that is how your problem can best be solved.

The entire application (consisting of cube manager and node processes) is developed in the cube manager. The actual development steps (compiling, binding, etc.) that you use will vary depending on the programming languages (C or FORTRAN) and whether the process is to be executed within the cube manager or on the nodes.

The cube manager can act as a host to the cube, creating node processes, starting the computation, and collecting the results. It lets you start and stop your application with XENIX commands.

Another way to view the cube manager is to consider it just *another node* in the cube. Although it does have access to additional facilities (such as the XENIX file system), it communicates with cube processes with similar message primitives that node processes use.

This chapter discusses how to design an application using:

- The two multitasking operating systems (XENIX and the node operating system)
- A message-based interconnection structure
- The four basic language routines for passing messages: SEND, SENDW, RECV, and RECVW
- The virtual communication links, called channels, that the four language routines require

20.1 CUBE SOFTWARE

Cube software consists of a Node Confidence Test (NCT) and a node operating system residing on each node.

Node Confidence Test   This PROM-based test runs automatically when the system is powered up or reset. It initializes each node by resetting and enabling the node memory, communication controllers, I/O controller, interrupt controller, and CPU. Node identity is also set by reading the slot ID from the backplane.

Node Operating System   A copy of the node operating system is loaded into each node after initialization and confidence testing have been successfully completed. The node operating system performs these basic functions:

Interprocess Communication. The node operating system provides users with a powerful set of communication routines in FORTRAN and C programming languages. The communication interface is consistent whether communicating with other processes in the same node, to remote nodes, or to processes in the cube manager. Sending and receiving can be synchronous or asynchronous. Messages are automatically routed from node-to-node, if necessary, to reach the destination process.

Reliable message delivery service is provided between nearest node neighbors. Data message length can vary from 0 to 16K bytes. Messages larger than 1K byte are automatically fragmented and reassembled at the destination node, transparently to the user process.

Process Management. Processes are executed for a given interval (50 milliseconds) in a round-robin fashion. The number of processes is limited only by available memory.

Physical Memory Management. Provides memory space for each process on the node as well as message buffering. Memory management is not directly visible to the user. Temporary message buffers are managed automatically.

Protected Address Space. Local descriptor tables storing code and data for each process provide a "firewall" between the node operating system and user space and between multiple user process spaces. This is hardware enforced so that the user cannot corrupt the node operating system.

20.2 CUBE MANAGER SOFTWARE

The cube manager software is divided into three basic categories: programming and development software, cube manager commands, and diagnostics.

Programming & Development Software

XENIX Operating System	XENIX/286 R3.0 is a fully-licensed derivative of UNIX System III. It includes enhancements from University of California at Berkeley as well as Microsoft and Intel. It is compatible with UNIX Version 7.
FORTRAN Compiler	Full implementation of ANSI X3.9-1978 FORTRAN Standard. Supports programs and arrays larger than 64K bytes and IEEE floating-point arithmetic.
Macro Assembler	Native 286 assembler ("ASM 286") plus macro extension.
Tools	All the standard XENIX tools are available. Additional tools developed at iSC.

Cube Manager Commands

These commands are developed by iSC and may be invoked from the terminal or can be executed by the XENIX program "exec". Some of the functions performed by these commands are:

Cube Access	Allows a user to gain exclusive access to the cube for running an application. When finished, another command allows the user to release exclusive access.
Load	Loads both the node operating system and application code into the cube.
System Logfile	Updated with events relating to the operation of the system, for example, when a system error occurs. Each entry is date and time stamped so that the sequence of events is preserved.

Diagnostics

The iPSC diagnostics provide both confidence and diagnostic tests. The confidence tests are used to verify overall system integrity prior to normal escape. The diagnostic tests isolate problems at the individual board or system module level.

System Confidence Testing	At power up, or upon reset, PROM-based confidence tests in the cube manager and cube verify individual module integrity and basic system

functionality. Immediately following, during the boot-up sequence, XENIX verifies the system configuration. If an error occurs during initialization confidence testing, you can invoke system diagnostic tests as appropriate.

System Diagnostic Testing   Using CDP (Cube Diagnostic Program) you can isolate problems at the board/system module level. The diagnostic strategy is to verify the functionality of the cube manager first, manager-to-cube communications next, and then the cube.

20.3 PROGRAMMING APPROACH

The approach to programming the iPSC consists of decomposing a problem into several parts. Many applications can be broken down into a few or many independent pieces. The approach to programming the iPSC is to identify these pieces and distribute them amongst the processors. These pieces could be identical programs which work on different data sets, or they could be unique programs, each contributing its part to the final solution.

The programming approach does not require that you formulate a computation to fit on nodes and on the physical communication links that exist only between certain pairs of nodes. Instead, you can formulate the problem in terms of "processes" and "virtual" communication channels that connect all processes. This is possible because the message system automatically routes messages from any process to any other process.

In general, the programming approach for the iPSC can be summarized in two steps:

1. At a fundamental level, formulate the problem by determining the set of processes that are required and the intercommunication that is necessary. For example, an application may require a set of nine processes as represented in Figure 20.1. The lines connecting the processes represent the necessary intercommunication paths.

2. The next step is to determine how to place these processes onto the nodes. Continuing the same example, Figures 20.2 and 20.3 show two possibilities for doing this. The dashed boxes represent single nodes. The first shows each process placed onto separate nodes. The second shows all nine processes placed onto a single node. As the example demonstrates, there may be more than one way to distribute the processes on the nodes. You should select a distribution that minimizes the number of messages and the distance these messages must travel. Other points to consider when selecting a distribution are keeping messages infrequent compared with computation and balancing the load so the nodes have approximately the same amount of work to do.

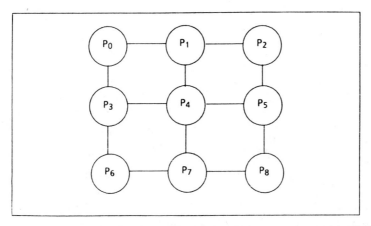

Figure 20.1 *Process and Communication Formulation. Courtesy and copyright ©1986 by INTEL and iPSC.*

20.3.1 Processes

The code for a process may be written in any combination of FORTRAN, C, or ASM286. The iPSC libraries (containing COPEN, SEND, etc.) are linked appropriately to cube manager and node processes using the XENIX link editor, Id. Node processes cannot perform I/O functions. If you do include I/O functions in node processes, you will receive errors when building the load modules. If you are a FORTRAN programmer, simply avoid I/O functions (READ, WRITE, etc.) when writing node processes.

Each node process will need its own copy of every routine used.

Here are a few more points to know about processes:

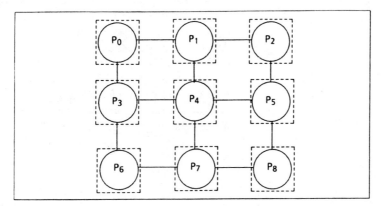

Figure 20.2 *Process Placement I. Courtesy and copyright ©1986 by INTEL and iPSC.*

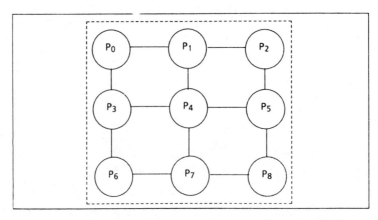

Figure 20.3 *Process Placement II. Courtesy and copyright ©1986 by INTEL and iPSC.*

Multiple Processes Per Node

Each node may contain up to 20 processes; the same number allowed in the cube manager. Therefore, the number of processes involved in a single computation may be more than the number of nodes in the system. The practical limit for the number of processes on each node is the available memory on the node and the size of the processes. User processes can take up to approximately 275 kilobytes per node in standard systems; Large Memory systems have an additional 4 megabytes. The remainder of the node's memory is reserved for the operating system and the message buffers.

Referring to Processes

The two key parameters used in the message-passing routines are process id (pid) and node id (or number). Node process id's are user-defined, and can be any number in the range of 0 to 32767. Although the system does not demand it, it is a good idea to consistently use the same pid when referring to a process.

Node numbers range from 0 to the number of nodes in the cube minus one. For example:

Cube Size	Node Number Range
16-node	0–15
32-node	0–31
64-node	0–63
128-node	0–127

The cube manager's node number is −32768. This value was chosen to allow future increases in the number of nodes per system without requiring you to modify portions of your program that refer to the cube manager.

Message Passing

Processes coordinate activities and exchange data by sending and receiving messages to and from other processes. No variables are shared among processes.

20.3.2 Channels

A channel, as used in the iPSC system, is a 64-byte block of memory that contains information about a message to be sent or received. Examples of the type of information a channel contains are:

- Source node and process ids
- Destination node and process ids
- Message length
- Message location

A sending process needs to establish a channel to contain this information before a message can be sent. Likewise, a receiving process must also establish a channel to receive this information before the message can be received. Processes use the COPEN routine to do this. Refer to Section 20.4 for more information about this routine.

Once an operation (send or receive) has been completed, the information is no longer needed and the channel can be used again by another message. If a process needs to send/receive more than one message simultaneously, the process needs to open a channel for each of the simultaneous send/receive operations.

20.3.3 Deadlock

The term "deadlock" refers to the permanent failure of a concurrent computation to make progress. For example, a computation is deadlocked if all processes are waiting to receive a message and no one has sent one.

A similar situation can occur if processes allow too many of its messages to pile up without processing them. This will lead to congestion of the message routing and could ultimately result in deadlock.

To avoid these situations, care should be taken when designing algorithms to make sure that not all processes will block without someone sending a message and to make sure that all processes do, in fact, consume messages.

TABLE 20.1 Cube Manager System Interface Library

Procedure	Description
MYPID	Returns the process id of the calling process.
PROBEMSG	Returns a value indicating whether a message is pending for a cube manager process.
SYSLOG	Allows a cube manager process to write a message into the system log file.
LWAIT	Waits for the selected process in the selected node (or nodes) to complete. It then returns the pid, node, and completion code. Enter −1 to return as soon as the first process completes.
LWAITALL	Waits for the selected process in the selected node (or nodes) to complete. Enter −1 to wait for all processes to complete.
CCLOSE	Destroys a specified communication channel created by a previous "copen" call.

20.4 CUBE MANAGER AND NODE SYSTEM INTERFACE LIBRARIES

This section introduces you to the cube manager and node system interface libraries and explains how the two libraries differ.

Tables 20.1, 20.2, 20.3 and 20.4 list the routines in the cube manager and node system interface libraries. The routines are the same for the two languages supported on the iPSC: C and FORTRAN. Assembly language programmers can use either library.

You will notice that the two libraries have a few routines that have the same name. For example, both libraries have a COPEN routine.

TABLE 20.2 Cube Manager System Interface Library

Procedure	Description
COPEN	Creates a communication channel for a cube manager process.
LOAD	Loads the file into the specified node (or all nodes if −1 is specified for the node number) and starts it.
SENDMSG	Initiates the transmission of a message from a cube manager process to a node or another cube manager process.
RECVMSG	Initiates the receipt of a message from a node or another cube manager process.
LKILL	Kills the selected process (or processes) in the selected node (or nodes).
CUBEDIM	Returns a value which indicates the dimension of the cube in which the program is run in.

TABLE 20.3 Node System Interface Library

Procedure	Description
COPEN	Creates a communication channel for a process.
SEND	Initiates the transmission of a message from a node process to a cube manager or node process. The user message buffer should not be rewritten until a "status" indicates that the send operation is complete.
SENDW	Initiates the transmission of a message from a node process to a cube manager or node process. Execution of this routine causes the calling process to be blocked until the message has been sent.
RECV	Initiates the receipt of a message from another process. The user message buffer is not available for reuse and the return values are not updated until "status" is performed.
RECVW	Initiates the receipt of a message from another process. Execution of this routine causes the calling process to be blocked until the message has been received.
STATUS	Allows a node process to determine the state of the process message buffer designated for sending or receiving a message.
PROBE	Allows a node process to determine if a message of a given type is available for reception.
FLICK	Enables a node process to defer execution to another process on the node.

TABLE 20.4 Node System Interface Library

Procedure	Description
CUBEDIM	Returns a value equal to the dimension of the cube in which the process is running.
MYNODE	Returns a value that is the node id of the requesting process.
MYPID	Returns the process id of the calling program.
GREENLED	Allows the process to turn its node board's green LED on or off.
REDLED	Allows the process to turn its node board's red LED on or off.
SYSLOG	Allows a process to write a message into the system log file.
CLOCK	Enables a node process to determine the number of elapsed millisecond intervals since the node was initialized, modulo 2^{32}.
CCLOSE	Destroys the specified communication channel created during a previous "copen."
HANDLER	Allows a process to assign the execution of a user-written exception handler to the occurance of a specific exception.

20.4.1 Differences Between the Two Libraries

The primary reason that the cube manager and node libraries are different is because the operating systems, which are the basis of the routines, are different. The cube manager operates under XENIX while the nodes have a unique operating system developed specifically for the iPSC.

The XENIX operating system dictates the way channels are treated for cube manager processes and thus the way certain cube manager, message-handling routines work. In XENIX, a channel is treated like a device. A process can only execute one device-related system routine at a time. Therefore, a cube manager process cannot perform concurrent sends and receives because that would require concurrent device operations.

Node processes, on the other hand, can perform concurrent sends and receives if the node process has multiple channels open.

The cube manager library has no analogous routine to the node library's asynchronous RECV or SEND. Consequently, the cube manager routine RECVMSG is more like the node routine RECVW than RECV. The cube manager routine SENDMSG is functionally identical to the node routine SENDW.

20.4.2 Difference Between SEND and SENDW; RECV and RECVW

SEND and RECV are non-blocking, asynchronous routines. When issued, they return to the calling process as soon as the node operating system records the request. The calling process continues to execute. The user message buffer should not be reused until "status" indicates that the send or receive operation is complete. "Status" indicates that the data can be reliably read. If a second send or receive request is issued before reading the data in the user message buffer, the data may be overwritten, corrupting both messages.

To explain it in terms of the routines and the channels that must be used, if a send or a receive is issued on a channel which already has a request pending, the second request is blocked until the first completes. If you issue a send or receive, and then issue yet another receive using a different channel, but the same buffer, data in the buffer will probably be overwritten. The way to avoid this is to never modify the buffer until "status" indicates that the buffer is ready for reuse.

Note that you can issue successive sends using the same buffer if your program does not change the data in the buffer.

You might use the SEND and RECV routines when the process has additional computations to complete which are not dependent on the information contained in the message. At the end of these computations, you can issue a "status" routine and further message processing can be done.

SENDW and RECVW, on the other hand, are blocking, synchronous routines. They do not return to the calling process until the node operating system has actually finished the operation and the message buffer is available for reuse. You might use these routines when the process has no other tasks it can do while the operation is being performed.

Note, however, that when the system returns from a SENDW, the message has simply been sent. It does not indicate that it has been received at the intended destination.

20.4.3 Using the Message Parameter "Type"

"Type" is one of the parameters in send and receive routines. Its value is user-definable, and its purpose is to identify the message content or to serve as a flag. Valid values are positive numbers in a range from 0 to 32767. The "type" parameter should not be confused with variable typing done in high-level languages.

The cube manager RECVMSG routine and the node RECVW routine receive messages differently.

On the nodes, a message is received based on its type. "Type" is an input parameter to RECV and RECVW which means that a message is received only if its "type" matches the request. That is, a pending receive on type 10 will only be fulfilled by a message sent as type 10.

On the cube manager, the "type" parameter is returned as a result of the routine. Cube manager processes cannot use message "type" to qualify message receipt, because the RECVMSG routine can be fulfilled by a message of any type. It is up to the programmer to look at the type after the message has been received in order to decide what to do with it.

Node processes, therefore, qualify message reception by "type" and cube manager processes do not.

This concept is illustrated on Figures 20.4 and 20.5 where a common use of "type" is shown.

Suppose process A can send three different messages to process B. The only way process B knows which of the three messages it has received is by the type value. Process A has defined type 10 to be an initialization message, type 15 as a floating point number, and type 20 as an error condition. Process B might then use the "probe" routine to determine the type of message that process A has sent, then branch accordingly. Or, Process B might execute three receive calls on separate channels to receive each message. Each receive specifies a different type.

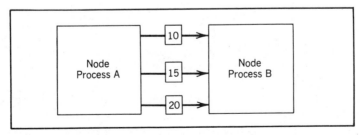

Figure 20.4 *Node Processes Using "Type." Courtesy and copyright ©1986 by INTEL and iPSC.*

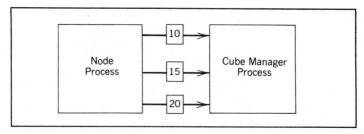

Figure 20.5 *Node and Cube Manager Processes Using "Type." Courtesy and copyright ©1986 by INTEL and iPSC.*

Figure 20.5 shows a cube manager process receiving messages. The cube manager process executes a RECVMSG and branches on the "type" *after* the message has been received. In this case, the cube manager process may execute three RECVMSG calls on three channels but cannot predict which message type will arrive at each channel.

20.5 APPLICATIONS EXAMPLE

This section gives an example of a FORTRAN application that may be run on the iPSC. This example describes all steps involved in getting the program running. The source code files (both cube manager and node) and makefile are supplied in the "/usr/ipsc/examples/rmfort_loader" directory. This application involves passing messages around a ring as illustrated in Figure 20.6.

Although a D5 is shown, the program will work, without modification, on any cube of dimension greater than zero.

The cube manager prompts for the message length and the number of times the message is to go around the ring. Node 0 receives this information and sends a message of the desired length to the next node (1). As each subsequent node receives the message, it sends it on to the next node in the ring. Every time the message completes a round trip, node 0 reports to the cube manager the current "ring count". At the end, when the desired number of rounds have been completed, it reports the time the message spent "circling" the cube.

This example allows you to inject messages of various sizes and have them circle the cube various times without having to reload or restart the program. When you are done with the example, simply type a negative number for the desired number of ring trips and the cube manager will clean out the ring processes and return you to XENIX.

Code in the node portion of the application is somewhat more involved than that running on the cube manager. Therefore, several elements deserve comment.

Notice first that, although the functions carried out by node 0 and node n (n ≠ 0) are not symmetric, the code is written in such a way that identical copies can be used on all nodes. However, also note that these functions are reflected in

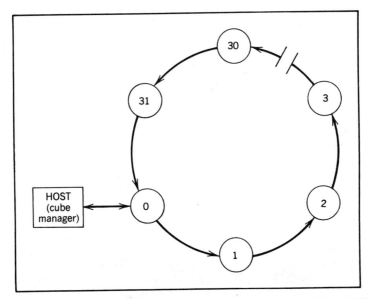

Figure 20.6 *Ring Application. Courtesy and copyright ©1986 by INTEL and iPSC.*

the example program's organization by having distinct pieces of the code execute on node 0 and node n. This approach has been found useful in developing and debugging application code.

Second, each node calculates the "next node" by simply adding 1 to its local node id, or wrapping around to node 0 if it has the largest node id. This method rarely selects next nodes that are nearest neighbors in the hypercube topology. Therefore, to reach them, messages have to traverse a number ($<$ cubedim) of intermediate nodes. If you watch the node LED's when passing long messages, you can see the consequences of this.

Finally, you might be puzzled by the status check on the cube manager channel in the main loop for node 0. There are two reasons for this. First, it protects the "count" variable from being updated (corrupted) before the previous count value has been received by the cube manager. Second, it allows node 0 to post its request to "send (. . .count. . .)" and not have to wait until the cube manager is ready to receive the message. Thus, node 0 goes on and sends the ring message to the next node and waits for the ring message to return from its trip. Node 0 only has to wait on the cube manager if the ring message completes its round trip before the cube manager can consume the count message.

You can compile and link the *cube manager* process, which is assumed to reside in a file called ring_cm.for, by typing:

```
rmfort ring_cm.for

cc -MI -o ring_cm ring_cm.o \
   /lib/Llibf.a \
   /usr/ipsc/lib/rmfhost.a
```

This produces a file, ring_cm, which can be executed on the cube manager.

The next two commands prepare the *node* process, which is assumed to reside in a file called ring_node.for.

```
rmfort ring_node.for

ld -Ml -o ring_node \
    /lib/Lseg.o \
    /usr/ipsc/lib/LfrtnO.o \
    ring_node.o \
    /usr/ipsc/lib/rmfnode.o \
    /usr/ipsc/lib/Llibfnode. \
    /usr/ipsc/lob/Llibcnode.a
```

This results in a node process, called ring_node, which can be loaded into the cube.

Or, you can generate *both* processes using the make utility (copy the makefile provided in the "/usr/ipsc/examples/rmfort_loader" directory) by typing: make all.

The following sequence of commands should be used to run the application:

getcube	Obtain permission to use the cube.
cubelog -l mylog	Transfers logging to a file called "mylog" in your current directory.
tail -f mylog &	Invoke XENIX "tail" command to display log file entries on the screen.
load -c 5	Load the dynamic loader into a D5 cube. Only needs to be executed once. Use "loadkill" to reset the cube once the loader is running.
ring_cm	Run the application. The cube manager process loads the node portion of the application using the "load" routine. It starts executing at that time. If your cube manager process does not require input during execution, you may want to invoke it with an "&" so it will run in the background.

Now, suppose that your application has errors. Do the following:

loadkill	Clear out the cube. If the dynamic loader needs to be loaded again, it will be done automatically.
cubelog	Return message logging to the default (/usr/ipsc/log/LOGFILE) log file.

relcube	Release the cube. This is particularly important in multi-user environments.
Kill [process id]	If "tail" is still running in the background, you should kill it using the "kill" command specifying its process id. You can list process ids using the XENIX "ps" command.
edit	Using any editor, correct the source code files(s).
make all	Create new application objects

You can now issue the first sequence of commands (starting with "getcube") to rerun the application.

The preceding procedure shows how to use the cube manager commands. Commands are invoked from a terminal and allow you to perform such tasks as accessing the cube, loading an application, and executing the application. Some commands use parameters from the cube configuration file. Refer to the iPSC Technical Description and iPSC Administrator's Guide for complete details about the cube configuration file.

The remainder of this section consists of the following:

Cube manager program	ring_cm.for
Node program	ring_node.for

The source code files and makefile are supplied in the "/usr/ipsc/examples/-rmfort_loader" directory.

Developing
FORTRAN Programs

Cube Manager Code - ring__cm.for

```
c*********************************************************************

       program ringhost

c*********************************************************************
c
c      This is the Host code (in Fortran) for the Ring demo.
c
c      It prompts the user for:
c        a) the length of a message to send around a RING in the cube, and
c        b) the number of times the message is to go around the RING.
c
c      It outputs:
c        a) a ring "count" each time the ring message goes past node 0,
c           and
c        b) the time it took the message to go around the ring the
c           specified number of times.
c
c*********************************************************************

c*********************************************************************
c
c      DECLARATIONS:
c
c
c      Declare & initialize CONSTANTS:

       integer NODEPID
       integer HOSTPID
       integer ALLNODES
       integer INITTYPE
       integer TIMEMSGSIZE
       integer CNTMSGSIZE
       integer INITMSGSIZE

c
c      Declare iPSC System Functions used:
c      (These declarations are contained in the "rmfhost.def" file.)
c
       integer copen

c
c      Declare program variables:
c
       integer ci,type,cnt,frnode,frpid
       integer msglen
       integer ringcount
       integer msgbuff(2)
```

Developing
FORTRAN Programs

```fortran
c       Declare time variable:
c
        real    ringtime

        DATA NODEPID            /1/
        DATA HOSTPID            /1/
        DATA ALLNODES           /-1/
        DATA INITTYPE           /10/
        DATA TIMEMSGSIZE        /4/
        DATA CNTMSGSIZE /4/
        DATA INITMSGSIZE        /8/
c
c*****************************************************************************

c*****************************************************************************
c
c       MAIN CODE:
c
c
        write (6,51)
51      format(' LOADING RING INTO CUBE ...')

c       load the cube:

        call load('ring_node', ALLNODES, NODEPID)

c       Open a channel for the host-to-node-0 communications.

        ci = copen(HOSTPID)

c*****************************************************************************
c
c       BEGIN MAIN PROGRAM LOOP:
c
10          write (6,100)
100         format(' *********************** READY ********************
       1*******')

c       get the number of times to go around the ring:

            write(6,101)
101         format(' Number of times to go around the ring (neg. value quit
       1s): ')
            read(5,102) ringcount
102         format(i7)

c       If ringcount is negative exit HOST program:
c
            if (ringcount .lt. 0) goto 600
```

Developing
FORTRAN Programs

```
c        Include ringcount in the message to the RING:

         msgbuff(1) = ringcount

c        get the message length:

         write (6,201)
201      format(' Length of Ring message in bytes (0-16,384): ')
         read (5, 202) msglen
202      format(i5)

c        Include msglen in the message to the RING:

         msgbuff(2) = msglen

c        ship the message buffer off to node 0:

         call sendmsg(ci, INITTYPE, msgbuff, INITMSGSIZE, 0, NODEPID)

c        Get the current ring count from node 0 and report to user:

         do 400 i=1, ringcount

            call recvmsg(ci, type, msgbuff, CNTMSGSIZE, cnt, frnode, frpid)

            write (6,310) msgbuff(1)
310         format('+Ring count: ',i5)

400      continue

c        Get the RING time from node 0 & report to user:

         call recvmsg(ci, type, msgbuff, TIMEMSGSIZE, cnt, frnode, frpid)

         ringtime = real(msgbuff(1))/1000.00

         write (6,306) ringtime
306      format(/,' Ring time :',F9.2,' secs.')

         goto 10

c
c        END OF MAIN PROGRAM LOOP.
c
c**************************************************************************

c**************************************************************************
c
c        CLEAN UP TIME!
c
```

```
600      write (6,601)
601      format(' CLEARING THE CUBE ...')

c        Kill RING processes in cube

         call lkill(-1,-1)
         call lwaitall(-1,-1)

         write (6,701)
701      format(' ************************* DONE *************************
     1******')

         end
c
c**************************************************************************
```

Developing
FORTRAN Programs

Node Process Code - ring_node.for

```
***************************************************************************

        program ringnode

***************************************************************************
*
*       This is the NODE part of the RING demo Program.
*
*       Node 0 will play the role of "controller" node.
*
*       It waits for a message from the host telling it:
*         a) the number of times to go around the RING, and
*         b) the length of the message to send around.
*
*       It then sends a message of the desired length to node 1 and
*       "controls" how many times the message goes around the RING.
*
*       At the end, Node 0 reports back to the host the time it took
*       the message to go around the RING.
*
*       All the other nodes wait for a message and then
*       pass it on to the next node in the RING.
*
***************************************************************************

***************************************************************************
*
*       DECLARATIONS:
*
*
c       Program CONSTANTS:

        integer HOSTNID
        integer HOSTPID

        integer INITTYPE
        integer NODETYPE
        integer TIMETYPE
        integer COUNTTYPE

        integer INITSIZE
        integer TIMESIZE
        integer COUNTSIZE
        integer MAXMSGSIZE

        integer NOTBUSY
```

```
                            Developing
                         FORTRAN Programs


c        iPSC System Calls used:
c        (These declarations are contained in the "rmfnode.def" file.)

         integer copen, status, mynode, mypid, cubedim
         integer clock

c        Program variables:

         integer hostchan, nodechan
         integer i, count, ringcount
         integer msglen
         integer nextnode, nextpid
         integer msgbuff(4096)
         integer ownnode, ownpid
         integer numnodes
         integer rtype, rcnt, rnode, rpid

c        Timing variables:

         integer starttime, ringtime

         data HOSTNID   /-32768/
         data HOSTPID   /1/

         data INITTYPE   /10/
         data NODETYPE   /20/
         data TIMETYPE   /30/
         data COUNTTYPE /40/

         data INITSIZE    /8/
         data TIMESIZE    /4/
         data COUNTSIZE   /4/
         data MAXMSGSIZE /16384/

         data NOTBUSY    /0/

****************************************************************************
*
*        MAIN CODE:
*
c        Each process identifies the node its running on and its pid:

         ownnode = mynode()
         ownpid  = mypid()
```

Developing
FORTRAN Programs

```
c       Each process determines the node id and the pid of the next node
c       in the RING:

        numnodes = 2**cubedim()
        nextnode = mod(ownnode + 1, numnodes)
        nextpid  = ownpid

        if(ownnode.eq.0) then

****************************************************************************
*
*       BEGIN NODE 0 CODE:
*
c       Open channels for communicating with both the next node in the
c       RING (node 1) & the host:

        nodechan = copen(ownpid)
        hostchan = copen(ownpid)

****************************************************************************
*
*       NODE 0 MAIN LOOP:
*
10      call recvw(hostchan, INITTYPE, msgbuff, INITSIZE, rcnt, rnode,
     >      rpid)

        ringcount = msgbuff(1)
        msglen    = msgbuff(2)

        starttime = clock()

        do 400 i=1,ringcount
            call sendw(nodechan, NODETYPE, msgbuff, msglen, nextnode,
     >          nextpid)

            call recvw(nodechan, NODETYPE, msgbuff, msglen, rcnt, rnode,
     >          rpid)

c           As soon as the host channel is not busy report the current
c           count to the HOST:

200         if (status(hostchan).eq.NOTBUSY) goto 300
                call flick()
                goto 200
```

Developing
FORTRAN Programs

```
300          continue

             count = i

             call send (hostchan, COUNTTYPE, count, COUNTSIZE, HOSTNID,
     >          HOSTPID)
400     continue

        ringtime = clock() - starttime

        call sendw(hostchan, TIMETYPE, ringtime, TIMESIZE, HOSTNID,
     >          HOSTPID)

        goto 10
*
*       END NODE 0 MAIN LOOP.
*
****************************************************************************
*
*       END OF NODE 0 CODE.
*
****************************************************************************

        else

****************************************************************************
*
*       BEGIN OTHER NODES' CODE:
*
c       All other nodes wait for a value from their left hand neighbor,
c       and pass it to their right hand neighbor.
c
c       They only have to open one channel for communication:

        nodechan = copen(ownpid)

****************************************************************************
*
*       BEGIN OTHER NODES' MAIN LOOP:
*
```

Developing
FORTRAN Programs

```
20        call recvw(nodechan, NODETYPE, msgbuff, MAXMSGSIZE, rcnt,
     >       rnode, rpid)
          call sendw(nodechan, NODETYPE, msgbuff, rcnt, nextnode,
     >       nextpid)

          goto 20
*
*      END OTHERS' MAIN LOOP.
*
*****************************************************************************
*
*      END OTHERS' CODE.
*
*****************************************************************************
      endif

      end
*
*      ... OF PROGRAM CODE.
*
*****************************************************************************
```

CHAPTER 21 ─────────────────

Transputer Family

INTRODUCTION AND SURVEY

The IMS T800 transputer is a 32-bit CMOS microcomputer with a 64-bit floating point unit and graphics support. It has 4 Kbytes on-chip RAM for high-speed processing, a configurable memory interface, and four standard INMOS communication links. The instruction set achieves efficient implementation of high-level languages and provides direct support for the OCCAM model of concurrency when using either a single transputer or a network. Procedure calls, process switching, and typical interrupt latency are submicrosecond.

The processor speed of a device can be pin-selected in stages from 17.5 MHz up to the maximum allowed for the part. A device running at 30 MHz achieves an instruction throughput of 15 MIPS.

The IMS T800 provides high performance arithmetic and floating point operations. The 64-bit floating point unit provides single and double length operation to the ANSI-IEEE 754-1985 standard for floating point arithmetic. It is able to perform floating point operations concurrently with the processor, sustaining a rate of 1.5 Mflops at a processor speed of 20 MHz and 2.25 Mflops at 30 MHz.

High performance graphics support is provided by microcoded block move instructions which operate at the speed of memory. The two-dimensional block move instructions provide for contiguous block moves as well as block copying of either nonzero bytes of data only or zero bytes only. Block move instructions can be used to provide graphics operations such as text manipulation, windowing, panning, scrolling, and screen updating.

Cyclic redundancy checking (CRC) instructions are available for use on arbitrary length serial data streams, to provide error detection where data integrity is

This chapter has been condensed from IMS T800 and IMS C004 Preliminary Data. Courtesy and copyright ©1987 by INMOS Group of Companies.

critical. Another feature of the IMS T800, useful for pattern recognition, is the facility to count bits set in a word.

The IMS T800 can directly access a linear address space of 4 Gbytes. The 32-bit wide memory interface uses multiplexed data and address lines, and provides a data rate of up to 4 bytes every 100 nanoseconds (40 Mbytes/sec) for a 30-MHz device. A configurable memory controller provides all timing, control, and DRAM refresh signals for a wide variety of mixed memory systems.

System services include processor reset and boot control, together with facilities for error analysis. Error signals may be daisy-chained in multitransputer systems.

21.1 IMS T800 BLOCK DIAGRAM

The standard INMOS communication links allow networks of transputer family products to be constructed by direct point-to-point connections with no external logic. The IMS T800 links support the standard operating speed of 10 Mbits per second, but also operate at 5 or 20 Mbits per second. Each link can transfer data bidirectionally at up to 2.35 Mbytes per second. Figure 21.1 shows an IMS T800 block diagram.

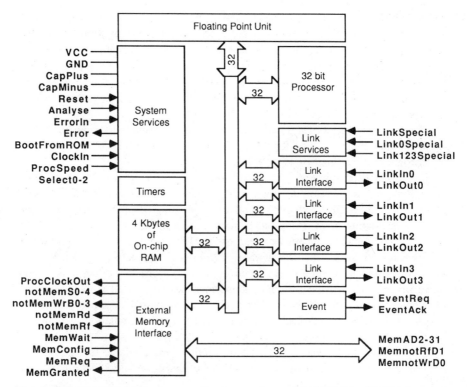

Figure 21.1 *IMS T800 block diagram. Courtesy and copyright ©1987 by INMOS Group of Companies.*

The IMS T800-20 is pin compatible with the IMS T414-20, as the extra inputs used are all held to ground on the IMS T414. The IMS T800-20 can thus be plugged directly into a circuit designed for a 20 MHz version of the IMS T414. Software should be recompiled, although no changes to the source code are necessary.

The transputer is designed to implement the OCCAM language, detailed in Chapter 22, but also efficiently supports other languages such as C, PASCAL, and FORTRAN.

The IMS T414 transputer is a 32-bit CMOS microcomputer with 2 Kbytes on-chip RAM for high-speed processing, a configurable memory interface, and four standard INMOS communication links. For example, a device running at 20 MHz achieves an instruction throughput of 10 MIPS.

The IMS T414 can directly access a linear address space of 4 Gbytes. The 32-bit wide memory interface uses multiplexed data and address lines and provides a data rate of up to 4 bytes every 150 nanoseconds (26.6 Mbytes per second) for a 20 MHz device. A configurable memory controller provides all timing, control, and DRAM refresh signals for a wide variety of mixed memory systems.

The IMS T212 transputer is a 16 bit CMOS microcomputer with 2 Kbytes on-chip RAM for high speed processing, an external memory interface and four standard INMOS communication links. For example, a device running at 20 MHz achieves an instruction throughput of 10 MIPS.

The IMS T212 can directly access a linear address space of 64 Kbytes. The 16-bit wide nonmultiplexed external memory interface provides a data rate of up to 2 bytes every 100 nanoseconds (20 Mbytes per second) for a 20 MHz device.

21.2 PIN DESIGNATIONS FOR THE T800

Table 21.1 shows the pin designations for the IMS T800.

21.3 PROCESSOR

The 32-bit processor contains instruction processing logic, instruction pointer, workspace pointer, and an operand register. It directly addresses 4 Gbytes of memory, 4 Kbytes of which are fast on-chip RAM.

21.3.1 Registers

The design of the transputer processor exploits the availability of fast on-chip memory by having only a small number of registers; six registers are used in the execution of a sequential process. The small number of registers, together with the simplicity of the instruction set enables the processor to have relatively simple (and fast) data-paths and control logic. The six registers (shown in Figure 21.2) are

The workspace pointer which points to an area of store where local variables are kept.

TABLE 21.1

System Services

Pin	In/Out	Function
VCC, GND		Power supply and return
CapPlus, CapMinus		External capacitor for internal clock power supply
ClockIn	in	Input clock
ProcSpeedSelect0-2	in	Processor speed selectors
Reset	in	System reset
Error	out	Error indicator
ErrorIn	in	Error daisychain input
Analyse	in	Error analysis
BootFromRom	in	Boot from external ROM or from link
HoldToGND		Must be connected to **GND**
DoNotWire		Must not be wired

External Memory Interface

Pin	In/Out	Function
ProcClockOut	out	Processor clock
MemnotWrD0	in/out	Multiplexed data bit 0 and write cycle warning
MemnotRfD1	in/out	Multiplexed data bit 1 and refresh warning
MemAD2-31	in/out	Multiplexed data and address bus
notMemRd	out	Read strobe
notMemWrB0-3	out	Four byte-addressing write strobes
notMemS0-4	out	Five general purpose strobes
notMemRf	out	Dynamic memory refresh indicator
MemWait	in	Memory cycle extender
MemReq	in	Direct memory access request
MemGranted	out	Direct memory access granted
MemConfig	in	Memory configuration data input

Event

Pin	In/Out	Function
EventReq	in	Event request
EventAck	out	Event request acknowledge

Link

Pin	In/Out	Function
LinkIn0-3	in	Four serial data input channels
LinkOut0-3	out	Four serial data output channels
LinkSpecial	in	Select non-standard speed as 5 or 20 Mbits/sec
Link0Special	in	Select special speed for Link 0
Link123Special	in	Select special speed for Links 1,2,3

Notes

Signal names are prefixed by **not** if they are active low, otherwise they are active high.

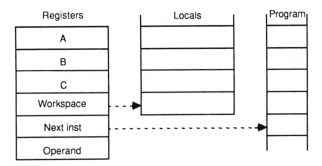

Figure 21.2 *Registers. Courtesy and copyright ©1987 by INMOS Group of Companies.*

The instruction pointer which points to the next instruction to be executed.

The operand register which is used in the formation of instruction operands.

The **A**, **B**, and **C** registers which form an evaluation stack.

A, **B**, and **C** are sources and destinations for most arithmetic and logical operations. Loading a value into the stack pushes **B** into **C**, and **A** into **B**, before loading **A**. Storing a value from **A**, pops **B** into **A** and **C** into **B**.

Expressions are evaluated on the evaluation stack, and instructions refer to the stack implicitly. For example, the *add* instruction adds the top two values in the stack and places the result on the top of the stack. Using a stack removes the need for instructions to respecify the location of their operands. Statistics gathered from a large number of programs show that three registers provide an effective balance between code compactness and implementation complexity.

No hardware mechanism is provided to detect that more than three values have been loaded onto the stack. It is easy for the compiler to ensure that this never happens.

Any location in memory can be accessed relative to the workpointer register, enabling the workspace to be of any size.

21.3.2 Instructions

The instruction set has been designed for simple and efficient compilation of high-level languages. All instructions have the same format, designed to give a compact representation of the operations occurring most frequently in programs.

Each instruction consists of a single byte divided into two 4-bit parts. The four most significant bits of the byte are a function code and the four least significant bits are a data value, which are shown in Figure 21.3.

Direct Functions. The representation provides for 16 functions, each with a data value ranging from 0 to 15. Thirteen of these are used to encode the most important functions. These include:

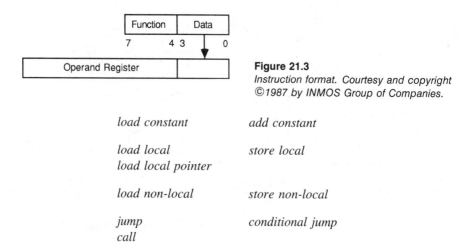

Figure 21.3
*Instruction format. Courtesy and copyright
©1987 by INMOS Group of Companies.*

load constant	*add constant*
load local	*store local*
load local pointer	
load non-local	*store non-local*
jump	*conditional jump*
call	

The most common operations in a program are the loading of small literal values and the loading and storing of one of a small number of variables. The *load constant* instruction enables values between 0 and 15 to be loaded with a single byte instruction. The *load local* and *store local* instructions access locations in memory relative to the workspace pointer. The first 16 locations can be accessed using a single byte instruction.

The *load non-local* and *store non-local* instructions behave similarly, except that they access locations in memory relative to the **A** register. Compact sequences of these instructions allow efficient access to data structures, and provide for simple implementations of the static links or displays used in the implementation of high-level programming languages such as OCCAM, C, FORTRAN, PASCAL, or ADA.

Prefix Functions. Two more function codes allow the operand of any instruction to be extended in length; *prefix* and *negative prefix*.

All instructions are executed by loading the four data bits into the least significant four bits of the operand register, which is then used as the instruction's operand. All instructions except the prefix instructions end by clearing the operand register, ready for the next instruction.

The *prefix* instruction loads its four data bits into the operand register and then shifts the operand register up four places. The *negative prefix* instruction is similar, except that it complements the operand register before shifting it up. Consequently operands can be extended to any length up to the length of the operand register by a sequence of prefix instructions. In particular, operands in the range −256 to 255 can be represented using one prefix instruction.

The use of prefix instructions has certain beneficial consequences. Firstly, they are decoded and executed in the same way as every other instruction, which simplifies and speeds instruction decoding. Secondly, they simplify language compilation by providing a completely uniform way of allowing any instruction to take an operand of any size. Thirdly, they allow operands to be represented in a form independent of the processor wordlength.

Indirect Functions. The remaining function code, *operate*, causes its operand to be interpreted as an operation on the values held in the evaluation stack. This allows up to 16 such operations to be encoded in a single byte instruction. However, the prefix instructions can be used to extend the operand of an *operate* instruction just like any other. The instruction representation therefore provides for an indefinite number of operations.

Encoding of the indirect functions is chosen so that the most frequently occurring operations are represented without the use of a prefix instruction. These include arithmetic, logical, and comparison operations such as *add*, *exclusive or*, and *greater than*. Less frequently occurring operations have encodings which require a single prefix operation.

Expression Evaluation. Evaluation of expressions sometimes requires use of temporary variables in the workspace, but the number of these can be minimized by careful choice of the evaluation order, as shown in Figure 21.4.

Efficiency of Encoding. Measurements show that about 70% of executed instructions are encoded in a single byte (i.e., without the use of prefix instructions). Many of these instructions, such as *load constant* and *add* require just one processor cycle.

The instruction representation gives a more compact representation of high-level language programs than more conventional instruction sets. Since a program requires less store to represent it, less of the memory bandwidth is taken up with fetching instructions. Furthermore, as memory is word accessed the processor will receive several instructions for every fetch.

Short instructions also improve the effectiveness of instruction pre-fetch, which in turn improves processor performance. There is an extra word of pre-fetch buffer, so the processor rarely has to wait for an instruction fetch before proceeding. Since

Program	Mnemonic	
x := 0	ldc	0
	stl	x
x := #24	pfix	2
	ldc	4
	stl	x
x := y + z	ldl	y
	ldl	z
	add	
	stl	x

Figure 21.4 *Expression evaluation. Courtesy and copyright © 1987 by INMOS Group of Companies.*

the buffer is short, there is little time penalty when a jump instruction causes the buffer contents to be discarded.

21.3.3 Processes and Concurrency

A process starts, performs a number of actions, and then either stops without completing or terminates when complete. Typically, a process is a sequence of instructions. A transputer can run several processes in parallel (concurrently). Processes may be assigned either high or low priority, and there may be any number of each.

The processor has a microcoded scheduler which enables any number of concurrent processes to be executed together, sharing the processor time. This removes the need for a software kernel.

At any time, a concurrent process may be

Active	Being executed
	On a list waiting to be executed
Inactive	Ready to input
	Ready to output
	Waiting until a specified time

The scheduler operates in such a way that inactive processes do not consume any processor time. It allocates a portion of the processor's time to each process in turn. Active processes waiting to be executed are held in two linked lists of process workspaces, one of high priority processes and one of low priority processes. Each list is implemented using two registers, one of which points to the first process in the list, the other to the last. In Figure 21.5, process S is executing and P, Q, and R are active, awaiting execution. In Figure 21.6, only the low priority process queue registers are shown; the high priority process ones perform in a similar manner.

Each process runs until it has completed its action, but is descheduled while waiting for communication from another process or transputer, or for a time delay to complete. In order for several processes to operate in parallel, a low priority process is only permitted to run for a maximum of two timeslices before it is forcibly descheduled at the next available descheduling point. The timeslice period is 5120 cycles of **Clockin**, giving ticks approximately 1 millisecond apart.

A process can only be descheduled on certain instructions, known as descheduling points. As a result, an expression evaluation can be guaranteed to execute without the process being timesliced part of the way through.

Whenever a process is unable to proceed, its instruction pointer is saved in the process workspace and the next process taken from the list. Process scheduling pointers are updated by instructions which cause scheduling operations, and should not be altered directly. Actual process switch times are less than 1 μs, as little state needs to be saved and it is not necessary to save the evaluation stack on rescheduling.

The processor provides a number of special operations to support the process

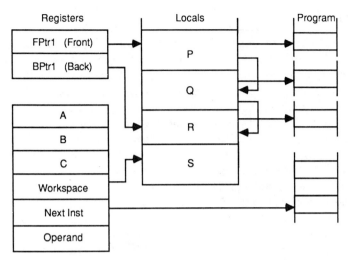

Figure 21.5 *Linked process list. Courtesy and copyright ©1987 by INMOS Group of Companies.*

model, including *start process* and *end process*. When a main process executes a parallel construct, *start process* instructions are used to create the necessary additional concurrent processes. A *start process* instruction creates a new process by adding a new workspace to the end of the scheduling list, enabling the new concurrent process to be executed together with the ones already being executed. When a process is made active it is always added to the end list, and thus cannot preempt processes already on the same list.

The correct termination of a parallel construct is assured by use of the *end process* instruction. This uses a workspace location as a counter of the parallel construct components which have still to terminate. The counter is initialized to the number of components before the processes are *started*. Each component ends with an *end process* instruction which decrements and tests the counter. For all but the last component, the counter is nonzero and the component is descheduled. For the last component, the counter is zero and the main process continues.

High Priority Queue Control Registers

Fptr0	Pointer to front of active process list
Bptr0	Pointer to back of active process list

Low Priority Queue Control Registers

Fptr1	Pointer to front of active process list
Bptr1	Pointer to back of active process list

Figure 21.6 *Priority registers. Courtesy and copyright ©1987 by INMOS Group of Companies.*

21.3.4   Priority

The IMS T800 supports two levels of priority. Priority 1 (low priority) processes are executed whenever there are no active priority 0 (high priority) processes.

High priority processes are expected to execute for a short time. If one or more high priority processes are able to proceed, then one is selected and runs until it has to wait for a communication, a timer input, or until it completes processing. If no process at high priority is able to proceed, but one or more processes at low priority are able to proceed, then one is selected.

Low priority processes are periodically timesliced to provide an even distribution of processor time between computationally intensive tasks.

If there are n low priority processes, then the maximum latency from the time at which a low priority process becomes active to the time when it starts processing is $2n$-2 timeslice periods. It is then able to execute for between one and two timeslice periods, less any time taken by high priority processes. This assumes that no process monopolizes the transputer's time (i.e., it has a distribution of descheduling points).

Each timeslice period lasts for 5120 cycles of the input clock **ClockIn** (approximately 1 millisecond at the standard frequency of 5 MHz). If a high priority process is waiting for an external channel to become ready, and if no other high priority process is active, then the interrupt latency (from when the channel becomes ready to when the process starts executing) is typically 19 processor cycles, a maximum 78 cycles (assuming use of on-chip RAM). If the floating point unit is not being used at the time then the maximum interrupt latency is only 58 cycles. To ensure this latency, certain instructions are interruptable.

21.3.5   Communications

Communication between processes is achieved by means of channels. Process communication is point-to-point, synchronized, and unbuffered. As a result, a channel needs no process queue, no message queue, and no message buffer.

A channel between two processes executing on the same transputer is implemented by a single word in memory; a channel between processes executing on different transputers is implemented by point-to-point links. The processor provides a number of operations to support message passing, the most important being *input message* and *output message*.

The *input message* and *output message* instructions use the address of the channel to determine whether the channel is internal or external. Thus the same instruction sequence can be used for both, allowing a process to be written and compiled without knowledge of where its channels are connected.

The process which first becomes ready must wait until the second one is also ready. A process performs an input or output by loading the evaluation stack with a pointer to a message, the address of a channel, and a count of the number of bytes to be transferred, and then executing an *input message* or *output message* instruction. Data is transferred if the other process is ready. If the channel is not ready or is an external one the process will deschedule.

21.3.6 Timers

The transputer has two 32 bit timers which "tick" periodically. The timers provide accurate process timing, allowing processes to deschedule themselves until a specific time, shown in Figure 21.7.

One timer is accessible only to high priority processes and is incremented every microsecond, cycling completely in 4295 seconds. The other is accessible only to low priority processes and is incremented every 64 microseconds, giving exactly 15,625 ticks of this timer in one second. It cycles in approximately 76 hours. The current value of a timer can be read by executing a *load timer* instruction. A process can arrange to perform a *timer input*, in which case it will become ready to execute after a specified time has been reached. The *timer input* instruction requires a time to be specified. If this time is in the "past" then the instruction has no effect. If the time is in the "future" then the process is descheduled. When the specified time is reached the process is scheduled again.

Figure 21.8 shows two processes waiting on a timer queue, one waiting for time 21, the other for time 31.

21.3.7 Instruction Set

For the function codes table consult the Transputer manual. Where the operand is less than 16 a single byte encodes the complete instruction. If the operand is greater than 15 one prefix instruction (*pfix*) is required for each additional four bits of the operand. If the operand is negative the first prefix instruction will be *nfix*.

The operation codes tables give details of operation codes. Where an operation code is less than 16 (e.g., *add*: operation code **05**), the operation can be stored as a single byte comprising the *operate function* code **F** and the operand. Where an operation code is greater than **15** (e.g., *ladd*: operation code **16**), the *prefix* function code **2** is used to extend the instruction.

21.4 PROGRAMMABLE LINK SWITCH

The INMOS communication link is a high-speed system interconnect which provides full duplex communication between members of the INMOS transputer fam-

Timer Registers

Timer0	Current value of high priority (level 0) process timer
Timer1	Current value of low priority (level 1) process timer
TNextReg0	Indicates time of earliest event on high priority (level 0) timer queue
TNextReg1	Indicates time of earliest event on low priority (level 1) timer queue

Figure 21.7 *Timer registers. Courtesy and copyright ©1987 by INMOS Group of Companies.*

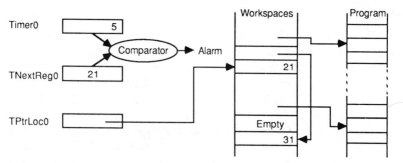

Figure 21.8 *Timer registers operation. Courtesy and copyright ©1987 by INMOS Group of Companies.*

ily, according to the INMOS serial link protocol. The IMS C004, shown in Figure 21.9, a member of this family, is a transparent programmable link switch designed to provide a full crossbar switch between 32 link inputs and 32 link outputs.

The IMS C004 will switch links running at either the standard speed of 10 Mbits/sec or at the higher speed of 20 Mbit/sec. It introduces, on average, only

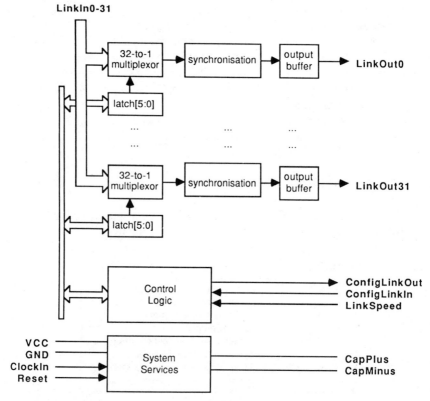

Figure 21.9 *IMS C004 block diagram. Courtesy and copyright ©1987 by INMOS Group of Companies.*

a 1.75-bit time delay on the signal. Link switches can be cascaded to any depth without loss of signal integrity and can be used to construct reconfigurable networks of arbitrary size. The switch is programmed via a separate serial link called the *configuration link*.

All INMOS products which use communication links support a standard communications frequency of 10 Mbits/sec, regardless of device type; most products also support 20 Mbits/sec. Products of different type or performance can, therefore, be interconnected directly and future systems will be able to communicate directly with those of today. System services include all the necessary logic to start up and maintain the IMS C004.

21.4.1 Power

Power is supplied to the device via the **VCC** and **GND** pins. Several of each are provided to minimize inductance within the package. All supply pins must be connected. The supply must be decoupled close to the chip by at least one 100nF low inductance (e.g., ceramic) capacitor between **VCC** and **GND**. Four-layer boards are recommended; if two-layer boards are used, extra care should be taken in decoupling.

Input voltages must not exceed specification with respect to **VCC** and **GND**, even during power-up and power-down ramping, otherwise *latchup* can occur. CMOS devices can be permanently damaged by excessive periods of latchup.

21.4.2 CapPlus, CapMinus

The internally derived power supply for internal clocks requires an external low leakage, low inductance $1\mu F$ capacitor to be connected between **CapPlus** and **CapMinus**. A ceramic capacitor is preferred, with an impedance less than 3 ohms between 100 KHz and 10 MHz. If a polarized capacitor is used the negative terminal should be connected to **CapMinus**. Total PCB track length should be less than 50mm. The connections must not touch power supplies or other noise sources.

21.4.3 ClockIn

Transputer family components require a standard clock frequency, supplied by the user on the **ClockIn** input. The nominal frequency of this clock for all transputer family components is 5MHz, regardless of device type. High frequency internal clocks are derived from **ClockIn**, simplifying system design and avoiding problems of distributing high speed clocks externally.

21.5 LINKS

INMOS bidirectional serial links provide synchronized communication between INMOS products and with the outside world. Each link comprises an input channel and output channel. A link between two devices is implemented by connecting a link interface on one device to a link interface on the other device. Every byte of data output on a link is acknowledged on the input of the same link, thus each signal line carries both data and control information.

A receiver can transmit an acknowledge as soon as it starts to receive a data byte. In this way the transmission of an acknowledge can be overlapped with receipt of a data byte to provide continuous transmission of data. This technique is fully compatible with all other INMOS transputer family links.

The quiescent state of a link output is low. Each data byte is transmitted as a high start bit followed by a one bit followed by eight data bits followed by a low stop bit. The least significant bit of data is transmitted first. After transmitting a data byte the sender waits for the acknowledge, which consists of a high start bit followed by a zero bit. The acknowledge signifies that the receiving link is able to receive another byte.

Links are not synchronized with **ClockIn** and are insensitive to its phase. Thus links from independently clocked systems may communicate, providing only that the communication frequencies are nominally identical and within specification.

Links are TTL compatible and intended to be used in electrically quiet environments, between devices on a single printed circuit board or between two boards via a backplane. Direct connection may be made between devices separated by a distance of less than 300 millimeters. For longer distances a matched 100 ohm transmission line should be used with series matching resistors **RM**. When this is done the line delay should be less than 0.4 bit time to ensure that the reflection returns before the next data bit is sent, as shown in Figure 21.10.

Buffers, as shown in Figure 21.11, may be used for very long transmissions. If so, their overall propagation delay should be stable within the skew tolerance of the link, although the absolute value of the delay is immaterial.

The IMS C004 links support the standard INMOS communication speed of 10

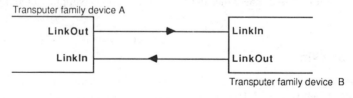

Links Directly Connected

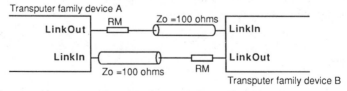

Figure 21.10 *Links. Courtesy and copyright ©1987 by INMOS Group of Companies.*

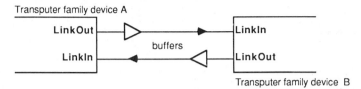

Figure 21.11 *Links connected by buffers. Courtesy and copyright ©1987 by INMOS Group of Companies.*

Mbits per second. In addition they can be used at 20 Mbits per second. When the **LinkSpeed** pin is low, all links operate at the standard 10 Mbits per second and when high they operate at 20 Mbits per second. A single IMS C004 inserted between two transputers which fully implement overlapped acknowledges causes no reduction in data bandwidth, the delay through the switch being hidden by the overlapped acknowledge.

21.6 SWITCH IMPLEMENTATION

The IMS C004 is internally organized as a set of thirty two 32-to-1 multiplexors. Each multiplexor has associated with it a six-bit latch, five bits of which select one input as the source of data for the corresponding output. The sixth bit is used to connect and disconnect the output. These latches can be read and written by messages sent on the configuration link via **ConfigLinkin** and **ConfigLinkOut**.

The output of each multiplexor is synchronized with an internal high-speed clock and regenerated at the output pad. This synchronization introduces, on average, a 1.75 bit time delay on the signal. As the signal is not electrically degraded in passing through the switch, it is possible to form links through an arbitrary number of link switches.

Each input and output is identified by a number in the range 0 to 31. A configuration message consisting of one, two, or three bytes is transmitted on the configuration link. The configuration messages sent to the switch on this link are shown in Table 21.2.

21.6.1 Link Switching

The IMS C004 provides full switching capabilities between 32 INMOS links. It can also be used as a component of a larger link switch. For example, three IMS C004s can be connected together to produce a 48-way switch, as shown in Figure 21.12. This technique can be extended to the switch shown in Figure 21.13. A fully connected network of 32 INMOS transputers (one in which all four links are used on every transputer) can be completely configured using just four IMS C004's. Figure 21.14 shows the connected transputer network. In these diagrams each link line shown represents a unidirectional link (i.e., one output to one input). Where a number is also given, that denotes the number of lines.

TABLE 21.2

Configuration Message	Function
[0] [input] [output]	Connects **input** to **output**.
[1] [link1] [link2]	Connects **link1** to **link2** by connecting the input of **link1** to the output of **link2** and the input of **link2** to the output of **link1**.
[2] [output]	Enquires which input the **output** is connected to. The IMS C004 responds with the input. The most signifigant bit of this byte indicates whether the output is connected (bit set high) or disconnected (bit set low).
[3]	This command byte must be sent at the end of every configuration sequence which sets up a connection. The IMS C004 is then ready to accept data on the connected inputs.
[4]	Resets the switch. All outputs are disconnected and held low. This also happens when **Reset** is applied to the IMS C004.
[5] [output]	Output **output** is disconnected and held low.
[6] [link1] [link2]	Disconnects the output of **link1** and the output of **link2**

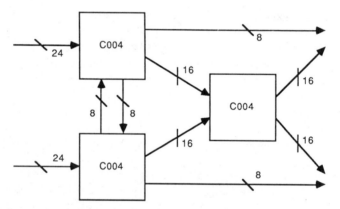

Figure 21.12 *48-way link switch. Courtesy and copyright ©1987 by INMOS Group of Companies.*

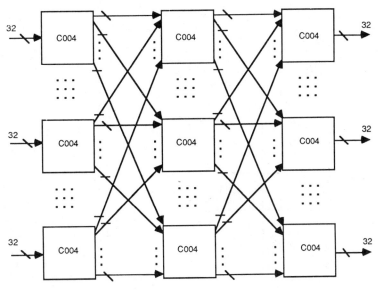

Figure 21.13 *Generalized link switch. Courtesy and copyright ©1987 by INMOS Group of Companies.*

21.6.2 Multiple IMS C004 Control

Many systems require a number of IMS C004s, each configured via its own configuration link. A simple method of implementing this uses a master IMS C004, as shown in Figure 21.15. One of the transputer links is used to configure the master link switch, while another transputer link is multiplexed via the master to send configuration messages to any of the other 31 IMS C004 links.

21.6.3 Bidirectional Exchange

Use of the IMS C004 is not restricted to computer configuration applications. The ability to change the switch setting dynamically enables it to be used as a general purpose message router. This may, of course, also find applications in computing with the emergence of the new generation of supercomputers, but a more widespread use may be found as a communication exchange.

In the application shown in Figure 21.16, a message into the exchange must be preceded by a destination token *dest*. When this message is passed, the destination token is replaced with a source token so that the receiver knows where the message has come from. The **in.out** device in the diagram and the controller can be implemented easily with a transputer, and the link protocol for establishing communication with these devices can be interfaced with INMOS link adapters. All messages from **rx[i]** are preceded by the destination output *dest*. On receipt of such a message the **in.out** device requests the controller to connect a bidirectional link path to *dest*. The controller determines what is currently connected to each

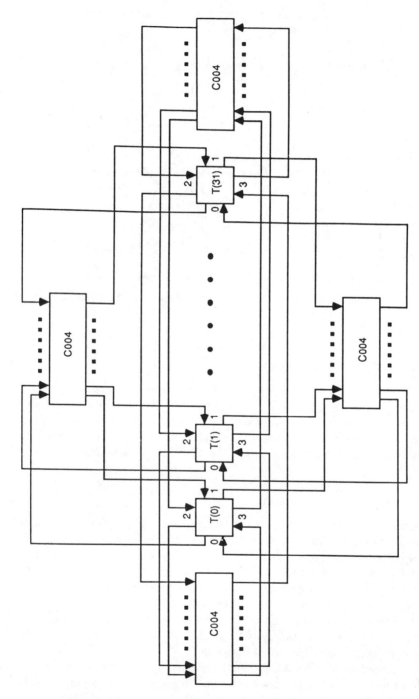

Figure 21.14 *Complete connectivity of a transputer network using four IMS C004s. Courtesy and copyright ©1987 by INMOS Group of Companies.*

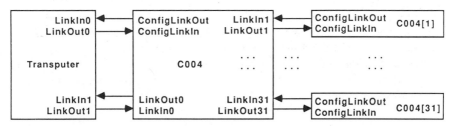

Figure 21.15 *Multiple IMS C004 controller. Courtesy and copyright © 1987 by INMOS Group of Companies.*

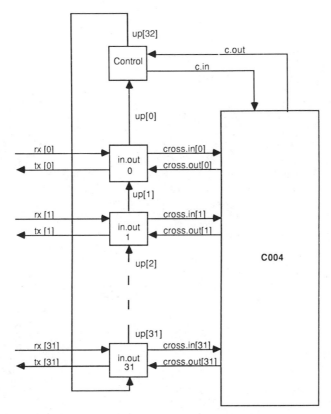

Figure 21.16 *32-way bidirectional exchange. Courtesy and copyright © 1987 by INMOS Group of Companies.*

end of the proposed link. When both ends are free it sets up the IMS C004 and informs both ends of the new link. Note that in this network two channels are placed on each IMS C004 link, one for each direction.

The IMS C004 can be used in conjunction with the INMOS IMS C011/C012 link adapters to provide a flexible means of connecting conventional bus-based microprocessor systems.

Concurrency and OCCAM Programming

INTRODUCTION AND SURVEY

Concurrency is so much a feature of the universe that we are not normally concerned with it at all. However it is worthwhile to reflect on the contrast between the concurrent nature of the world, and the sequential nature of the digital computer. Since the main purpose of the computer is to model the world, there would seem to be a serious mismatch.

In order to model the world with a computer, programmers of conventional computers have to find ways to mimic concurrent events using a sequence of instructions. This is not a problem in an application like accounting, where it is perfectly reasonable to regard goods despatched, materials and moneys flowing in and out as happening sequentially in time. It is more of a problem when you wish to control a petro chemicals plant by computer. Every process in every part of the plant must be monitored and controlled at the same time, all the time. It is not acceptable for a crisis in one reaction vessel to be overlooked because the computer happened to be looking at a different reactor at the time.

To adequately model the concurrency of the real world, it would be preferable to have many processors all working at the same time on the same program. There are also huge potential performance benefits to be derived from such parallel processing. For regardless of how far electronic engineers can push the speed of an individual processor, 10 of them running concurrently will still execute 10 times as many instructions in a second. Conventional programming languages are not well equipped to construct programs for such multiple processors as their very design assumes the sequential execution of instructions. Some languages have been

This chapter has been adapted from Occam Tutorial (D. Pountain). Courtesy and copyright © 1987 by INMOS Group of Companies.

modified to allow concurrent programs to be written, but the burden of ensuring that concurrent parts of the program are synchronized (i.e., that they cooperate rather than fight) is placed on the programmer. This leads to such programming being perceived as very much more difficult than ordinary sequential programming.

OCCAM is the first language to be based upon the concept of parallel, in addition to sequential execution, and to provide automatic communication and synchronization between concurrent processes. In OCCAM programming we refer to the parts of a program as processes. A process starts, performs a number of actions, and then finishes. This definition fits an ordinary sequential program, but in OCCAM more than one process may be executing at the same time and processes can send messages to one another. More importantly, OCCAM doesn't mind whether the two programs which so communicate are running on different computers, or are just two processes running concurrently on the same computer. A channel is a one-way, point-to-point link from one process to one other process. The two novel features which distinguish channels from variables are:

1. A channel can pass values either between two processes running on the same computer, or between two processes running on different computers. In the first case the channel would in fact be just a location in memory, rather like a variable. In the second case the channel could represent a real hardware link, such as a Transputer link or other serial communication line. Both cases are represented identically in an OCCAM program.

An OCCAM channel describes communication in the abstract, and does not depend upon its physical implementation. You can thus write and test a program using channels without having to worry about exactly where the different processes will be executed. The program can be developed on a single processor workstation; when it's finished and proved you may decide to distribute various processes in the program onto different computers, and do so by making a few simple declarations at the beginning of the program.

2. Channels are patient and polite. If an input process finds that no value is ready it will wait until one is supplied, without any explicit instruction from the programmer. Equally an output will not send until the receiver is ready. This introduces the time factor into programming, but in a way which lifts much of the responsibility for "timekeeping" off the programmer's shoulders.

22.1 PRIMITIVE PROCESSES

All OCCAM programs are built from combinations of three kinds of primitive process. They are assignment, input, and output.

22.1.1 Assignment Process

An assignment process changes the value of a variable, just as it would in most conventional languages. The symbol for assignment in OCCAM is := . So the assignment process:

```
fred := 2
```

makes the value in variable fred two. The value assigned to a variable could be an expression such as:

```
fred := 2 + 5
```

and this expression could contain other variables:

```
fred := 5 - jim
```

Be sure not to mix up = and := . In OCCAM = means a test for equality, not an assignment.

22.1.2 Input Process

An input process inputs a value from a channel into a variable. The symbol for input in OCCAM is ?. The input process:

```
chan3 ? fred
```

takes a value from a channel called chan3 and puts it into variable fred. Input processes can only input values to variables. It is quite meaningless to input to a constant or to an expression. An input process cannot proceed until a corresponding output process on the same channel is ready. As an aid to memory think of the question mark as meaning "Where's my value?"

22.1.3 Output Process

An output process outputs a value to a channel. The symbol for output in OCCAM is !. The output process:

```
chan3 ! 2
```

outputs the value 2 to a channel called chan3.

The value output to a channel can be anything that you could assign to a variable, so it may be a variable or an expression, and the expression may contain variables. An output process cannot proceed until a corresponding input process on the same channel is ready. As an aid to memory, think of the exclamation mark as meaning "Here's your value!"

22.2 CONSTRUCTIONS

Several primitive processes can be combined into a larger process by specifying that they should be performed one after the other, or all at the same time. This larger process is called a construction and it begins with an OCCAM keyword which states how the component processes are to be combined.

22.2.1 SEQ Construction

The simplest construction to understand is the SEQ (pronounce it "seek"), short for sequence, which merely says "do the following processes one after another." Here is an example:

```
SEQ
  chan3 ? fred
  jim := fred + 1
  chan4 ! jim
```

This says, "do in sequence, input from chan3 to fred, assign fred + 1 to jim and output jim to chan4". In sequence means, to be more precise, that the next process does not start until the previous one has terminated. A SEQ process therefore works just like a program in any conventional programming language; it finishes when its last component process finishes.

Notice the way that the processes which make up this SEQ process are indented by two characters from the word SEQ, so that they line up under the Q. This is not merely to make the program look prettier, but is the way that OCCAM knows which processes are part of the SEQ.

Whenever a construction is built, we indicate the extent of the new process by indenting all its component processes by two characters. Other languages use special characters like { ...} or begin ...end for this purpose, but OCCAM uses indentation alone. A SEQ construction terminates when its last process terminates.

SEQ is compulsory in OCCAM whenever two or more processes are to run in sequence. In conventional programming languages, sequence is taken for granted and merely writing one statement after another guarantees they will execute in sequence. Because OCCAM offers other modes of execution apart from the sequential, sequence must be explicitly requested.

22.2.2 PAR Construction

The PAR construction, short for parallel, says "do the following processes all at the same time" (i.e., in parallel). All the component processes of a PAR start to execute simultaneously. For example

```
PAR
  SEQ
    chan3 ? fred
    fred := fred + 1
  SEQ
    chan4 ? jim
    jim := jim + 1
```

says "at the same time, input from chan3 to fred and then add one to the result, while inputting from chan4 to jim and then adding one to the result."

Notice again the indentation. The first two character indent tells OCCAM that the PAR process consists of two SEQ processes. The second level of indentation shows that each SEQ is composed of two primitive processes. Notice also that the processes which are to run in parallel are still written in sequence just as in any ordinary program. This is purely a matter of writing convenience. The designers of OCCAM could have chosen to make us write parallel processes side by side, which would give a stronger impression of what is happening.

22.3 CHANNEL TYPE AND PROTOCOL

Channels are all of the type CHAN OF *protocol*. It is necessary to specify the data type and structure of the values that they are to carry. This is called the channel protocol. For the present we shall be content to regard channels as able to carry single values of a single data type, rather like variables.

A channel which carries single integer values would be specified by:

```
CHAN OF INT chan3 :
```

where the INT specifies the type of values which may pass along the channel chan3. The type of chan3 is CHAN OF INT. In general the protocol of a channel is specified by CHAN OF *protocol*.

Communication between parallel processes is the essence of OCCAM programming. At its simplest it requires two processes executing in parallel and a channel joining them

```
INT x :
CHAN OF INT comm :
PAR
   comm ! 2
   comm ? x
```

This trivial program merely outputs the value 2 from one process and inputs it into the variable x in the second. Its overall effect is exactly as if we had a single process which assigned 2 to x.

22.4 ALTERNATIVE PROCESSES

In OCCAM choice has an extra dimension lacking in ordinary programming languages. We can make choices according to the values of variables in a program using IF. But we can also make choices according to the state of channels. This is made possible by the ALT construction, whose name is short for alternation. Like IF, ALT joins together any number of components into a single construction, but the component parts of an ALT, called *alternatives* are rather more complicated than IF choices.

The simplest kind of ALT has as each alternative an input process followed by a process to be executed. The ALT watches all the input processes and executes the process associated with the first input to become ready. Thus ALT is basically a first-past-the-post race between a group of channels, with only the winner's process being executed:

```
CHAN OF INT chan1, chan2, chan3:
INT x:
ALT
    chan1 ? x
      . . . first process
    chan2 ? x
      . . . second process
    chan3 ? x
      . . . third process
```

If chan2 were the first to produce an input, then only the second process would be executed. Here choice is being decided in the time dimension, the inputs causing the program to wait until one of them is ready.

An alternative may start with a test in addition to an input, just like the tests in an IF. If this is done, the associated process can only be chosen if its input is the first to be ready and the test is TRUE. OCCAM makes this easy to remember by using the & sign, as in:

```
CHAN OF INT chan1, chan2, chan3 :
INT x:
ALT
    (y < 0) & chan1 ? x
      . . . first process
    y = 0) & chan2 ? x
      . . . second process
    y > 0) & chan3 ? x
      . . . third process
```

If y is, say, 3 and chan3 is the first to be ready then the third process will be executed. This form of alternative is most often used to impose limits on some process, by using a test such as (voltage < maximum). As with IF, ALT behaves like STOP if there are no alternatives. Also like IF, an ALT can be nested as inside an outer ALT.

The ALT is an extremely powerful construction. It allows complex networks of channels to be merged and switched in a simple and elegant way.

Because of this power, and because it is unlike anything in conventional programming languages, ALT is far-and-away the most difficult of the OCCAM constructions to explain and to understand. Fortunately we have now seen enough of OCCAM to be able to work through some more serious examples, which should clarify its usage.

22.5 REAL-TIME PROGRAMMING IN OCCAM

OCCAM concerns itself with the time dimension in a far more profound way than do most conventional languages; the issues of concurrency and synchronization are tackled in its deep structure. This being so, it is necessary to have ways of measuring and apportioning time in OCCAM programs.

22.5.1 Timers

Timing in OCCAM is provided by declaring named objects of the type TIMER. A timer behaves like a channel which can only provide input. The value input from a timer is, not surprisingly, the current time represented as a value of type INT.

The simplest kind of timer process would look like this:

```
TIMER clock:
INT time:
clock ? time
```

Technical Note: The "ticks" of this clock will vary from one implementation of OCCAM to another, depending upon the hardware on which it is running. On the INMOS Transputer, the ticks will be in units of (input clock rate)/(5*64) which will normally work out at 64 microseconds per tick; details must be obtained from the hardware manuals for a given system. The time starts from the moment at which the system was switched on, unless the system is provided with a battery backed clock and suitable software to synchronize the OCCAM clock with the real time. Whenever the value of time exceeds the maximum value that can be represented by an INT it will become negative and begin to count back towards zero (in accordance with 2's complement signed arithmetic). With a 64 microcsecond tick and a 16-bit INT this would happen approximately every 4.2 seconds, with a 32-bit INT approximately every 76 hours. Time differences must therefore exclusively be calculated using the modulo arithmetic operators, and a long interval can only be timed by breaking it into a series of shorter intervals. Note that one second is exactly 15,625 ticks of 64 microseconds each.

It can be useful to declare more than one timer in a program, even though the value returned from all of them may be the same (if the program is running on a single processor). If there are several independent parallel processes which all require timing, their independence is better expressed if they each have their own timer. For the same reason it may sometimes be useful to declare an array of timers.

22.5.2 Delays

Delays can be added to a program by using a delayed input. This is an input from a timer which cannot proceed until the time reaches a stated value. The operator AFTER followed by an expression representing a time is used to cause the delay.

The crude delay procedure is:

```
PROC delay (VAL INT interval)
    TIMER clock :
    INT timenow :
    SEQ
        clock ? timenow
        clock ? AFTER timenow PLUS interval
```

An instance of this procedure, say delay (6000), would pause for 6000 ticks before terminating.

Notice that the delayed input is not an ordinary input process because no variable has its value changed; the value from clock is only compared with the value of the expression. Timers are in general rather different from ordinary channels; several components of a PAR are allowed to input from the same timer, which would be strictly forbidden for an ordinary channel.

A delayed input could be used in an ALT to provide a real-time wait:

```
TIMER clock :
VAL timeout IS 1000 :
INT timenow :
SEQ
    clock ? timenow
    INT x :
    ALT
        input ? x
            . . . process
        clock ? AFTER timenow PLUS timeout
            warning ! (17 :: "Timeout on input!")
```

This process will send the timeout warning message if input doesn't produce an input within the prescribed time of 1000 ticks.

AFTER can also be used as a comparison operator which returns a truth value; x AFTER y is equivalent to (x MINUS y) > 0. In other words AFTER subtracts y from x, modulo the largest INT, and sees if the result is positive. Modulo arithmetic must always be used for times, hence the use of PLUS instead of + in the two preceding examples.

AFTER can be used in conditionals to check whether one time is later than another:

```
TIMER clock:
INT proc1.time, proc2.time:
SEQ
   PAR
      SEQ
         ... process 1
         clock ? proc1.time
      SEQ
         ... process 2
         clock ? proc2.time
   IF
      proc1.time AFTER proc2.time
         ... rest of program
```

This provides a check on which of the two parallel processes terminated first.

When writing programs of this kind it is essential to be aware of the physical details of time representation (see Technical Note above). This test is only meaningful if the difference in the two times is small compared to the largest value represented by an integer. Otherwise a more complex program will be needed.

22.5.3 Priority

So far, the question of priority among processes has been ignored. But when real-time programs are concerned, priority becomes a matter of considerable importance. In the discussion of ALT for instance, no mention was made of what would happen if two inputs became ready simultaneously. Which process (if any) would be executed?

The answer to that question is "it depends". In an ordinary ALT, OCCAM will make an arbitrary choice if the inputs guarding two processes become ready simultaneously. By arbitrary we mean that the outcome is not defined by the language, and may vary from one implementation to another; this does not imply that a random choice will be made, (though that would be one option open to implementors). The crux of the matter is that the programmer cannot predict what will happen in such a case.

In real-time programs it will sometimes be necessary to know what will happen in such a case, and so OCCAM allows both ALT and PAR processes to be prioritized. This is signified by preceding the construct with the word PRI.

In both a PRI ALT and a PRI PAR, the component processes are assigned a priority according to the textual order in which they appear in the program—the first has highest priority and so on. In a PRI ALT, when two inputs become ready simultaneously, the component process with the higher priority will be executed.

A special example of the use of a PRI ALT is this routine to guarantee that a channel carrying an important signal will be looked at:

```
WHILE cycling
    PRI ALT
        quit ? any
            cycling := false
        TRUE & SKIP
            ... main cycle
```

The TRUE & SKIP option is always ready, and if used in an ordinary ALT this path could be taken at every cycle without quit ever getting a look in. The PRI ALT however forces the program to inspect the channel quit, because it has a higher priority, and thus guarantees that the cycle can be broken when desired.

In a PRI PAR, processes with a lower priority will only be executed if no higher priority process can proceed. So in:

```
PRI PAR
    SEQ
        input1 ? x
        output1 ! x
    SEQ
        input2 ? y
        output2 ! y
```

the second SEQ cannot proceed, even when input2 is ready, unless the first (higher priority) SEQ is waiting on its input or output. PRI PAR can be used in certain real-time applications to service a hardware device sufficiently quickly when the computer has other things to do as well.

```
VAL blocksize IS 1024 :
CHAN OF [blocksize]BYTE nextblock :
PRI PAR
    WHILE TRUE
        [blocksize]BYTE block :
        SEQ
            nextblock ? block
            SEQ i = 0 FOR blocksize
                squirtout ! block[i]
    ... main process
```

In this program, the main process is allowed to proceed only in the slack moments when the device connected to squirtout is not being serviced (i.e., when waiting to output). Like a spoiled child, the device must always be given full attention when it demands it, so the main process is halted to devote the processor's full power to the SEQ loop.

22.5.4 Buffering

If PRI PAR is used, the question of buffering may well arise. It is pointless to run a process at high priority to service an impatient device if, while servicing that device, it can be kept waiting to communicate with another process. A high priority process of this kind should have all such communications with other processes buffered, so that data can be sent without delay. The size of buffer needed would be tuned to the actual timings of the processes involved.

```
VAL blocksize IS 1024 :
CHAN OF [blocksize]BYTE nextblock :
PRI PAR
    CHAN OF [blocksize]BYTE bufferedblock :
    PAR
        WHILE TRUE – buffer process
            [blocksize]BYTE block :
            SEQ
                nextblock ? block
                bufferedblock ! block
        WHILE TRUE – service process
            [blocksize]BYTE block :
            SEQ
                bufferedblock ? block
                SEQ i = 0 FOR blocksize
                    squirtout ! block[i]
    . . . main process
```

In this example the input from nextblock has a one block buffer added. This reduces the chances of the service routine having to wait to input the next block, which would cause it to delay service to the device.

PRI PAR should only be used when it is necessary to impose explicit priority and should not be lightly used when an ordinary PAR will do. If you find that you are relying heavily on PRI PAR, reexamine your problem carefully; perhaps a differently structured program would work with ordinary PAR.

22.6 PRIORITY AND CONFIGURATION

Priority is, strictly speaking, a configuration issue because it does not affect the logical behavior of a program. Configuration issues are those which allow performance criteria to be met, but which in no way alter the program logic; hence a program can be developed without considering them until the very last stage. Programs should be developed using ordinary PAR and ALT, and priority, if it is required, should be left until the logic has been correctly established and the program works.

In most computer languages I/O is a problem area. It is always an afterthought, because conventional languages are designed to manipulate data only inside the computer's memory space. As a result I/O tends to be tied to specific hardware devices, and it often violates principles adhered to elsewhere in the language. In OCCAM this is not the case. We could safely ignore I/O until now, because we already know almost all there is to know about it. OCCAM performs I/O over channels and all we need to know further is how to attach OCCAM channels to real-world hardware devices, which can then be treated just as if they were further OCCAM processes. All the programs that have been developed so far can be made into "real" programs by the addition of a bit of notation tying the abstract channel names to real hardware channels.

In any particular OCCAM implementation there will be a number of I/O channels which can be used by programs. These channels may in some cases lead directly to the hardware, via driver programs which the OCCAM compiler links to your program. In other cases they may lead to the operating system of the host computer, which then handles I/O on behalf of OCCAM.

A typical OCCAM system will support at least channels for a VDU screen, a keyboard, and a filing system. These channels are given numbers which can be found in the manual for the particular OCCAM implementation.

Let us suppose that the "hard" channels are numbered as follows:

1. Output to screen
2. Input from keyboard

These numbers are associated with the channel names used in an OCCAM program as follows:

```
PLACE screen AT 1 :
PLACE keyboard AT 2 :
```

Inside the program these channels can all be input to and output from in the usual fashion. So

```
VAL message IS "Hello world!" :
SEQ i = O FOR SIZE message
    screen ! INT message [i]
```

would display the message on a VDU screen, and:

```
keyboard ? x
```

would input the code for a single character typed at the keyboard into variable x.

GLOSSARY ─────────────────

ADA. A computer language named for Lord Byron's daughter, Augusta Ada, who is referred to as the first programmer. ADA was developed for internal use by the U.S. Department of Defense. The language is difficult to work with and has received little commercial software support.

Adaptive coefficient. Weighting value associated with each input to a processing element. It gaits or weights the effect of that input on the output of the processing element. Adaptive coefficients can be self-adjusting; that is their values can be self-modified in response to external input. The process of self-adjusting is called *learning*.

ANZA. General purpose neurocomputing coprocessor for a PC AT compatible computer. It off-loads the neurocomputing tasks from the host PC resulting in more efficient network implementations.

Artificial Intelligence (AI). The study to make computers more useful by performing tasks that, until recently, only humans could perform. AI addresses the methods and concepts of symbolic inference by a computer. Artificial intelligence software packages draw conclusions from given sets of facts and rules, following the laws of logic.

Asymmetric system. A system whereby one processor acts as a host, performing system functions, while other processors execute code by function or task.

Automatic Programming. The study of how to create computer programs, called *application generators*, that in turn write other computer programs. Programs are explained to the application generator in a non-programming language. The application generator constructs the program to solve the problem. In the future, application generators will automate major portions of computer programming.

AXON. A language capable of describing any neural network.

Brain-Behavior Intelligence (BBI). The study of hardware and software that mimics intelligent behavior in man and animals and approximates some brain functions. In the brain, a signal fired from one neuron can trigger a cascade of thousands of other neurons; consequently BBI hardware is massively parallel with a high interconnectivity between a large number of simple processors. Programming is frequently replaced by learning and training. Presently, the hardware solutions, based on LSI and WSI, are called *sixth-generation computers*. The sixth-generation project started in the late 1980s.

Concurrency. Independent operation of a collection of simultaneous computing activities. Also an asynchronous operation of processors in a multiprocessor system concurrently is called interactive parallelism.

Compiled knowledge. Knowledge organized into chunks and association sets. An expert system is composed of large amounts of compiled knowledge.

Cube. An ensemble of microcomputers connected by high-speed communication channels into a concurrent, hypercube architecture.

Cube manager. Host computer that serves as the link between the cube and the external environment.

Chunk. A collection of facts stored and retrieved as a single unit. Also, the amount of information stored in the human short-term memory. The capacity of human/computer memory is defined by the number of chunks that can be handled simultaneously.

DARPA. Acronym for the U.S. Defense Advanced Research Project Agency.

Data flow. The process whereby the programmer analyzes the flow of data through the system, how individual data packets move, what their sequential dependence is, and so on.

Decomposition. The degree to which an application and its tasks are divided into subtasks between processors for simultaneous execution.

Distributed Memory. The independent memory of each processor in parallel systems. This allows each processor to work on a small portion of the overall computational problem thus distributing the load.

Expert system. A software package that could perform at, or near the level of a human expert. It draws conclusions from a knowledge base that has been structured from human experts in a given field. Applications include medicine, geology, financial planning, integrated circuit design, and so on.

Fifth-generation computers. A new generation of computing machines, defined by the fifth-generation project of the early 1980s. These machines are optimized towards symbolic processing, artificial intelligence (AI), expert systems, PROLOG, and LISP languages. Included in the fifth-generation technologies are new supercomputers, improved storage devices, parallel processing, and large-scale integrated circuits.

Fine grain. Decomposition of the application at the instruction level.

Frame. A knowledge representation that associates an object with a collection of features, facts, and rules, stored in slots. A frame is the set of slots related to a specific object. The frame is also used to specify a segment of time in an utterance. A single frame usually represents 10–25 milliseconds.

Goal-driven system. The system that is programmed "What to do," rather than "How to do it." The feedback information received from the goal leads the system through the process of adaptation until the goal is achieved.

Heterogeneous system. A system whereby all processors are identical, equal, and perform the same functions.

Heuristics. Rules-of-thumb or other devices of simplification. Also, knowledge derived from experience. Knowledge is not based on defined sets of facts, but rather on inferences made from experience in similar situations. Unlike algorithms, heuristics do not guarantee correct solutions.

Human information processing. A process that analyzes human usage of information, and asks how one could design a computer program that would use the same information and reach the same conclusion.

Hypercube. A network for connecting a collection of microcomputers (nodes) together. The dimension, d, of the cube represents the number of directly connected nodes. For example in a five-dimensional cube, each node is connected to its five nearest neighbors. Such a cube would have $2^5 = 32$ total nodes. Nodes communicate by passing a message.

Inference. The process by which new facts are derived from known facts. An inference engine's program is designed to make logical assumptions, cross-references, and inferences about knowledge programmed into an expert system.

Input data. Any item used to drive the state of the network. It can be a binary or gray-scale value that describes the external process on which the network is operating.

Input pattern. A collection of input data items that is sent to the neurocomputer to act as the external stimulus to the network.

Interconnect. Unidirectional information channels that provide connections between processing elements.

Kernel. A core set of software that runs on the neurocomputer board to control the operation of the board and implements the neural network processing functions.

Knowledge base. Computer storage that keeps an unstructured set of facts and a set of inference rules for determining new facts.

Large grain. Decomposition of an application, function, or task into logical and functional units that can be computed concurrently.

Learning law. The equation specifying how the adaptive coefficients or weights are self-modified. Usually a first-order, ordinary nonlinear differential or difference equation.

LIPS (logical inferences per second). Measurement of processing speed for symbolic computing. Each logical inference requires from one to several hundred instructions per second. Current machines operate in thousands of LIPS. Improvement by a factor of 1000 or more is expected with new machines.

LISP. The shortened name of the program: "list processing language." Easy-to-use AI programming language favored in the United States. Europe and Japan prefer PROLOG.

Long-term memory. A high-capacity human memory that contains an enormous quantity of information not currently being processed.

Machine learning. A research effort that seeks to create computer programs that can learn from experience. It includes formation of general rules, adjustment of coefficients of decision function, discovery of heuristic rules, and the guidance for goal-oriented behavior.

Medium grain. Decomposition of an application to allow concurrent execution of sequential operations; typically of related but independent processes, such as FORTRAN DO loops.

MIMD (multiple instruction multiple data) stream. A computer architecture in which several processors perform different operations on several different data streams.

MIPS. Million instructions per second.

MISD (multiple instruction single data) stream. A computer architecture in which several processors perform various operations on the same data stream.

Molecular intelligence (MI). A study on the premise that the cytoskeleton within the living cell presents the molecular level of cognition and information processing. Research in this direction could result in the interface between biological and technological information devices. Ultimate goals would be biosensors, biochips, and biocomputers, and useful results are expected by the early 1990s, as a tail of the sixth-generation, or possibly as the beginning of the seventh-generation.

Natural language. Techniques that allow computer systems to accept inputs and produce outputs in a conventional language, such as English. They include natural language processing, representation of knowledge, deduction, learning, AI and artificial neural networks, speech understanding, speech production, parsing, discourse analysis and generation, sentence generation, and so on. Natural language is an ideal form of man–computer communication.

Netware. A body of AXON code or its compiled equivalent. Also used to describe the binary or textual representation of a network, netware is typically supplied on a disk that can be loaded directly into the neurocomputer.

Neural network. A cognitive information processing structure based on models of brain function. In a more formal engineering context, a highly parallel dynamic system with the topology of a directed graph that can carry out information processing by its state response to continuous or initial input.

Neurocomputer. A neural network hardware/software implementation that is attached as a coprocessor to a standard computer, allowing software on a host computer to call neural networks as procedures (which are then executed on the neurocomputer). Neurocomputers allow neural networks to be integrated into almost any computer hardware and software environment, whenever their unique information processing capabilities are needed.

Neurocomputing. The process of implementing and executing neural networks.

Node. One of the microcomputers in a concurrent processing machine. Each node contains the processor, memory, and a communication channel. It could be a very simple system with a limited set of functions, like those found in neurocomputers, or a complete computer with operating system like those found in hypercubes.

Parallel processing. The operation of a computer in which several programs are executed concurrently as opposed to serially. Also the data could be distributed between a large number of independent processors that can function on different data simultaneously. Applications include scientific processing, real-time systems, expert systems, neural systems, image and speech processing, and robotics.

Pattern recognition. A technique that classifies data into predetermined categories, using statistical methods, template comparisons, or learning algorithms.

Processing element. The fundamental computational element in a neural network. A network consists of a large collection of highly interconnected processing elements. A processing element is composed of a number of input values from other processing elements. These are weighted by a set of adaptive coefficients and then used to generate a single output value that branches to form input programs to other processing elements.

Procedure-driven. A program whereby a programmer writes the code to accomplish some task. In other words, the programmer creates a new program that exploits parallelism.

Production rules. Knowledge representation based on IF-THEN rules (also called condition and action). A production system is composed of a database of production rules and of some control mechanism that selects applicable production rules to reach some goal state.

PROLOG. The shortened name of the program "programming in logic." A symbolic or AI programming language based on predicate calculus. It is the choice language of Japan's fifth generation and also used in Europe. The main U.S. rival is LISP.

Pruning. The process of selecting the most useful subset of rules in an expert system. The rules or decision branches that prove less efficient are cut off or ignored.

RISC (reduced instruction set computer). A SISD computer designed to increase performance and cut execution time by reducing the number of instructions.

Scalar. A quantity characterized by a single number.

Short-term memory. That portion of human memory that is actively used in new data acquisition and temporal storage. It contains all the data that is instantly available to the system and its capacity is measured in chunks. It is believed that human short-term memory can contain and manipulate about seven chunks at one time.

SIMD (single instruction multiple data) stream. A computer architecture in which a single set of operations is performed on a number of different types of data. Most commonly, this is an array processor with several processing elements governed by a single control unit with limited memory-to-processor communication for high efficiency in repetitive calculations.

SISD (single instruction single data) stream computer. A serial processor that executes sequential instructions.

Sixth-generation computers. The new generation of computing machines defined by the sixth-generation project in the late 1980s. These machines emulate information processing in the brain and neural networks. The features include massive parallelism, machine learning, adaptability, goal directed, processor/memory elements, associative memories, concurrency, and event trains. Presently, the machines are based on very large-scale and wafer-scale integration. In the future the trend towards optical and molecular machines is possible.

Slab. A collection of processing elements that use the same transfer and learning functions.

State value. The output of a processing element.

Transfer equation. The difference equation that describes how the processing element output signal evolves in time as a function of its weighted input signals.

UISL (user interface subroutine library). A collection of subroutines designed to provide complete access to all ANZA functions by allowing the user to embed subroutine calls to the library in their software.

Vector. A quantity represented by an ordered set of numbers.

Weight. An adaptive coefficient that can be self-adjusted in response to external input. (See also "adaptive coefficient").

AUTHOR INDEX _____

455

SUBJECT INDEX _____